April 30, 1972

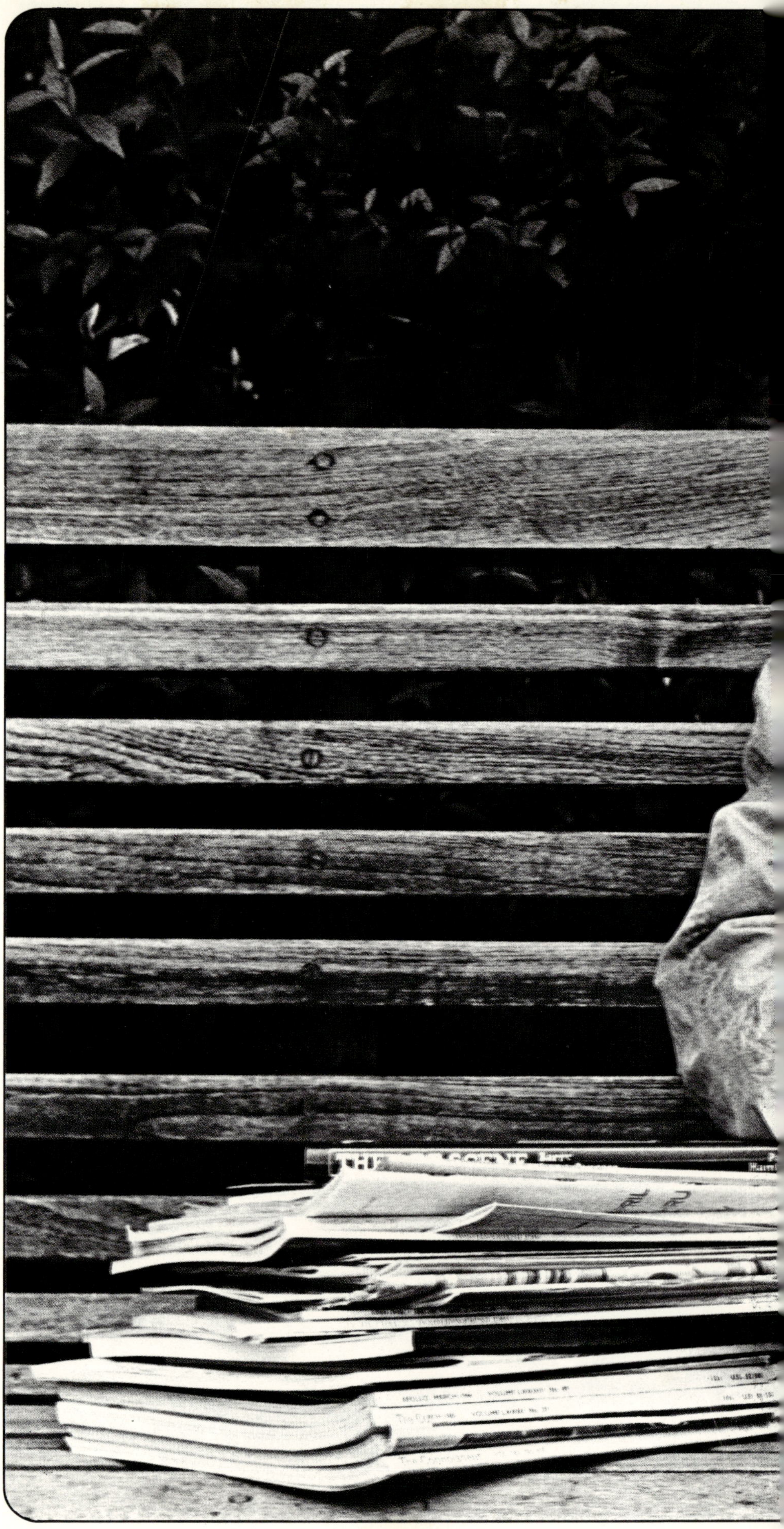

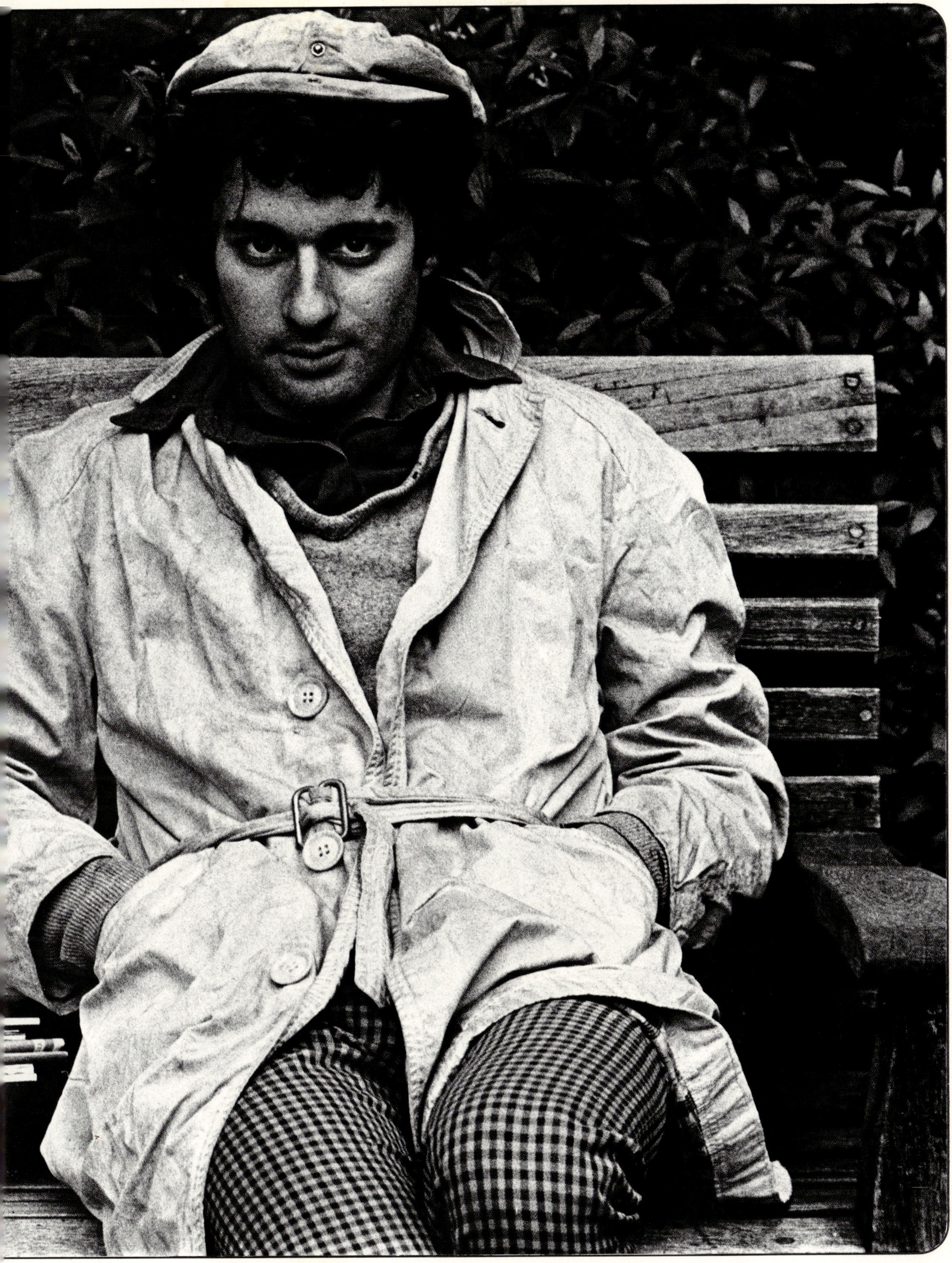

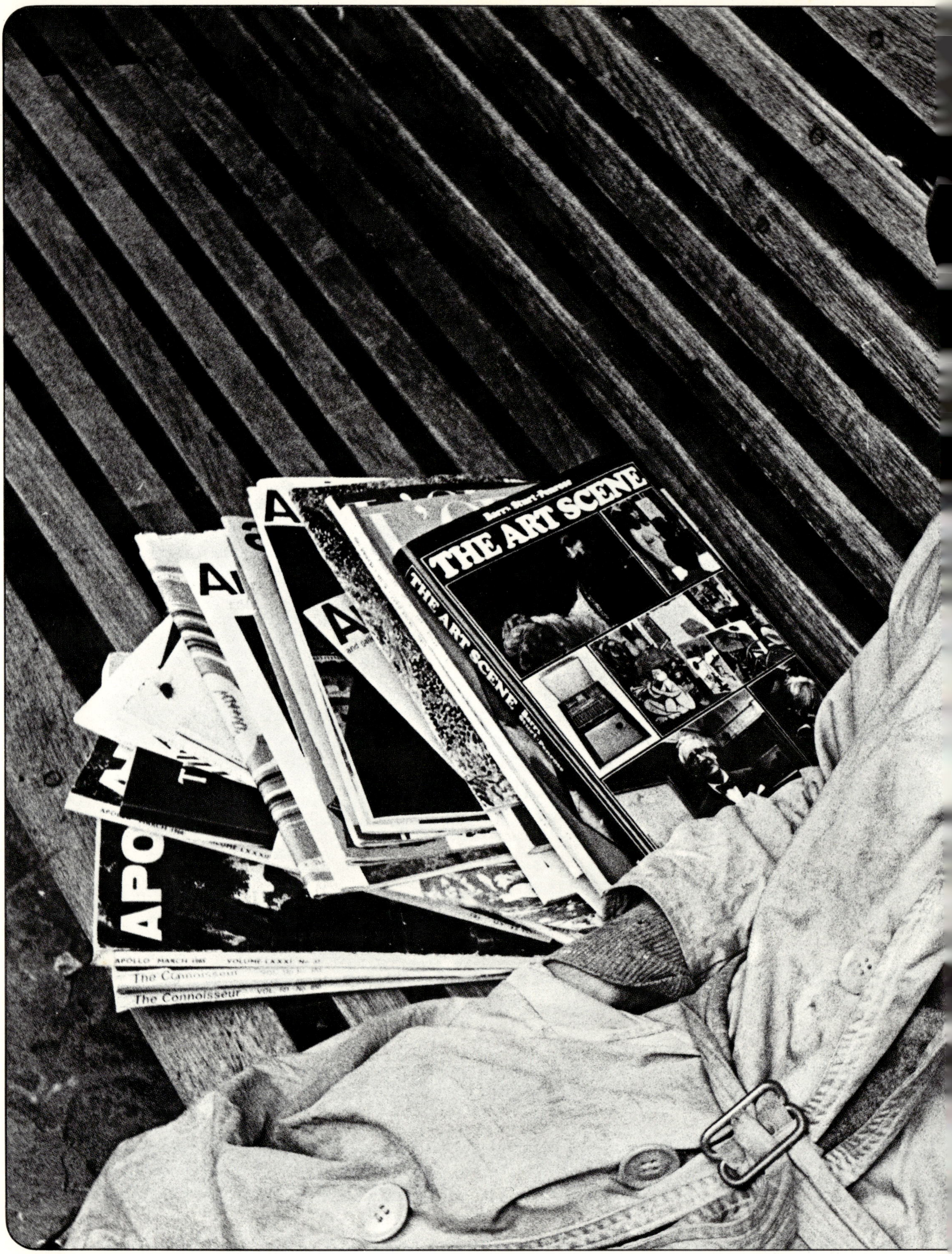
THE ART SCENE
THE ART SCENE
The Connoisseur
The Connoisseur

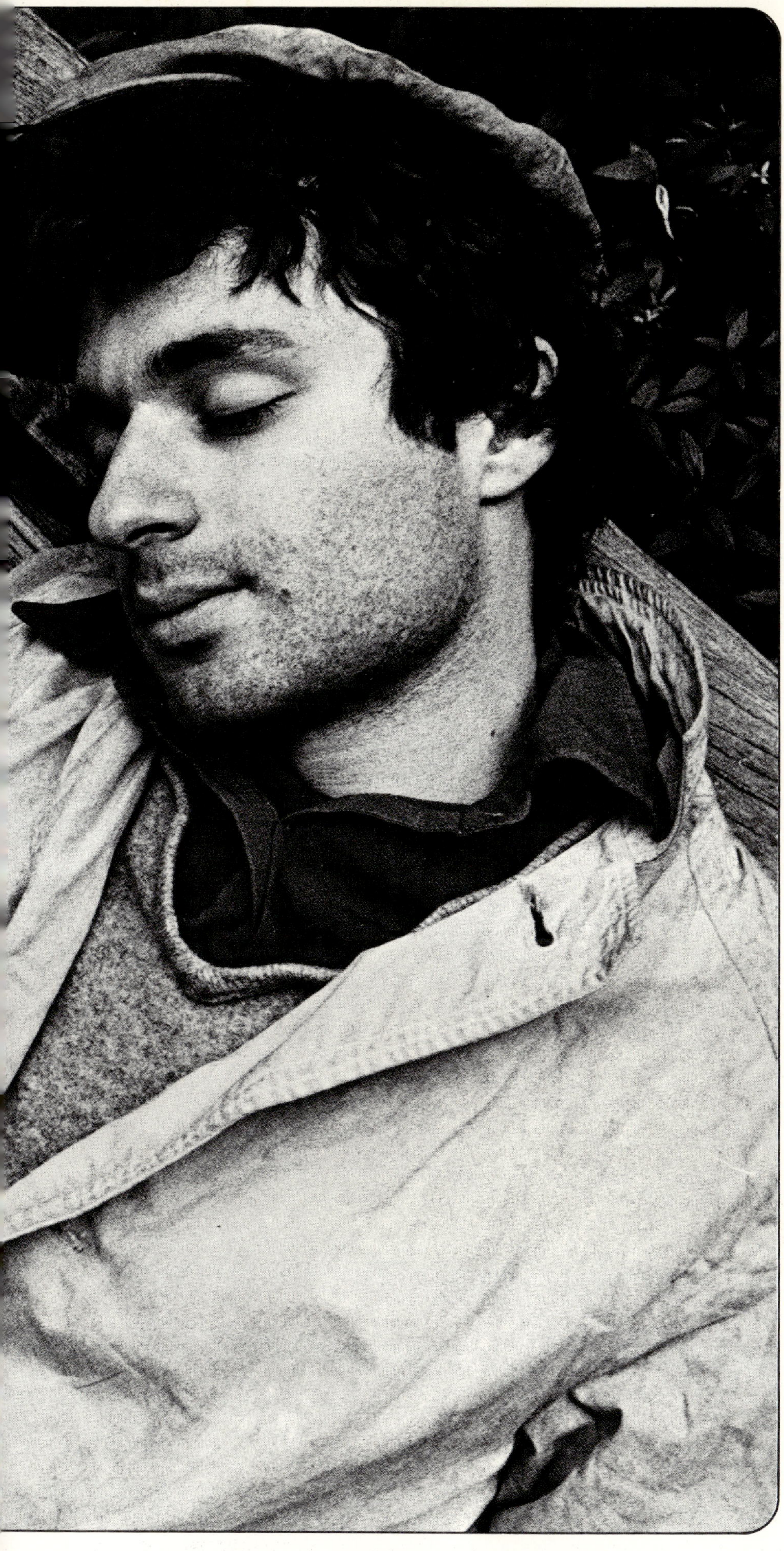

THE ART SCENE

THE ART SCENE

Barrie Sturt-Penrose

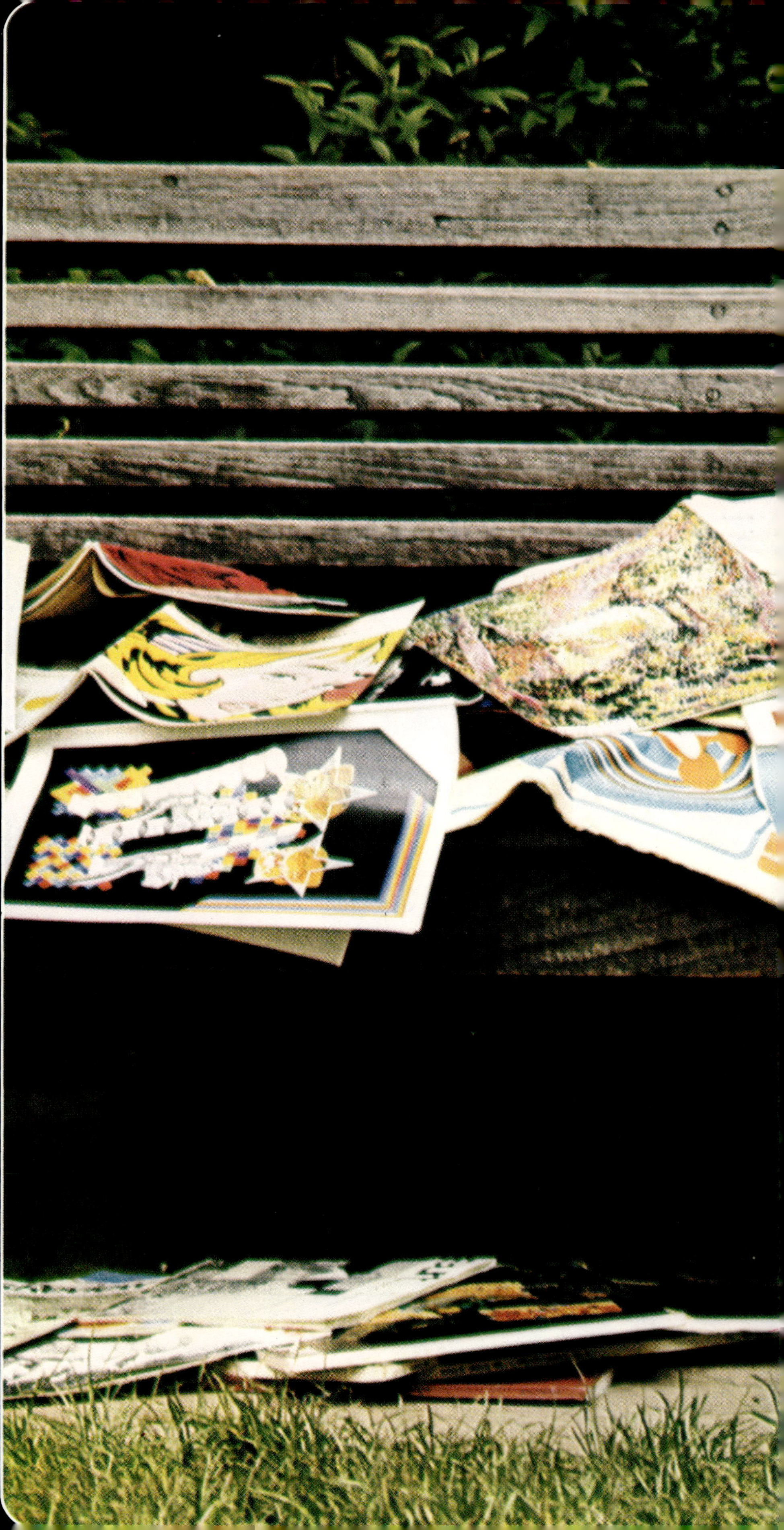

PAUL HAMLYN
LONDON · NEW YORK · SYDNEY · TORONTO

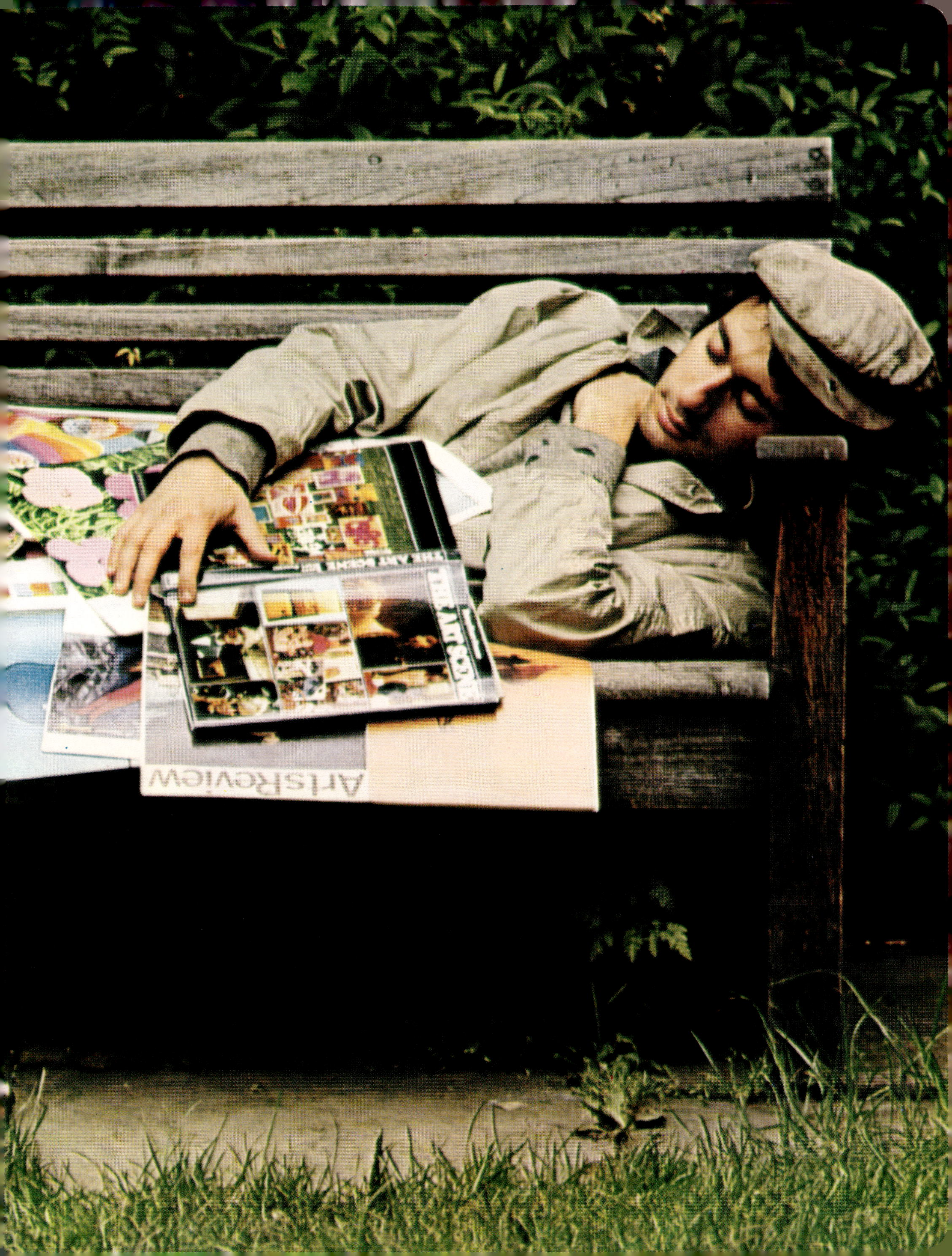
THE ART SCENE
ArtsReview

I would like to express sincere thanks
to Stan Hardy, Ian Laurie,
Keith Davis (design), Dr Tode
Curuvija, Mara Curuvija and
Nicole Colella
for their advice, patience and
kindness
B.S-P. January 1969

Published by
The Hamlyn Publishing Group Limited
London · New York · Sydney · Toronto
Hamlyn House,
Feltham, Middlesex, England

Printed in Hong Kong by
Continental Printing Co. Ltd.

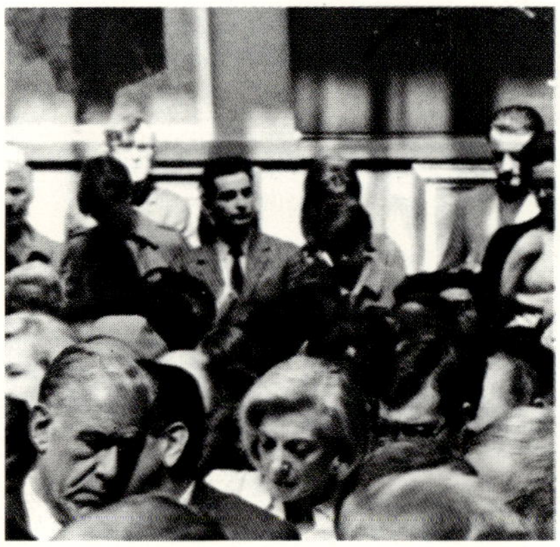

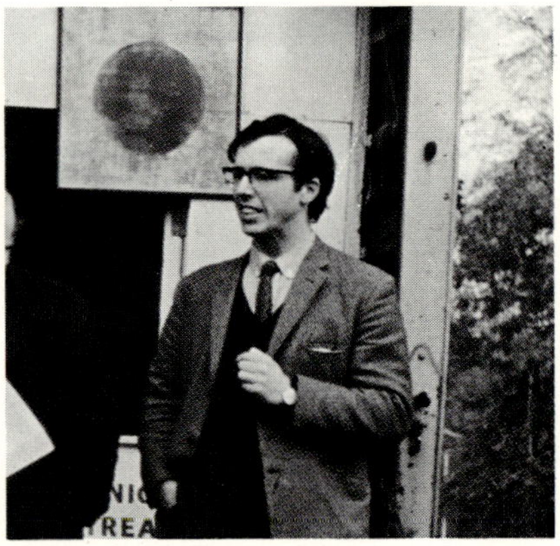

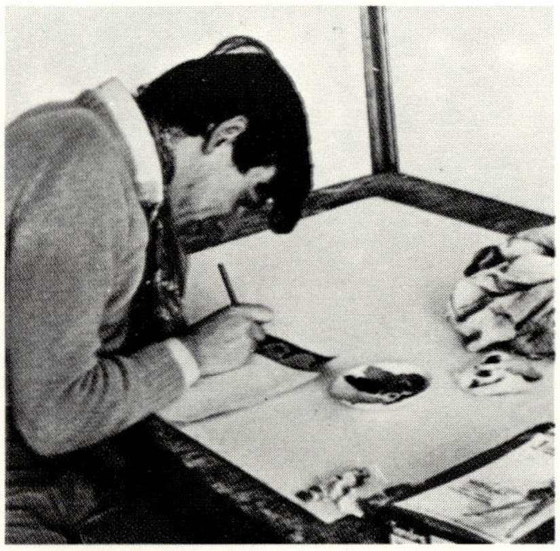

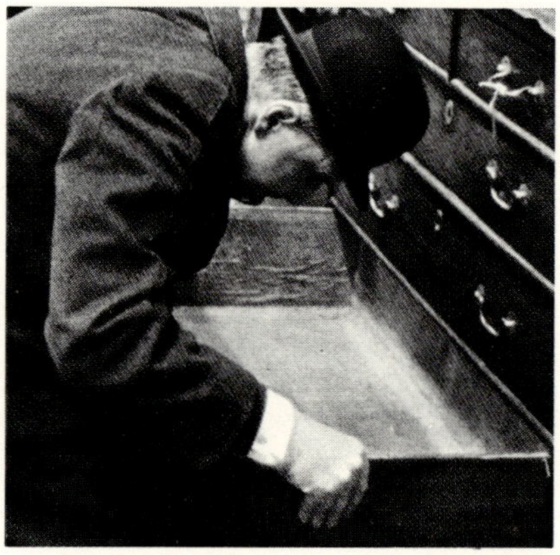

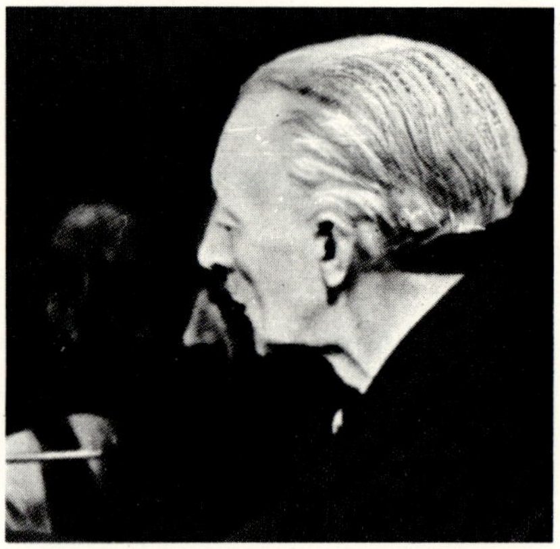

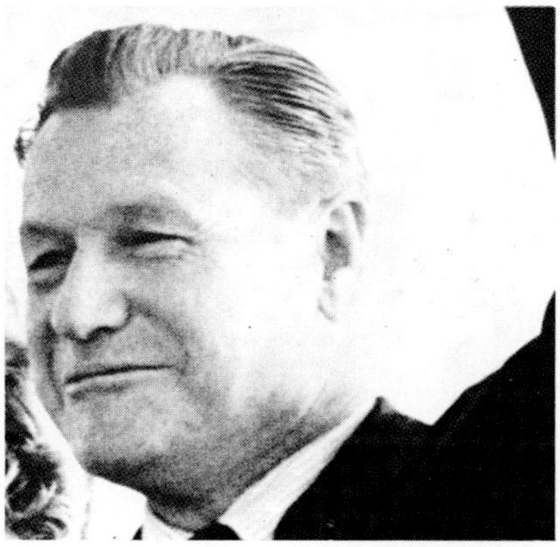

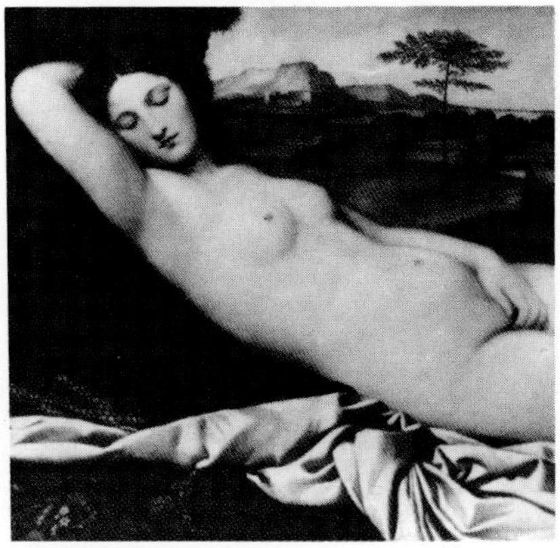

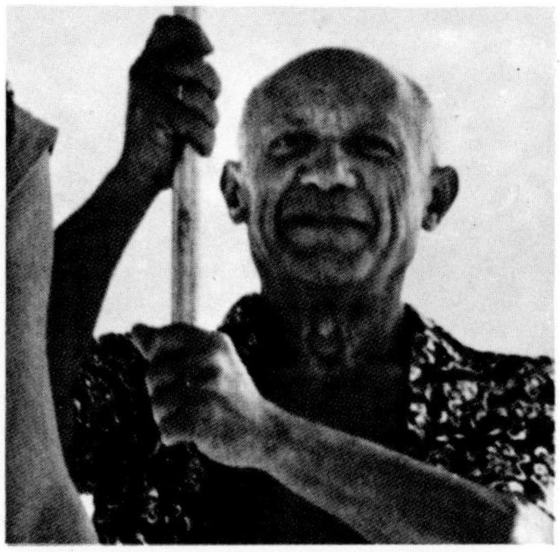

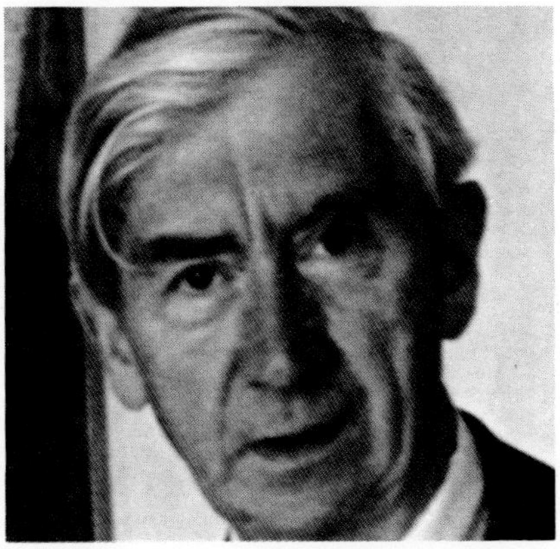

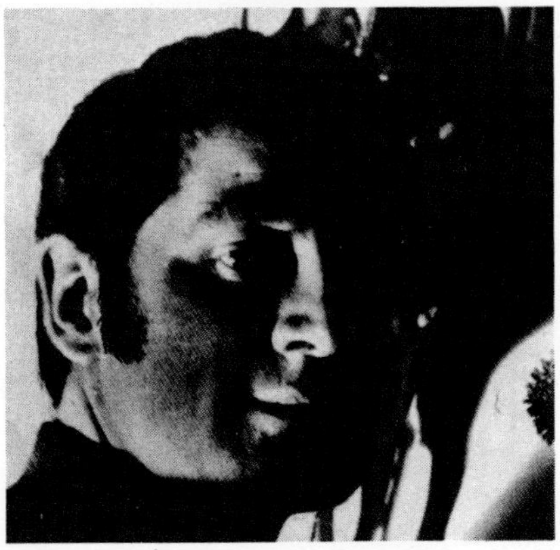

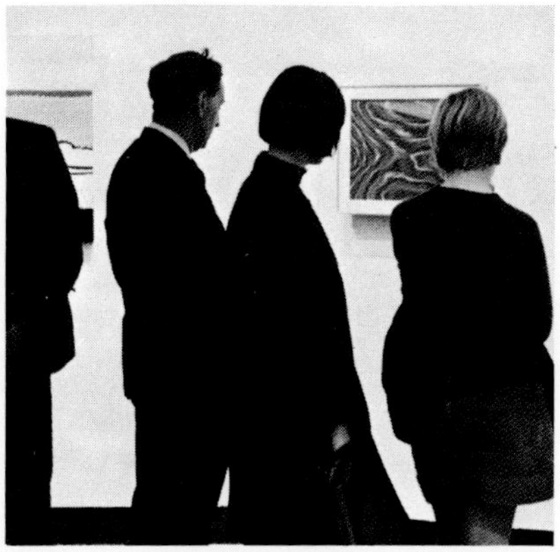

INTRODUCTION

Art reflects many human attributes: love, beauty, sex, history, glory, riches even decadence. Nations have both cherished and despised it; men have pillaged, raped and murdered in pursuit of it. Few are totally indifferent about art, especially in the twentieth century. When the world's most valuable pictures are worth millions and supermarkets sell paintings for a few shillings, we can scarcely be accused of indifference.

Art has become the opium of more people than ever before. It has even created its own world with its popes, priests, its faithful and its devils. They exist to buy and sell, to produce and hoard objects we call art. Around them is a flock of followers who believe that art is precious, perhaps sacred; others think is it merely rubbish.

Despite art being a multi-billion dollar business and big news in the press, on television and radio, misunderstanding and ignorance about it has never been greater. It's a safe bet that your neighbour won't know who painted *The Madonna Alba* or *Guernica*—two of the world's most famous pictures.

Perhaps we take a truly astonishing phenomenon too much for granted? Why do our ears prick up when the word art is mentioned? Whether it is that Leonardo's *Mona Lisa* has been insured for forty million pounds for its trip to America or that the National Gallery has paid £500,000 for a Cézanne, it's certain to provoke comment and controversy. But few people are bothered when even greater amounts are spent by property speculators or the army.

What is so special about art? Why do we feel the need to buy countless art books, art magazines and gallery guides, and troop in our thousands through museums and private collections? How can we explain the fact that some people *need* to own works of art themselves? And why should we be interested in the portraits of others, pictures of oranges and lemons, landscapes or an abstract doodle? Why don't we just settle for a photograph, look at a *real* bowl of fruit, a *real* landscape, or produce our own doodles?

To art is attributed qualities which are rarely given to other art forms such as books or the cinema, for example. Art has aesthetic merits and a monetary value, just like stocks and shares. In other words art is considered valuable both in and outside itself. A book or a film may have enormous literary and visual qualities, but as objects, as so much paper and celluloid, they are expendable and relatively worthless.

Art then is an international currency, in terms of value, scope, standards and in its audience. If you buy a Henry Moore sculpture in London you will be able to sell it in New York, Palm Beach or Stockholm. Buy a picture by Andy Warhol in Rome and you can sell it in Paris. Take a drawing by Umberto Boccioni or Modigliani from Rome and you may sell it to the Tate Gallery in London.

Similarly, today's art students can follow their studies in many of the major capital cities. They can learn the same techniques and employ the same images in Tokyo, Belgrade, Paris, London or New York. Art has, like pop music, become international.

The world's museums and galleries are among the best free universities and a necessary part of everyone's education. Wealthy Italians fly to the United States to see the work of the New York School of abstract expressionism. American and German tourists flock to Italy to visit the Sistine Chapel, the Uffizi, and St Mark's Square. Art fans will travel far and wide to see their favourites.

People don't simply look, of course. They also buy works of art which, if placed together, would make the great collections of the past seem almost nothing. There are now more than 400 art galleries in New York alone, more than 250 in Paris, and more than 150 in London. Art is clearly a part of big business, whatever else it may be.

Works of art are fast becoming another medium of exchange. Like money, they can be used in some countries to pay estate duty when a person dies. Collectors use them as securities, for tax avoidance and, perhaps last of all, for furnishing their homes. Economists have already pointed out that since the war sections of the art market have out-played the stock market.

If your grandfather bought a painting by Cézanne for £26, as Thèodore Duret did in 1894, the profit, even allowing for the drop in the value of money, would be astounding. Cézanne's *Le Paysan* was bought in 1911 for £960 and was sold, forty-nine years later, for £145,000.

But, of course, buying paintings is not always a profitable experience. If your grandfather bought a picture by the Victorian artist Lord Leighton he would have lost, not made, any money. Leighton's *The Syracusian Bride* was bought by a London art dealer for £1,200 in 1866; sold in 1874 for £2,677, it brought only £200 when it was sold at auction in January 1961. So uncertain and eccentric is the great art game that

London's distinguished sale rooms (below) have helped to make it the centre of the international art trade
Andy Warhol (above right): a cult leader of the avant-garde. Buy a picture by him in Rome and you can sell it in Paris
A New York 'Happening' (below right) They often have a strong dose of lunacy about them

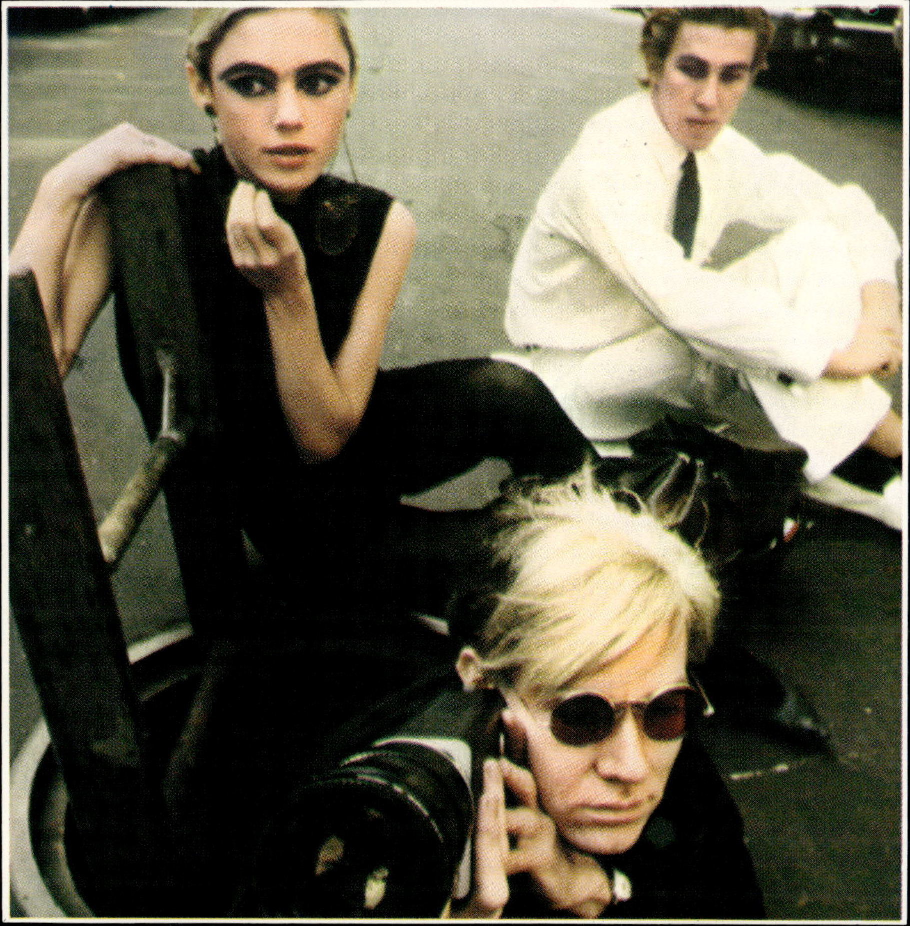

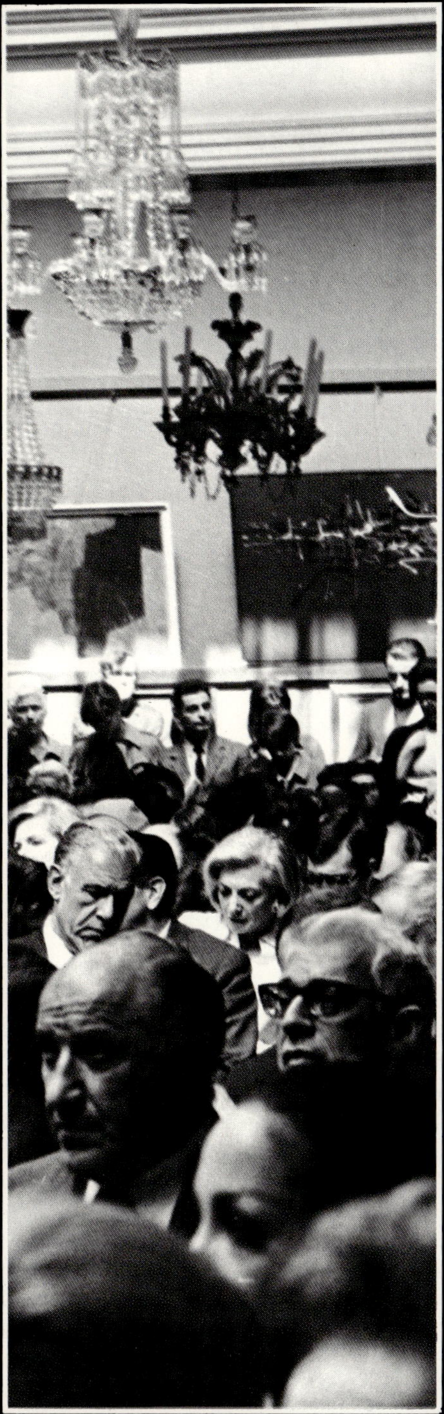

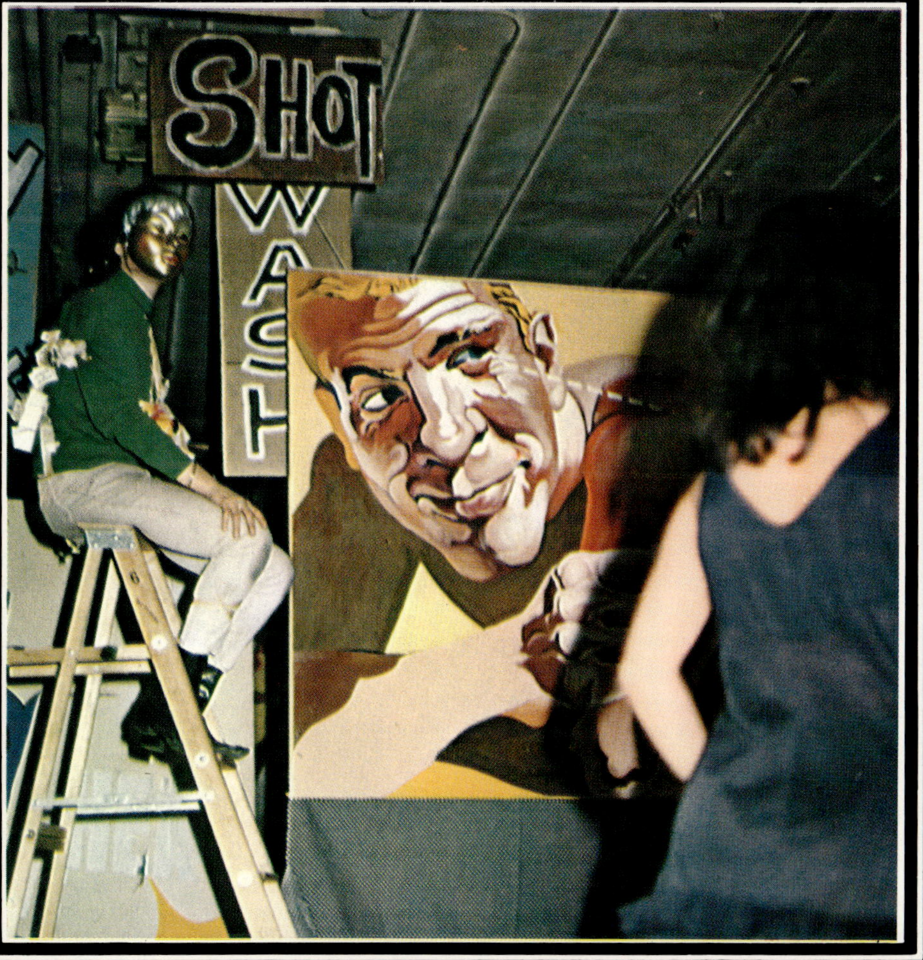

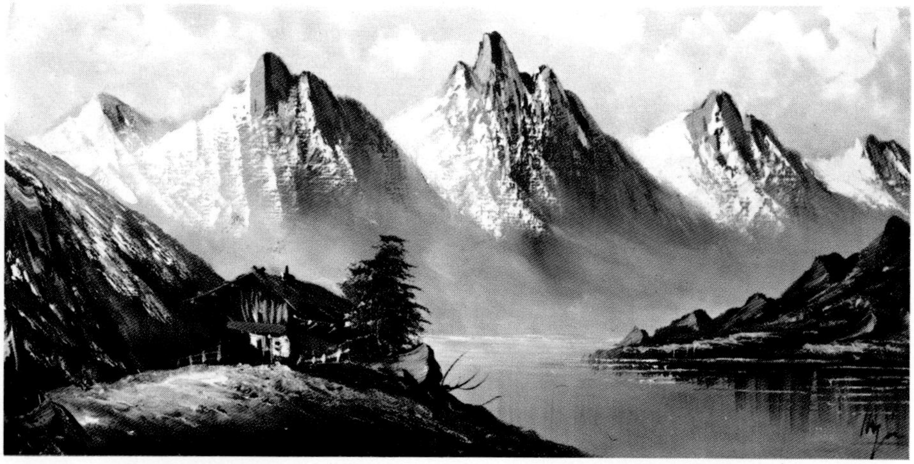

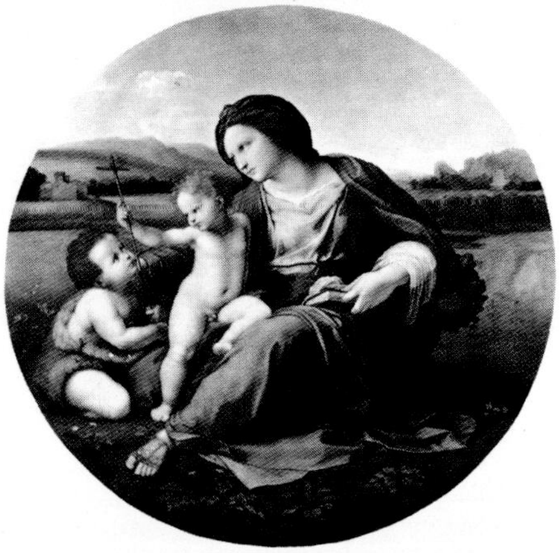

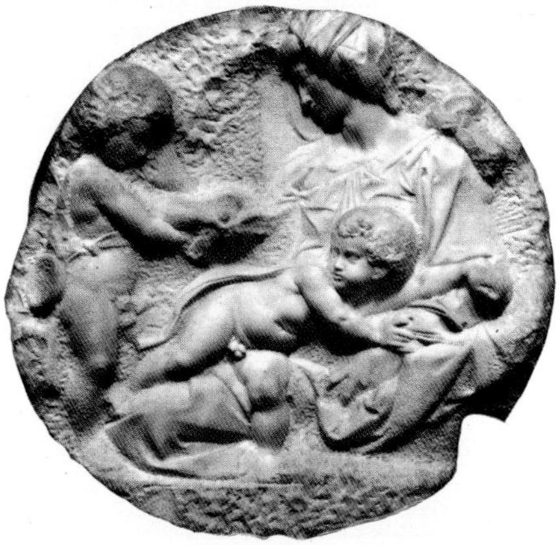

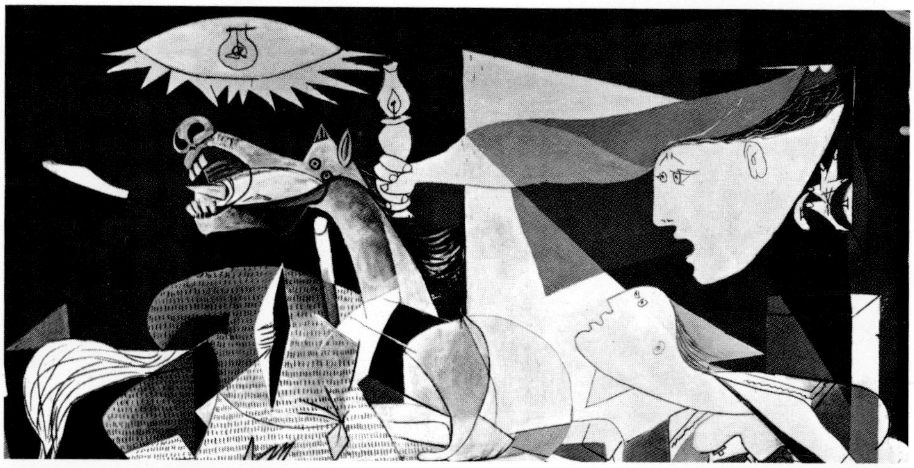

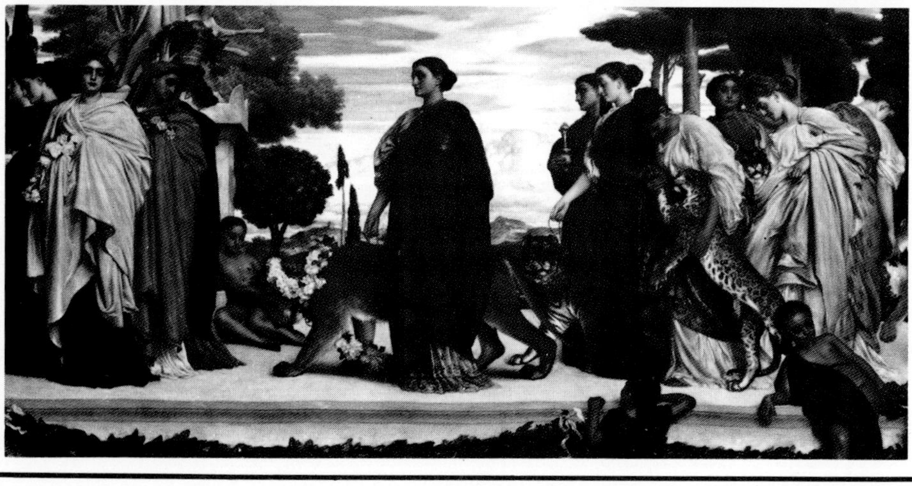

This alpine scene (left) may be bought for about thirty shillings at Woolworth's. Michelangelo's *Taddeo Tondo* (below right) was insured for £1 million.
It's a safe bet that your neighbour won't know who painted the *Alba Madonna* (below left, in the National Gallery of Art, Washington D.C., Andrew Mellon Collection) or *Guernica* (below, on extended loan from the artist to the Museum of Modern Art, New York) two of the world's most famous pictures.
Lord Leighton's *The Syracusian Bride* (bottom) was sold in 1874 for £2,677. In January 1961 it fetched only £200 at an art auction

Museums and galleries are no longer places to take a nap or eat sandwiches away from the city crowds (right)
Tourists flock to Italy to visit the Sistine Chapel, the Uffizi, and St Mark's Square, shown here (right)
Leonardo da Vinci, *Mona Lisa* (above right): insured for forty million pounds for its trip to America
Cézanne's *Le Paysan* (below right) was bought in 1874 for £960 and sold in 1960 for £145,000

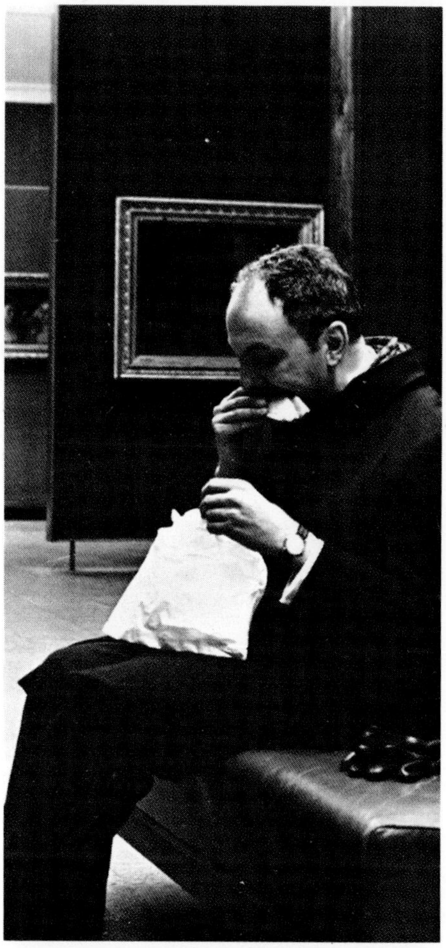
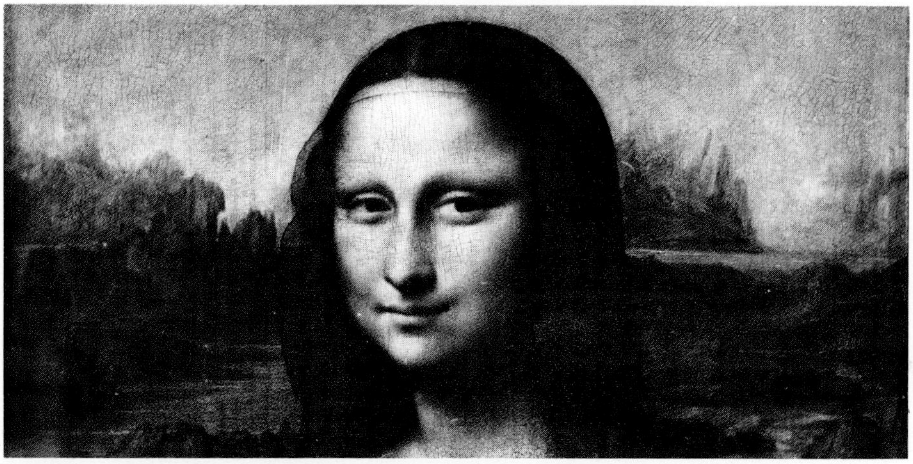
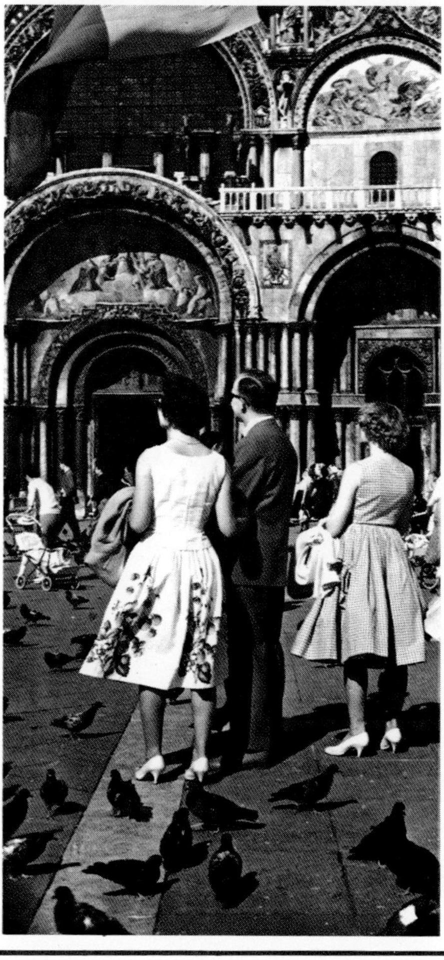
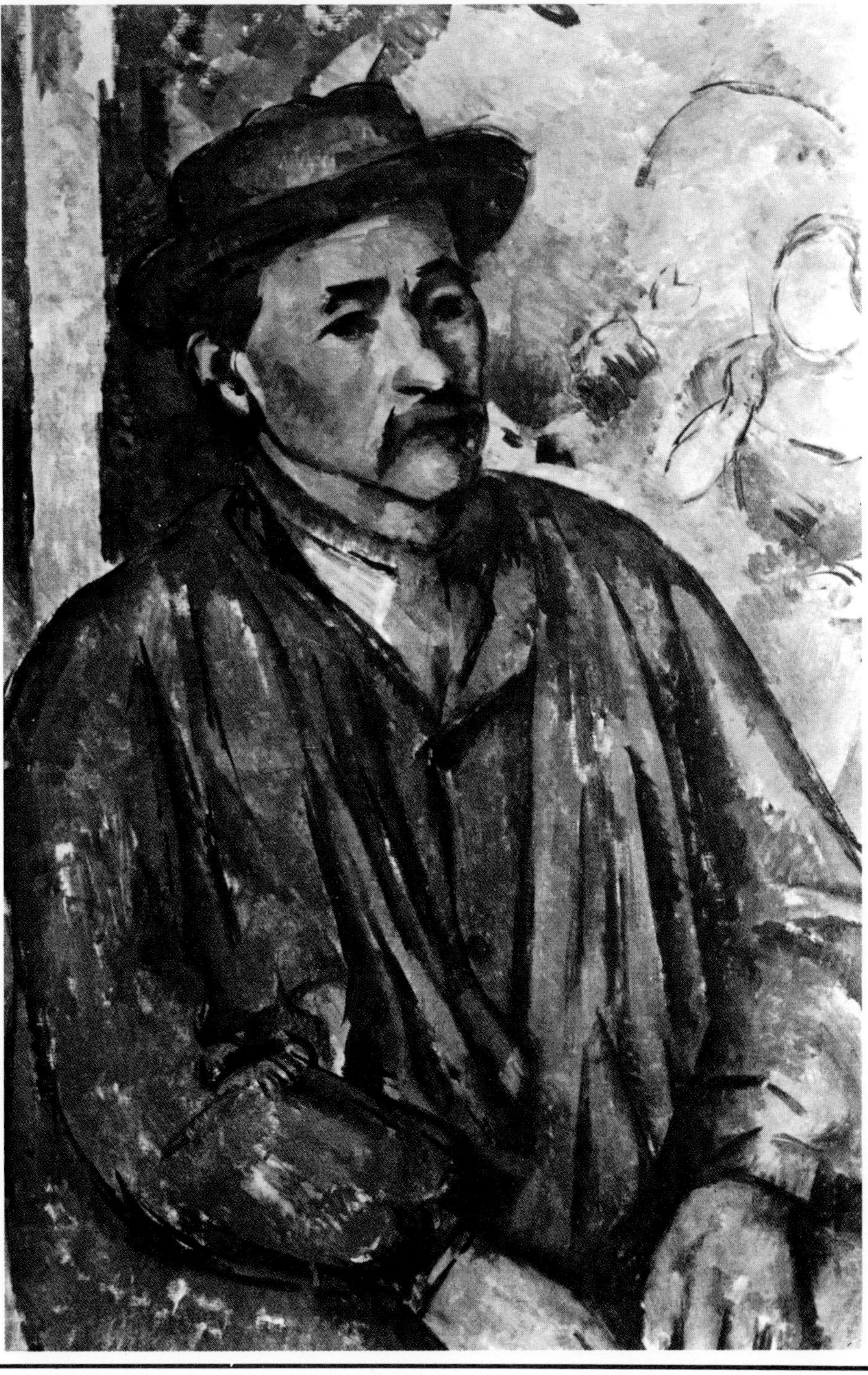

The Syracusian Bride could well be worth a king's ransom in five, ten, or perhaps a hundred years from now.

In September 1967 four London galleries felt so confident about the kind of paintings they were selling that they offered the following paintings for sale with a guaranteed profit in five years time:

Albert Houthuesen: *Winter coast with dark cloud*, oil	£150	£300
Marie Laurencin: *Le chapeau bleu*, watercolour	£500	£800
Amedeo Modigliani: *Tête d'une Femme*, pencil	£950	£1,500
Felicien Rops: *Portrait d'une Femme*	90 gns	135 gns
Gustav Klimt: *Standing Dancer*	£265	£395
Alfred Kubin: *Death Blows Everything Away*	£140	£210
Michael Ayrton: *Demeter and Kore*	£260	£325
Erte: *Guadalquivir*	£150	£200
Oskar Rabin: *A Sunny Day*	£400	£475

Fans and fan clubs play a part in the great art game, but they have little in common with fans in the pop music or football worlds. They rarely scream or shake rattles, and their active interest in art is largely kept to themselves.

Nevertheless, their all-round support at galleries and museums is generally measured by the clicking of the turnstile and the jingle of the cash register. Last year the Tate Gallery had nearly a million visitors, the Museum of Modern Art, New York, and the Louvre, Paris, even more, and a private gallery like the Redfern in London's Mayfair claims that more than a thousand people pass through its exhibitions every week.

The gaiety of modishly-dressed fans at the Tate Gallery or in a private gallery like Dwan's in New York often finds a direct correlation in the gay poster-box colours of the art they go to see. The more bizarre fans at the more bizarre shows occasionally appear like a colourful annex of the local fairground. 'Happenings' and 'Events' often have a strong dose of lunacy about them. New York artist Al Hansen enjoys pushing pianos from the top of high buildings. Who can blame the fans if they get excited? 'Several times I've pushed a piano off a building', he says. 'It is a wonderful experience'.

The tourists, teenagers and art students seen every summer outside the world's major art museums, with rows of ice-cream vans and pop-corn sellers, create a playful holiday atmosphere. It is only a few soirée enthusiasts and private view fans who help give the art scene its exclusive upper-class moments. One thing is certain: museums and galleries are no longer places to take a nap or eat sandwiches away from the city crowds.

Art isn't just a sport for devotees and private patrons—nations and governments also get involved. Culture is now a weapon in the armoury of diplomacy. Countries don't send gunboats, they send the *Mona Lisa* or Tutankhamun's treasure. Winning the Venice Biennale, the top art competition, brings more prestige than winning a battle.

The art manufacturers, at least most of the living ones, appear to play a comparatively backroom role. The limelight is often stolen by the auctioneers and the dealers, the collectors and the critics, the forgers and the art thieves.

Artists may live in a more comfortable and enlightened age, but few earn their living from painting pictures. Nevertheless, the Bohemian image of the painter is almost as dead as Van Gogh or Toulouse-Lautrec.

Only the internationally established grandees of modern art or the publicity-seeking off-beat artists regularly make the headlines. Like King Midas, everything that Picasso, Henry Moore or Andy Warhol touch seems to turn into hard currency. Picasso holds the world's record for a living painter: £190,000 for his *Mère et Enfant*. If one of his best-known works like *Guernica*, now on loan to the Museum of Modern Art, New York, came on to the market it would probably fetch more than a million pounds.

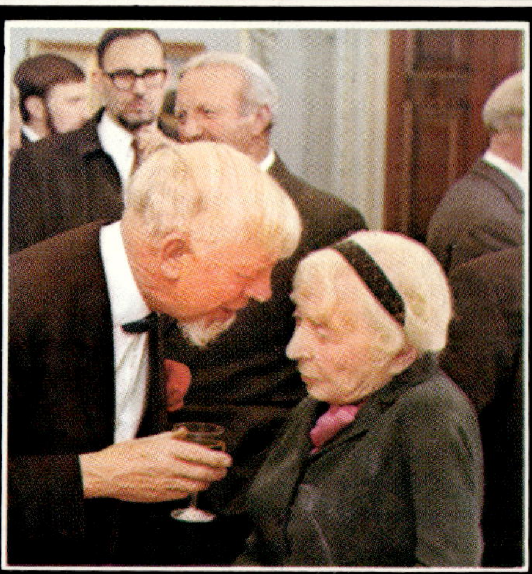

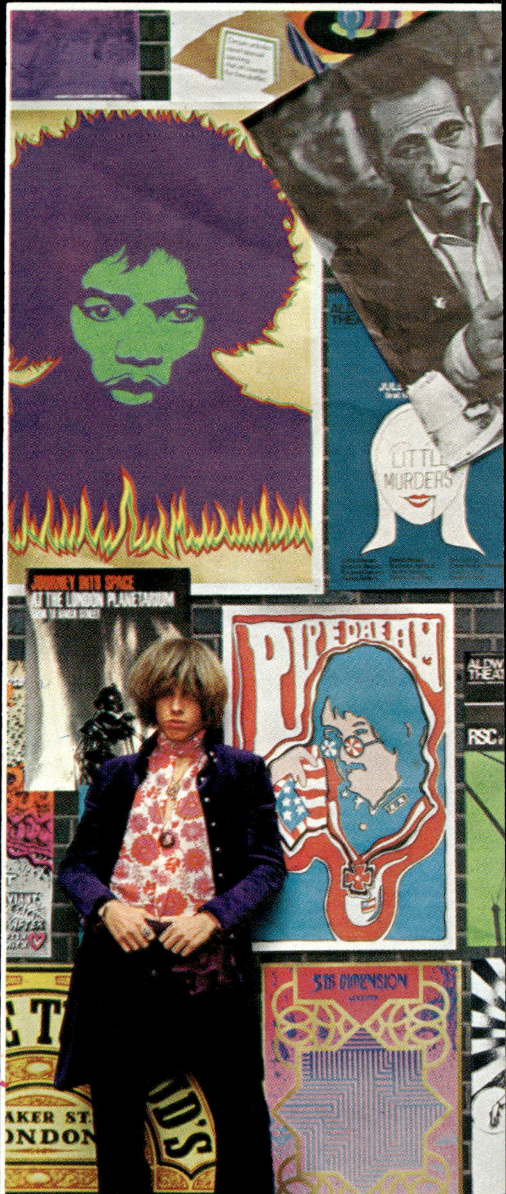

Distinguished guests at an Establishment art function (left)
Picasso's *Mére et Enfant* was sold in London for £190,000 (right)
Posters costing a few shillings are an important part of pop culture (below)

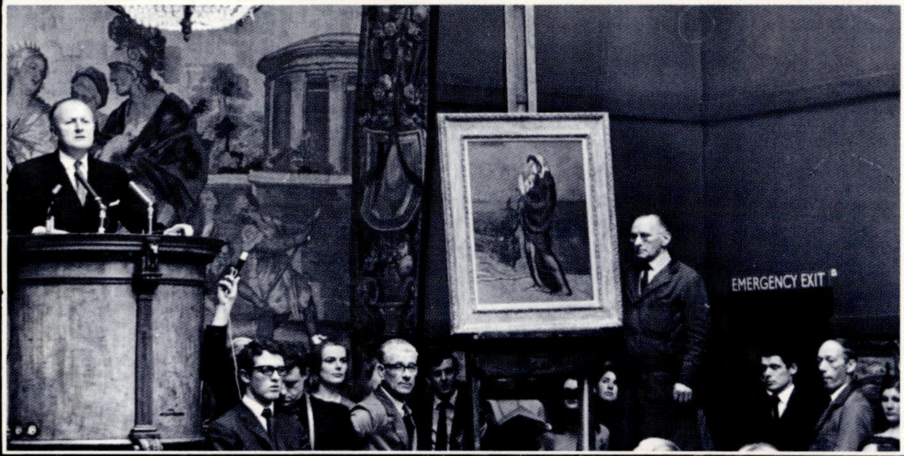

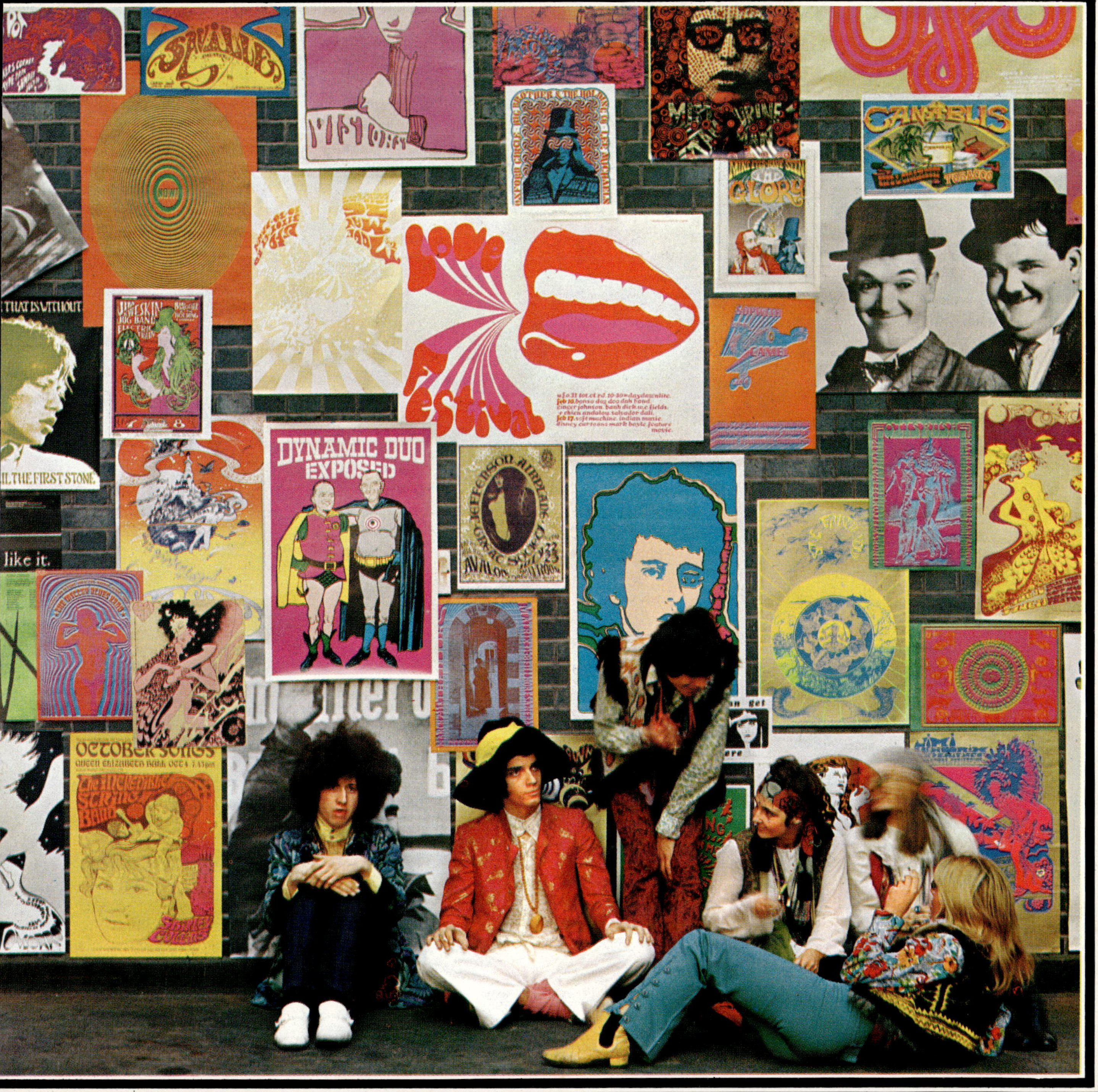

THE DEALERS

The art dealing game is very old and, luckily for many participants, it can still be played without worrying too much about rules. Conduct which would be considered foul by some players is, for others, sound day-to-day business strategy. For the Brobdingnagians of the game selling art to a richer, larger and more gullible public than ever before can be a highly profitable way of making money. If the market collapsed, as well it could in time, they would probably do almost as well selling brass tacks, butter or brocade. Few dealers are very fussy about how or what they sell.

Then again, there are players who find art dealing a rather special way of life. Apart from the financial rewards, it is culturally and socially respectable to be an art dealer. It is one of the few kinds of shopkeeping, apart from hairdressing, which *could* provide an entrée to Buckingham Palace, the White House, the Elysée Palace and even the Kremlin. Dealers have, of course, an entrée to many less illustrious but nevertheless prosperous households. Hanging about on the touchline are the minor officials and supporters who help the dealers reach their goal: the artists, the collectors, the museum-men, the auctioneers and the critics. Naturally, in a sport without rigidly defined rules the play can sometimes be rough, sometimes skilful, even dainty, but seldom, if ever, *dull*.

In fact, when the definitive history of modern art comes to be written, the chapter on art dealers is going to provide one of its richest and purplest passages. Few areas of our cultural and business life are so rich in extremes: you can buy anything from a thirty shilling original oil painting at Woolworth's to avant-garde Soviet paintings or a picture like Rembrandt's portrait of his son Titus, sold in London for £798,000. A little oil painting by Raoul Dufy brought in 1945 for thirty guineas is worth four to five thousand pounds today. This gives some idea of what can be done with buying and selling pictures.

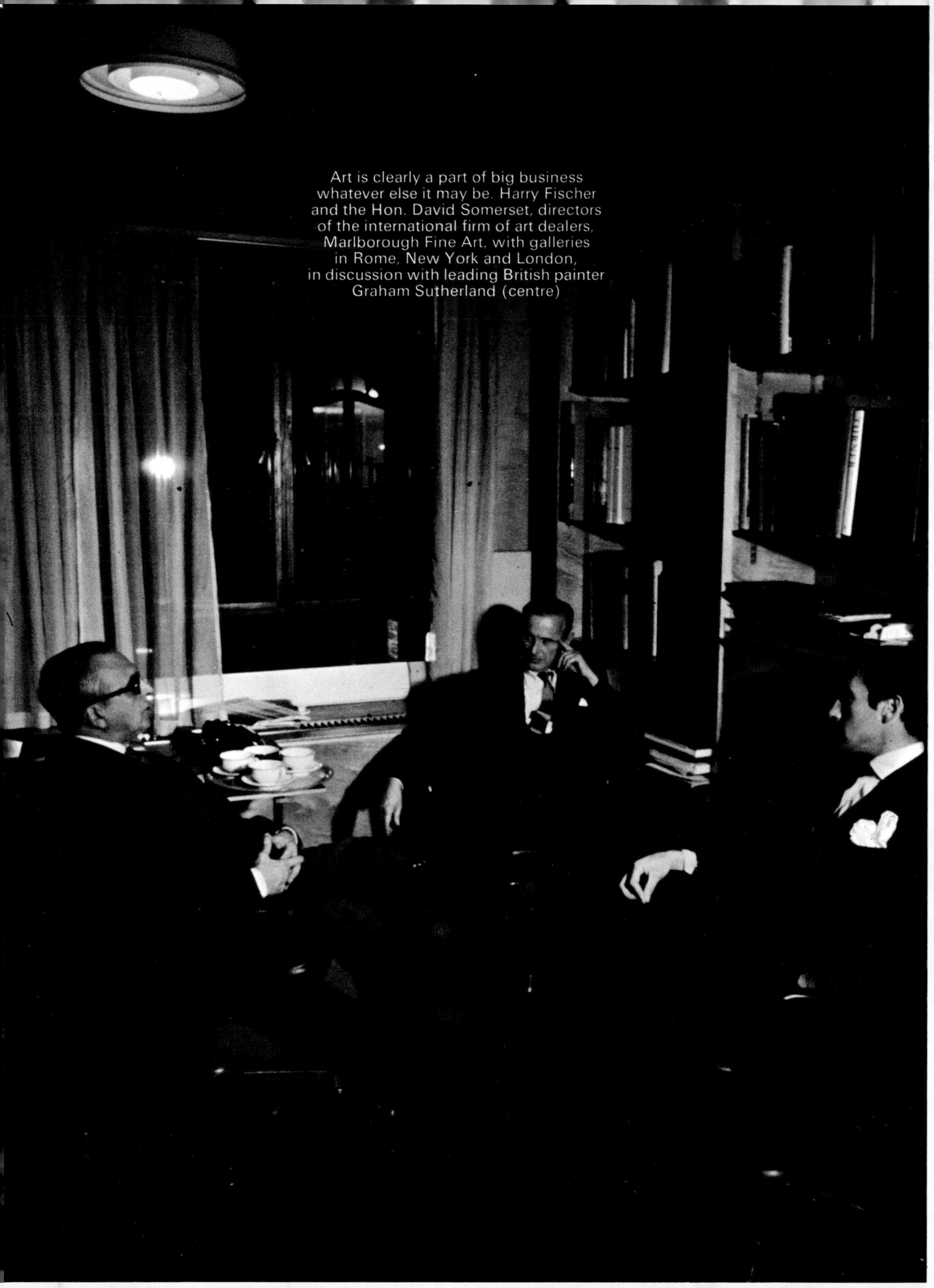
Art is clearly a part of big business whatever else it may be. Harry Fischer and the Hon. David Somerset, directors of the international firm of art dealers, Marlborough Fine Art, with galleries in Rome, New York and London, in discussion with leading British painter Graham Sutherland (centre)

The international art market now has an annual turnover of more than £500 million in pictures, sculptures and other works of art. Centred upon London, which in the saleroom field alone has a higher turnover than that of the New York and Paris salerooms combined, the art market is fatter and richer than at any time in the past. Fortunes and more modest profits are made, and yet bankruptcy is an occupational hazard. Marlborough Fine Art is today a multi-million dollar empire with galleries in London, New York and Rome. Opened in 1946 by two ex-privates from the British Army's Pioneer Corps, Marlborough Fine Art is now a dominant force in the world's modern art market. On the other hand, in the last two years four important galleries have closed in London, eight in New York and ten in Paris. One of the fallen London galleries closed shop with outstanding debts amounting to just over £30,000 and information from a usually reliable source suggests that another London gallery is in the red to the tune of £200,000 and is likely to close in the near future. If one added up the number of galleries opening and closing their doors from one month to the next, often without being noticed by collectors and critics, the figure would be startling. The fact is, however, that there are more private galleries than ever before and, therefore, more opening than closing.

Dealers have multiplied with the boom in international art. Working through more than 150 galleries in London, 400 in New York and 250 in Paris, and through many more in other countries, in provincial cities, country towns and even isolated hamlets, they are largely responsible for the enormous number of privately organised exhibitions. Gallery owners are the impresarios of the art world. Few of them are art historians or great collectors. In the Bond Street area, for example, one leading dealer formerly ran a chain of petrol stations; two other dealers run a garage for vintage cars and a discothèque in Spain; one was once a tailor, one is an Irish aristocrat and another is a large clothing manufacturer. In the Rue de Seine in Paris, the street with most of the Left Bank galleries, a dealer allowed an artist to fill his gallery with refuse collected from the city's streets. It was the central spectacle of the artist's one-man show. It was considered a coincidence, however, that the gallery owner had been a refuse collector a few years before he decided to enter the art trade. Another well-known Paris gallery owner is also a member of the Rothschild family. Without any previous experience in selling art she launched her avant-garde gallery. One of her first exhibitions was devoted to discarded but very colourful articles of underwear, which were stitched together and hung on the gallery's walls.

Rather more than three-quarters of the private galleries in Europe and the United States show the work of living artists. The majority of dealers charge from one-third to half the price of a work sold in a one-man exhibition or mixed show. Galleries like the Upper Grosvenor and the Alwin Gallery in Mayfair sometimes charge an artist a three-figure fee for showing his work. If the artist sells nothing during his exhibition he may still have to pay for the opening party, catalogue, publicity, framing and the gallery's fee. Perhaps the most popular dealer is the one who is prepared to place an artist under exclusive contract. Galleries such as the Marlborough, Gimpel Fils, the Leslie Waddington Gallery and the Grosvenor have, in effect, made some of their artists–Francis Bacon, Henry Moore, Graham Sutherland and Ben Nicholson, for example–salaried employees by paying them monthly or quarterly and giving them a percentage on the work they are able to sell.

The relationship between an artist and a dealer–in other words the producer and retailer–has invariably taken different forms through the centuries. The art-dealing game is very old, although it did not take on its modern appearance until the end of the eighteenth century. From the moment when man wanted works of art for himself or his nation, an instinct which is almost as old as the human race, agents were around to make certain he got it–but at a price, of course. When the Greeks began keeping inventories of their works of art in the fifth century B.C., then the property of the community as a whole, the wealthy classes wanted their own private collections. The fact that they were soon able to furnish their houses with art treasures was largely through the activities of the first Greek art dealers.

Whenever there is a profit to be made from the buying and selling of art, dealers and their agents have always been close at hand in any age. They even had their own quarter in ancient Rome, near the Villa Publica, and here works of art were bought and sold, restored and faked, for large sums of money. The art was supplied by soldiers and agents from the lands conquered by the Roman legions.

The Romans had a passion for the 'antique' and they often scorned 'contemporary' works of art. Pliny records that most art collections in Rome consisted of 'old' paintings and sculptures. Dealers found that the demand invariably outran the supply of genuine works of art.

Dealers have rarely been fussy about where their stock comes from, especially in times of war. Marco Polo was what the modern art trade would call a 'runner', an agent who looks out for saleable works of art and sells them directly to dealers or collectors. When Marco Polo visited the Emperor of China he brought back huge amounts of treasure to his native Italy. Later few ships returned from China without having rich treasure on board.

The Quattrocento was a golden age for artists, collectors and dealers. Because the great families of the Renaissance–families like the Medici –venerated art, demand for rare works increased, and so, of course, did the price. Francis I of France paid 4,000 scudi for Leonardo da Vinci's *Mona Lisa*. In today's terms 4,000 scudi, which is about twelve tons of pure silver, would be worth about £145,000. Although it is difficult to put a price on the priceless, the *Mona Lisa* must be worth upwards of a million pounds of any nation's money in prestige alone.

Agents for the great collectors of the 16th and 17th centuries were really pioneer dealers. They searched everywhere for works of art for the collections of such men as Cardinal Richelieu, the Grand Duke of Tuscany and Charles I of England. 'The Prince of Wales,' wrote Rubens in a letter of January 10, 1625, 'is of all princes the most enthusiastic amateur of painting in the world.' Charles I, as he became four months later, formed one of the finest collections of his day, and at a time when there was tough competition from other zealous collectors. Charles paid vast amounts for drawings by Leonardo

An original oil painting does not have to cost you a fortune like the profile on the right by Boltraffio, a pupil of Leonardo da Vinci. Woolworth's sell 'originals' like the one on the left for as little as 77s. 6d. Producing these paintings is a cottage industry in Belgium. A number of artists work either at home or in special studios, under the direction of Martin Dawen, owner of a large framing factory. Roman collectors often commissioned copies in bronze of older Greek sculptures. The original of *Aphrodite Arranging Her Hair*—(below) dates from the fourth century B.C. Gallery owners are the impresarios of the art world where age is no barrier. Michael Findlay (below right) is the young Vice-President of a well-known New York gallery. One of his artists, Charles Hinman, stands with arms folded in the background

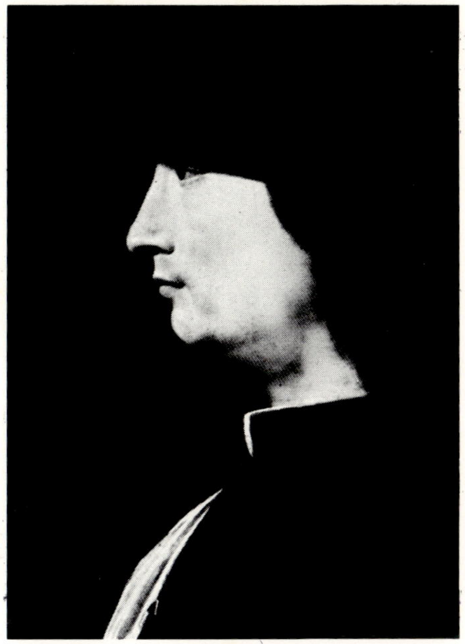

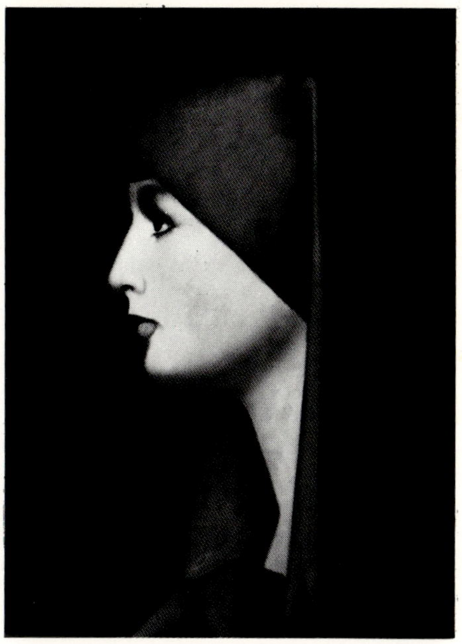

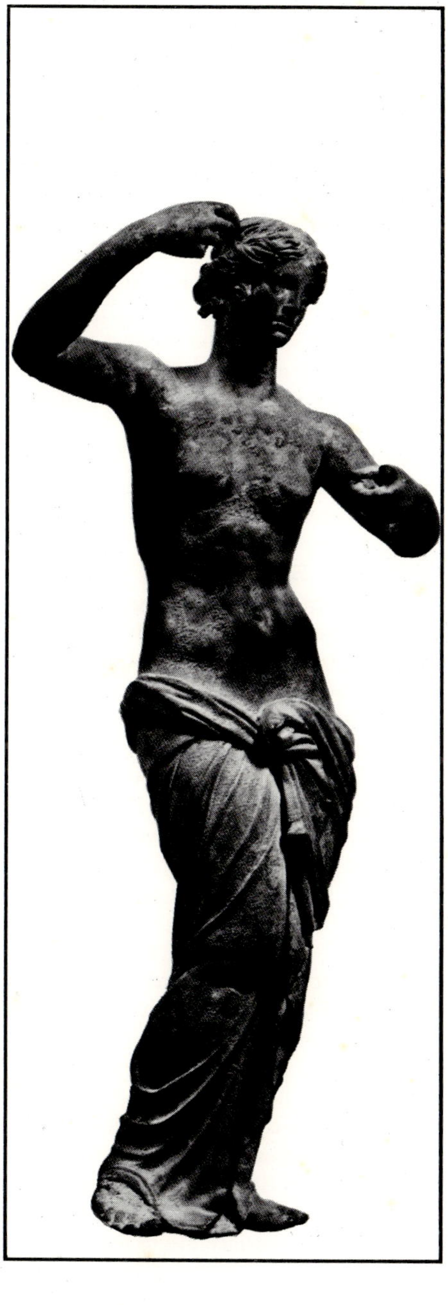

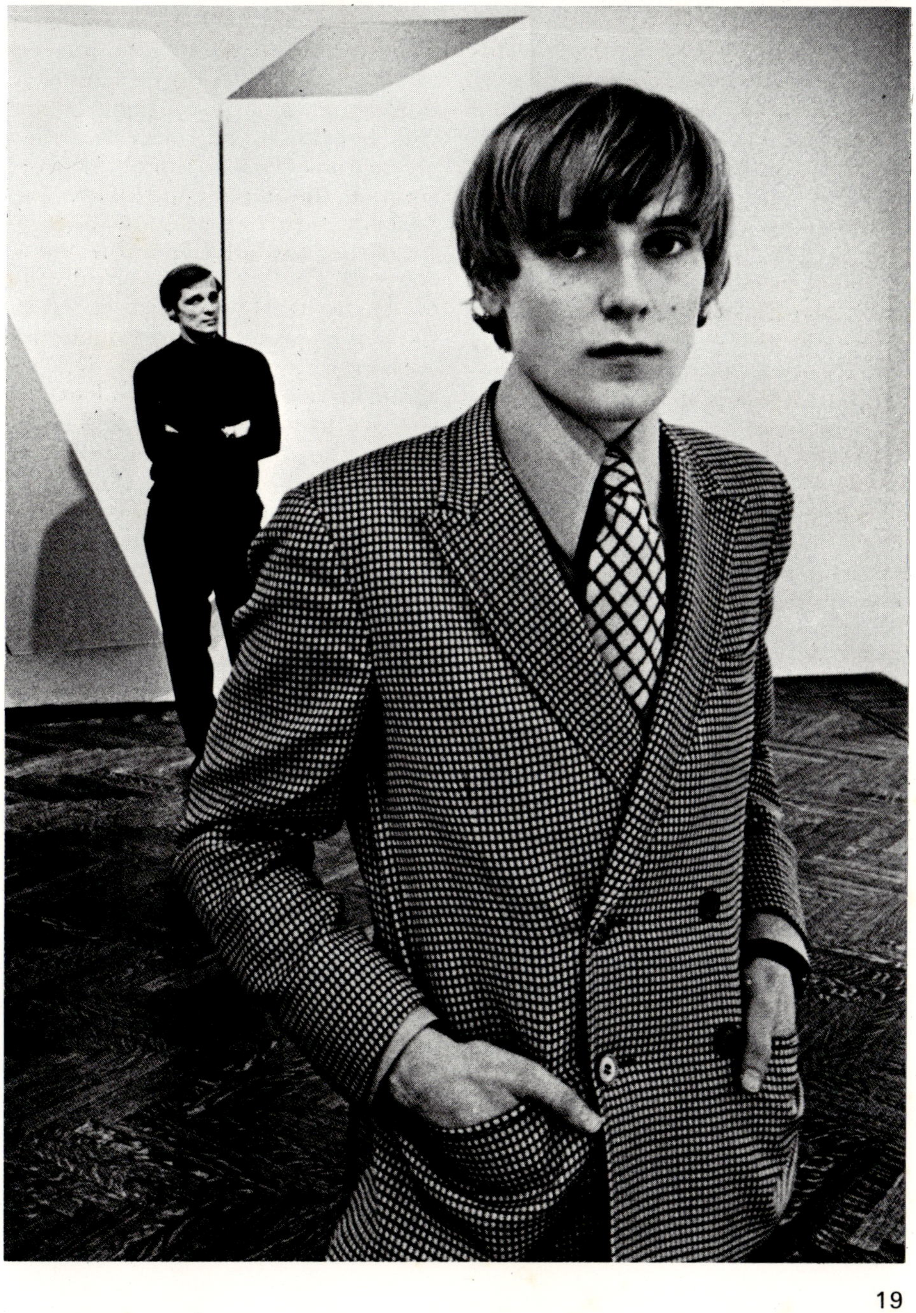

da Vinci, paintings by Correggio, Titian and Holbein. In 1629 he spent £18,000 on important works from the Gonzaga collection. When he visited Madrid to woo Philip of Spain's sister he commissioned Velasquez, then almost unknown in England, to make sketches for his portrait. He also bought paintings in large quantities in Spain. The King of Spain gave him a Correggio and a Titian, and Charles had copies made of work in the Spanish Court which he was not able to buy.

After the execution of Charles I in 1649, Parliament ordered the sale of many of Charles's pictures. Three commissioners were appointed—a poet, a painter and a civil servant—to dispose of the collection. Some of the pictures were used to pay some of the Court debts while others were sold directly to those who were either buying for themselves or acting as agents for others. Buyers came from all over Europe. The Archduke Leopold William of Austria, Cardinal Mazarin and the King of Spain, Philip IV, were among the principal collectors represented. The Spanish Ambassador in London, acting for his king, employed a tailor, a timber merchant, a cobbler and other equally obscure people to buy magnificent paintings by Raphael, Titian, Tintoretto, Andrea del Sarto and Dürer. Among the pictures sold by Cromwell's Commonwealth were Giorgione's *Concert Champêtre*, a superb group of Titians, all now in the Louvre in Paris, and Raphael's *La Perla*, now in the Prado in Madrid.

One of the greatest dealer-cum-agents of the 18th century was Count Algarotti, an intelligent, cultivated and courageous Italian. Algarotti was employed at different times during his career by Frederick the Great and the Elector Augustus III, King of Poland and Saxony. He helped supply some of the hundreds of paintings which entered their collections. Partly through Algarotti's influence and ability to acquire fine works of art, Augustus III devoted more time to his collection than to the affairs of state. In 1745 he acquired the magnificent collection owned by the Duke of Modena, which included four paintings by Correggio, four by Veronese, other masterpieces by Holbein, Rubens and Velasquez, and Titian's painting *The Tribute Money*. Later he got his hands on the Waldstein collection, which had well-known paintings by Vermeer, Frans Hals and Van Dyck. From Paris he was sent a steady supply of pictures by Rembrandt, Rubens and Watteau. But perhaps the finest work in his collection, at least in the opinion of other collectors, was Raphael's *Sistine Madonna*.

Algarotti's remarkable reputation as a dealer can be judged from a letter which Frederick the Great sent to him in September, 1742. Algarotti had joined the court of Augustus III, a desertion which greatly annoyed Frederick. He wrote: 'The rules of good taste would forbid me to reply to your letter. Its style and expressions are so immoderate that silence would certainly best become me. But a residue of goodwill towards you induces me to ask you (for the last time in my life, mark you) whether you will come back to me and on what terms. Put all official duties out of your head; they do not suit you; think only of a good pension and your liberty. If you reject this offer, please think of me no more.' Algarotti ignored the letter and five years passed before he again became Frederick's art adviser and friend.

Algarotti's letters to Count Brühl, one of Augustus III's ministers, reveal some of the mysteries, intrigues and dishonesty which surrounded the acquisition of beautiful and expensive works of art. In 1742 he was asked to buy the Pallavicini collection and other paintings from collections nearby. Not surprisingly, other dealers were also after the same collection. The methods described by Algarotti and his contemporaries would not have disgraced James Bond. One rival wore a silk mask to confuse other dealers and owners and also used a string of false names. The man in the mask, a dealer called Rossi, was the subject of a letter Algarotti wrote to Count Brühl:

'These pictures, with those I have already bought or would have bought if Rossi had not got in front of me, are the pick of an enormous number seen up to date in Venice. I have ransacked every corner in case anything might escape me, and I have been on the search for famous paintings in all the great palazzi. In the course of all this I have been shown many copies, many fakes, many poor and patched up and badly preserved originals. But, with me, the brew soon clears. My collection, by the excellence and splendour of each special work, shall be to other collections what the green diamond in the royal treasure in Dresden is to all other diamonds, their assay-piece and measure.'

By the 1780s London was becoming the centre of the international art market, a profitable honour she has held off and on ever since. London's traditional rival, Paris, suffered a serious setback with the French Revolution. Fleeing aristocrats, and even those who didn't get away, often entered some of their possessions in the London auction rooms. Christie's, the London saleroom, sold the collection of pictures belonging to John Trumbull, an American Embassy attaché, and Madame du Barry's jewels in 1797. Five years before, the collection belonging to Philip, Duke of Orléans, who had joined the French revolutionaries, found its way to the London market where it was finally sold and dispersed. One English art dealer who succeeded in temporarily getting his hands on part of the collection was Michael Bryan, an ex-cloth salesman, actor and schoolmaster. In 1783, this strange but charming man had married the Earl of Shrewsbury's sister whom he had met quite by chance on a cross-Channel ferry. Later he went to live in Belgium where he began dealing in pictures, a profitable career for many after the expropriation of the Belgian monasteries.

Interned by the French during their invasion of Belgium he was repatriated to England in 1794, whereupon he opened a small gallery in London's Savile Row. There he made a comfortable living from selling paintings brought to him by other refugees from the Continent. It is significant that by 1800 dealers like Cox, Moreland, Harris, Erard, John Smith and, of course, Michael Bryan were a force to be reckoned with in the salerooms. Before, the aristocracy and the landed gentry only had the competition they created amongst themselves to worry about. By opening their own galleries in the fashionable quarters of London, the dealers showed that they no longer had to rely on one or two rich patrons for their living. The dealer now cast his net for large and small fishes alike.

With the creation of a new industrial aristocracy—the cutlery, cotton and coal kings—a rich market was open for the growing number of dealers to exploit. The industrialists were often

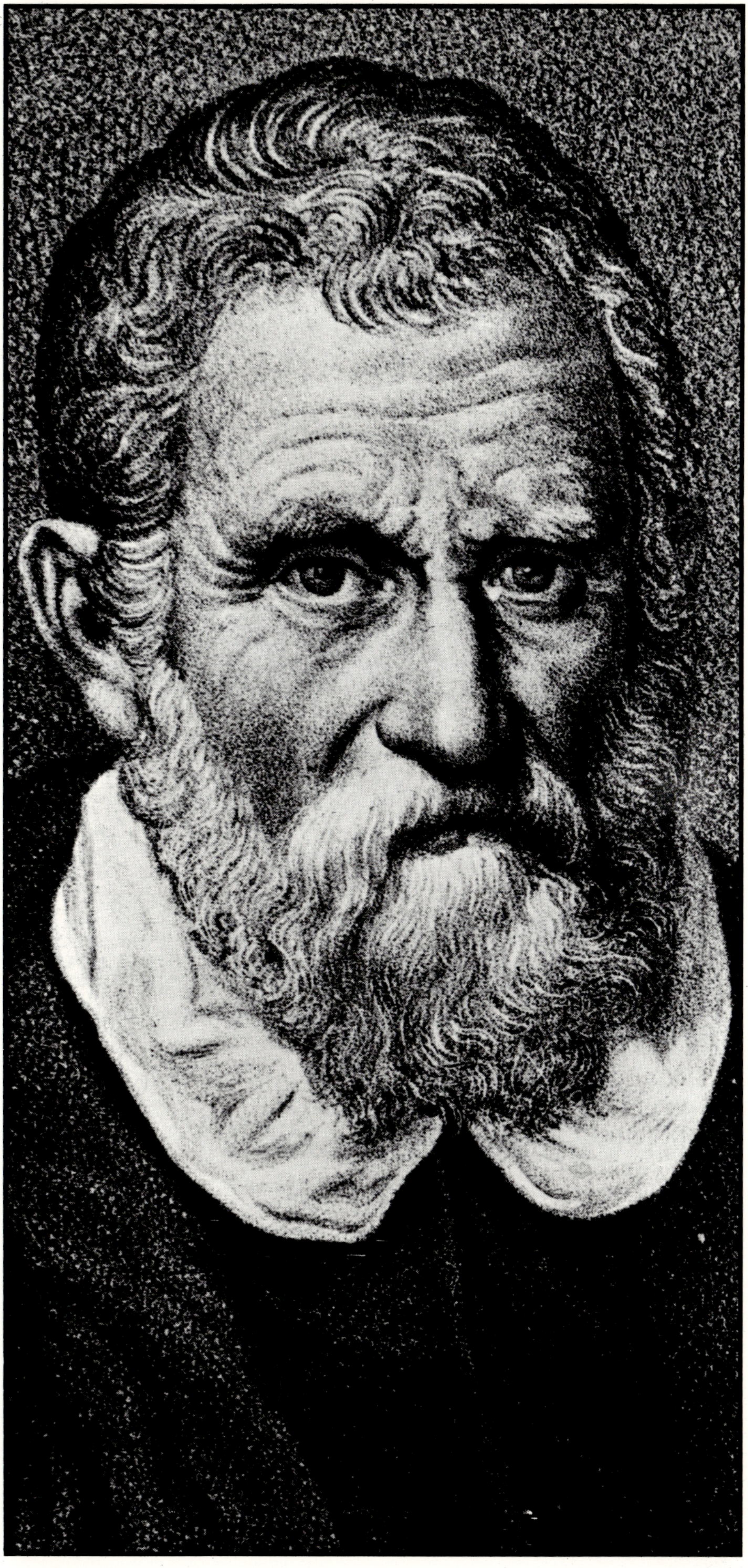

Marco Polo, the first traveller to trace a route right across Asia. Famous for his travels throughout thirteenth-century China, where he was employed in the service of Kublai Khan, he made a fortune trading in oriental art

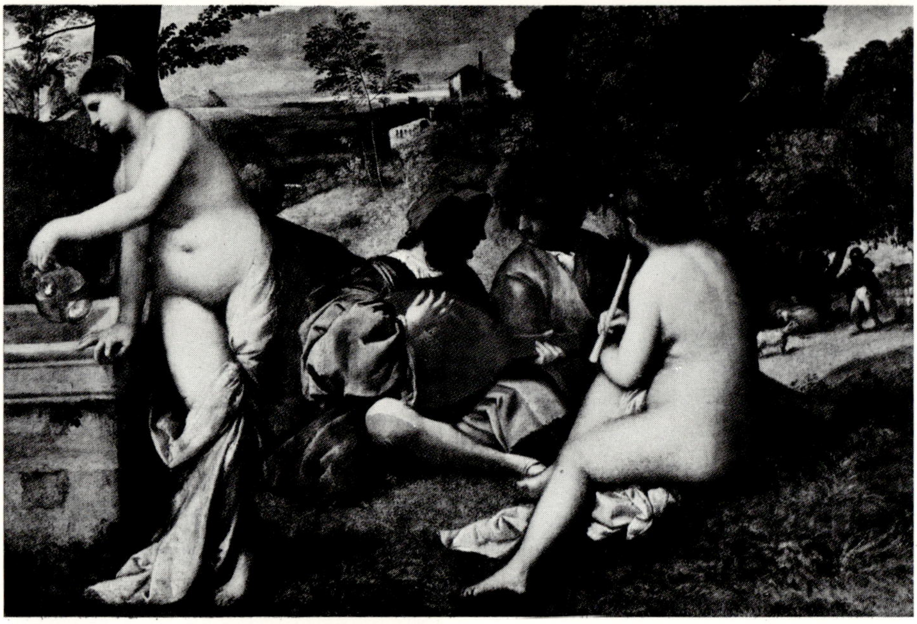

Giorgione's *Concert Champêtre* once belonged to Charles I of England. After his execution in 1649 Parliament ordered it to be sold to help pay court debts

Edwin Long, *The Babylonian Marriage Market*, bought in 1875 for 7,000 guineas. At that time a record for a living English painter . . . what would it fetch today?

men of humble background and they turned to the art dealer to help them acquire a 'background' more in keeping with their sudden wealth. Like the Roman and Renaissance *nouveaux riches* before them, they invariably admired 'antique' painting and sculpture; contemporary artists were quick to take the hint. A hundred years ago Victorian paintings of the *When Did You Last See Your Father?, Broken Vow, Hylas and the Nymphs, Sir Galahad at the Ruined Castle, The Doubt: Can These Dry Bones Live?* and *Cherry Ripe* variety became extremely popular in England.

Scenes of courting curates, rustic lovers, rosy-cheeked children and drunken sots, with sentimentality dripping from the ornate picture frames, captivated our great-grandfathers. The Tate Gallery and the Victoria and Albert Museum, municipal galleries like Birmingham and Manchester, are full of them–even if most of them are collecting dust in the basements. Sunday School virgins learning the Ten Commandments by heart, husbands catching their wives having some illicit fun, tales of financial ruin through gambling–pictorial morality often well painted but only found nowadays in Russia. Technically, the paintings are often well composed, colourful, even beautiful. But they are made up of bits and pieces. Bits of Leonardo, Michelangelo and Raphael, pieces of della Francesca and Greek sculptures. The rich and poor alike loved them. Whether they will always be considered something of a bad joke is purely academic.

Take Augustus Leopold Egg's triptych, which was recently rehung during the reorganisation of the Tate Gallery. When it was first exhibited at the Royal Academy it had no title but bore the quotation: '4 Aug: Have just heard that B. has been dead more than a fortnight; so his poor children have now lost both their parents. I hear *She* was seen on Friday last, near the Strand, evidently without a place to lay her head–What a fall hers has been!' In the first of these three paintings a Victorian husband holds a letter from his wife's lover. She lies sprawled on the ground while her children play in a corner of the room. The next picture shows her in a seedy bedsitter in Whitechapel and in the final picture she is seen with her child, dejected and poor, beneath the Adelphi arches looking across the river. Great stuff. Very different from the bands of flat colour which are hung in so many galleries today. Fortunately for art dealers few of them ever have to worry about the style of painting they sell. Naturally enough, they always serve the taste of their own age and leave the final reckoning of what is priceless or worthless to the only judge in art speculation worth listening to, time. A glance at any Victorian saleroom catalogue would show that pictures which cost thousands of pounds would now be knocked down for less than a thousand shillings. Edwin Long's large and splendid but also vulgar and boring picture *The Babylonian Marriage Market* was bought by Edward Hermon, M.P., in 1875, for 7,000 guineas. Seven

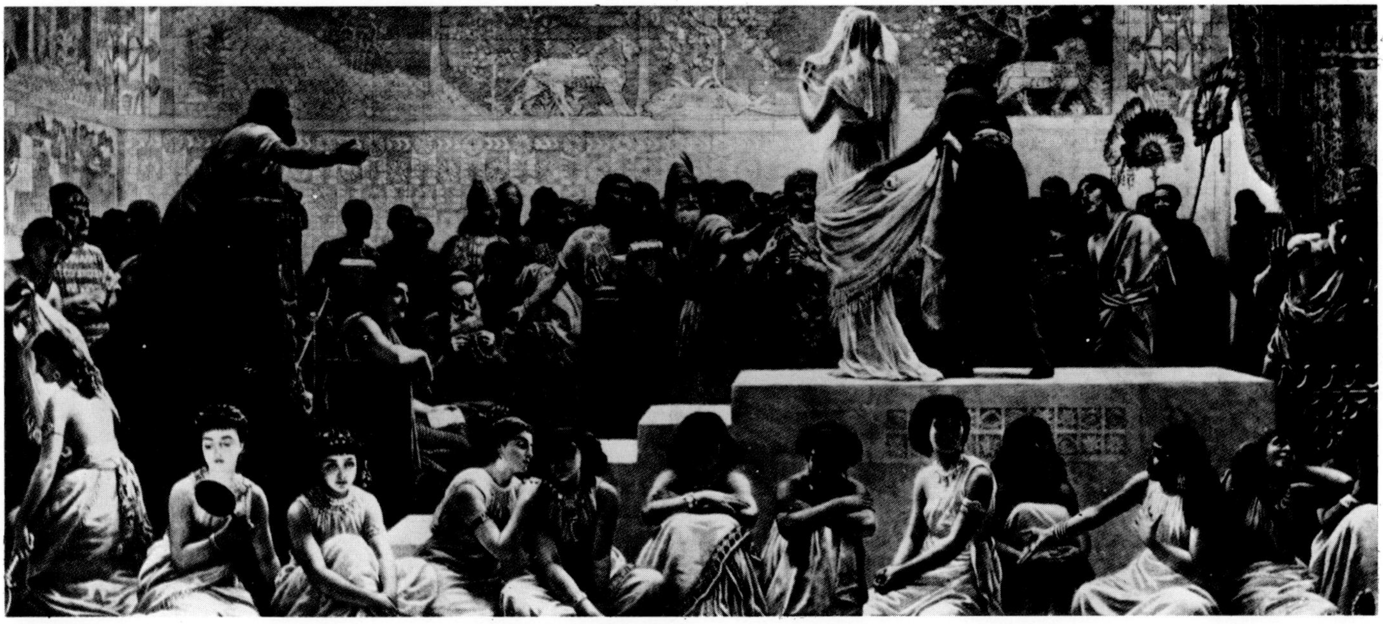

years later it was sold at auction for £6,615, at that time a record for a living English painter. But how many people today have even heard of Edwin Long? The reader should observe the examples and moral of Victorian collectors and ask themselves: How many of today's favourites will be remembered in a hundred years from now? Robert Wraight, the author of *The Art Game*, suggests that less than 1 per cent of contemporary works of art will survive the rampages of time.

The greatest and most famous art dealer of them all, 'Joe' Duveen, later Lord Duveen of Millbank, outsold, outspent and outwitted more dealers and collectors than anybody else in any age. Duveen became an art dealer when the industrial aristocracy in the United States were ready to spend their newly-acquired fortunes. Duveen noticed one significant characteristic of his time: America had much too much money and much too little art, whereas Europe had too much art and comparatively little money. Duveen observed that he could redress the balance while making a commensurate profit for himself. The fact that he succeeded was largely because he knew the kind of collector he was selling his art to.

Ernst Fischer in his challenging book, *The Necessity of Art*, suggests that industrialists in 1860 or 1960, were different in their habits from art-loving feudal princes. 'The capitalist's increasing wealth also brought new luxuries with it, but, as Marx pointed out, ". . . the capitalist's extravagance never has the genuine character of unbridled prodigality which was typical of certain feudal magnates . . . behind it there lurk sordid avarice and anxious calculation." For the capitalist, luxury may mean the purely private satisfaction of his desires, but it also means the chance of displaying his wealth for prestige reasons. Capitalism is not essentially a social force that is well disposed to art or that promotes art; in so far as the average capitalist needs art at all, he needs it as an embellishment of his private life or as an investment.' Fischer also suggests: 'For a long time capitalism regarded art as something suspect, frivolous, and shady. Art "did not pay". Pre-capitalist society had tended towards extravagance, carefree spending on a vast scale, lavish entertainments and the promotion of the arts. Capitalism meant sober calculation and the puritanical slide-rule.'

Capitalist princes like J. P. Morgan, Henry Clay Frick, Joseph E. Widener, Samuel H. Kress or Andrew Mellon may have been mean to their employees and even mean to their friends, but when it came to buying art from a dealer like Duveen they threw 'sober calculation and the puritanical slide-rule' to the wind. Fifty-five of the 115 pictures, exclusive of the American portraits, in the Mellon Collection, which is now in the National Gallery in Washington, came to Mellon through Duveen. Of the 700 paintings in the Kress Collection, also in the National Gallery, more than 150 were supplied by Duveen and these are considered among the very finest in the collection. According to the American art scholar, Dr Alfred M. Frankfurter, the United States has the largest aggregation of Italian pictures outside Italy, apart from the English collections which were formed during the 18th and 19th centuries. Of these pictures in the United States 75 per cent are believed to have passed through Duveen's hands.

When Duveen said: 'If I had the Sistine Chapel, I could sell it tomorrow half-a-dozen times over' it was no idle boast. Dealers today would have no trouble selling the choicest pickings from the world's finest museums. The only problem is that the museums don't want to sell their treasures. Because there are comparatively few masterpieces and good quality items about, dealers and collectors have turned to more modern pictures. The scarcity factor largely explains why Impressionist and modern works of art have enjoyed such an enormous rise in popularity since the war. For example, Cézanne's *Le Paysan* was sold for £960 in 1911; in 1959 it was sold for £145,000. In 1913 his *Garçon au gilet rouge* was sold for £3,600; in 1958 it was sold for £220,000. Encouraged by the gold-strike proportions of these increases in values, dealers have been suggesting ever since that almost every modern work of art will *eventually* rise in value. The breakthrough for modern art came in the mid-1950s. Gerald Reitlinger observes in his book *The Economics of Taste* that 'the prices of 1956 included surprising advances by distinctly

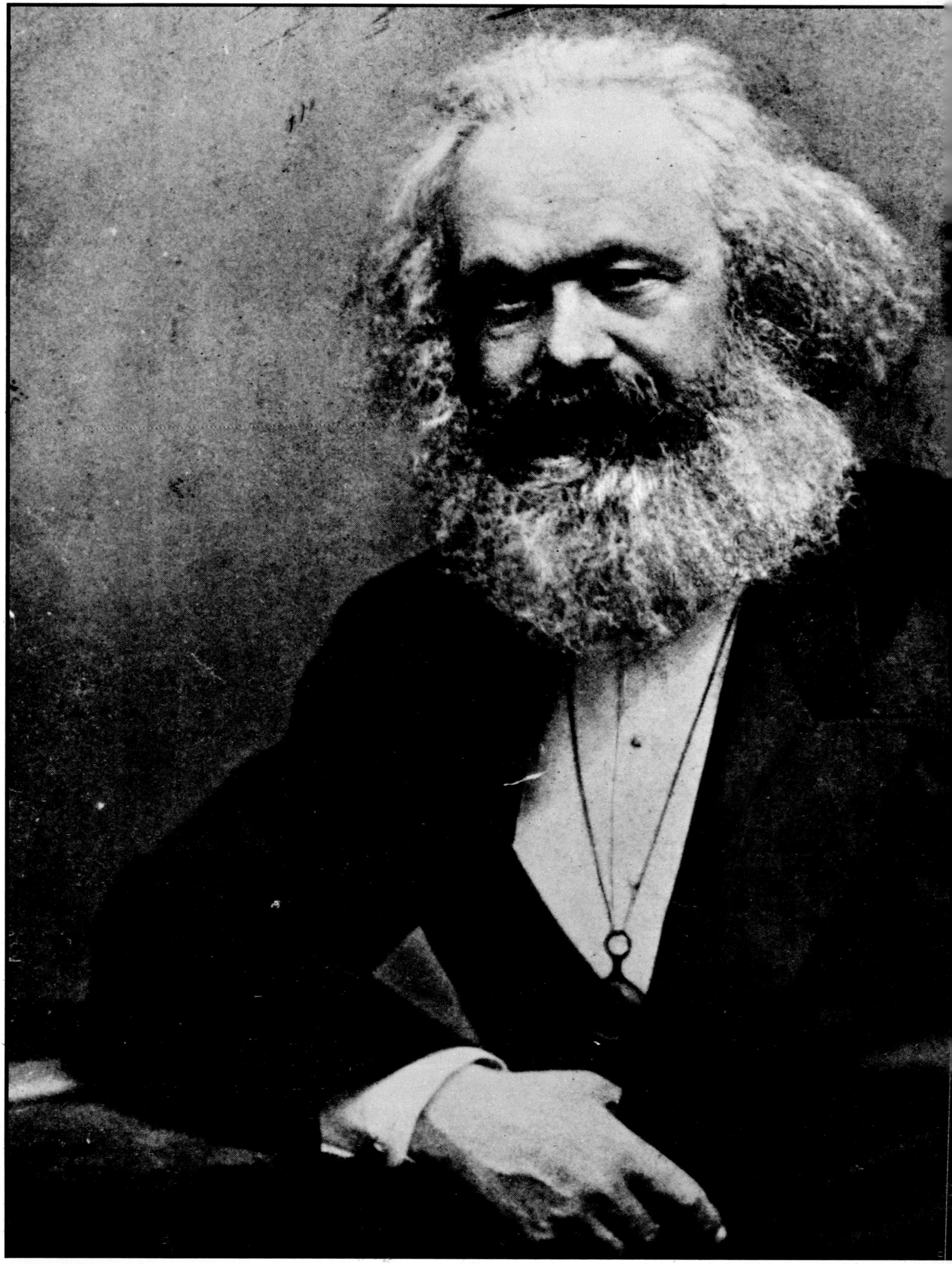

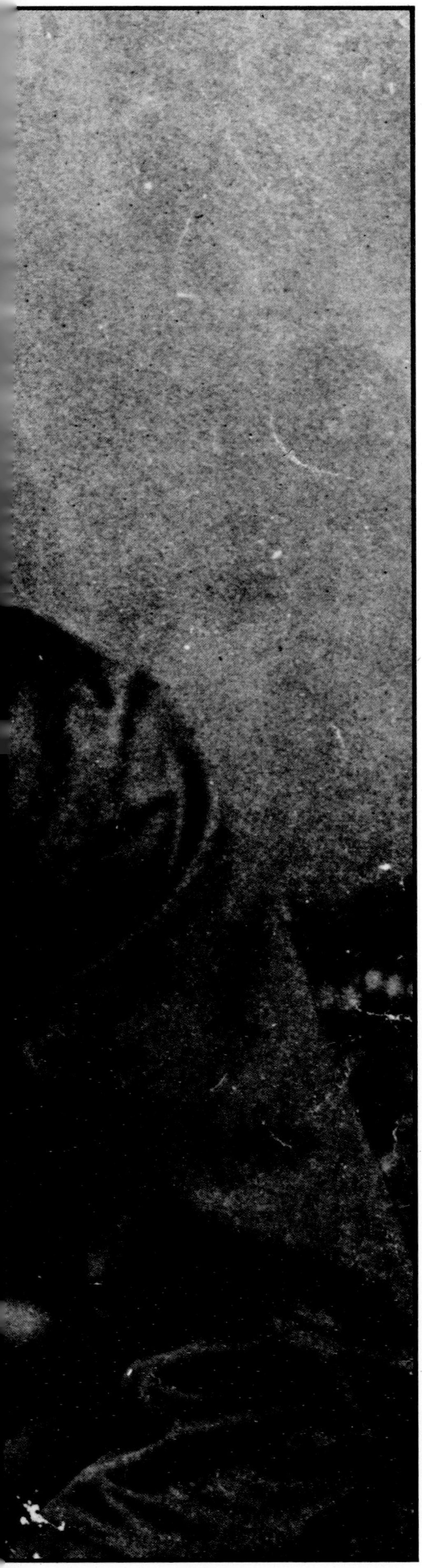

Karl Marx (left), not surprisingly, was out of sympathy with the nineteenth-century art trade. 'Capitalist extravagance,' he wrote, 'never has the genuine character of unbridled prodigality typical of certain feudal magnates. Below it there lurk sordid avarice and anxious calculation'

The Doubt: Can These Dry-Bones Live? A characteristic painting of the Victorian era (below)

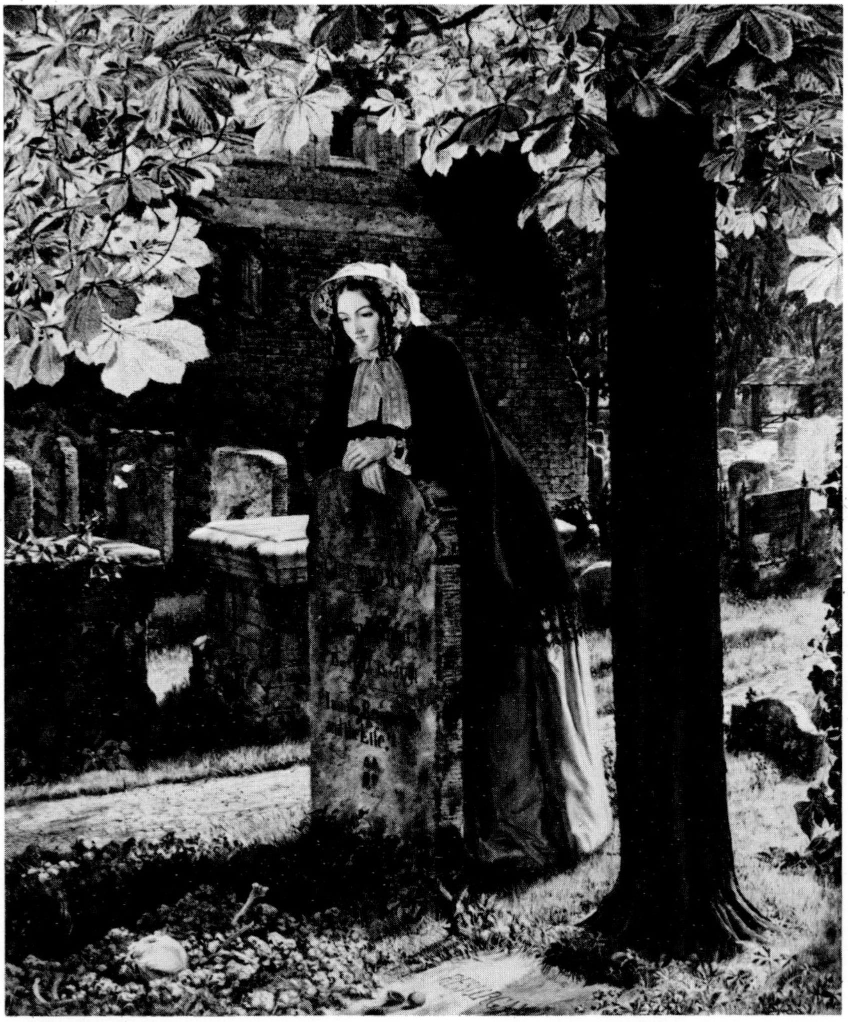

minor men: £7,350 for a Bonnard and about £5,000 each for a Vuillard and a Utrillo. It was a sign that, as a millionaire's market, the modern French school had now taken the place of the English eighteenth-century portraits in the 1920s. Compared with the large number of modern works at prices over £10,000, the London salerooms in 1952–56 produced only twelve old masters that made as much.' In October 1958 the moderns marched on in triumph with the sale of seven pictures in the Goldschmidt sale. The prices, given here, staggered the art world.

Cézanne	
Garçon au gilet rouge	£220,000
Van Gogh	
Public gardens at Arles	£132,000
Manet	
Rue Mosnier aux drapeaux	£113,000
Cézanne	
Les grosses pommes	£90,000
Manet	
La promenade	£89,000
Renoir	
La Pensée	£72,000
Manet	
Self-portrait	£65,000

Five weeks later the moderns were again seen to be catching up their elders, this time at the Arnold Kirkeby sale in New York:

Picasso	
Madonna and Child	£54,285
Cézanne	
Garçon, couché sur l'herbe	£44,500
Renoir	
Jardin à Sorrento	£37,500
Bonnard	
Fenêtre ouverte	£34,140
Renoir	
La couseuse	£31,070
Monet	
Child in a Cradle	£30,350
Degas	
Dancers on a Landscape Stage	£23,680
Matisse	
Fleurs et céramiques	£23,215
Modigliani	
Half-length portrait, Male	£23,600
Portrait of Mme Eynaud-Vaillant	£23,250
Pissarro	
Route d'Auvers	£23,425
Van Gogh	
Barge at Arles	£24,150
Signac	
Fishing boats	£12,140
Manet	
Half-length Portrait of a Girl	£14,000

Although an early picture by Picasso fetched £190,000 at Sotheby's in 1967, the highest price ever paid for the work of a living artist, the moderns and the ultra-moderns still have a great deal of ground to catch up. If we compare the best and most popular of the moderns with performances recently set up by some old masters the dead are still well in front of the living and the recently demised. Rubens's *Adoration of the Magi* was sold in 1959 for £275,000; Frans Hals's *Unknown Cavalier* for £182,000 in 1960; Gainsborough's *Mr and Mrs Andrews* for £132,000 in the same year, and Rembrandt's portrait of his son Titus was recently sold for £798,000. What would Raphael's *Alba Madonna* fetch, one wonders, in the unlikely event of it reappearing on the world market? In 1808 it was bought for £4,000; in 1836 it was sold to the Tsar of Russia for £14,000; and in 1931 it was sold to the American millionaire Andrew Mellon for £240,800. If the *Alba Madonna* continues its extraordinary rise in value and esteem, and there is nothing yet to suggest it couldn't, the work might fetch up to five million pounds by the year 2000. In other words, expensive as some modern art has become it is still cheap compared with the most popular old masters.

Despite the increased value of some modern painting and sculpture since the war, the international art market has become more democratic. With improved living standards has come an enormous demand for *original* works of art. Prints of popular favourites like Millais's *Cherry Ripe* may have been good enough for 'granny' sixty years ago, but it's certainly not good enough for people today. Picture owners are probably a larger group than car owners in the 1960s. Thousands more people are painting in the hope of selling their wares in this expanding new industry. At one end, 'factory' artists are producing 'original' pictures in the thirty-shilling to five-pound range of prices, which chain stores like Woolworth's have discovered. In Belgium, one painting 'factory' has had an enormous demand for Swiss landscapes. One man paints the sky, one the fluffy cotton wool clouds, another adds trees and a blue lake, and yet another signs the finished composition. Then at the other end of the scale is the made-to-measure art market.

Not surprisingly, a host of new dealers have appeared on the scene to exploit this situation in art. Always eager to spread the gospel of art collecting, they have helped speed up the cultural revolution. They have nevertheless made quite sure that the producer—the artist, rarely meets the consumer—the buyer. They have, after all, got a living to make, and this is not always easy. Dealers have to convince clients that they should buy work by comparatively little-known artists, the giants of tomorrow. They know that the big names of modern art get more of the publicity and the big prices ('Agnew's pays more than half-a-million pounds for a Monet' and 'Multi-million pounds art swindle—Picassos and Braques faked' were two recent newspaper headlines) but they can still make a comfortable profit selling a lot of pictures at less than a hundred pounds each and the occasional item at anything up to five thousand pounds. For the moment I'm forgetting the Moguls of the trade and concentrating on the average dealer. Many dealers play on their client's passionate hope that the paintings or sculpture of their choice will steadily, perhaps even outrageously, jump in value. Nowadays many people treat works of art like piggy banks, but with two major differences. One is that they don't need to fill up their picture and the other that their 'piggy bank' is wrapped in an aura of mystery and culture. Dealers also play on the snob value when talking to clients in their galleries. Higher up the social scale surrounding oneself with canvases and bronzes by well-known artists is much less vulgar than three cars, servants and a house in the country, though if you have these as well so much the better. When David Frost, the television personality, had bought his house in Belgravia, his Mercedes and his other cars, he turned to several thousand pounds' worth of modern art for that extra bit of individuality. And so it is with many more of us, except perhaps that we buy on a shoestring budget.

The modern artist has made the dealer's task simpler by painting, paradoxically, things we can understand immediately and non-representational pictures. On one hand, art uses the symbols of its age in much the same way as the Renaissance once used antique sculptures of

The fifteen pictures shown here all fetched high prices at recent art auctions. Together they represent a substantial fortune. Anyone buying them all would have to be a millionaire. Arranged in three columns they are as follows.
Left-hand column: Velasquez, *Jester Calabazas*. 170,000 guineas. Christie's; Frans Hals, *Male Portrait*. 70,000 guineas. Christie's; Matisse, *Femme à la Fontaine.* $70,000. Parke-Bernet Galleries; Frans Hals, *Portrait of Pieter Jacobsz Olycan, Burgomaster of Haarlem*. 50,000 guineas. Christie's.
Centre column: Edgar Degas, *Répétition de Ballet.* $410,000. Parke-Bernet Galleries; Picasso, *Femme au Corsage Bleu*. $115,000. Parke-Bernet Galleries; Claude Lorrain, *View of Carthage with Dido, Aeneas and Their Suite Leaving for the Hunt*. 52,000 guineas. Christie's; Nicolas de Largillière, *Portrait of Elizabeth Throckmorton*. 62,000 guineas. Christie's; Camille Pissarro, *La Route d'Osny, Pontoise.* 35,000 guineas. Christie's; Antonio d'Ancona, *The Virgin and Child with Saints.* 58,000 guineas. Christie's.
Right-hand column: Braque, *Bouteille de Rhum.* $120,000. Parke-Bernet Galleries; Edouard Vuillard, *Portrait de la Comtesse de Noailles.* $74,000. Parke-Bernet Galleries; Hubert Van Eyck, *St George and the Dragon.* £220,000. Sotheby's; Jan van de Cappelle, *Coast Scene with Fishing Boats in a Calm Sea.* 52,000 guineas. Christie's; Van Gogh, *Portrait of Mademoiselle Ravoux*. 150,000 guineas. Christie's

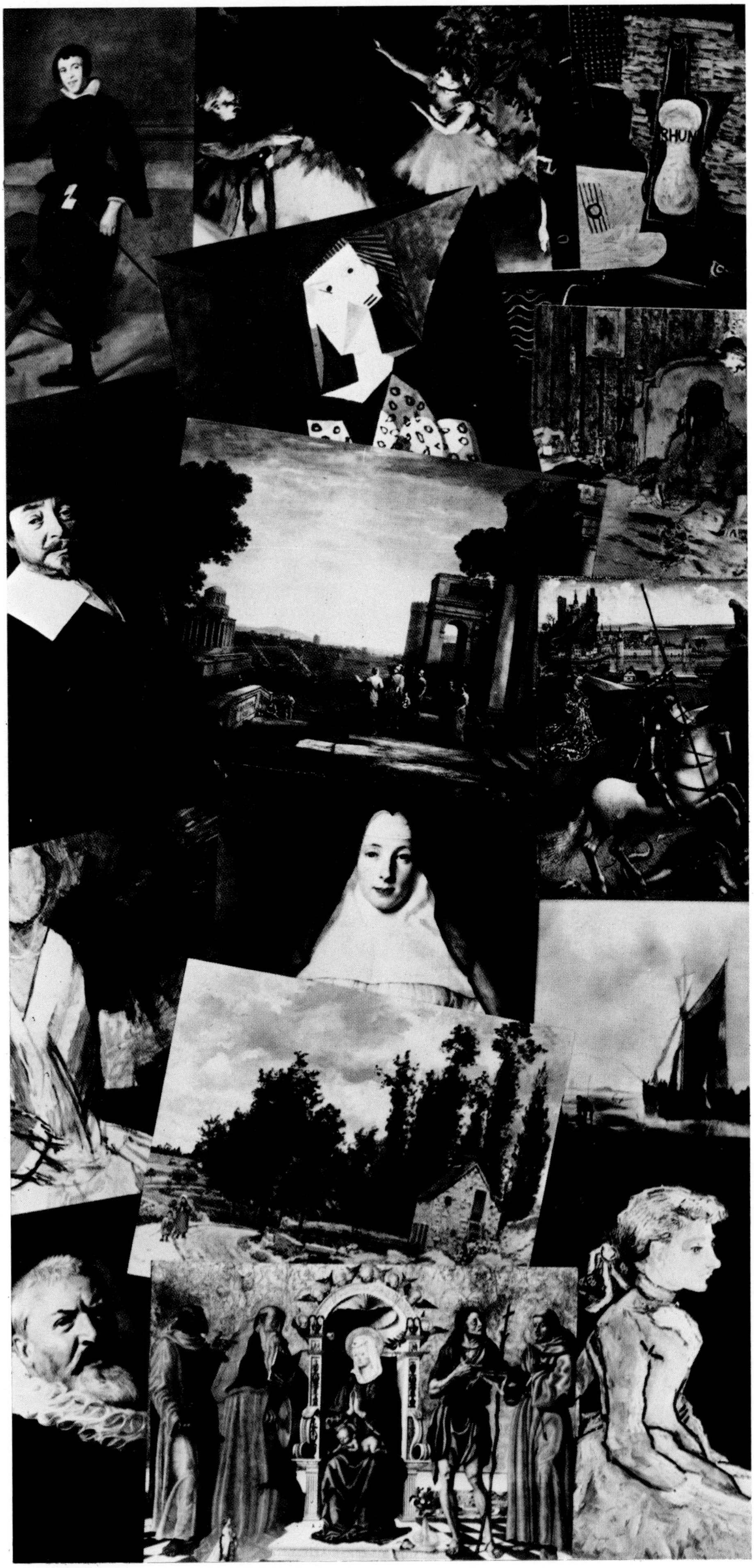

Apollo and Venus. Modern artists perpetuate in new forms the whole mythology of affluence, the common man, expendable culture, candy-coloured neon lighting, fun-making, love-ins and even the threat of the bomb. The so-called gap between art and life has perhaps never been narrower. At its most superficial, an Op painting by Vasarely or Bridget Riley has an equal chance of becoming the very latest dress design or entering a very recherché gallery. We have come a long way from the time when Sir Lawrence Alma-Tadema was every cultured person's ideal painter. A hundred years ago, dealers had to persuade collectors to buy pictures of Roman scenes, eastern marriage markets and other High Renaissance hangovers. Nowadays artists are more than likely to paint ordinary scenes and ordinary people. On the other hand, when they paint abstract pictures they provide the dealer with the heaven-sent opportunity to bring their own 'gallery' language into play. This consists of whimsical expressions about 'a painter's creative and dramatic use of colour', 'his inexplicable ability to handle paint', or 'the extraordinary way he filled each corner of the canvas with explosive feeling'. The language is normally accompanied by the dealer extending his arms in elegant gestures and occasionally pursing his lips as he stares bewitched at the picture he hopes so desperately to sell. The fact that people sometimes laugh at the antics of the art world doesn't in any way detract from its good qualities. It certainly has variety, which can be seen from random lists of exhibitions on view during the past two years.

During one month recently these exhibitions could be seen in LONDON, among more than a hundred others:

Appleby Bros
Watercolours prior to 1850
Couper Gallery
Barbizon School/French 19th century paintings
Don Quixote Gallery
Spanish paintings
Gallery 43
Oceanic, African and Eastern art
ICA Gallery
Picasso & Concrete: photographs
Imperial War Museum
Sir Muirhead Bone
Marlborough New London
Kandinsky and His Friends
Mermaid Theatre
Theatre Posters from the German Democratic Republic
Tryon Gallery
Sporting and Natural History Pictures
Upper Grosvenor Galleries
Seven Contemporary Indian Artists
Whitechapel Gallery
A Box of Bricks, Composing in Units

The following exhibitions were on view in the following cities at the same time:

NEW YORK
AAA
Homage to American Art
Art Fair
Grosz, Beckmann
Brooklyn Museum
Ancient Art
Cisneros
Latin America 1966
Ella Lerner Gallery
Daumier, Goya
Gallery of Modern Art
Highlights of the Dali Exhibition
IBM
French posters
Phyllis Lucas Old Print Center
Old Oriental Prints and Watercolours
Royal Marks
Randell, Richard: Air Frame Sculpture
Stix
Five Hundred Million Years of Inspired Design

PARIS
Arditti
Fontana, Hartung, Mathieu
Du Fleuve
Baj, Adzak, Buri
Fernand Depas
Figurative Masters of the 20th Century
Jacques Massol
McAllister, Gerolds
L'Oeil Galerie
Old and Contemporary Masters
Messine
Braque, de Stael, Landskoy
Percier
Bauchant, Van Dongen, etc

AMSTERDAM
Espace
Lucassen
Galerie 20
Schippers, Postma, van Amen, etc
Krikhaar
Paul de Lussanet
Stedelijk Museum
Niki de St Phalle

It is extraordinary just how international the world's art market has become. Swop any of the above exhibitions around from city to city and few art devotees would even notice. Parisians would certainly enjoy the New York list of exhibitions and there is no reason why Londoners shouldn't appreciate the shows from the Amsterdam list. In many cases, of course, an exhibition is toured from one city to another. Discussing the problem of a contemporary artist who's been quite well known and is now out of fashion, the London art dealer Leslie Waddington describes the 'mobile' exhibition. 'Let's assume that this painter doesn't go over in New York, then have shows in Chicago, he doesn't go over in Chicago, then move further West but don't go as far as California because California has already become sophisticated . . .' But international giants like Picasso and Henry Moore can be expected to be successful in any city, town or hamlet, almost anywhere.

Gallery owners are the impresarios of the clannish, competitive and mysterious network which makes up the international art market. Many of them are tempted or 'forced' to help their deadly rivals, because sooner or later their rivals will probably help them in return. 'A great deal of backscratching goes on between dealers,' explained one New York gallery owner, 'and if it didn't how do you think I organised that Braque show. I haven't got that kind of money so I scoured the city for items by Braque. I did many of my major rivals a favour, but I didn't do too badly either.' Many of the art galleries in London have been forced to co-operate on different occasions, partly because of powerful galleries with larger resources. Suppose a dealer organises an exhibition of work by Chagall. He will build the exhibition around his own stock, but the other items he will borrow from other people. If he sells any of the pictures he has borrowed he will pay a commission to the owners. Normally it is in the region of twenty per cent of the purchase price.

Consider for a moment the economics of running a modern art gallery in London, Paris or New York. Few dealers can make much of a living by arranging exhibitions for little or unknown artists. If he does this at all, it is merely the dressing on the gallery cake. Selling the work of artists who command high prices is the major interest of a successful dealer. Avant-garde galleries like Signals and Indica in London failed to learn that 'dealing pictures' are the very backbone of the art trade. They went out of business, and they won't be the last to fail for this reason. Dealers must have sound financial backing and a certain amount of time to build up a stock of dealing items. Unlike grocers and furniture shops they can't just order their stock from a parent organisation. If he has a quarter of a million pounds to spend on stock he could spend it on forty quality paintings by the favourites of the century Picasso, Matisse, Braque, Dali and Chagall, etcetera, and have no change left to pay for the staff and the rent of his gallery. A dealer must have money and a great deal of patience.

There is a very reliable rumour that a newly-opened London gallery cost £19,000 to build and decorate, and the stock a solitary and undistinguished £1,000. The dealer's total resources when he started amounted to £20,000. He was last seen pleading with a rival and long-established gallery to lend him pictures from their stock. When one stops to consider the resources of firms like Marlborough Fine Art, the Palm Beach Galleries and the Wally Findlay Galleries in New York, Palm Beach and Chicago, it is perhaps astonishing that newcomers even enter the field.

Wally Findlay has been variously described as 'the multi-millionaire tycoon of business and art . . . third generation member of an art dynasty . . . owner of three burgeoning art galleries located in strategic centres where the great American wealth is concentrated: New York, Palm Beach and Chicago . . . tireless globe-trotter, in perennial search of art that will please his exclusive clientele . . . bon viveur whose opening night parties are famous on two continents . . . an aesthete whose handsome penthouses above his Regency style New York and Palm Beach galleries are filled with Impressionist and Post-Impressionist masterpieces and fine 18th-century French furniture . . . a man who prefers white for his two Rolls-Royces and his Bentley, to complete the cycle of his extraordinary, individualistic taste.' Guests, and one assumes that many were also clients, at a recent opening at the Wally Findlay Gallery in Palm Beach included: the Duke and Duchess of Windsor, Mr and Mrs

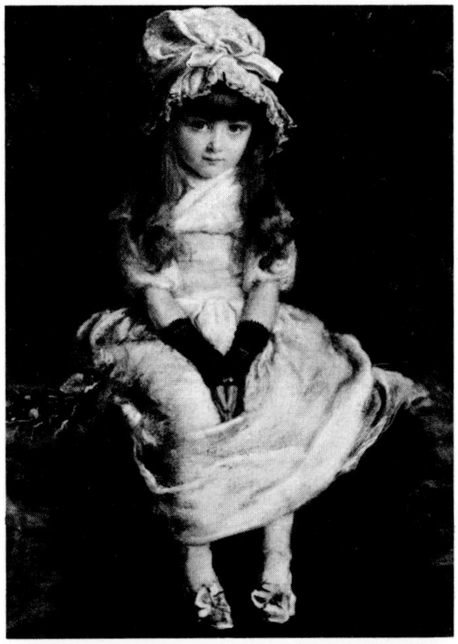

Millais, *Cherry Ripe* (right): Good enough for granny sixty years ago . . . still a favourite today.

Most dealers hope that the price of their artists' work will steadily or phenomenally jump in value. Dutch-born artist Albert Houtheusen (below) has seen a remarkable rise in the value of his paintings in the past three years

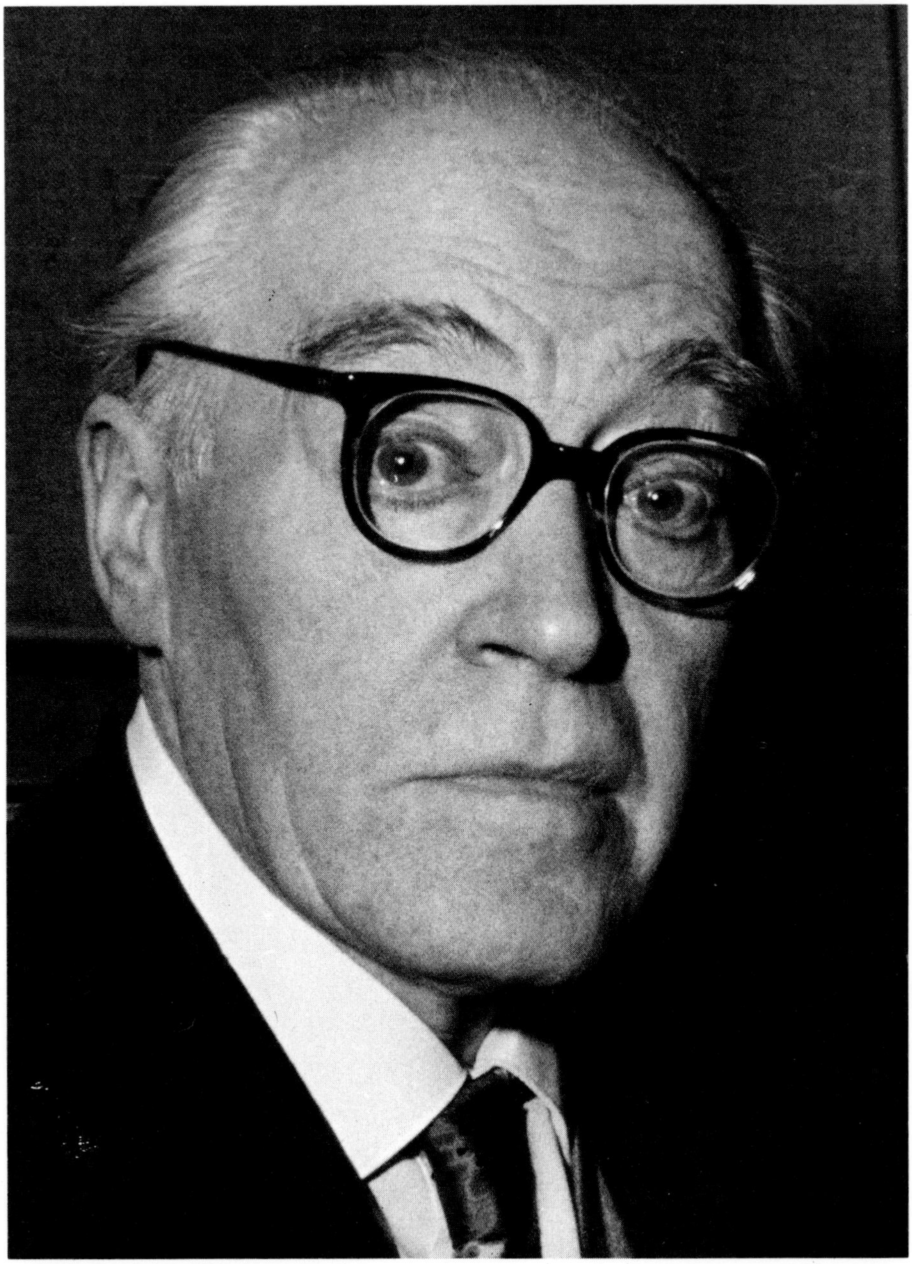

We have come a long way from the time when Sir Lawrence Alma-Tadema was every cultured person's ideal painter

If the giants of yesterday are out of fashion and the giants of tomorrow are still unknown, the work of today's successful artist can reach a vast public in the form of framed reproductions. This striking picture, *Blaze IV* (1964), by Op artist Bridget Riley, is having a wide sale thanks to modern marketing methods

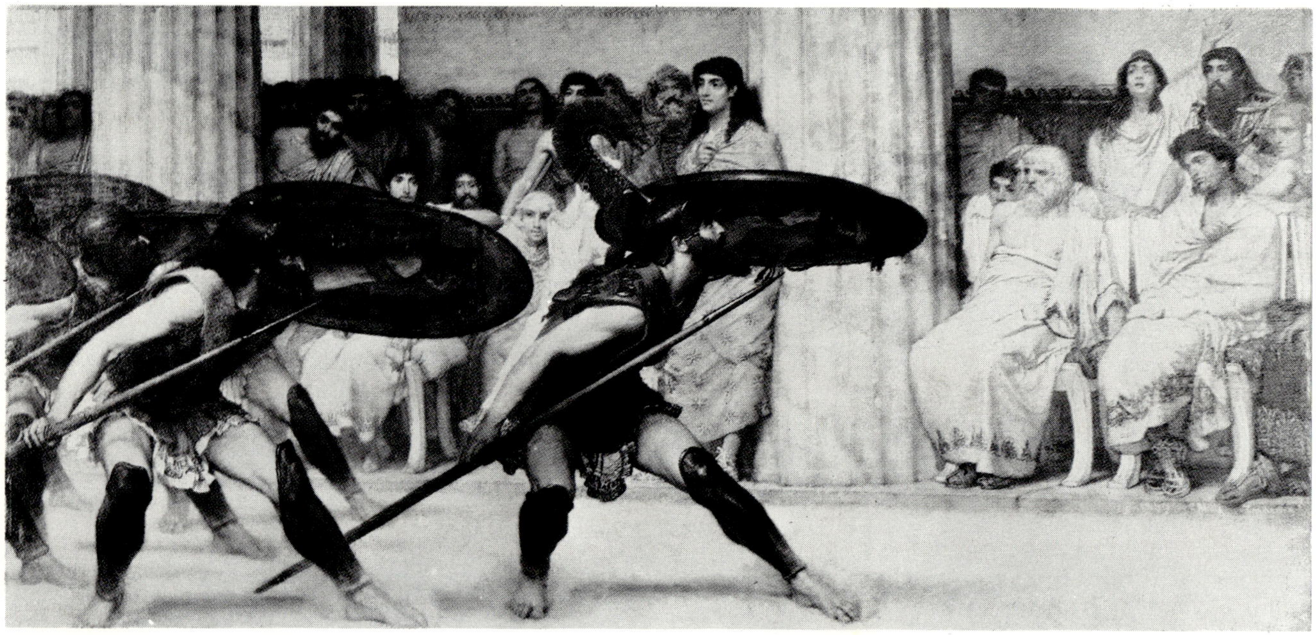

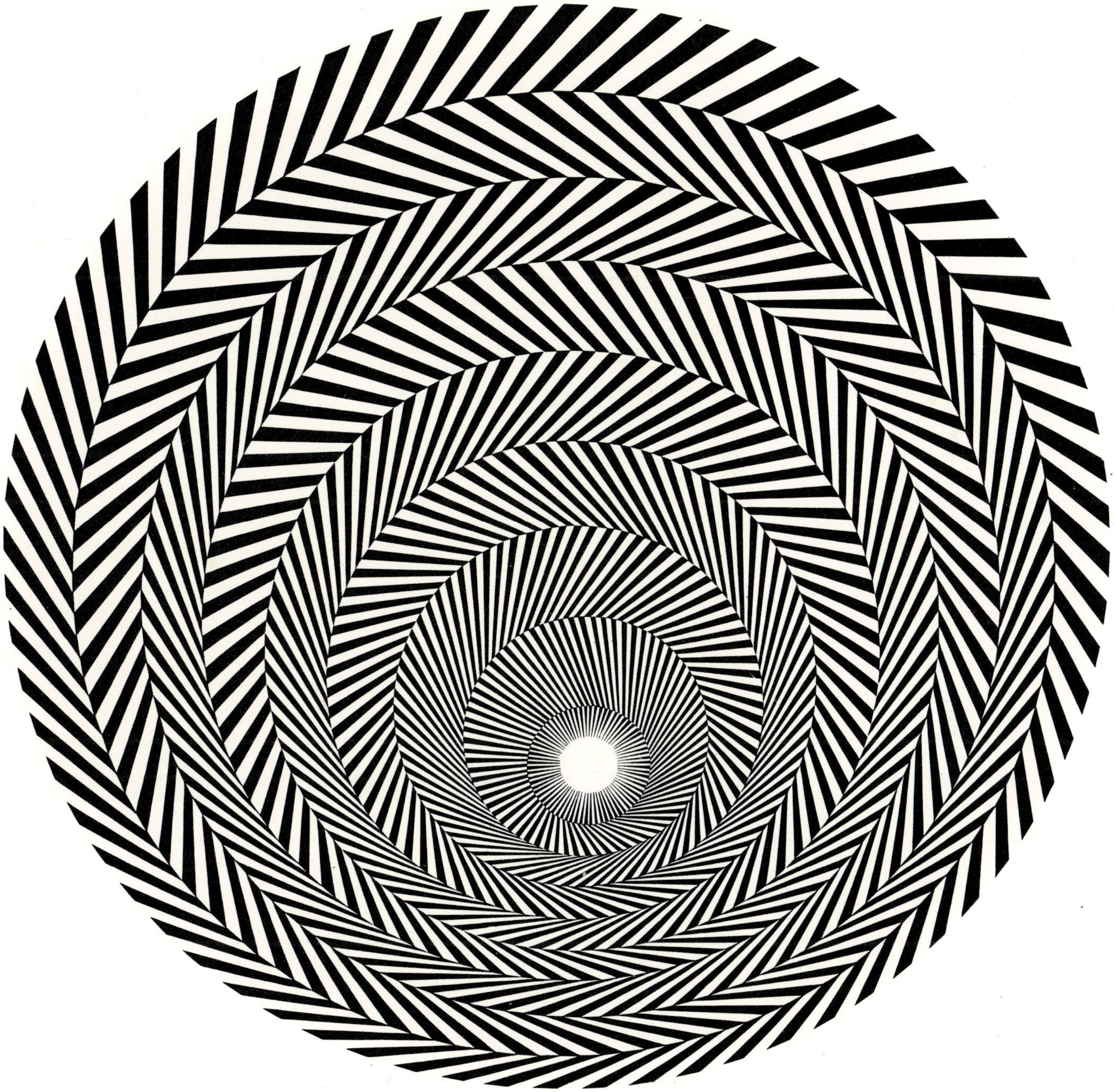

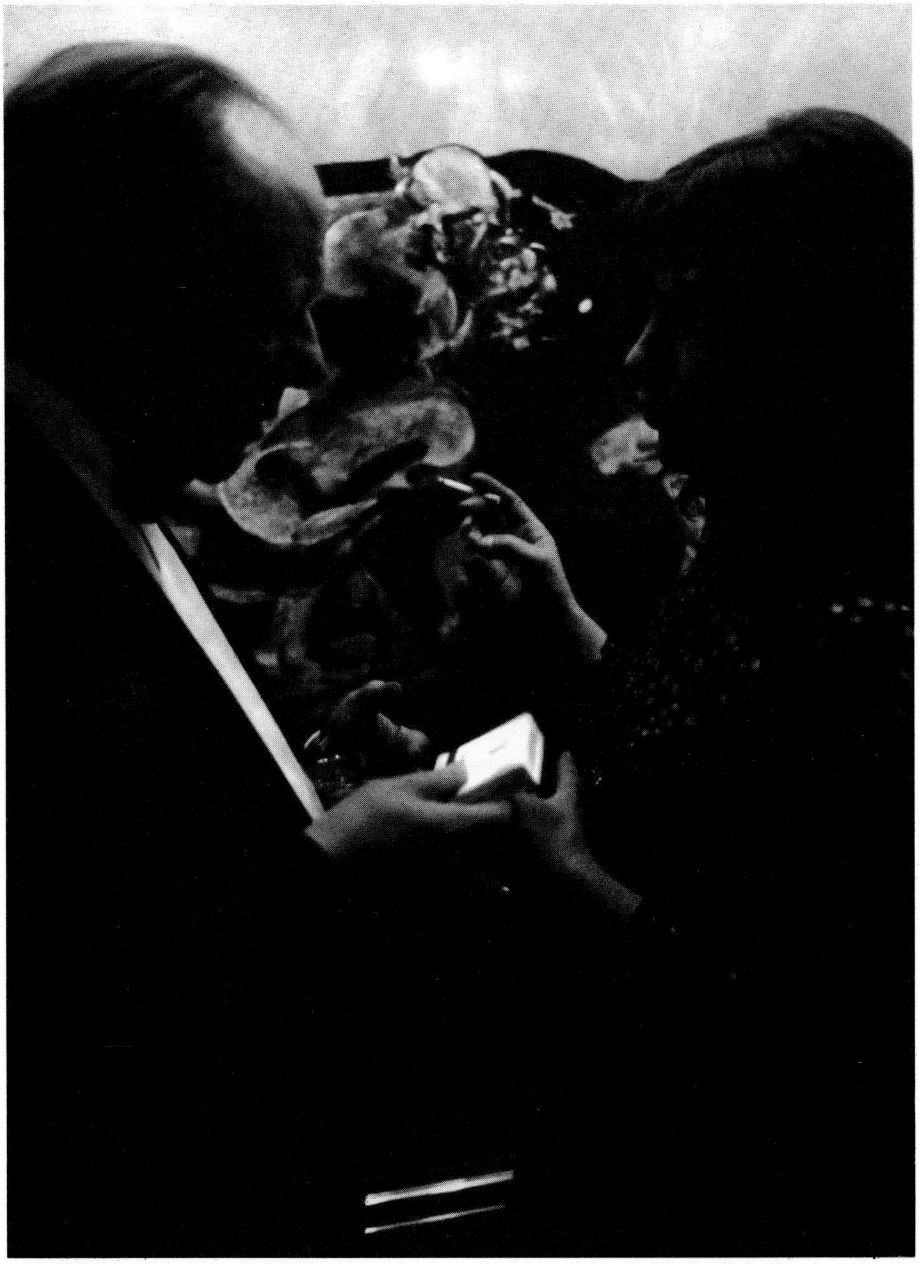

First night parties (left) are merely the dressing on the gallery cake. All successful gallery owners know that the very backbone of the art trade is 'dealing pictures'

Sailing, yachting, golfing, dancing and gambling are all part of the diamond studded social round. Today art adds another dimension to the colour and excitement of the international 'dolce vita' (right)

Joseph P. Kennedy, parents of the late President of the United States, Dame Alicia Markova, the ballet dancer, automobile magnate Benson Ford, Mr Peter A. B. Widener, and the Duchess of Leeds.

A writer in the American magazine *Art Voices* described Palm Beach as the fastest growing art centre in the world. 'A galaxy of old and new galleries has spread like shooting stars down Worth Avenue, the multi-million dollar centre of this fabulous Floridian resort,' he wrote. 'They are now reaching for wider horizons in their spectacular bid for a sizeable share of the art market held by that older constellation, the New York-Paris-London-Rome axis . . . we have captured the quintessence of the Palm Beach art scene by presenting the prime-movers of this phenomenal art explosion. We call them art enthusiasts—for have they not been seen, time and again, at lively vernissages, art receptions and dinner parties where art is the main topic of conversation? That is where their latest acquisitions and the art treasures in their collections are seriously discussed . . . Sailing, yachting and lying in the sun, golfing, dancing and card-playing are probably the most integral parts of the diamond studded Palm Beach ambience. Today, the wondrous art explosion adds another dimension to the color and excitement of Palm Beach's extravagantly glamorous "dolce vita".'

Whether a dealer sells art in Palm Beach or London he is still governed

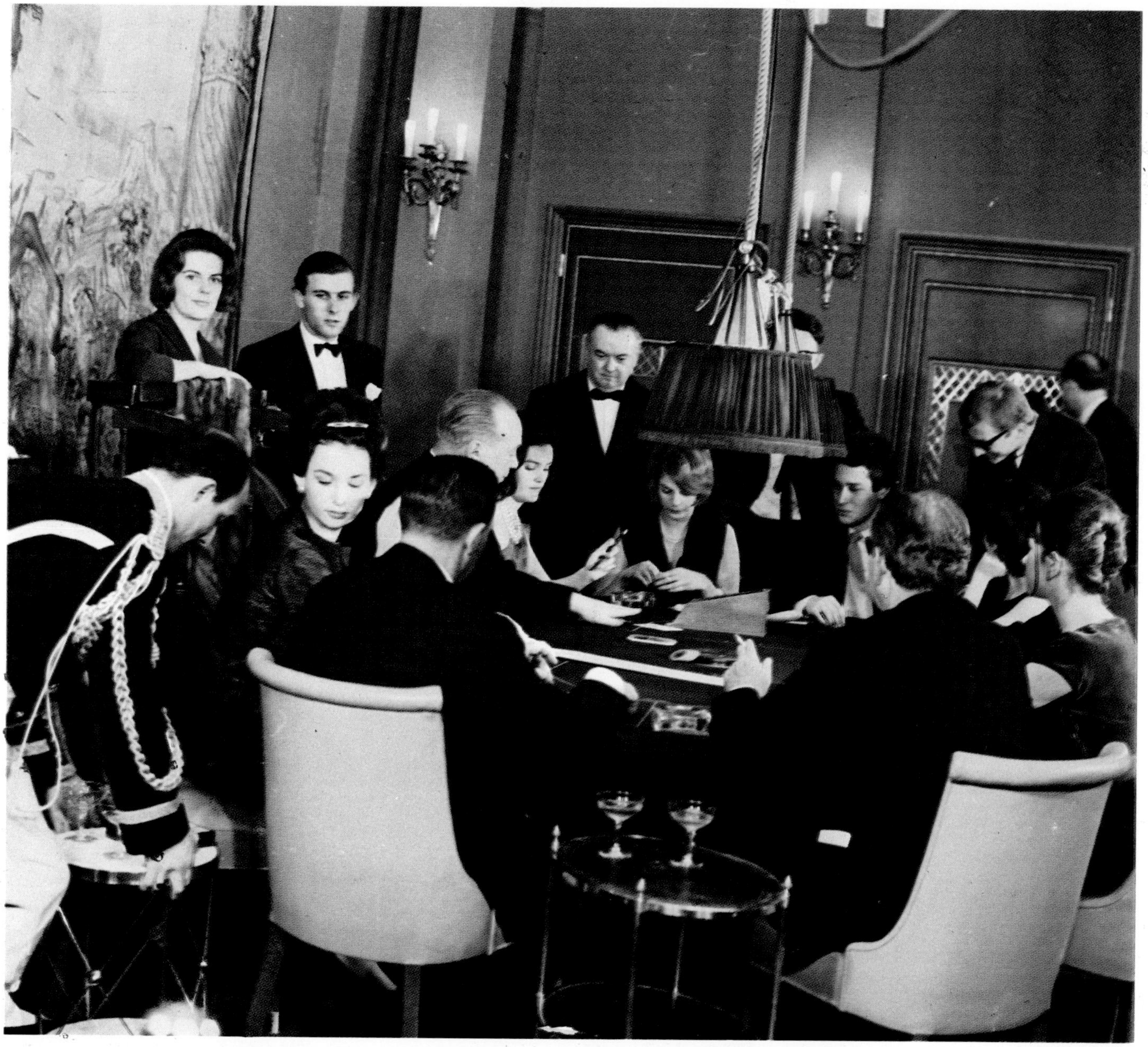

by important economic factors. To stay in business he must attract collectors and casual buyers to his gallery. He must poach clients from his rivals, if it becomes necessary. Private parties, impressive vernissages and special openings are designed to make the small minority of buyers feel that they are *special*. A dealer must keep the drink flowing freely in order to loosen tongues and open cheque books. He depends on information, tittle-tattle and gossip to know who is selling what, and who is prepared to buy what he can't get rid of from his stock. He must remember names of critics, newspaper reporters and the other people who often make his task easier. If needs be, he will have to pay them, flatter them, bribe them or even blackmail them for good publicity. Sometimes, he is just able to ask them. Art today is a saleable commodity like any other and the gallery owner must increasingly make use of modern marketing techniques. Advertising is now an expensive item in most dealers' budget expenses. The extent of their publicity can be seen from the full and half-page advertisements which fill the pages of the art magazines like *Art International*, *Art and Artists*, *The Arts Review*, *Studio*, and *Art Voices*. Campaigns to outshout their competitors have even trickled over on to the arts pages of newspapers like the *New York Herald Tribune* (European Edition), the *New York Times*, *The Daily Telegraph*, *The Times*, and most of the European papers.

Illustrations of the way many dealers make money, and are therefore able to subsidise the one-man exhibitions by unknown artists, can be seen from the following examples. A small Henry Moore sculpture (maquette) was bought privately at a Mayfair gallery for £95 in 1953. The work was kept until 1958, whereupon it was bought by a dealer for £800. The new owner passed it to a 'runner' telling him he wanted £950 for it. The 'runner' approached four leading dealers and eventually sold it to one of them for £1,050. This buying-and-selling process went on until the maquette entered the collection of an American industrialist who paid £2,100. Similarly, a dealer collected together a number of paintings and drawings by the Mancunian artist

L. S. Lowry because he knew that the Tate Gallery and two private galleries were organising retrospective exhibitions. He expected there would be a great demand for this artist's work, and he turned out to be right. Not only was he able to sell many of the items to collectors and the trade, he also did well in the auction rooms. Before the London exhibitions opened he entered a 'nice' Lowry drawing in a London saleroom. When the bidding began he swiftly took the price up to a figure hitherto unknown for a Lowry drawing. The dealer was, in effect, buying his own drawing back at a loss because he had to pay the saleroom charges of 8 per cent, the normal commission charge to the trade. But the dealer had succeeded in drawing the attention of other people to the higher prices good quality Lowry drawings were now fetching in the market. Later the same dealer placed two comparable Lowry drawings in a sale of modern art and made, as he'd hoped, a handsome profit for all his pains.

Many dealers don't have to use these rather complicated, not to say crude, techniques. They can afford to sell their wares directly to the collectors who patronise them. Nevertheless, they often make use of the saleroom to ensure that they keep their clientele. It's no secret that most artists would like to destroy some of their work they now feel is not up to their usual standard. Top artists like Henry Moore, Graham Sutherland, Ben Nicholson and Francis Bacon are no exception. If bad examples of their art appear in the salerooms it is more than likely that galleries will buy the work in, especially if the bidding looks as though it might be low. Occasionally a gallery will support an artist's prices in the salerooms until they have established, at least for a few months, an artificially high level. Not only does this often help make an artist's name, but it establishes a new level of prices in the dealer's own gallery. One well-known gallery in London's Cork Street recently launched a young painter who had not long left the Royal College of Art. Few people doubted that the young artist had talent, but few thought that his paintings were worth three to five hundred pounds in his first one-man exhibition. Nevertheless, the show was almost a sell-out and the owners presumably congratulated themselves on their strategy. The artist's next exhibition was as great a failure as the first had been a success. People were more wary about paying high prices for an unknown and largely untested painter a second time round. The reputations of the dealer and the artist suffered what has proved to have been a temporary setback, but pitfalls like these are constant hazards in the art scene.

The relationship between a dealer and his artists rarely remains a solely business affair. Frequently a dealer becomes an artist's confidant, public relations officer, secretary, investment adviser, psychoanalyst, marriage guidance counsellor and general mentor. Occasionally a dealer and his artist become bitter enemies for reasons we touch upon in another chapter. Whatever the relationship, the business of grooming an artist for fame and fortune is both risky and expensive. Unlike the pop singer, who may become successful with one hit record, the artist needs more than one hit exhibition to establish himself with his rivals, with the collectors and critics and in the salerooms. First one-man shows are rarely sell-outs and, in any case, a dealer will seldom sell the work of a young artist for more than fifty or sixty pounds.

The now-defunct Gallery One had the Indian painter Francis Souza in its stable of artists from 1955 to 1963. His prices rose steadily and his work was snapped up by several noted collectors and, a strong point in Souza's favour, by a number of artists, including Ivon Hitchens. When Gallery One closed its doors Francis Souza was placed under contract by the Grosvenor Gallery. They organised large exhibitions of Souza's work but they were noticeably less popular than the exhibitions at Gallery One. Critics either attacked or ignored Souza and his prices dramatically dipped to an all-time low in the London salerooms. Whatever the reasons for Souza's falling popularity in the period 1963 to 1967, and they may have had little to do with the Grosvenor Gallery, it is easy to understand how the relationship between a dealer and an artist can, to say the least, be tricky.

In a business like art dealing the variable and the undependable are so potent that galleries, like artists, are constantly in a state of flux, some rise and others fall. I have no evidence for suggesting that bankruptcy is more common among art dealers than among dentists, booksellers and butchers, but I nonetheless think it is probably true. When a commodity is basic like razor blades or, like bread, a necessity, demand tends to be fairly constant. Art is neither a necessity nor a timeless luxury like gold or silver, which can always be melted down and sold again. At the moment of writing (September, 1967) strong rumours suggest that at least three well-known Mayfair dealers are on the brink of closing, but at the same time there are at least two galleries about to open in the same area. Moreover, before readers begin organising a flag day for distressed art dealers it might be fair to point out that some owners expect to run at a loss. The majority of them don't mind in the least. Several dealers run their galleries in the same way and for the same tax-saving reason as rich industrialists buy farms. One or two galleries are run solely as a source of cultural amusement for the owner's wife. There is no doubt whatsoever that a number of firms do not make a profit—at least in the ordinary sense of the term.

Although some galleries exist on a shoestring budget and others with the backing of a rich businessman, others make sound profits out of selling art. Few of them, however, disclose their annual profits, which is probably just as well because a number of collectors on hearing the news might stop buying art. A few years ago one of Britain's top painters gave his wife a large collection of drawings and sketches he had made in preparing an important public commission. He gave them as a present to his wife and she eventually sold them to a well-known London dealer. She was paid about £35,000 for them. Shortly afterwards the same dealer was able to sell them to an English collector for a price which rumours put as high as £90,000. Few galleries need the benefit of a flag day!

Well-established firms, especially old family businesses like Agnew's, Colnaghi and Leggatt Brothers, give the appearance that they will go on for ever. And they succeed in creating this appearance without the visitors feeling that their existence and future depend on commercial realities. Agnew's, to cite perhaps the obvious example, suggests to the casual visitor that it is an unusually

Less than twenty years ago a maquette like this (right) would have cost about £100; today one would have to pay more than £2,000.
Art today is a saleable commodity like any other and the gallery owner must increasingly make use of modern marketing techniques. Sidney Janis, shown here together with his sons, advertises on an international scale. This photograph appeared in one of their advertisements

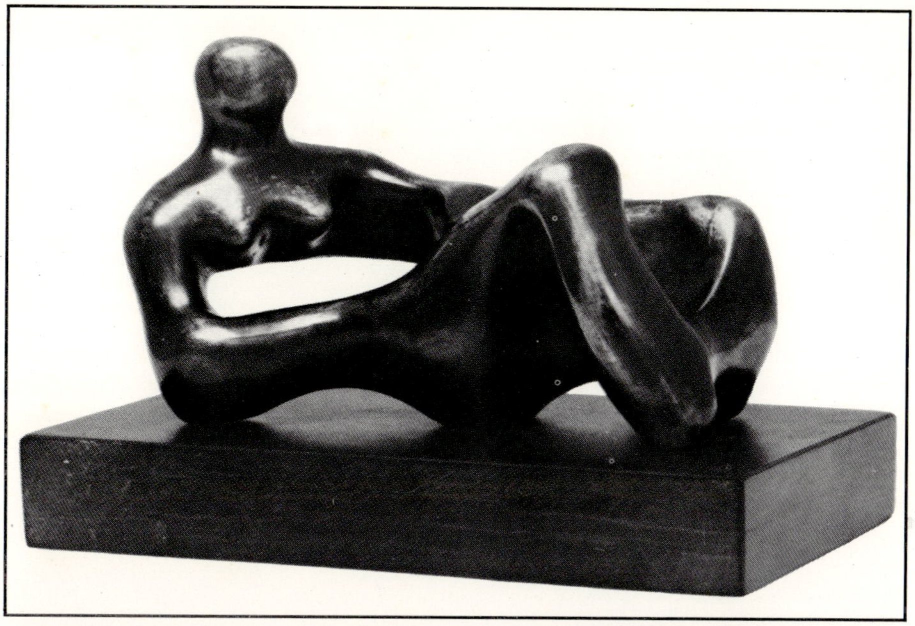

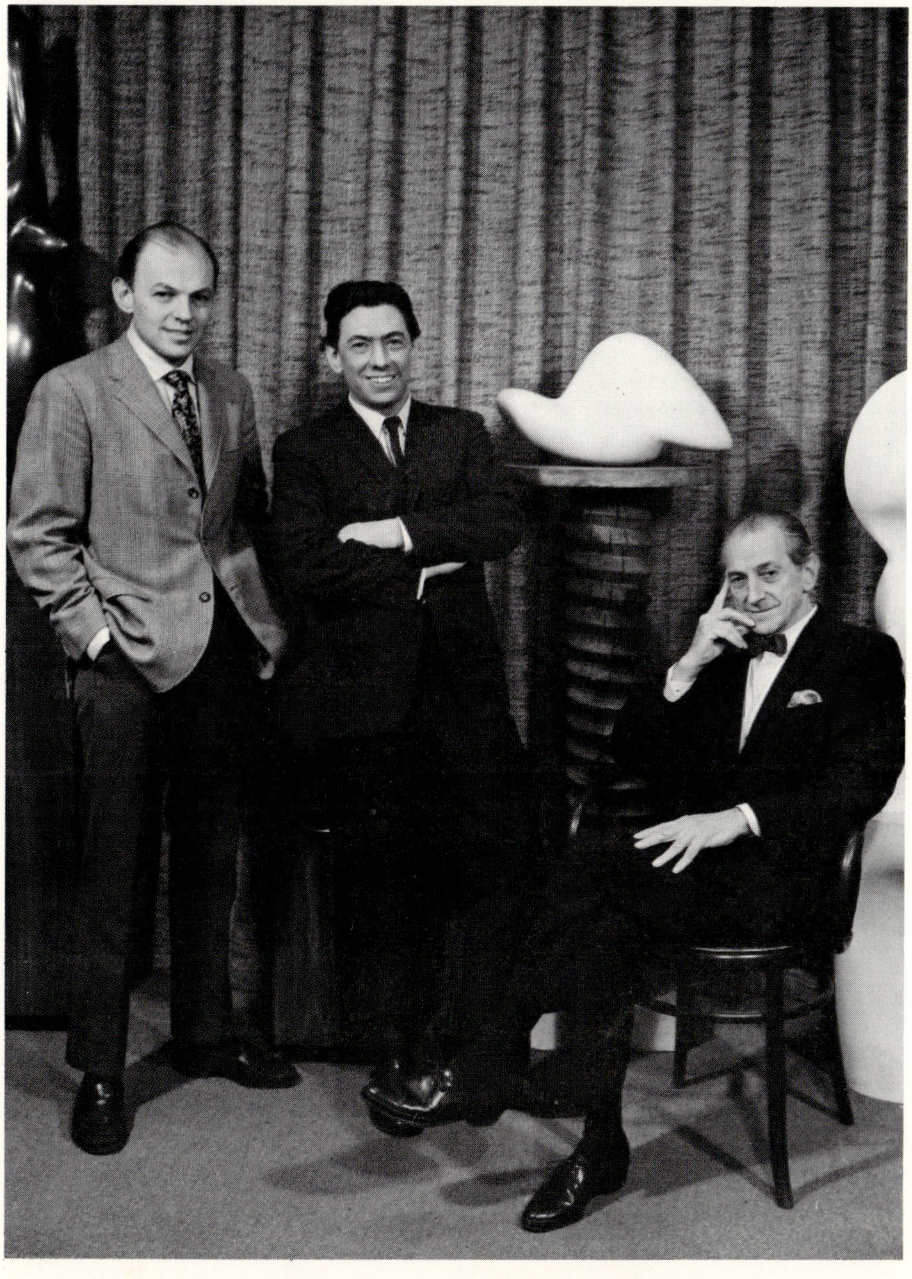

vell-stocked provincial museum. The ·ery mention of money would, one night imagine, only bring a frown 'rom one of Agnew's assistants.

Not surprisingly, it has been the nodern galleries who have led and :reated fashions since the war. How s a fashion for a certain style of painting started? Who creates or :hanges the direction of public taste? 'ohn Russell, the art critic of the *Sunday Times*, has suggested that Marlborough Fine Art helped start 'ashions and altered the course of public taste in art. 'They (Marlborough) foresaw,' he wrote, 'that n Switzerland, in Scandinavia, and n a recovered Germany people would want works of art and be able to pay 'or them. They also saw that, there and elsewhere, British artists could be sold if they were promoted with push and drive. Greying heads were wagged at this point, but the artists saw nothing to complain of in the 'act that they suddenly became persons of international consequence and could get on with their work without having to worry continuously about money . . . . The Marlborough also saw that if a dealer takes enough trouble with his exhibitions they become, in effect, an annexe of our non-existent Modern Museum. Detractors may blow themselves black in the face, but the fact remains that the student of Schwitters, or Pollock, or Bomberg, will simply not know his subject unless he has the relevant Marlborough catalogue to hand.'

One art critic has remarked that if the Marlborough were ever nationalised England would have one-and-a-half museums of modern art. One would be the Marlborough and the other half the Tate Gallery. For critics, collectors, artists, and a good many dealers, the Marlborough is something of a Mecca in the British art scene. Envied, attacked and even hated, the Marlborough was a vital fifth column in the revolution in the modern art trade. Begun shortly after the war by Harry Fischer and F. K. Lloyd, who first met as privates n the Pioneer Corps of the British Army, the Marlborough helped stimulate interest in the British avant-garde and in contemporary European movements like Expressionism, which had been neglected n Britain and the United States.

The Marlborough's reputation for organisational finesse is perhaps

A Gallery of Gallery Personalities

Gallery owners play an important part in the world of art. They are to the artist what the publisher is to the writer. The thirty well-known dealers, shown here, between them represent many of the world's leading artists

Top Row (left to right): Jacques O'Hana, the O'Hana Gallery, London; Martha Jackson, the Martha Jackson Gallery, New York; Crane Kalman, Crane Kalman Gallery, London, Diana Kingsmill, Rowan Gallery, London; Klaus Perls, Perls Galleries, New York

Second Row: Dr Henry Roland, Roland, Browse and Delbanco, London; Alfred Schmela, Galerie Alfred Schmela, Düsseldorf; Charles Durand-Ruel, Galerie Durand-Ruel, Paris; Denise René, Galerie Denise René, Paris; Giorgio Marconi, Studio Marconi, Milan

Third Row. Bruno Bischofberger, Galerie Bischofberger, Zürich; Baroness Beatrice Monti-Rezzori, Galleria dell'Ariete, Milan; Dudley Tooth, Arthur Tooth and Sons, London; James Crabtree, Axiom Gallery, London; Virginia Zabriskie, Zabriskie Gallery, New York

Fourth Row. Mino Pater, Galleria Pater, Milan; Robert Estorick, Grosvenor Gallery, London; Gillian Raffles, Mercury Gallery, London; Alfredo Bonino, Galleria Bonino, New York, Rio de Janeiro and Buenos Aires; Mateusz Grabowski, Grabowski Gallery, London

Fifth row. Laddie Andrews, Lord and Taylor, New York; Felix Landau, Felix Landau Gallery, California; Kas, Kasmin Gallery, London; Yvon Lambert, Galerie Yvon Lambert, Paris; Carla Panicali, Marlborough Galleria d'Arte, Rome

Bottom row. Leo Castelli, Leo Castelli Gallery, New York; Dr Rundqvist, Galerie Bonnier, Lausanne and Svensk-Franska Konstgalleriet, Stockholm; Hans-Jurgen Müller, Galerie Müller, Stuttgart; Betty Parsons, Betty Parsons Gallery, New York; Godfrey Pilkington, Piccadilly Gallery, London

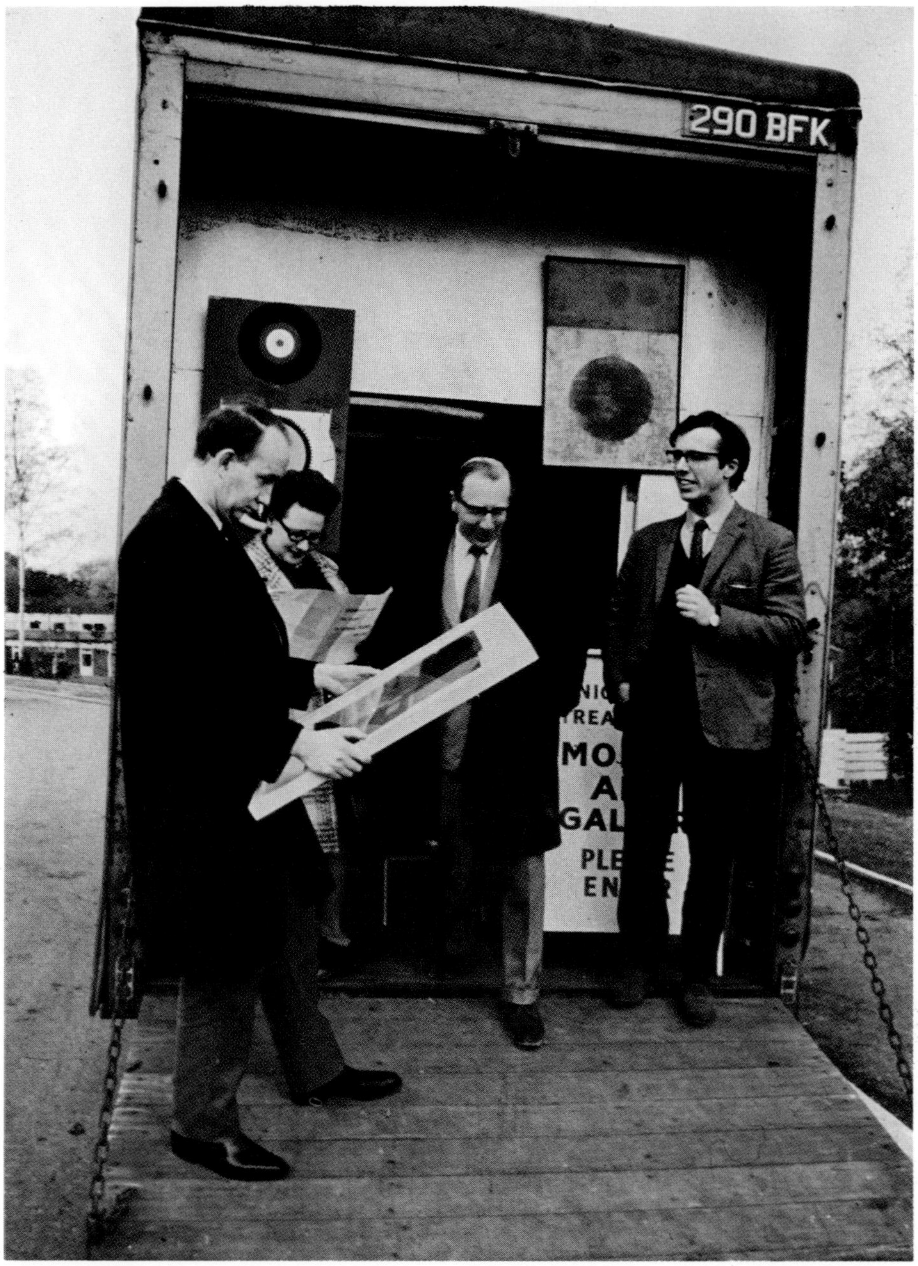

gallery with a picture tucked under their arm. Although London is right at the centre of the world's art market our dealing is based entirely on international buying and selling. We also have a truly international clientele. Collectors vary in every way you can conceive of–and some that you can't. Some collectors take ages to make up their minds about a picture and others decide directly they see a picture.'

Not every dealer is tied to his gallery. Nicholas Treadwell sells modern paintings and sculpture from a large blue furniture van he has converted into a mobile art gallery. He started with £100 capital four years ago and now has his large furniture van and two Mini-vans as mobile art galleries and an art gallery-cum-pottery shop in Surrey. The main mobile gallery has fluorescent lighting and carpets, and the pictures hang closely together on the inside walls. Small sculptures are strapped down at one end of the van. The gallery's stock includes Abstracts, Pop art, modern figurative painting, and even an example of 'joke' art, a brightly-coloured lavatory seat which lifts to reveal a picture underneath.

'I like to handle the work of young painters before they become expensive', says Treadwell. 'I sell roughly six picture a week at prices from £8 to £80. The new private estates are good because there are many young couples and they don't have much in the way of pictures, but council estates are murder, believe me.'

Geoffrey Agnew (left), chairman of the respected family firm of Thomas Agnew and Son, standing near a Turner painting, which his firm sold for a five-figure sum

Nicholas Treadwell (right) sells paintings and sculpture from a large blue furniture van he has converted into a mobile art gallery. Before selling modern art he sold pottery and chinaware to American service families in Europe and North America

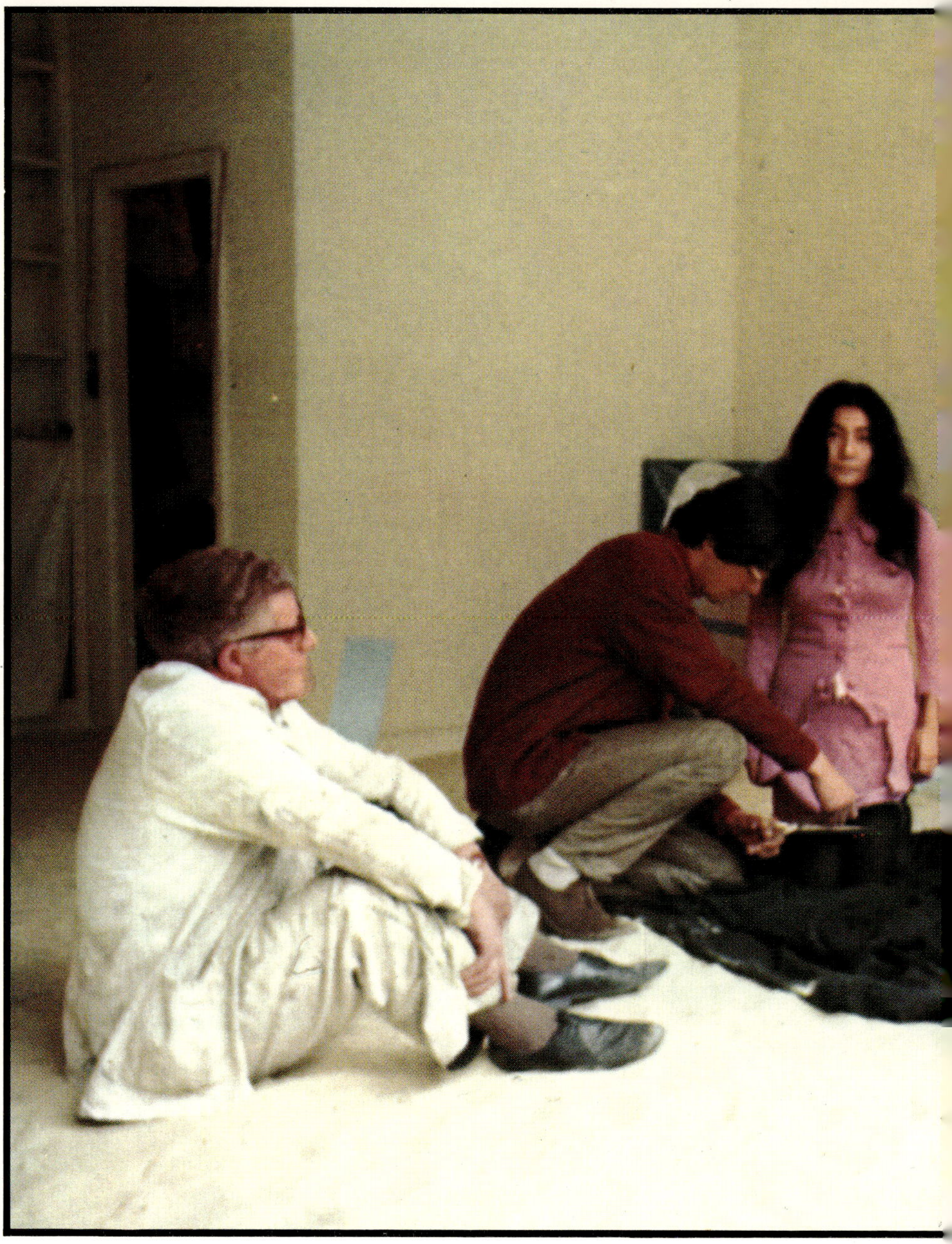

The 'pace-making' galleries who often steal a good deal of publicity for their activities and antics in and out of their galleries include firms in London like Kasmin, Axiom, Rowan, Robert Fraser and, until their recent closure, the Indica Gallery in Mason's Yard, Duke Street, St James's. New York and Paris have a greater percentage of galleries who are prepared to show avant-garde art. New York galleries like Leo Castelli, Tibor de Nagy, Dwan and Pace provide much of the art and fun to be seen along the east coast. When Andy Warhol's show opened at the Castelli Gallery in 1966 it was perhaps inevitably bizarre. The back room of the Gallery, otherwise bare, was papered in Warhol-inspired wallpaper. The wallpaper design was basically a large cow's head in fluorescent pink, photographically silk-screened on a bright yellow ground. The rest of the gallery was full of helium-inflated balloons made of aluminised polythylene and shaped like coal sacks. Warhol's balloons were called 'clouds' and wandered aimlessly as, one would expect, about the room. One critic remarked, 'On the whole, it was a new experience to be confronted by closed forms that were soft and resilient, and which, for all their inertness and passivity, seemed to exist in enviable freedom.'

I watched an 'event' organised by Yoko Ono and her American husband, Anthony Cox, during her exhibition at the Indica Gallery. 'If it's indecent to show your bottom

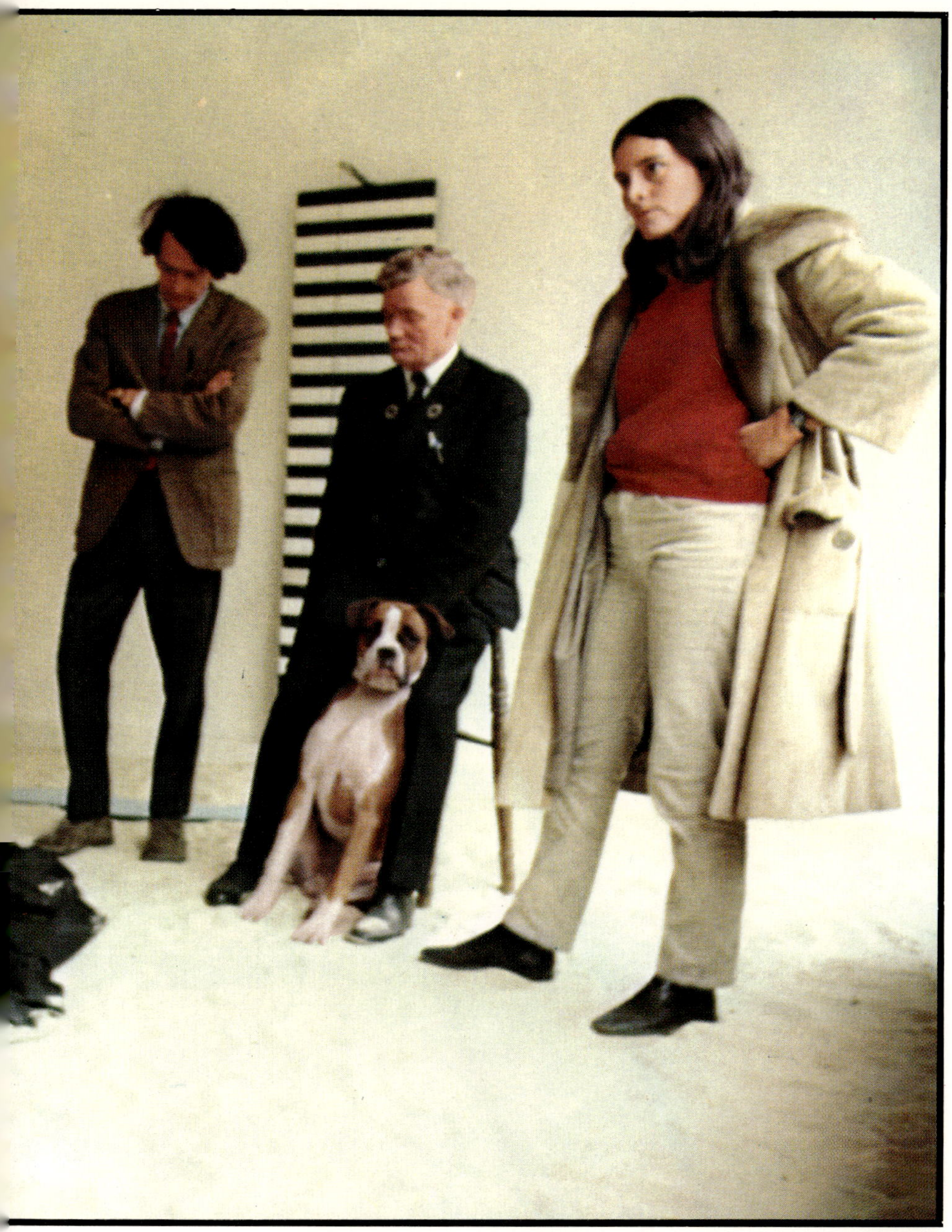

it follows that it is indecent to show other parts of the human body, say the mouth,' says Yoko Ono, a tiny Japanese woman who looks much younger than her thirty-five years. 'We cover our mouths with clean linen handkerchiefs and when people walk into the gallery we ask them to do the same. We are trying to fight the whole business of people not being able to communicate with one another.'

Indica was run by John Dunbar, one-time Cambridge student married to pop singer Marianne Faithfull. Slim, bespectacled and often taken for one of the Beatles in his Edwardian-styled pin-striped suits (the Beatles were regular visitors to Indica), Dunbar was something of an enigma. Exhibitions like Yoko Ono's Events could hardly show much of a profit and Dunbar didn't have a reputation for 'dealing', up to now the life-blood of most galleries. When Indica closed it was a chilly reminder of the risks involved in the art trade.

Most of the conservative-minded modern art dealers prophesy ruin for London galleries who specialise exclusively in what is best described as ultra-avant-garde. Few were surprised, therefore, when Signals London in Wigmore Street, a gallery which had spent large sums of money to promote kinetic art, went out of business. Its director, Paul Keeler, started his gallery because he believes in the importance of kinetic art.

He may still be proved to have been right.

Lilianne Lynne (standing right), American-born wife of the Greek sculptor Takis, with Yoko Ono, Japanese art impresario (centre) at an Event. Members of the public were given the opportunity to cut off Yoko Ono's clothes. A tipsy Irish labourer, a student and a porter with a boxer dog agreed to snip

The art boom in Australia began in the early fifties. Now dealers are reaping the rewards of their perseverance

Frank Watters (above left) holds programmes of jazz and poetry in his Sydney gallery.
Rudy Komon (above right) ex-journalist, ex-chauffeur. Now the elegant and wealthy stream through his South Yarra Gallery. Here seen with Dame Mary Gilmore beside her portrait by Dobell.
Barry Stern (below left) began as a collector before turning his talents to art dealing.
Georges Mora (below right) now director of the successful Tolarno Gallery has seen more frugal days in the past

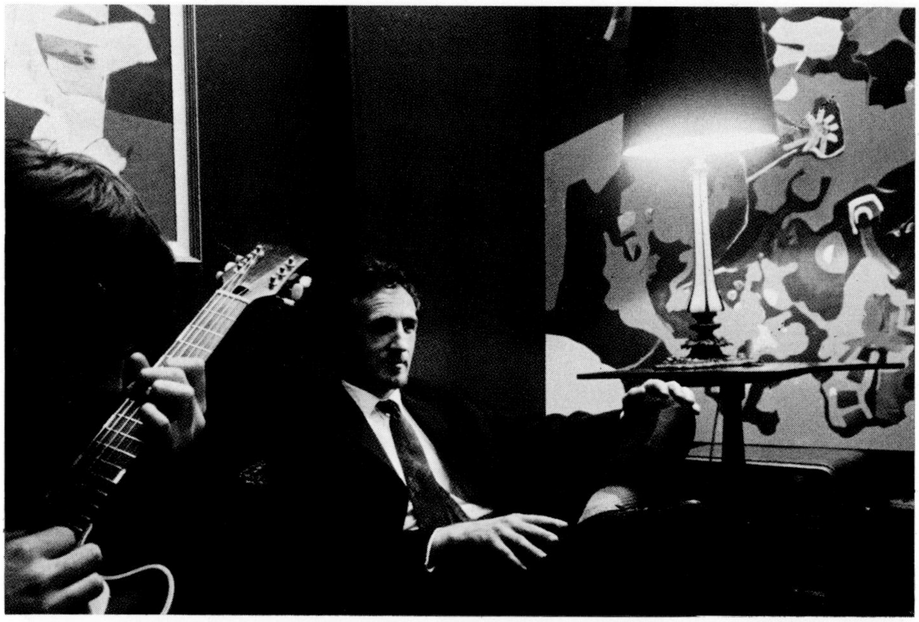

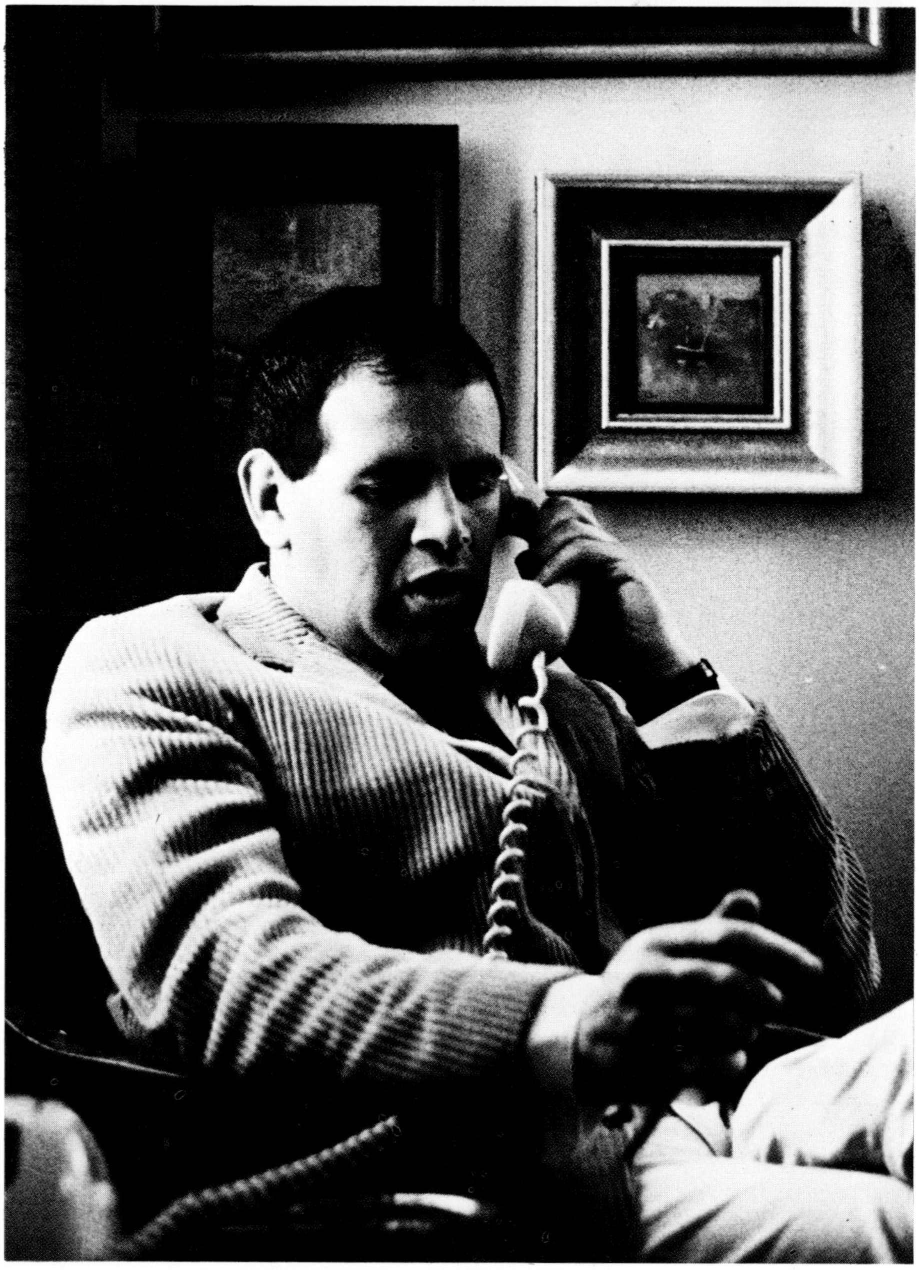

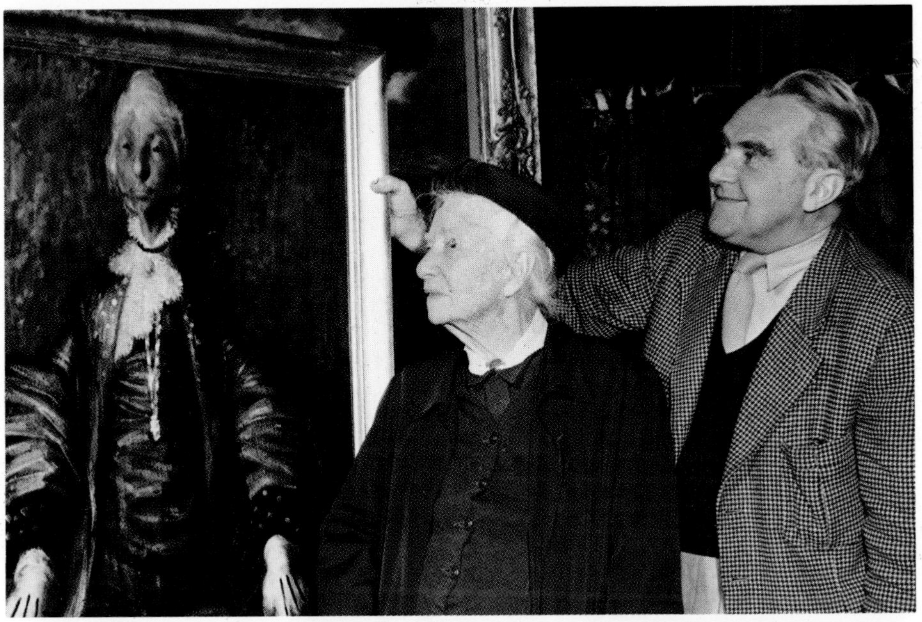

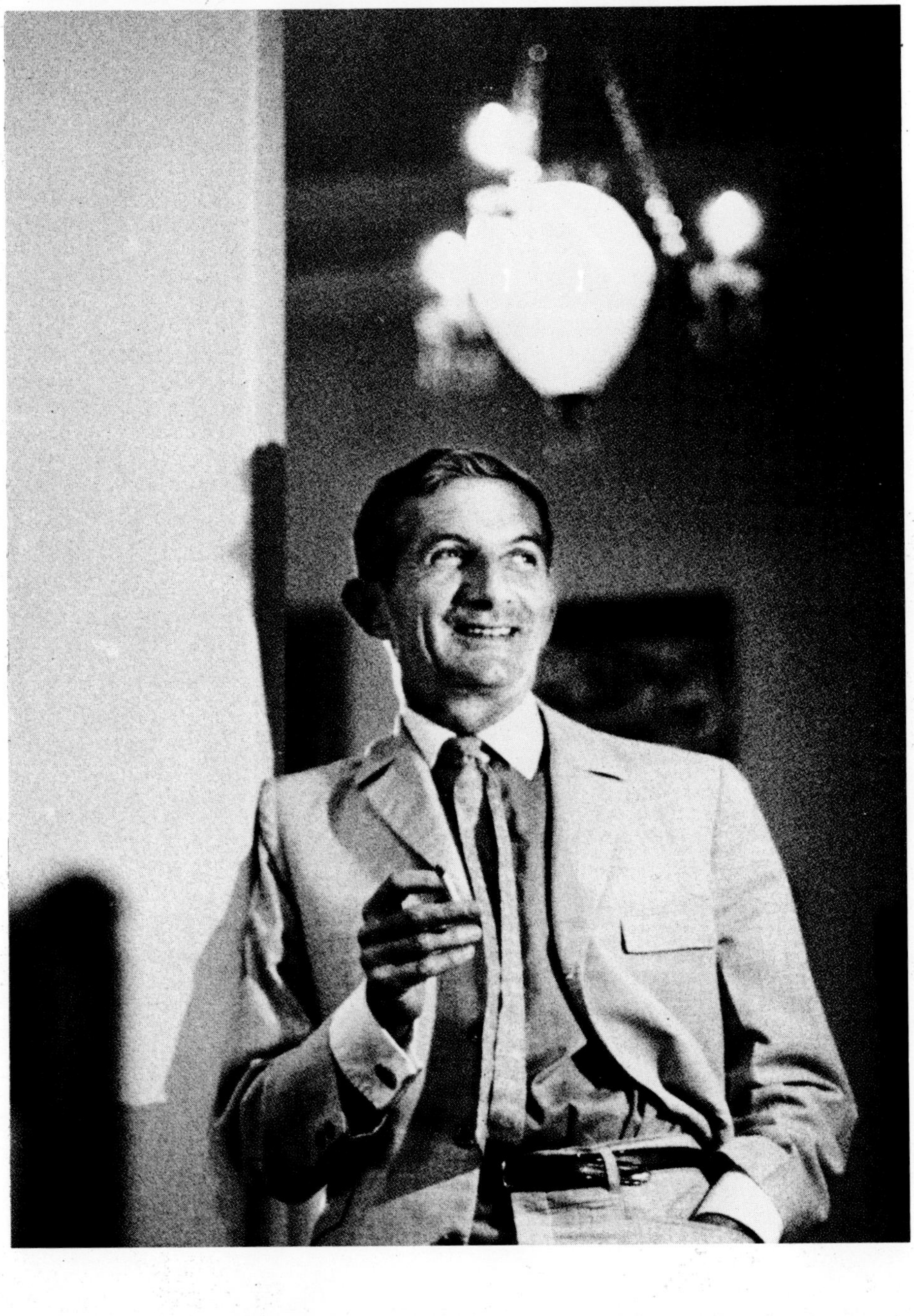

The present Australian pattern of marketing art was established early in the fifties with the boom in private galleries. A key figure in the story is Rudy Komon, a journalist who arrived from Czechoslovakia in 1950 with a handful of etchings. He took a job as a chauffeur and sold art in his spare time. The painters he has encouraged and helped include Dobell, French, Olsen, Molvig and Cassab. Now his handsome South Yarra Gallery, Paddington (complete with extensive wine cellar) is the centre of the Australian art scene.

Georges Mora and his wife Mirka came from France in 1951 and opened a small gallery in Collins Street, Melbourne. He recalls that in two one-man exhibitions of paintings by Charles Blackman, he sold only three works out of some eighty on display. In 1958 he opened the Museum of Modern Art and Design of Australia with collector John Reed. This lasted only eight years before it ran out of funds, but it was a powerful influence on public taste. Mora is now director of the Tolarno Gallery in Melbourne's St. Kilda.

Brian Johnstone's gallery in Brisbane has quickly won a reputation, and his Blackman exhibition in 1966 set a new record in prices. Perhaps Johnstone's experiences as an aide to the Governor gave him an entrée to the right circles, and helped him to become established in a city not prone to artistic indulgence.

The Watters Gallery in Sydney and the Argus Gallery in Melbourne sell the work of avant-garde experimental painters such as John Peart, Richard Larter and Vivienne Binns, whose work can still cause a stir in an increasingly blasé world.

Some collectors deal directly with the painters, and commission works from them. One collector who discovered he had an affinity for art dealing is Barry Stern who recently made headlines when he sold a Nolan painting *Burke and Wills Leaving Melbourne* for a record $A35,000.

Easily one of the best and largest private galleries in the country is the new Bonython Gallery in Paddington. Hidden behind a row of terraced houses, the gallery's splendid Japanese-style inner courtyard and modern viewing courts is an indication of the degree of sophistication which the Australian art world has so quickly achieved.

Yoko Ono (below) listening to her *Eternal Clock* with a stethoscope. 'I was asked to produce something for about 250 dollars for a couple living in New York. I bought a clock at Tiffany's, removed the hands, and had it inscribed "Eternal Clock, Happy Birthday Julius, Love Sylvia"'

John Dunbar (right) one-time Cambridge student, ran London's most way-out art gallery until it closed in 1967

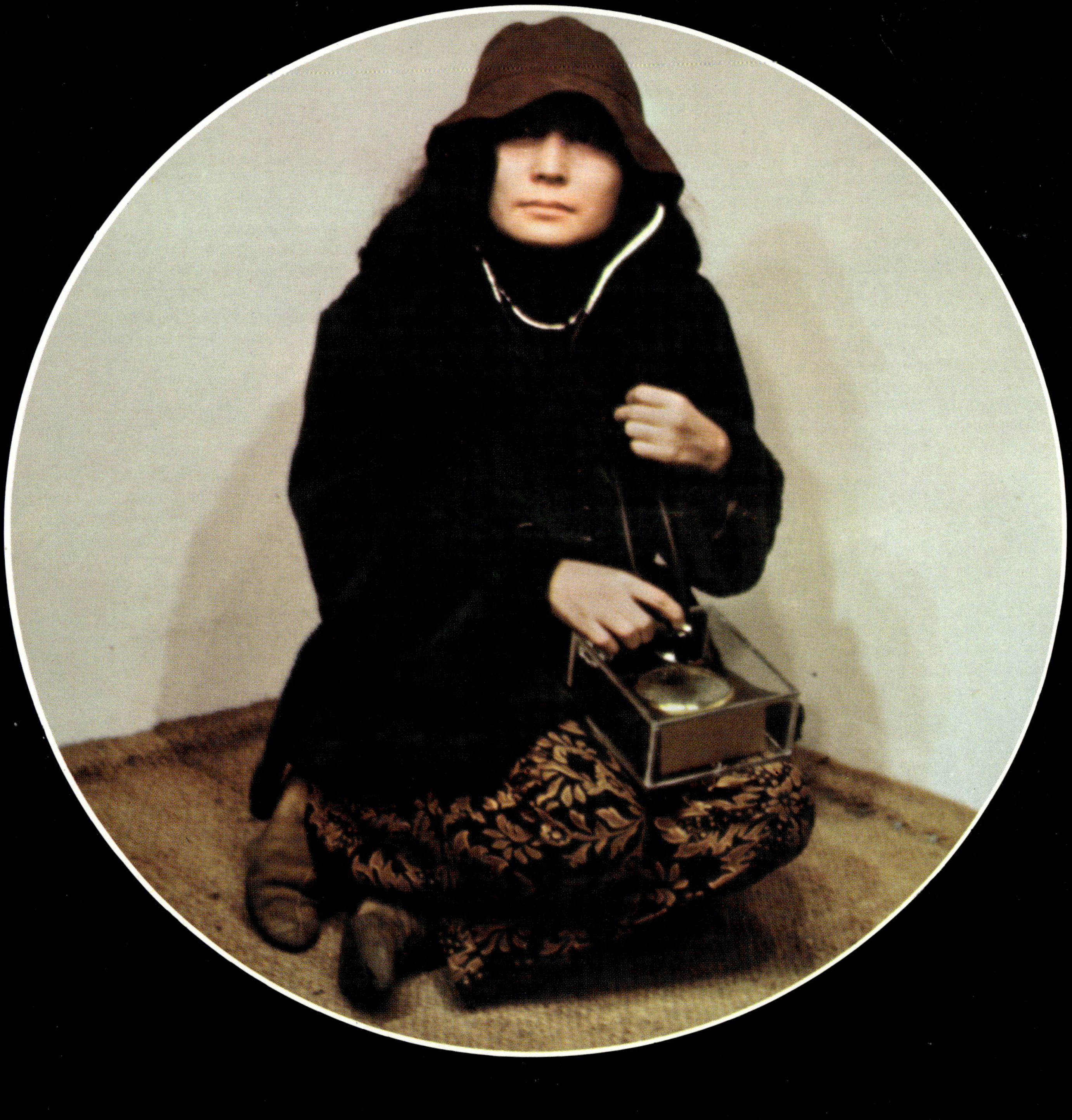

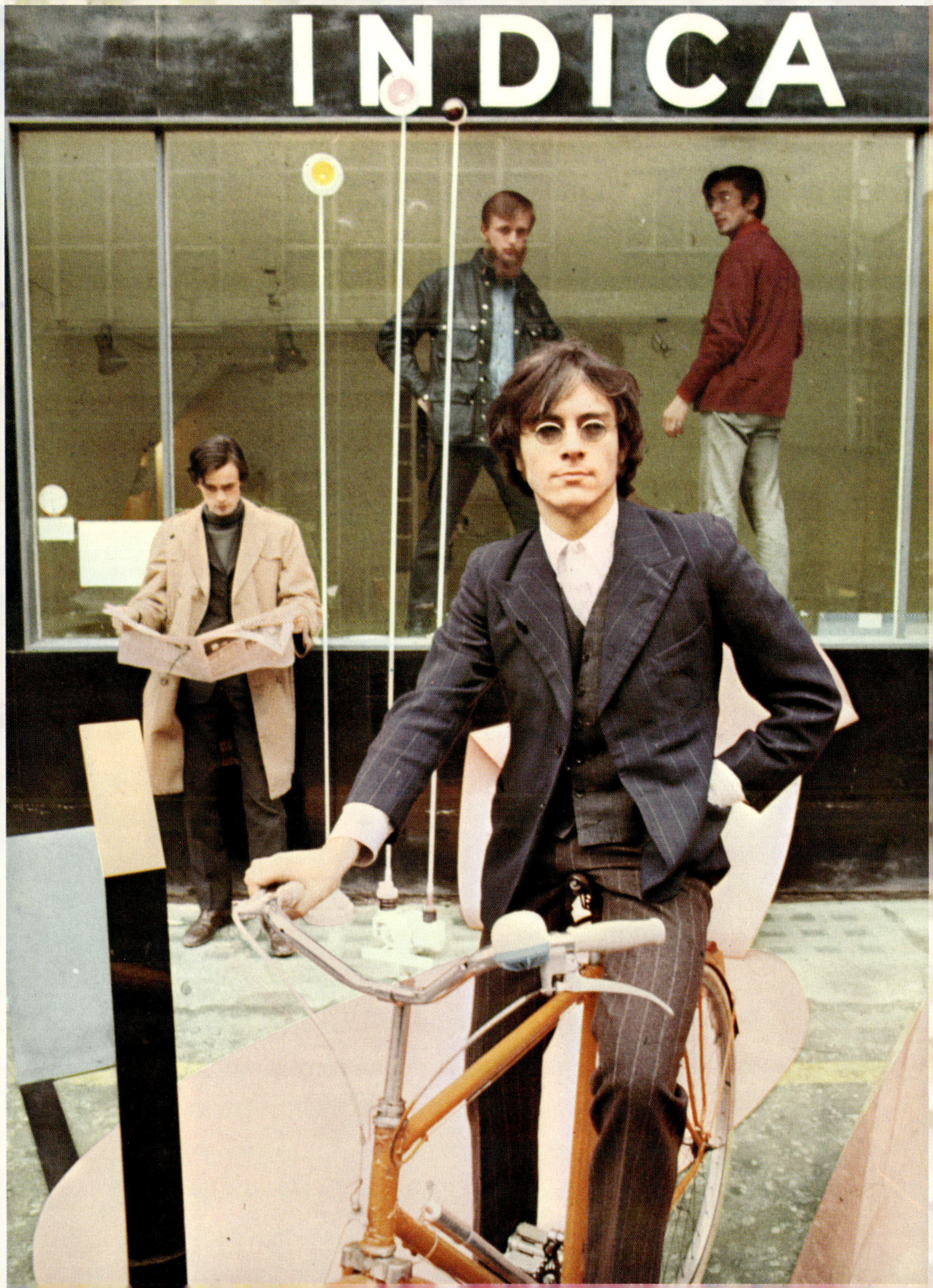
INDICA

THE COLLECTORS

Art collectors are rarely straightforward lovers of art, although they feel passionately for it. They tend to be mysterious, acquisitive almost by definition, occasionally cunning, sometimes ruthless or neurotic in their pursuit of the rare, beautiful and fashionable. Their relationship with fellow collectors, artists and the under-privileged is often a mixture of pride and jealousy. But the collectors are an important and indispensable part of any sophisticated age. They hoard some of the most valuable litter of their time.

Why some people passionately enjoy *possessing* works of art is still a considerable mystery. Dr Luzier dealt with victims of the collecting disease at the 1953 Paris Congress of Neurologists and Mental Specialists but he came to no firm conclusions. Dr Codet wrote as early as 1921 that there were at least four major factors in the collector's make-up: the acquisitive instinct, the need for a spontaneous activity, the wish to surpass oneself and the desire for social prestige. Princess Marie Bonaparte, a follower of Freud, claims that she has discovered that collecting is akin to anal eroticism.

The world's top collectors live in the United States, Britain, France, Italy, Switzerland and Germany. Altogether there are less than 250 individual collectors who are in the market for the world's most expensive works of art. Collectors like Nelson Rockefeller, Henry Ford II, Paul Mellon, Paul Getty, Walter P. Chrysler Jr and Stavros Niarchos are in constant touch with major dealers and auction houses and have agents who watch for news of important works which may come on the market.

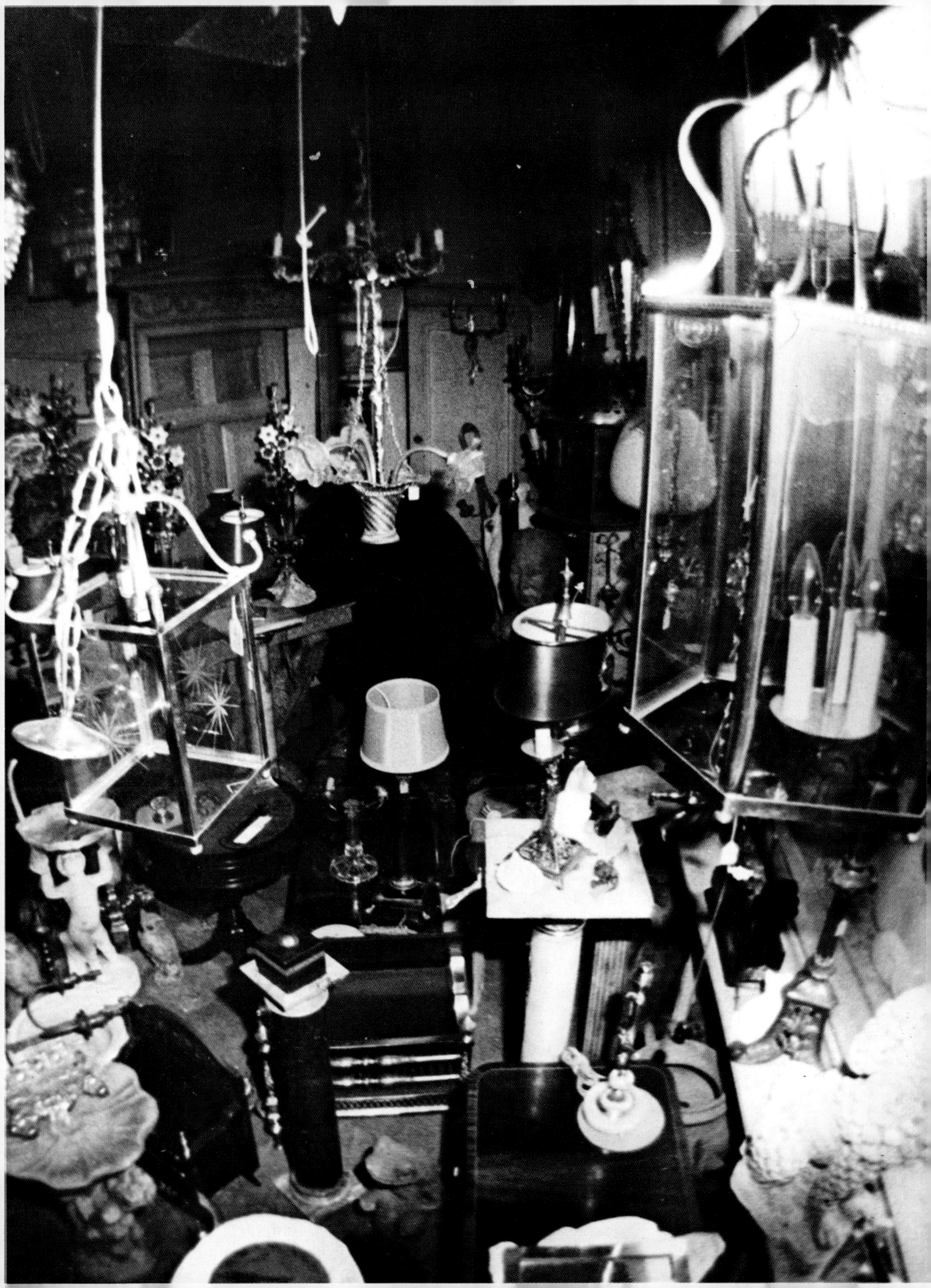

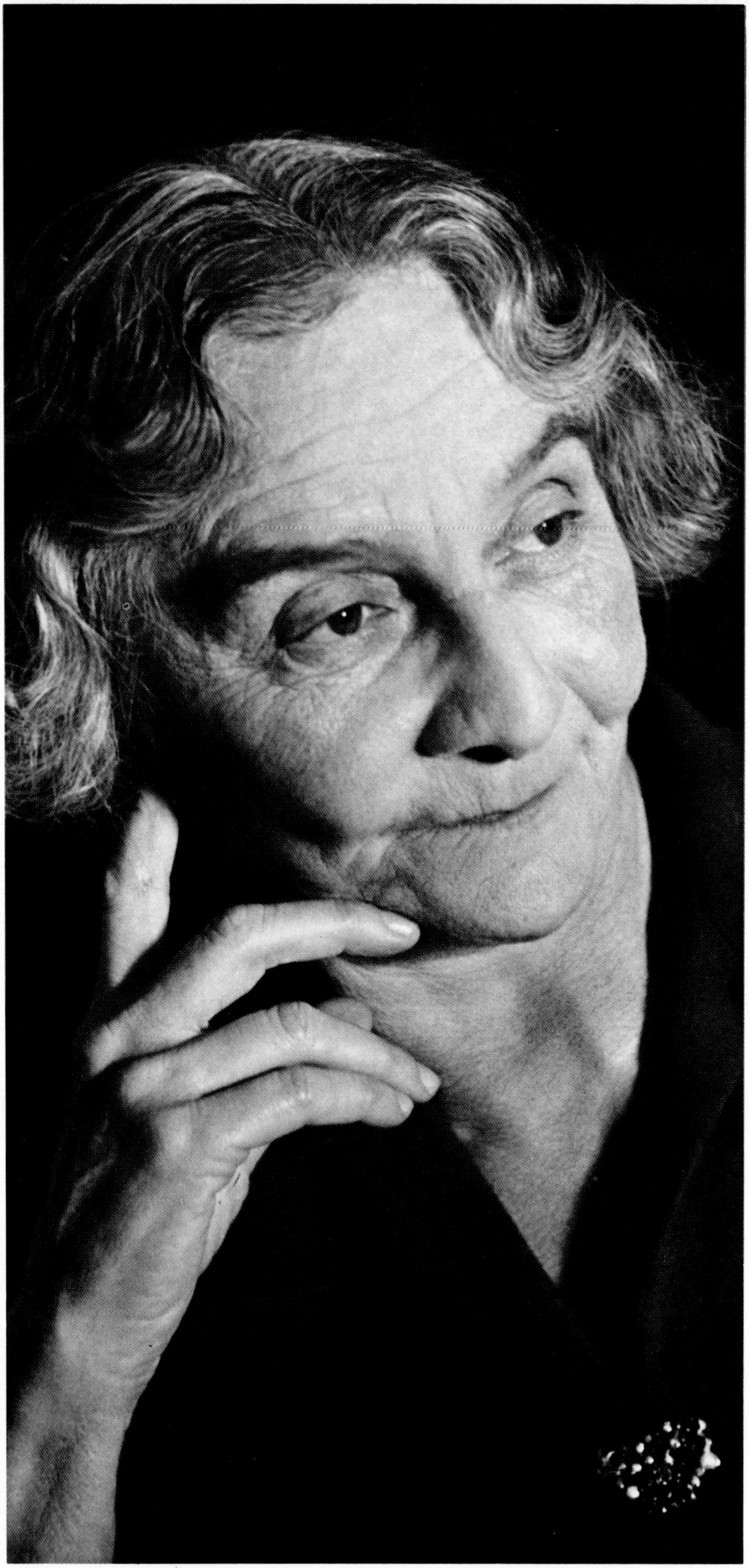

Collectors, an important and indispensable part of any sophisticated age, hoard some of the most valuable litter of their time

Princess Marie Bonaparte: 'Collecting is akin to anal eroticism'

Sir Kenneth Clark, the art scholar and collector, once asked himself the question: 'Why do men and women collect? As well ask why they fall in love: the reasons are as irrational, the motives as mixed, the original impulse as often discoloured or betrayed. The collector's instinct, if animals and children are any guide, has two roots: the desire to pick up anything bright and shining and the desire to complete a series; and these primitive instincts, under the stress of competition, memory, wealth, and other evolutionary factors, produced the first stage in collecting, the treasury and the cabinet of coins.'

But although art collectors, whether they are rich or poor, have many of the most obvious human weaknesses they have also proved their worth through the centuries. What would Michelangelo have done without the early support of Florentine bankers, Rubens without his wide circle of admirers, the Impressionists without Caillebotte or Chocquet, Soutine without the American collector Dr Barnes, and even Picasso without his early supporters.

Catherine of Russia, Charles I of England, Louis XIV of France, Lord Hertford, J. P. Morgan, H. E. Huntington, Samuel Courtauld, Albert Barnes and Peggy Guggenheim are among the greatest of the world's art collectors. Nowadays, museums and public art galleries have replaced many of the important individual collectors. Nonetheless, the lust for collecting paintings and sculpture still thrives at different levels.

Today, most powerful private collectors of modern art are Americans and Europeans and they often have understanding governments on their side. In America, a man who invests in art has a 'public bequest' arrangement whereby he can get immediate tax concessions if he agrees to leave his collection to the nation when he dies. British collectors are not so happily provided for, nor indeed are they as rich.

Moreover, the fact that many private British collections may seem modest in comparison with similar collections abroad is because their owners joined the art race so late in the day. Thus when most British collectors were buying work by Lord Leighton and Sir Lawrence Alma-Tadema, European and American competitors were choosing from the pick of the emerging avant-garde movements.

British collectors in this century have rarely shown that collecting mania and love of risk and speculation which history certainly suggests is a necessary part of art collecting. And heavy taxation and death duties have helped clip the enthusiasm of many budding collectors. Nevertheless, more and more people, rich and poor alike, are entering the art hoarding stakes.

Collectors of the stature of the nineteenth century and the beginning of this century are few and far between and may never be emulated in this age of large public institutions, more powerful than private individuals.

In the past a private collector like Dr Albert C. Barnes was a prince of the art world. Barnes was particularly important because, although he collected old masters, he also bought the work of living painters. In fact, he bought the work of artists who are now household names all over the world: Renoir, Cézanne, Matisse, Juan Gris, Picasso, Braque.

Barnes grew up amid poverty and ignorance and only escaped from his early environment when he won a scholarship to the Central High School, a secondary school with good academic standing. Later, Barnes studied medicine at Pennsylvania and eventually did research preparing a thesis for a doctorate in chemistry. His particular interest was in producing an antiseptic which he succeeded in doing with his student-friend and collaborator Herman Hille. Barnes later bought the sole rights for his product, which was called Argyrol, from Hille and went on to make a fortune estimated at several million dollars. In 1914 the United States Government bought the rights for the sale and manufacture of Argyrol from Barnes and the latter was left to follow his only hobby—collecting paintings.

Barnes's interest in art began with his own efforts on canvas, but he soon realised that his talents lay elsewhere. Finally, he decided that collecting could be made a genuine creative activity with far-reaching and worthwhile results. His taste at the beginning was conventional: Théodore Rousseau, Diaz, Daubigny and Corot being among his early favourites. Before the First World War Barnes sent an agent to buy 20,000 dollars' worth of modern paintings.

The agent's early purchases included a Renoir: *Girl Reading,* for which he paid 100 dollars; the *Portrait of the Postman Roulin* by Van Gogh and other works by Sisley, Gauguin, Pissarro, Monet, Seurat, Degas and Renoir. Barnes was not impressed and felt his agent had taken advantage of him because he was rich. The agent asked him to keep the twenty pictures for six months. If he didn't like them then he would buy them back from Barnes. Barnes soon became a staunch supporter of the modern forms of art, which at that time were misunderstood and unpopular.

Following his conversion to art's latest manifestations, Barnes visited Europe. Firstly, he went to the finest museums—the National Gallery in London, the Kaiser Friedrich Museum in Berlin and the Louvre in Paris—to study the finest art of the past. With knowledge, he believed, he could start a magnificent collection of his own.

Visiting Europe every year he began collecting large numbers of paintings. The American art critic and specialist in Renaissance painting, Bernard Berenson, once asked Barnes: 'Why have you got the same Renoir fifty times over, and fifty times the same painting by Matisse?'

A French art dealer, Paul Guillaume, agreed to show ninety-four works from Barnes's collection at his Paris gallery from January to February 1923. Barnes wrote at the time of the show: 'The work of these modern artists is the product of French influence on different cultures and racial dispositions. All, except Modigliani, are living artists and only three, Matisse, Picasso and Derain, are over thirty.' Barnes offered the entire collection to the Pennsylvania Academy of Fine Arts. The show was not the success in the United States that it had been in Paris. Barnes was furious and attacked the critics who had described the exhibition as 'unwholesome' and 'morally degenerate'.

In 1924 Barnes started the Barnes Foundation in Philadelphia. People who disagreed with his ideas about art were not admitted. Barnes enjoyed controversy and even his death started a legal battle concerning his collection. Before the war the collection was unofficially estimated to be worth something in the region of $100,000,000.

Baron Thyssen

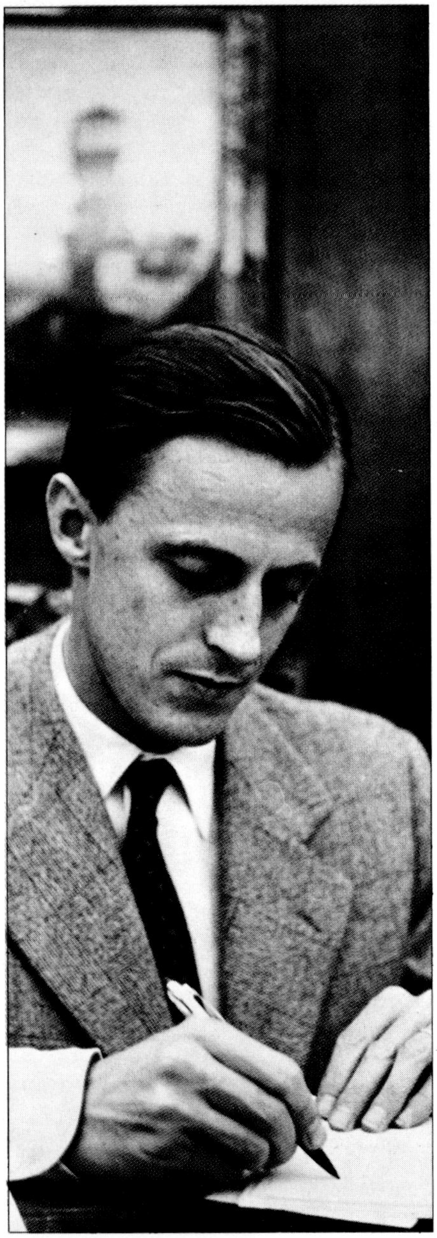

Millionaire industrialist, Baron Heini Thyssen, in his study at the Villa Favorita. Hungarian by birth, he is now a naturalised Swiss. The family fortune was built by his German grandfather

Although he is perhaps better known for having married four times, Baron Heini Thyssen-Bornemisza de Kaszon also has one of the world's richest private art collections. Baron Thyssen is now married to Brazilian heiress Denise Shorto, 28; his own private fortune is estimated at around £100 million, derived from his family's steel interests.

His collection is centred at Castagnola on the outskirts of Lugano in Ticino, Switzerland. There at his palatial home, Villa Favorita, art treasures worth several million pounds are hung in the museum-like picture gallery.

The Thyssen collection first became world famous when it was shown in the Neue Pinakothek at Munich in 1930. Since then parts of his collection have been seen in Germany, Holland and Britain. An important picture, Holbein's *King Henry VIII,* has visited the National Gallery in London on two occasions since the war.

Fra Angelico, Fra Bartolommeo, Bellini, Caravaggio, Carpaccio, Chardin, Joos van Cleve, Correggio, Lucas Cranach, Albrecht Dürer and Goya are particularly well represented in the collection.

One picture in the Thyssen collection is still the cause of an interesting and scholarly controversy. *Head of a Man,* attributed to the Master of Flémalle, an early Netherlandish artist who is thought by some to be Robert Campin (*c.*1378–1444), has belonged to the picture gallery at Berlin since it was bought at Christie's in 1901. A similar picture was recently acquired by Baron Thyssen. The sitter in both the pictures, which differ only slightly, is thought to be Robert de Masmines, one of the original Knights of the Golden Fleece. Both pictures have been examined by X-ray, revealing that the Thyssen version has stronger outlining and less modelling. Although the Berlin version has been widely accepted as the original, two well-known scholars, Tolnay and Panofsky, believe it to be a copy.

A rich collection like Baron Thyssen's must make one ask whether, supposing one doesn't have forbears who collected old masters, plus a personal fortune, it is possible to start collecting works of art?

The beginner will largely be guided by his purse. Aware of this he should concentrate on schools of art which have not risen in price and importance at the same speed as, say, the Italian and Flemish Primitives.

An obvious course is to patronise little or unknown contemporary painters and sculptors. Here taste and foresight are more important than cash.

If, however, like Baron Thyssen, you prefer old masters but have a modest income, the schools to buy now include eighteenth- and nineteenth-century British and American artists. The contemporaries of Gainsborough and Reynolds, often little-known and under-priced, can still be discovered in unlikely places. Junk shops and dust are often the collector's best friend.

Oscar Weiss

owner, is also a passionate collector of modern paintings. His interest in collecting is comparatively recent, but already he has brought together a number of notable works.

Cynics might suggest that every painting has its price; therefore for a wealthy man like Niarchos acquiring important pictures is not a great problem.

Nevertheless, although money is the key to most important collections money does not necessarily guarantee a first-class collection.

But apart from well-known paintings by Degas, Renoir, Gauguin, Modigliani, Van Gogh, Matisse and Rouault, Niarchos has also purchased examples, and incredibly fine ones, by El Greco, Goya, Corot and Delacroix. Why does he collect works of art? 'I want to decorate my homes in the finest and most tasteful way I can,' he says.

Oscar Weiss, consultant geophysicist, brings a coldblooded scientific approach to his systematic collection of modern art. 'I don't like things in life which have been done before,' he says. 'Why should I collect another cosy array of this and that? Anyhow, I hate competition and I've found that imagination is the main thing to encourage in oneself. Imagination is the mainspring of anything I do whether it's searching for oil deposits or searching for pictures by my favourite painter Nicolas de Stael, the Russian émigré painter who worked in Paris until his suicide in 1955.

'I've helped sustain the popularity

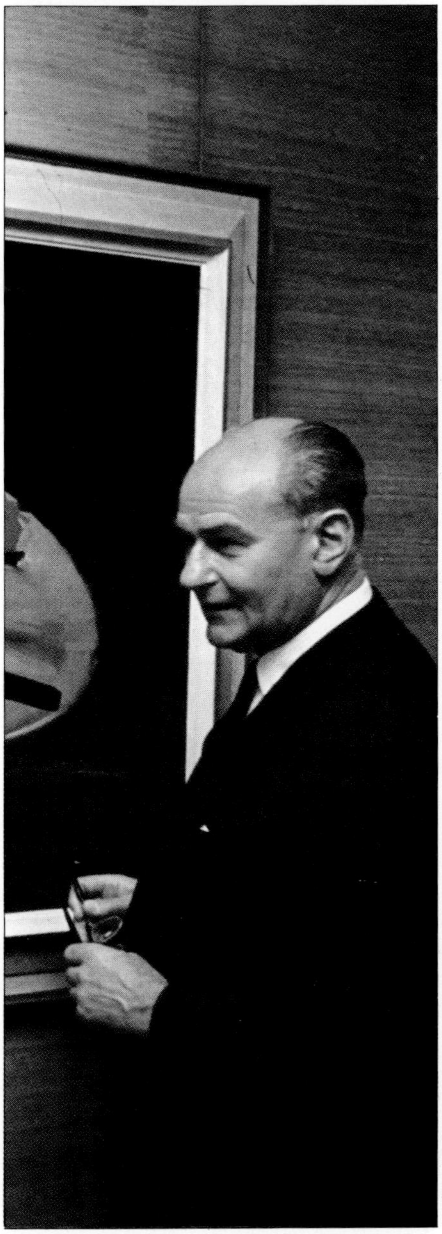

Oscar Weiss. He brings a coldblooded scientific approach to his systematic collection of art

of de Stael. I know both his wife and his children well. The man fascinates me. He has exactly my temperament and mentality. He approaches technical problems in his work just as a scientist would. Look at this simple study of fruit and then the sheer majesty of this larger, more abstract composition. Magnificent.

'I've walked miles to find good examples of his work. It's difficult now because his work is so rare and the prices are high. Fortunately, I know exactly what a certain painting of a certain period and quality should cost. I've got an example of every major period in de Stael's development as a painter except 1947. I'm still waiting.

'Dealers know that I'm a de Stael fan and I'm always being called to see things. The other day I went to see a collage by de Stael. It turned out to be a fake. The next day I got another telephone call to see a de Stael collage. It was from another dealer and again it was the same work, the same fake. This happened several times and I eventually lost my temper about the whole business.'

Apart from a small painting by Braque, the drawing-room of their spacious flat is devoted entirely to de Stael. The Weisses live in a fashionable row of Nash terraced houses overlooking Regent's Park. In the hallway there is a large portrait of a man by Francis Bacon, sculpture by Eduardo Paolozzi, and in the bedroom are two Modigliani drawings. Each room, however, is not without its examples of de Stael.

ART INVESTMENT

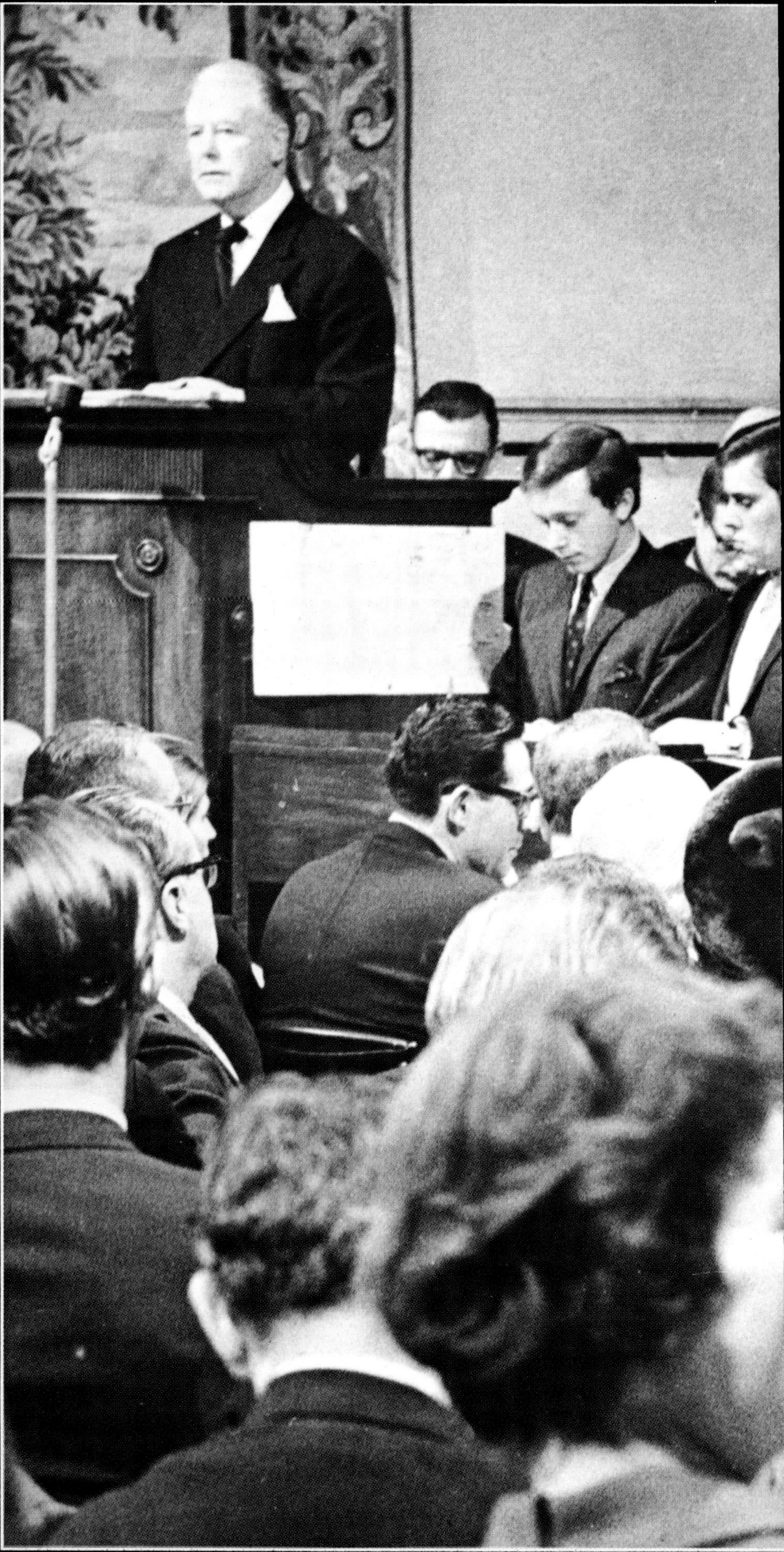

A recent sale at which Manet's *La Terrasse* was sold for 560,000 guineas—a record for a work by this artist

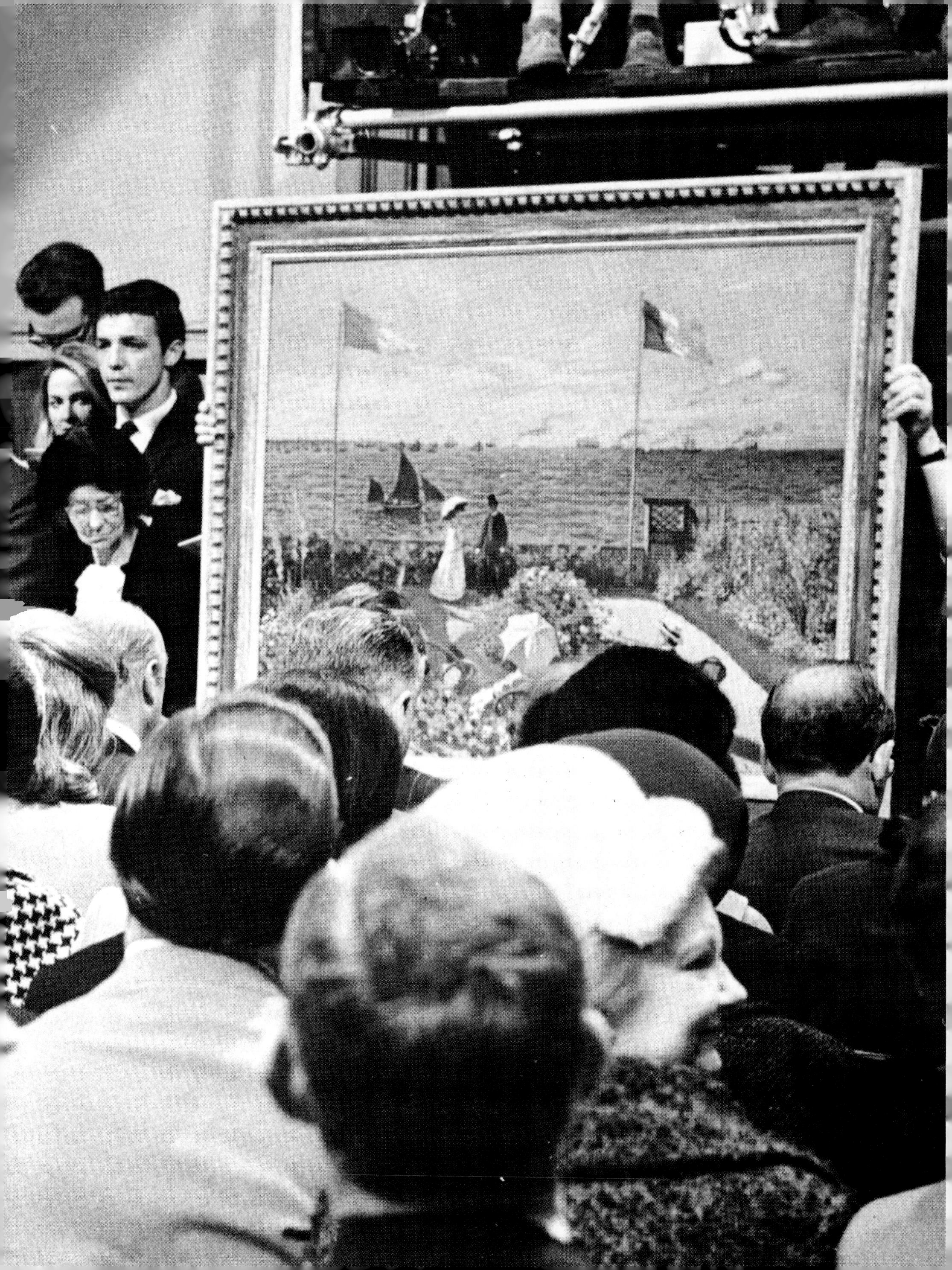

Few people like the idea that art has a lot to do with money, but only the naïve would deny it. Never before has the public bought original works of art in such quantity. And never before have so many people bought works of art with one eye on their subject matter and the other on their prospects as an investment.

Few believe in the once-popular myth that art is priceless; every painting and sculpture has its price. Most dealers, museum curators or insurance experts know the market value of an item down to the last nought, pounds, shillings or pence. Before the last war Lord Duveen, the great art dealer, claimed: 'If I had the Sistine Chapel, I could sell it tomorrow half a dozen times over.' No doubt Duveen also had a price in mind too.

There is, of course, no intrinsic value in a painting or sculpture. Prices are wholly artificial, and as changeable as the weather. They are subject to the machinations of dealers and auctioneers, museum-men and scholars, collectors and critics, and the related questions of time, scarcity and fashion. Recently a painting by Rembrandt was sold in New York for £821,400 ($2,300,000) and a painting by Picasso was sold in London for £190,000.

Why? Any painting is, after all, only made of canvas, oil colours, wood and dust. The artist's skill and dexterity are *not* always the answer to the tricky question of price and value. There are, for example, two versions of Rubens's *Diana and her Nymphs*. One belongs to the Cleveland Museum of Art, who are believed to have paid more than £100,000 for it in 1958, and the other to Mr Paul Getty, the multi-millionaire, who is believed to have paid £200,000 for it in 1962.

The *Sunday Express* posed the question: 'Which twin has the master touch? Only one painting can be the original. The other is likely to be a studio copy with finishing touches added by the master, and worth only a small fraction of its price.' It is unlikely that Rubens would have painted two versions so meticulously similar, so one would probably have been painted in his studio with perhaps finishing touches by the master.

If the controversy is ever settled one of them will be declared relatively worthless. And either the Cleveland Museum or Mr Getty will be poorer according to the remarkable 'logic' of the art market, but the twin versions of *Diana and her Nymphs* will not change as pictures.

The art market is engineered just as the stock market, a nation's currency or the pop record charts can be engineered. Art is a legitimate and highly profitable area of the business world and, as far as most of the art-men are concerned, has little to do with aesthetics. Wildly fluctuating fashions and prices are nothing unusual. In a sale of pictures at Houghton Hall in 1779, Catherine the Great of Russia paid £3,500 for a Guido Reni; £1,600 for a Van Dyck; £1,000 for a Pietro da Cortona; £600 for a Rembrandt; £100 for a Veronese; £100 for a Titian; and £60 for a Bellini. Today, the prices would probably be reversed, apart from Rembrandt who would no doubt realise the highest price.

The price and fashion for paintings by Rembrandt, a painter who most people would now consider to be one of the all-time 'greats', has taken an extraordinary course since his death in 1669. The graph here shows that Rembrandt enjoyed three periods of great popularity. In England during the first quarter of the nineteenth century; in Germany and the United States during the 1870s and 1880s; and throughout the world before the Second World War. The £128,000 which the National Gallery advanced towards the undisclosed sum paid for the large equestrian portrait from Panshanger, and the £821,400 paid for *Aristotle Contemplating the Bust of Homer* suggests that Rembrandt may be rising to another peak of popularity.

Rembrandt has had a bumpy career in the art market; despite occasional high prices his periods of popularity have been very short. Compared with his near-contemporary Rubens, who has always enjoyed popularity and relatively high prices, Rembrandt's performance has been rather unreliable. Thinking of the distant future, rather than short-term profits, Rubens would seem a better investment than Rembrandt. But most experts (and laymen) would consider Rembrandt a better painter than Rubens.

Top of the pops in the late eighteenth century included the paintings of Claude Lorrain (1600–1682). A pair of Claudes, the Altieri Claudes, have appeared at Christie's several times. In 1798 they were bought by an English dealer for £2,000; sold in 1799 for £6,825; sold in 1808 for £10,000 and in the same year £12,600; sold in 1940 for £2,600; and in 1947 they realised £5,300.

If your great-grandfather bought a painting costing thousands by Alma-Tadema (see page 30) or Lord Leighton (see page 12) it would long ago have proved a financial disappointment and an aesthetic embarrassment. Henry Moore is now the world's most highly-paid sculptor, and although his reputation will probably survive our generation it could be a dim memory by the time our grandchildren are looking at their contemporary favourites. Moore is now enjoying a peak of success; might possibly be out of fashion in the year 2000 and rise again in 2225.

Why are some pictures worth thousands and a place in the museum and seemingly identical pictures only £10 and a corner in a junk shop? Why is an average Impressionist landscape by Monet worth more than an average Impressionist landscape of the same subject by his contemporary, Sisley? And why does the price of a picture attributed to Giorgione fall dramatically when it turns out to be by Titian?

There is no single answer, but scarcity and scholarship, the market and fashion, are all general factors. A Giorgione is more expensive than a Titian because Titian painted many more Titians than Giorgione painted Giorgiones. Monet's pictures are more expensive because, by and large, art writers consider that Monet has the edge over Sisley as a painter. The fact that Rembrandt has been in and out of fashion, the possible value of work by Henry Moore in the year 2225 and the changing tastes of different generations suggest three important characteristics of the art market. Firstly, art tastes and values vary from century to century. Secondly, that anybody who wants to invest in art should employ caution and acquire as much knowledge about the subject as possible. Finally, if one is looking for profits rather than pleasure, short-term buying and selling is advisable.

There is little doubt that since the war more and more people have been making money out of investing in art. One American writer claims that 'the art market outperformed the

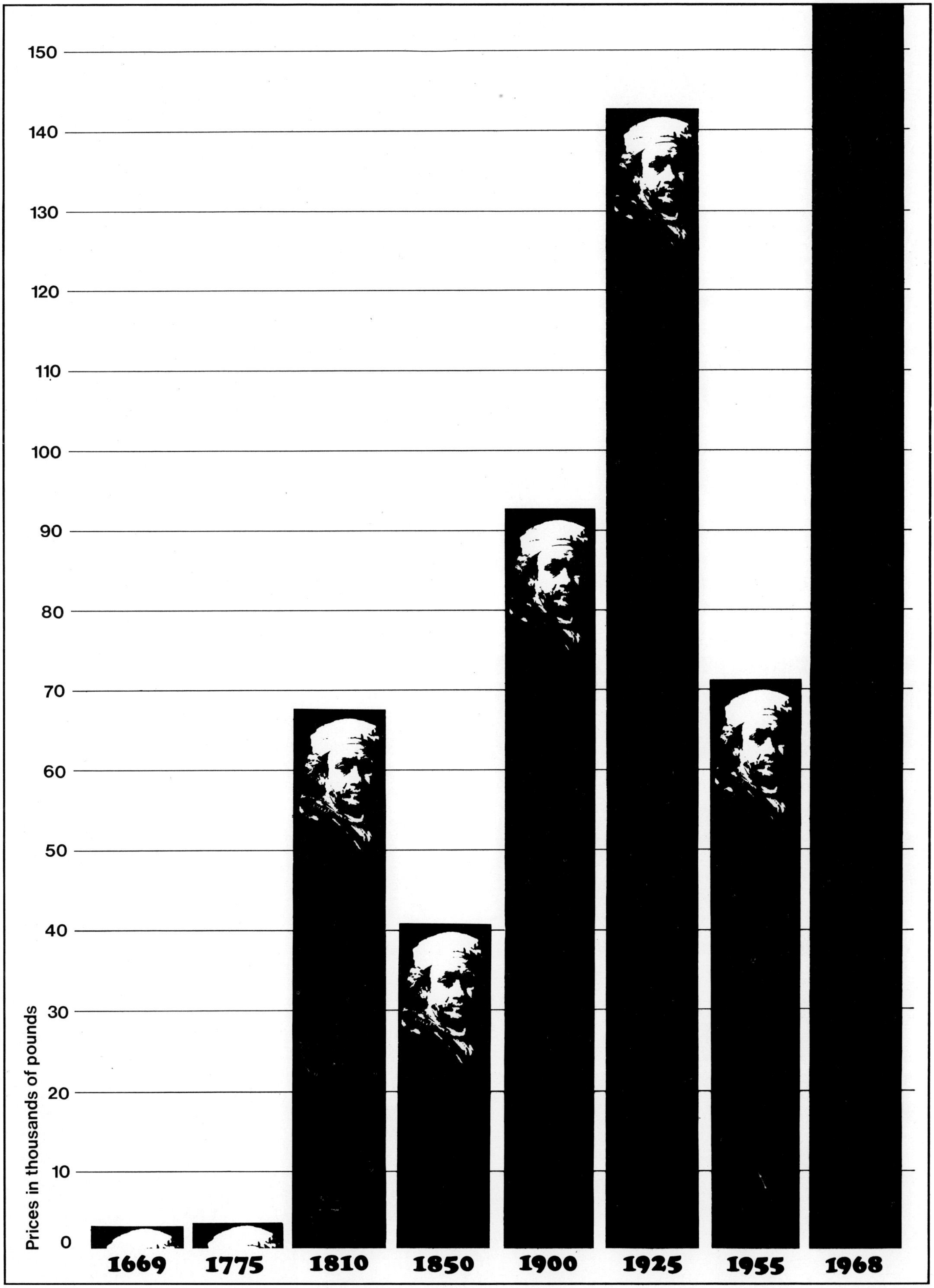
Prices in thousands of pounds
150
140
130
120
110
100
90
80
70
60
50
40
30
20
10
0
1669
1775
1810
1850
1900
1925
1955
1968

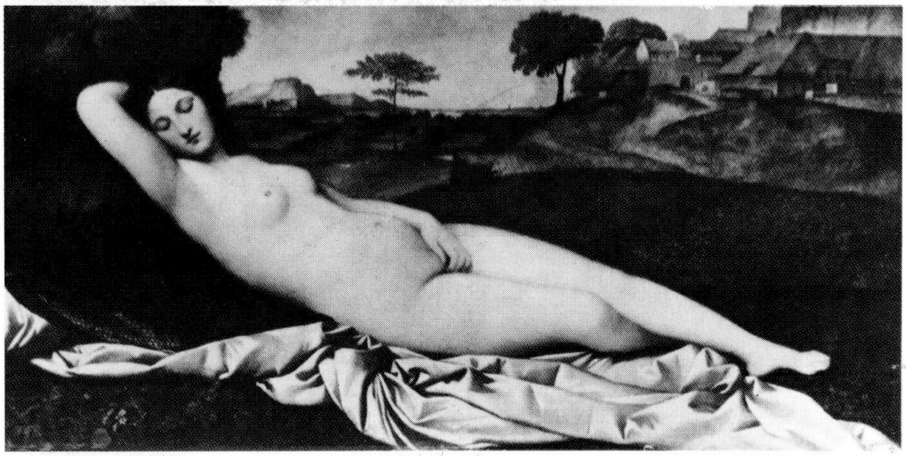

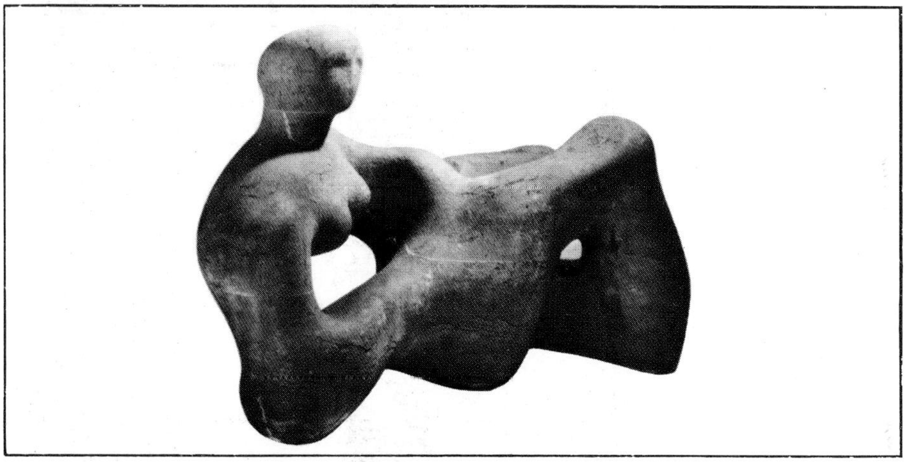

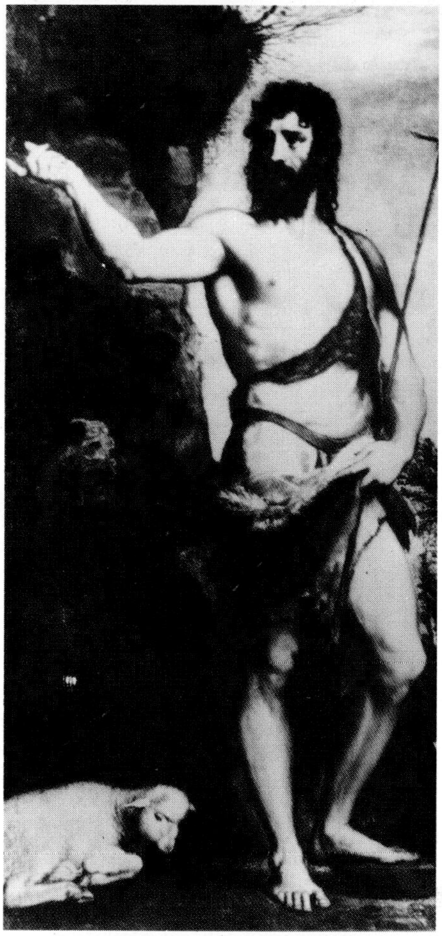

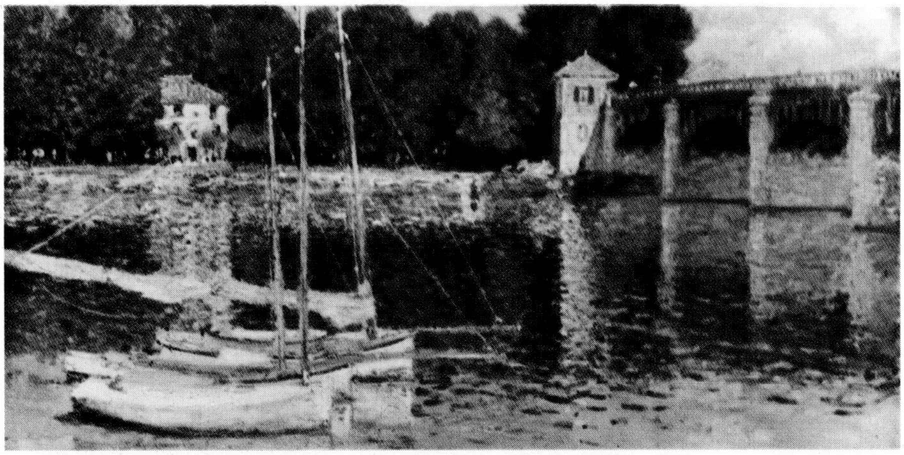

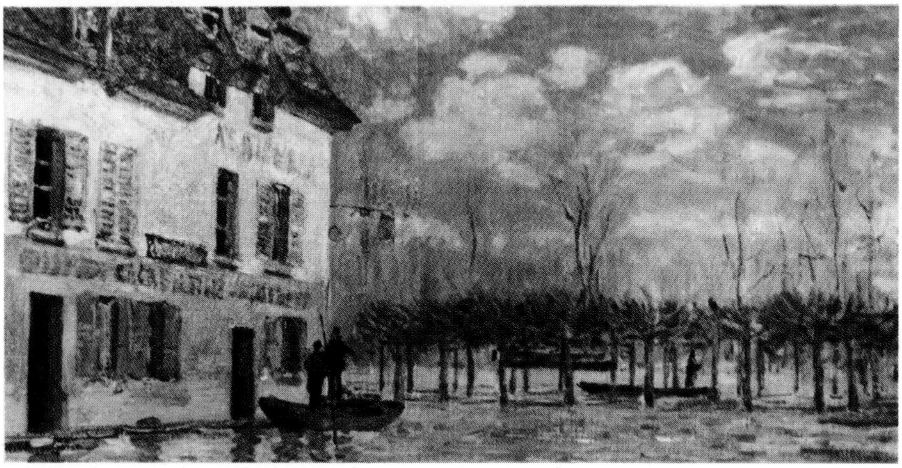

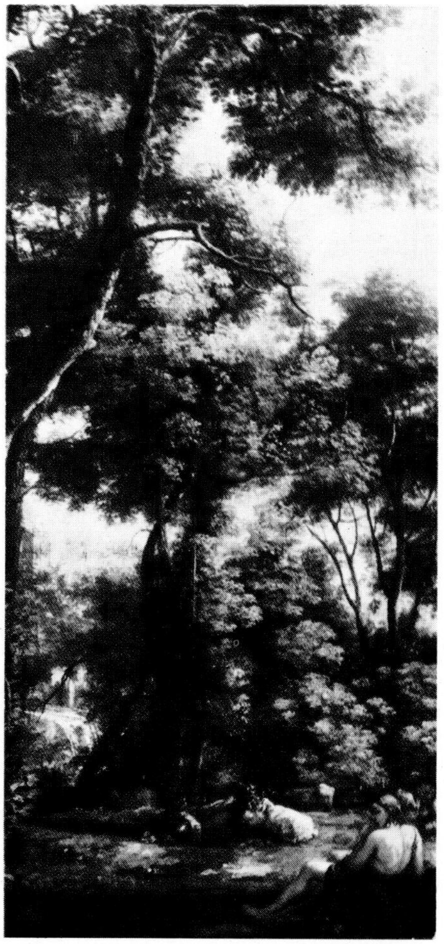

Rarity as well as quality makes some works of art more valuable than others. Pictures by Giorgione (1477–1510) are very rare, and prices very high indeed. Titian (*c.* 1487–1576), on the other hand, painted more, and pictures by him are sold for less. It is unlikely, however, that Giorgione's *Sleeping Venus* (top left) at Dresden, or Titian's *St John the Baptist* (top right) in Venice, will ever come on the market.

Fashion, too, plays a large part in deciding prices. Sculptures by Henry Moore (left) are enjoying a peak of success. Will they be out of favour by AD 2000? During the 18th century Claude Lorrain (bottom right) was top of the pops. Two paintings by him were sold in 1947 for only £5,300.

Sometimes it is very difficult to explain why the work of one artist outprices that of another. For example, pictures by Monet (left) fetch ten times as much as similar paintings by Sisley (bottom left)

stock market in the boom of the 1950s.' Even the squeeze has not affected the growing interest in art as an investment. Many auctioneers and dealers say the squeeze helped them considerably.

Robin Sanderson, who was a member of the Stock Exchange for 20 years and recently established a firm of fine art counsellors, is one of the few businessmen who actually claim to have benefited from the squeeze. Because the general run of British Ordinary shares yields only $5\frac{1}{2}$ to 6 per cent, Sanderson encourages people to invest in works of fine art. He has been so successful, he says, that he has widened his activities and now advises people on forming stamp collections for investment.

He suggests that people sell their British Ordinary Shares and immediately reinvest 70 per cent to 75 per cent of the proceeds in high-yielding, fixed-interest securities. This replaces their income, he says, since fixed-interest securities give a return of over 7 per cent; it also assures a much greater stability of capital value.

He then advises his clients to put the balance of their total assets into well-selected, 'international-type' works of art 'which will steadily increase in value.'

Several investment experts are sceptical about this idea and about the efficacy of art investment generally. Two writers, however, would seem to share Robin Sanderson's confidence in buying works of art rather than stocks and shares.

In his *World Currency Report,* Dr Franz Pick claims that in 1965 French porcelain appreciated on average by 15 per cent; Chippendale furniture by 30 per cent; silver by 40 per cent; French Impressionists by 40 per cent; and old masters by 50 per cent. Snuff-boxes were down by 30 per cent.

Richard H. Rush, an American investment banker, in his *Art as an Investment* (Prentice-Hall, 1961) claims that the works of Van Gogh, Gauguin and Cézanne appreciated by 4,833 per cent between 1930 and 1960.

The recent example of Van Gogh's painting *Les Déchargeurs* certainly seems to support what Rush is saying. Sold at Sotheby's in 1959 for £30,000, it was up for auction at Sotheby's again four years later but failed to reach its reserve price and was bought in at £45,000. In April it was sold at Parke-Bernet's, the New York auction house owned by Sotheby's, for £85,700.

A trap for the post-war investor was to buy those artists who appeared on the art scene in the early 1950s only to disappear shortly afterwards, seemingly for ever. Presumably any money invested in them has also, at least for the time being, disappeared. In *Young Artists of Promise,* a book published by Studio in 1957, Jack Beddington listed nearly one hundred artists who showed outstanding talent. Ten years later the West-End dealer, Eric Lister of the Portal Gallery, recognises only five names in the book. One wonders what happened to all those other artists?

In a discussion between six investment specialists part of which appears here on pages 70–71, Leslie Waddington, a prominent modern art dealer in London, suggested that 'only the main people in the modern movements will hold their prices and keep rising in value: in other words the top six Impressionists, the top six Fauves, the top six Surrealists, the top four Abstract Expressionists. I'm not talking about the peripheral people who joined in later but the main painters of the main movements.'

Art movements such as Waddington mentions are likely to last at the *top* of the investment stakes for as long as the generation who first backed them financially and aesthetically. In other words the generation of people, mostly Americans, who helped launch the Impressionists as a major movement in the art investment market in the 1920s, has largely died off. With their disappearance we are beginning to see a gradual slow-down in the inflated prices of Impressionist paintings. The Goldschmidt sale in London in 1958 and the 1960 sale of Impressionist works, also in London, probably represent the peak of Impressionist prices, although individual works will probably fetch eye-catching prices in the salerooms. Many of the best-known Impressionist paintings are now secure in museums and are unlikely to return to the commercial market. And with the death of their early and often wealthy protagonists, it is not surprising that the Impressionists are being edged out of the top price positions. Each generation of collectors and investors has its favourites

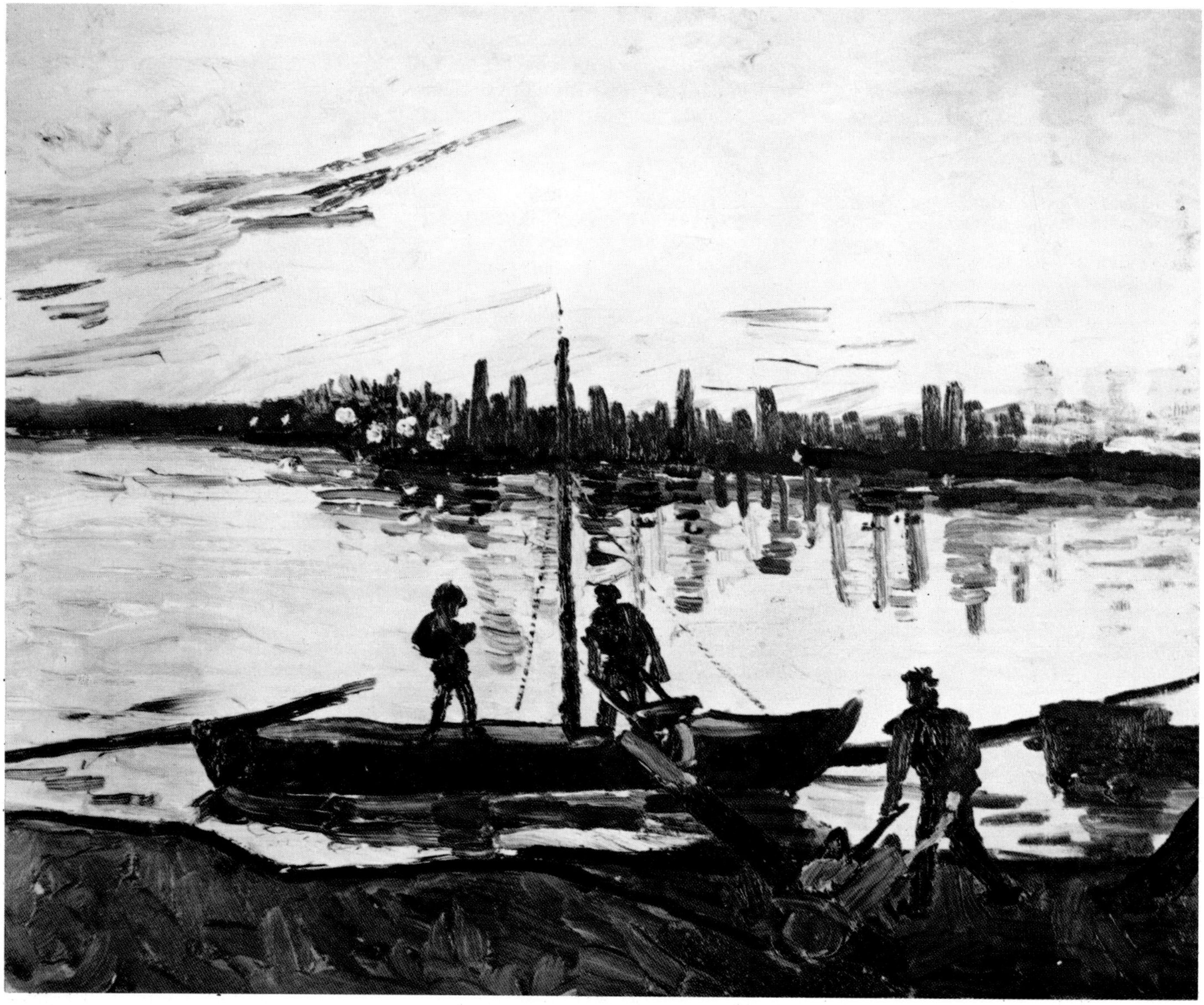

in any age and this helps force up high prices. In the pop group world few would expect the Beatles to be top of the pops in 50 years from now. People will expect new groups, fresh sounds and new sentiments to match their age. If history is any guide, this process also takes place in the art world.

In a review of his book, the Wall Street Journal said that 'Mr Rush had almost succeeded in applying Dow-Jones averaging techniques to the suddenly expanding world of art brokerage' but had not 'quite managed to come up with a suggestion for an "art exchange" page that would be the equivalent to an ordinary stock exchange page, because the 6,000 extant Renoir paintings, for example, can't be averaged for a useful ticker-tape quotation.'

The major problem is the way we compare the rise and fall in the value of works of art. Robert Wraight, the author of a book called *The Art Game* (Frewin), says: 'The first thing that should be remembered when we read of some spectacular new record price is that we are living in an inflationary period. The devaluation of the pound since the pre-war period means that today's prices must be divided by approximately four to make real comparisons with pre-war prices.' In America prices should be divided by three to allow for currency depreciation.

Richard H. Rush gives an idea of the profits which have been made from art in his book *Art as an Investment*. In two graphs he shows the percentage of price increase of several well-known twentieth-century artists and the price increase of four of them in dollars. *If* one bought work by Matisse, Braque, Picasso, or some of the other leading names of modern art, at the right time and the right price, one's profits would be astonishingly high. But suppose money had been invested in prominent artists in the same period, 1945–1960, who subsequently did not rise in value? Artists like Edzard, Picabia, Soulages and Alan Reynolds had a considerable following among collectors and museum-men in the 1950s, but during the past five years their performance in the salerooms has been disappointing. The future may reverse this current trend in their favour (not an uncommon happening in the past) but their post-war record is shown in the graphs on pages 68 and 69.

The graphs are a salutary reminder that for every winner there are a dozen also-rans. Favourites do not always live up to their form, and the carefree punter who backs his fancy in the art stakes can easily find himself flogging a dead horse.

Cliché perhaps, but life is short and this chapter should guide the would-

Artists

Four Contemporaries

Prices in Pounds 1945-1965

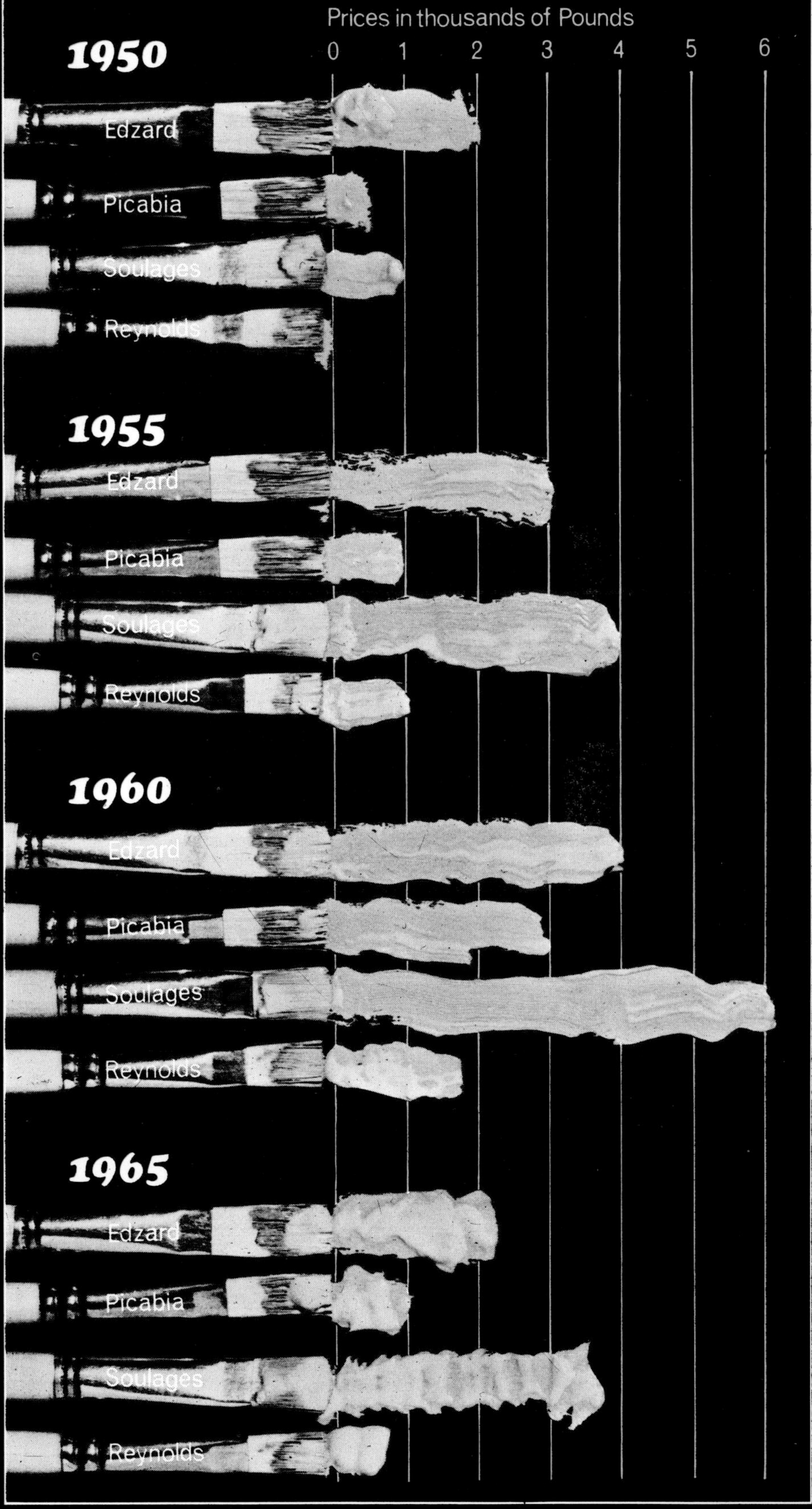

The author and six experts on art as an investment. Left-hand column: Peter Wilson, Chairman of Sotheby's; Michael Dormer, fine art investment adviser; Peter Chance, Chairman of Christie's. Right-hand column: Barrie Sturt-Penrose; Leslie Waddington, owner of the Waddington Gallery; Margot Naylor, financial journalist and author; Robert Wraight, art critic, journalist and author

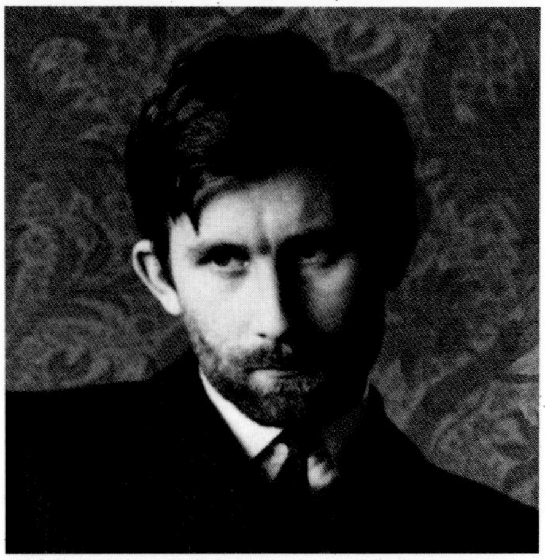

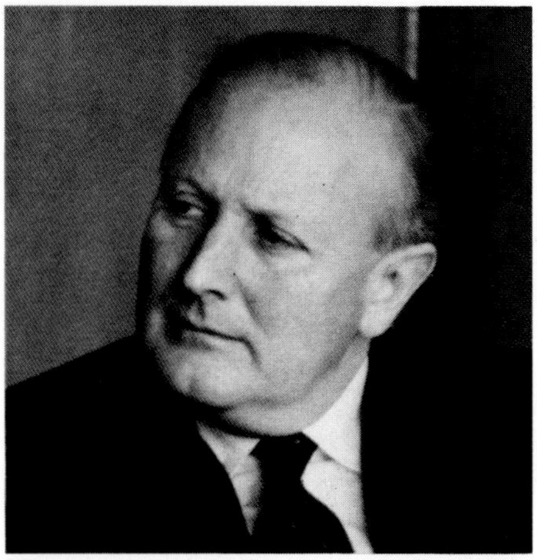

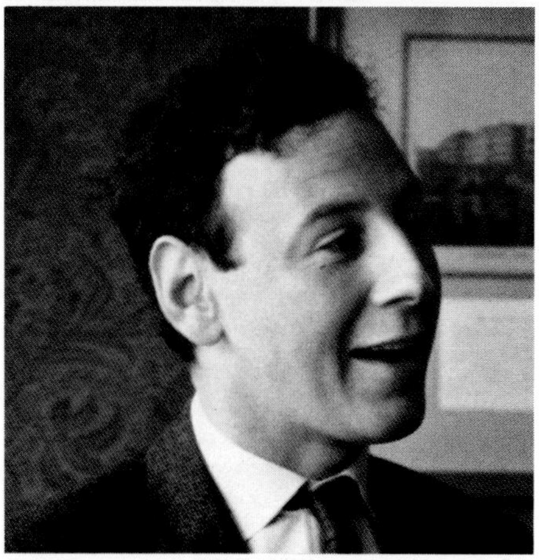

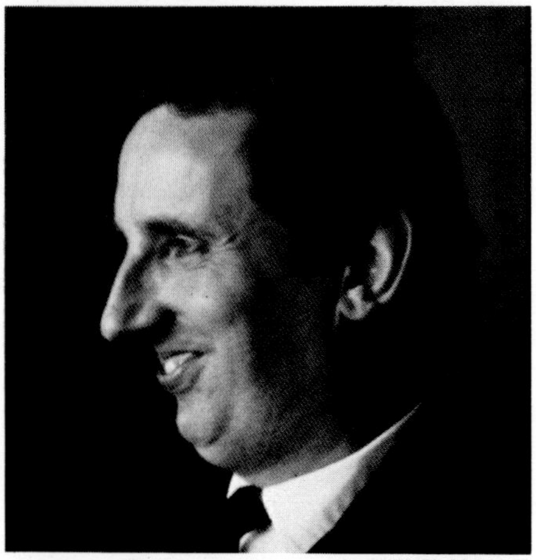

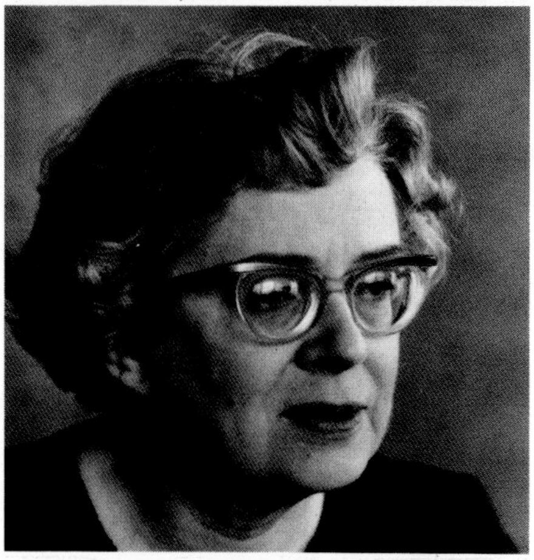

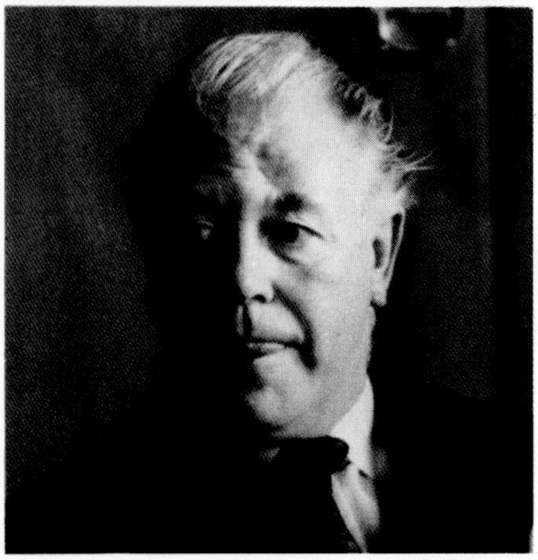

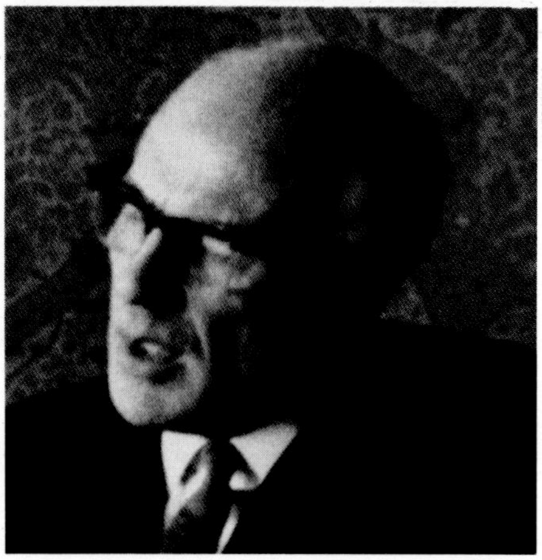

Sturt-Penrose: Art investment as a means of making money is still frowned upon by many people, even by some of the people who have a vested interest in the buying and selling of art. Would you agree?

Wraight: Even experts who write about art, and people like Rush who wrote the American book, are still frightened of talking about art as an investment. It's too nice a thing, too grand a thing for one to use this horrible word 'investment' in relation to it. Leslie Waddington has told me he doesn't believe in art as an investment, and he's a dealer.

Waddington: There used to be an élite who bought pictures; now people from a much wider circle of society are buying. We can see the same process here as the spreading of share-buying to the ordinary salaried class. For every picture that's sold at £10,000 probably a thousand are sold at £100, and most of these pictures within a year of sale are worth only about £40 on the market.

Naylor: Then that's bad investment.

Wraight: From my own experience it is easier to buy a picture that is a good investment at under £100, but if you are talking about investment as a percentage of gain there are plenty of opportunities in the great salerooms in this country to buy things, well under £100. I hesitate to say this in front of Peter Chance and Peter Wilson, but you can buy at Sotheby's and sell at Christie's or vice-versa at a profit, in fact, quite quickly.

Wilson: I think in this country people do not buy a picture to sell it at a profit within a few weeks, a few months or a few years. I think the vast majority still buy because they like works of art, although as a secondary thought it's always nice to have something that, if need be, we can sell at a profit.

Chance: I think the people who buy works of art totally without the idea of investment do not exist in any country in the world. If you buy something for £50 you expect it to be worth something in the future. Often it may be better to buy a very good picture by a less-known artist than a rather bad picture by a great man. Buying by name must be disastrous. Buying paintings by name doesn't exist as much as it did in the 1920s and 1930s.

Waddington: Yes, the good paintings go high in price and the bad ones go low. You only had to sit in the sales for the last few months to see the good pictures shoot right up and the bad ones just not go.

Wraight: This is very gratifying to anybody who wants to see more discrimination in buying. But the fact is that a third-rate Monet, and there are a lot of them, will sell for a lot more than a good-class painting by a less-known Impressionist.

Wilson: But I think a bad painting by Monet can still fetch £12,000 while a good one can fetch £200,000. Since the squeeze, I think buyers have been more discerning and discriminating in our Impressionist sales. I think we have been more informed since the war.

Waddington: The major painters of one period are influenced normally by the major painters of a period before. For example, Picasso and Matisse were both influenced by Cézanne. Picasso had an influence on the Surrealists. Surrealist paintings were being bought by Americans in the 1930s–the French didn't buy them–and post-war American painting grew under their influence. Going on this rule, and there must be exceptions to the mainstream art, the main schools of 30 years ago in the art world will gradually creep up. You'll find the Cubists are starting to shoot up now, and next you'll get Surrealists, and next the American Abstract Expressionists; besides that you'll get all the idiosyncrasies like Henri Rousseau.

Wraight: I think all paintings that have got a very high price eventually stop; some go back, but if, as Leslie Waddington says, they are in the mainstream of painting, they eventually find a high level in the art world as works of art, and the appropriate value. I personally think that the Impressionists are just in the first sort of surge and will probably in the not too distant future level off and even drop.

Wilson: I'm not so certain about this. After all, there is a very disagreeable economic situation at the moment. In spite of that the Impressionists have really increased in value lately.

Wraight: Do you really think prices have really increased, actual prices, since the extraordinarily high prices reached at the Goldschmidt sale in 1958?

Wilson: Fantastically, and I can prove this with an index.

Wraight: But the great masters of the past have not gone on, but have gone back and come up again: W. H. Hunt, for example, the man who painted birds' eggs and once brought enormous prices; Romney and Reynolds were at their highest in the 1920s.

Chance: The English Schools and a few curiosities were terribly valuable and then went right down, but except for the English Schools things have increased in value over the years.

Wraight: If you look at certain Dutch painters you will find they had a tremendous vogue in the early nineteenth century and yet by the late nineteenth century they faded.

Waddington: But not the main ones like Rembrandt–my point is that the important people keep going up. You may get slight setbacks with the peripheral people, but rarely with the giants. There were 3,000 painters working in Holland in 1630, of whom 10 or 15 were people who broke new aesthetic ground.

Sturt-Penrose: But if people have some money they want to invest in art they can hardly afford to buy a Rembrandt, a Cézanne, a Renoir or any of the other painters Waddington has mentioned. Wraight, in your book *The Art Game* you say that less than 1 per cent of contemporary art will survive. That's hardly an encouragement for people who are thinking of investment.

Wraight: That's just a figure relating to the absurd production of painting and pseudo art; everybody's on the bandwaggon to paint. Of course, very little of it will survive. There are 50,000 painters working in New York alone–how much of their work will live?

Wilson: The survivors are the best of every school, the best of every school of painting. This remains more or less constant throughout the ages, but as the paintings get scarcer and scarcer, because they go into museums and private collections, on purely economic grounds they must go up in value as long as there are people who appreciate paintings.

Naylor: By definition, this is an investment for millionaires, isn't it?

Wilson: No, because you can do the same with some of the less-known schools.

Dormer: We had a client the other day who wanted to buy an Impressionist. We found two or three selections for him in various galleries in London and, in the week he was making up his mind, well over half of the pictures we had suggested had been sold.

S-P: Going back to Waddington's contention that people who have stuck to the main painters of this century have made a good investment, I would like to ask about someone like Bernard Buffet. Shortly after the last war he was highly regarded–Picasso called him one of the most promising young painters–and now he would seem to have been a bad bet for any investor.

Waddington: He wasn't a mainstream artist, he was incidental.

S-P: Quite a few influential collectors bought paintings by Buffet–they must have done, or prices would not have risen so astonishingly high.

Chance: Very often one looks at something one bought oneself 10 or 20 years ago and one wonders why one bought that, and says 'I see that's wrong and this is wrong and maybe now I've grown a little older and a little wiser.' If you make a profit then you realise that maybe you weren't such a fool when you bought it, and if you make a loss then you've learnt your lesson.

Waddington: Well I've been a big private collector outside the gallery and 70 per cent of the things I've bought five, six years ago, I don't like. They are bad things, but I still get enjoyment out of them. They were things I couldn't advise my clients to buy. I agree with Wilson that most people buy pictures because they like them, and they are the people who also in the end make money on them.

Wraight: I don't think this alters the fact that the percentage of people who are now interested in investment has gone up. It has, because you do find the people who buy purely, as they think, for investment. They buy with their ears not with their eyes–they buy a thing because it's reputed to be going up in value, and in my experience these people very often do come croppers.

Chance: The people who have made absolutely incredible profits are widows who bought pictures in the 1930s out of their dress allowances because they loved them. They thought: 'Here's something I like, I want it and I'm sure it will be worth what I'm paying for it if I sell it again and that I won't lose money.' People who buy purely for investment can lose a lot of money unless they are very well advised.

THE ARTISTS

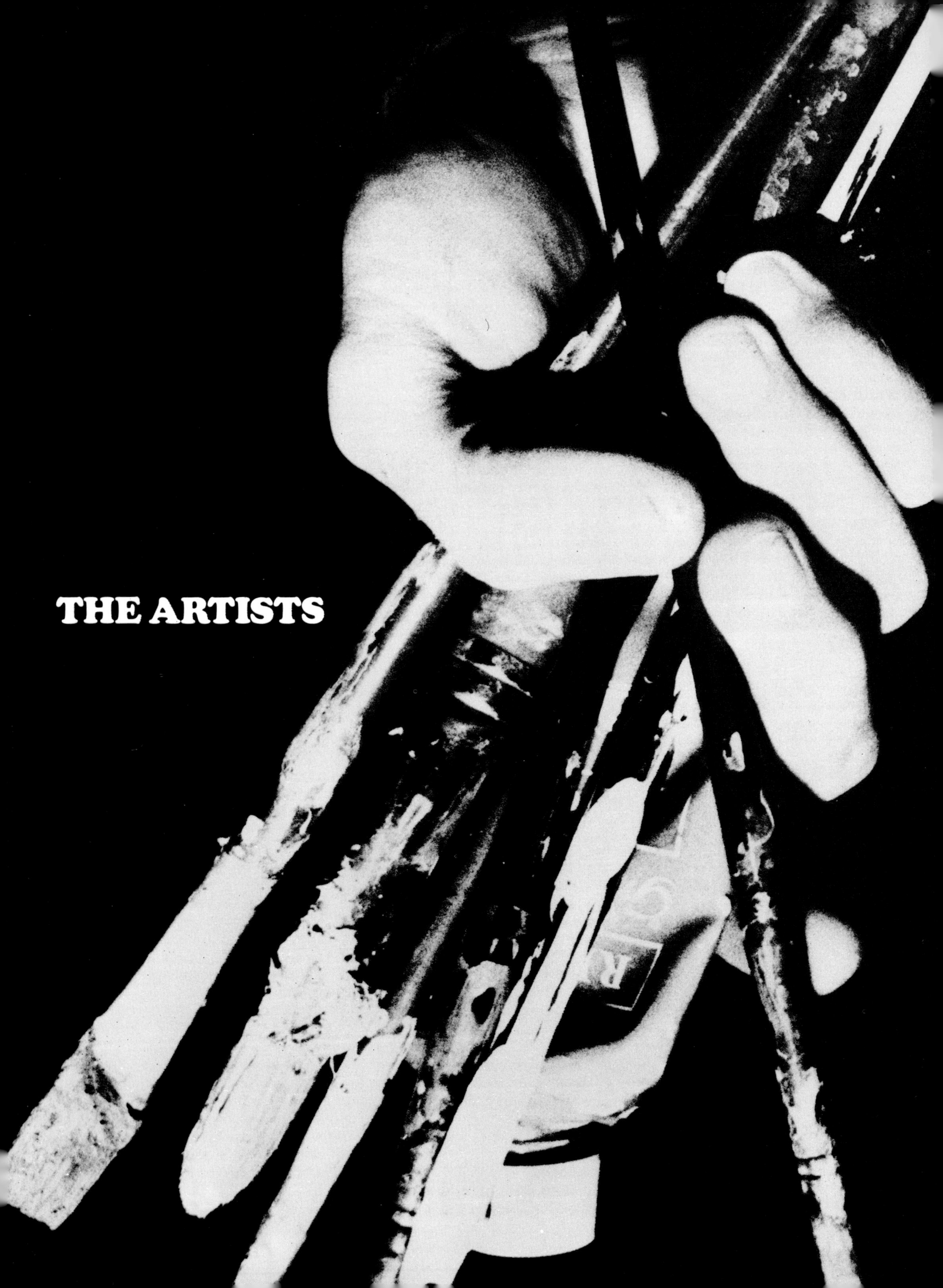

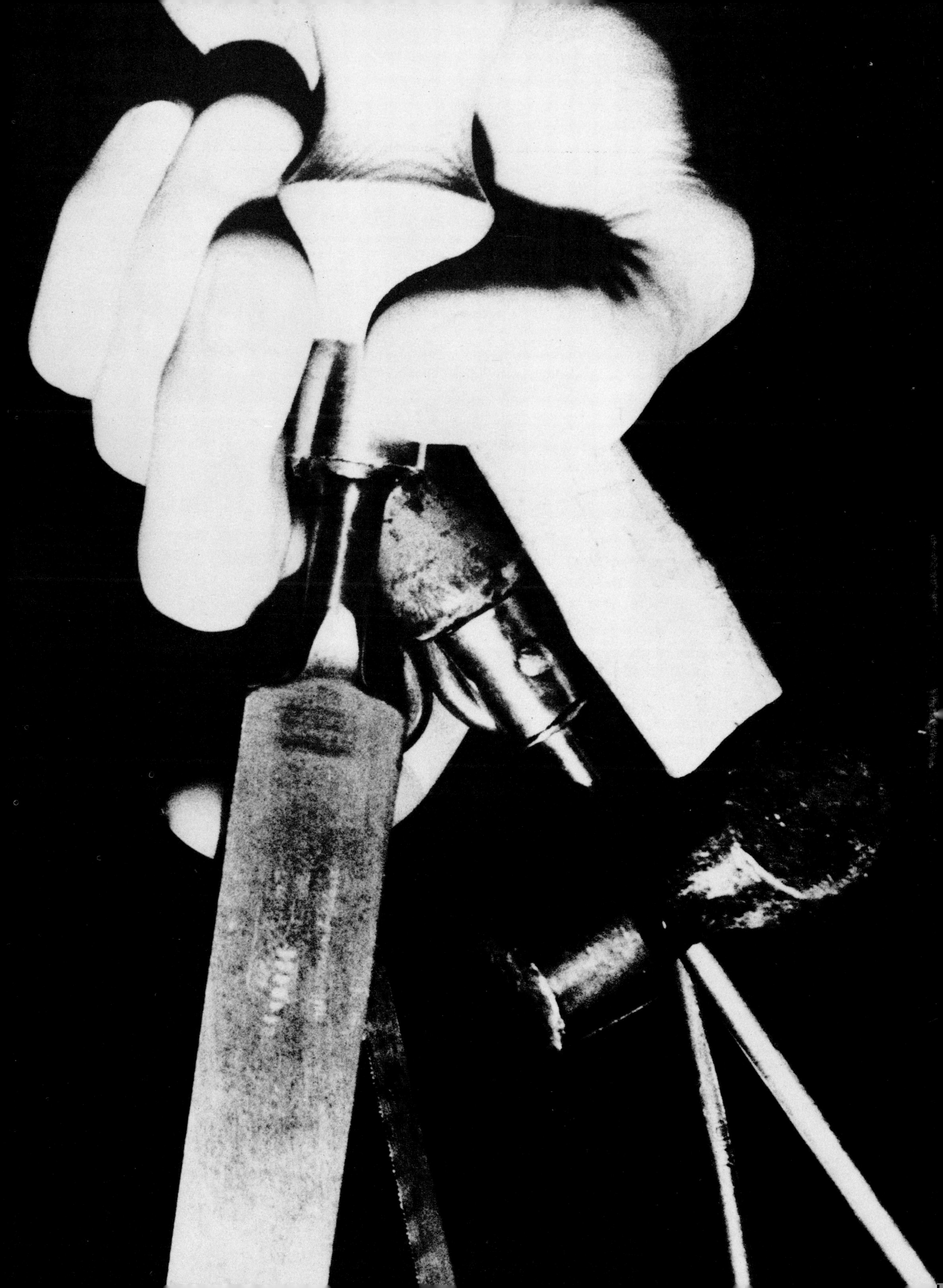

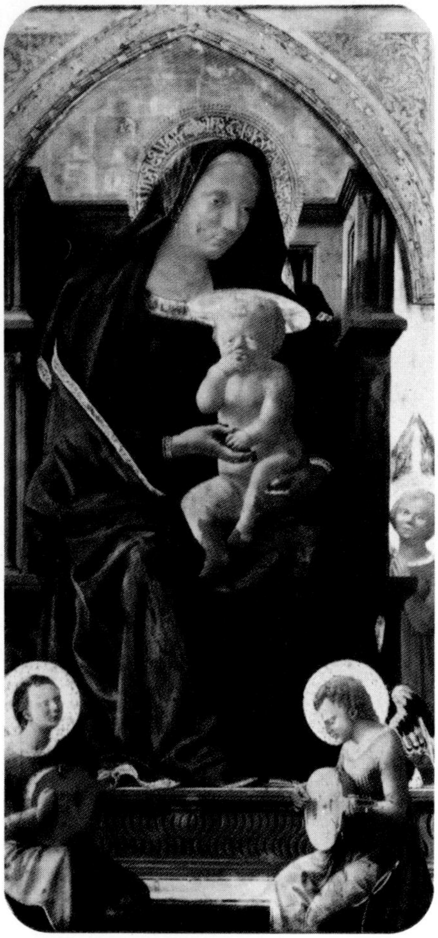

Art is a reflection and an integral part of man's history, progress and culture. Today, as in the past, artists help us to come to terms with our environment—or to escape from it. The four works shown here each reflect the age in which they were made

Left to right: Masaccio, *Virgin and Child with Angels*. 1426. National Gallery, London; Parmigianino, *Madonna with the Long Neck*. *c.* 1535. Uffizi, Florence; François Boucher, *Cupid a Captive* (Detail). 1754. Wallace Collection, London; Claes Oldenburg, *Soft Toilet*. 1966. Ganz Collection, New York

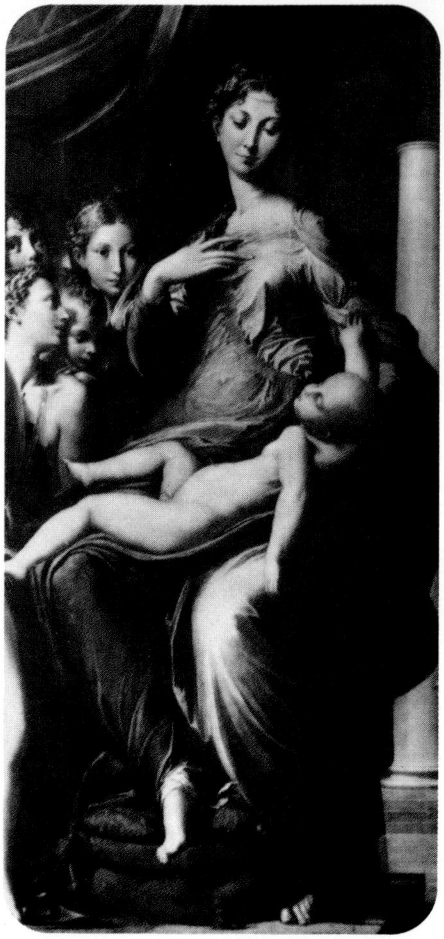

Few people believe that art is unnecessary and that man could live happily without it. After all, art is almost as old as himself. But if art is indispensable what do we need art for? Questions like these have never been so urgently in need of a reply as they are today.

Art is a reflection and an integral part of man's history, progress and culture. Artists today, as in the past, reflect and record our beliefs and superstitions, our moments of magnificence and failure, our fears and our ambitions. They help us to recognise ourselves.

It is because every human being has an aesthetic sense that we respond to art, however differently and irrespective of our intellectual standing. Donatello's sculpture and Cézanne's painting may mean nothing to us, but the latest Rolls-Royce, a beautiful building or the shape of a Boeing 707 may evoke an immediate aesthetic appreciation.

The art of primitive peoples has an aesthetic quality, even though to many people who are more familiar with the style of Michelangelo and Raphael, it may appear crude. Prehistoric man painted hunting scenes on cave walls because they suggested to other cave-dwellers that they could out-wit and out-chase animals upon whom they depended for their survival. The famous cave-pictures of animals at Altamira in Spain are outstanding examples of the aesthetic impulse working in man. Rarely has art been so real and meaningful about the basic day-to-day realities of life.

But prehistoric art and the work of primitive peoples which survives today also have much to do with magic and religious feeling. Anthropologists investigating the art of 30,000 to 10,000 B.C. and the more recent art of the Bushmen of Southern Rhodesia and South-West Africa have discovered that paintings were often repainted and that the caves where they were kept were regarded as sacred.

The development of art from its primitive stage to its most civilised accomplishment in Classical or Gothic art is paralleled and interwoven with the evolution of man's view of his universe. Art helped take us from magic and animism to religion and science. But because the art of primitive man is different from the art of civilised man it cannot be said that one is superior to the other: they are just different stages in man's evolving culture.

Neither can it be said that there has been a profound change in the psychological workings of the artist's mind. The way we live in societies may change, but the artist's sensibility is a fairly constant factor. Art is rich and varied because artists respond exactly to the demands, the needs and the potentiality of their environment and fellow-men.

When we compare Masaccio's *Madonna and Child* and Parmigianino's *Madonna with the Long Neck* with, for example, Boucher's *Cupid a Captive* and Claes Oldenburg's *Soft Toilet*, we can see from the subjects chosen and their style how each artist is responding to a different situation.

The history of art until the Renaissance expressed the overwhelming importance which religion played in man's daily life. The medieval painter in Europe was very powerful and could put the fear of the Devil or the love of God into those who saw his work in churches and great cathedrals.

With the Renaissance some five

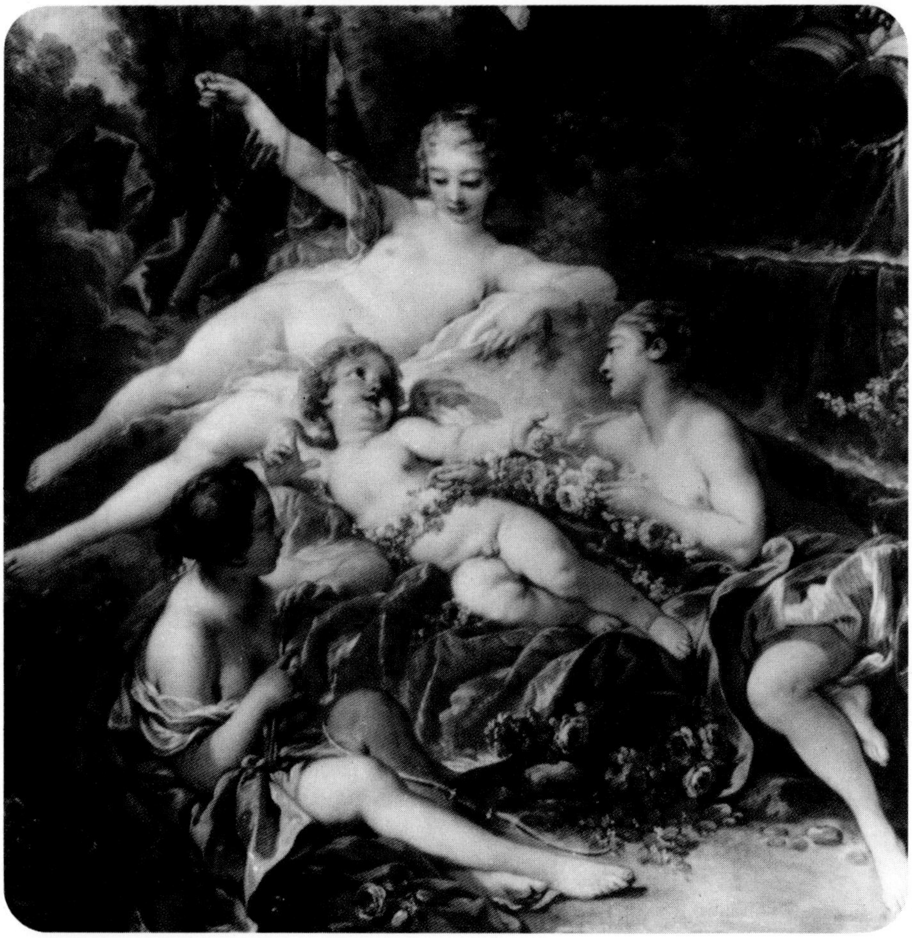

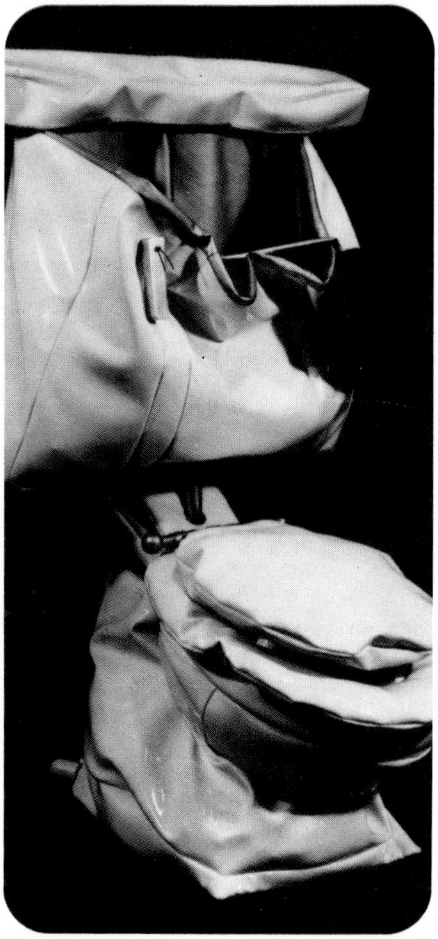

hundred years ago art changed its emphasis and its more rigid traditions. Artists and writers turned to the classical humanism of Greece for their subjects and inspiration. They also helped turn the minds of people from religion in the medieval sense to thoughts about man and his world. Through the influence of the great patron-popes and rich merchants, painters like Leonardo da Vinci began producing portraits of private citizens as well as saints. Art began to widen its base and its preoccupations.

The Protestant reformation had a lasting effect upon the art and architecture of Northern Europe. Religious art was savagely attacked in Britain, Holland, Scandinavia and Northern Germany and subsequently became much more austere and puritan in character. The Council of Trent (1545–1563) and the rise of the Jesuits led by Ignatius Loyola, did a lot to restore religious art in Southern and Central Europe, especially in the great Hapsburg domains stretching from Spain to Austria. In order to win people back to the Catholic Church every available artistic device was used in a universal appeal to the senses. Extravagantly ornamental Baroque churches, more like theatres than places of worship, became the setting for lavish religious ceremonies performed to an accompaniment of orchestral music, by such great composers as Monteverdi and Scarlatti.

In Holland and England the establishment of Protestantism saw power pass from the old religious and aristocratic patrons into the hands of wealthy merchants and traders. They wanted portraits of themselves, and their families, domestic scenes, interiors and landscapes. Both Vermeer and Rembrandt painted ordinary people engaged in everyday tasks, and even Rembrandt's religious pictures are subdued and puritan in feeling.

The age of Louis XIV, the Sun King (1643–1715), saw the rise of Baroque art in France. More restrained than in Prague and Vienna, it was pressed into the service of the monarchy rather than the church, and is epitomised by the Palace of Versailles, built to glorify the person of the great king.

By the middle of the eighteenth century, however, Frenchmen like Boucher, Watteau and Fragonard were reflecting the frivolity, the prettiness, the charm of their age and their own new and privileged positions as painters.

David, in pictures like *The Death of Marat,* characterised the mood of the French Revolution, and it is in fact revolution which has characterised European art since 1789. One might say that the history of modern art begins with the fall of the Bastille. The French Revolution, the revolution of 1848 and the Paris Commune of 1871 are as important for art and literature as for politics.

In nineteenth-century France, Italy, Germany, Austria, Poland, Russia and other European countries, revolutionary movements and actions sprang up dedicated to the overthrow of conservative governments and feudal systems.

Under the assorted banners of freedom, republicanism, marxism, socialism and anarchism, new classes and political parties aimed for a new European order, a new independence and a place in the modern world which they were helping to form. The art of Boucher and Fragonard, which stood for old Europe, was replaced with the art of men like David and Goya. Soon other artists came along

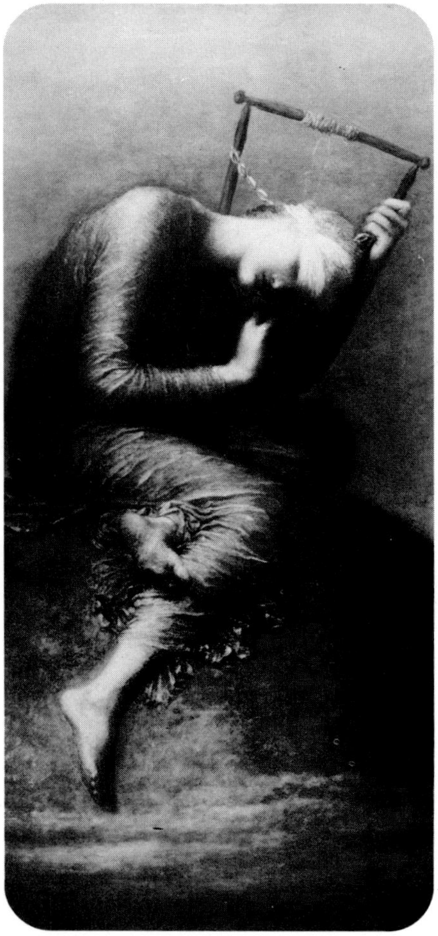

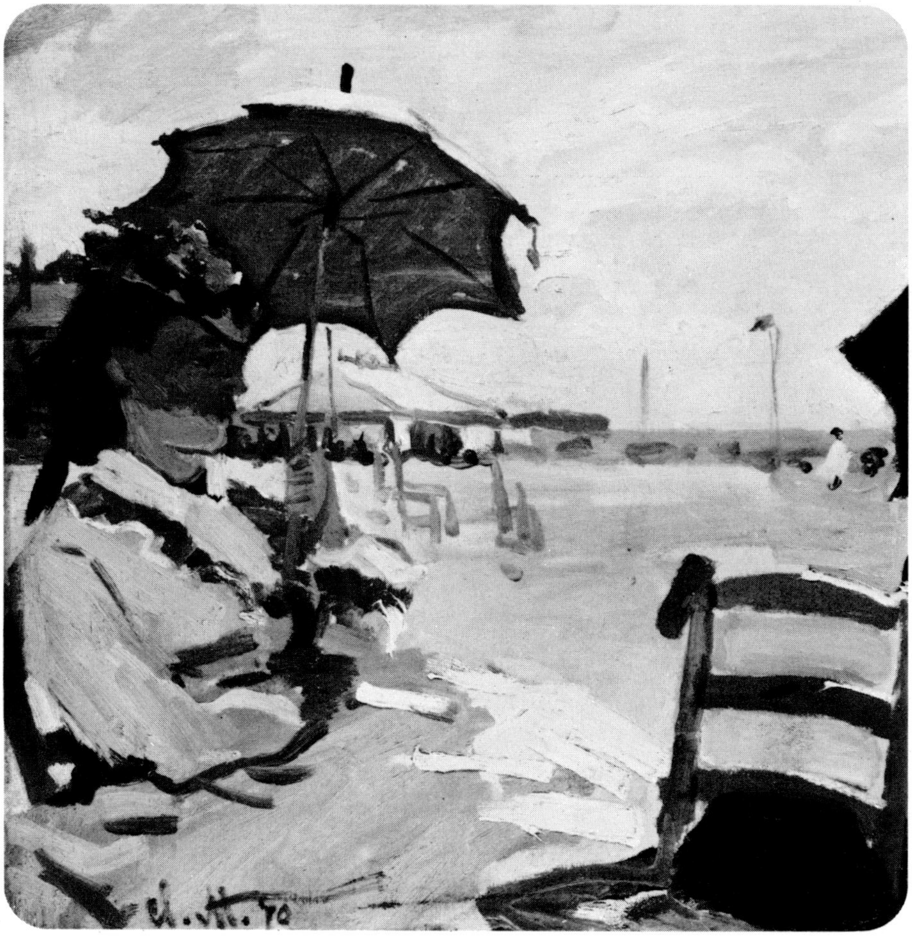

to take the artistic revolution several stages further.

With social revolution came scientific and industrial advances of enormous importance. The theories of Charles Darwin and Karl Marx, the invention of complicated machinery, the telephone, the introduction of railways and mass production and the appearance of the photographer, all had dire consequences for the future of art and literature.

All over Europe and the United States people drifted towards the towns and cities, forming for the first time an urban working class. Because people lived closely together in large numbers communication became much easier. The Crimean War which involved Britain, France and Russia was the first general European war in which the popular Press and the telegraph brought war to the attention of the whole country.

Although the underlying spirit of the last century was revolutionary, financial power was still in the hands of the middle classes – the *bourgeoisie* – the capitalists who owned the factories. But with wars, social unrest, the spectre of revolution, and the assassination of rulers like Tsar Alexander II of Russia, the European monied classes found they were under fierce attack. Writers like Zola and painters like Millet used their art to fight tradition in whatever form they discovered it.

The nineteenth-century European artist was forced to take political sides; either he was a reactionary or he was a progressive. The reactionary painter showed his work in the official salons; the progressive either had nothing to do with such circles or he was totally rejected by them.

The Impressionists and a few of their forerunners, men like Courbet and Millet, were the first revolutionaries in nineteenth-century art. It is no coincidence that the founders of Impressionism – Manet and Monet – were both rebels. After the Paris Commune, in 1871, Manet was arrested as an insurgent and accused of painting revolutionary pictures. Monet was avowedly left-wing in his views, and had little time for the bourgeois circles which Manet found so vital to himself and his art. Later adherents to the Impressionist movement – Pissarro is the striking example – declared themselves enemies of tradition, both in art and in politics.

Impressionism had its origins in Realism, a style which emerged forcefully at the time of the 1848 revolution. In the hands of Courbet, Millet and Daumier and others, Realism was in opposition to the official salon style of art: a style characterised by scenes of classical mythology and an overall fancy-dress appearance.

Millet was significantly the first painter to protest at the life of the peasant in the first half of the nineteenth century. Whereas Breughel painted peasants as peasants – neither idealised nor protesting – Millet, who was himself of peasant origin and an ardent supporter of the 1848 revolution, presented them as exploited slaves of a system he considered both vicious and outmoded.

The Impressionists also rejected art which depicted an ideal (and therefore an unreal) world. They were materialists who were vitally concerned with the world they lived in. Their pictures were concerned with 'impressions' of nature and humanity as they saw it in the countryside and in the streets. Later, Post-Impressionists like Van Gogh represented

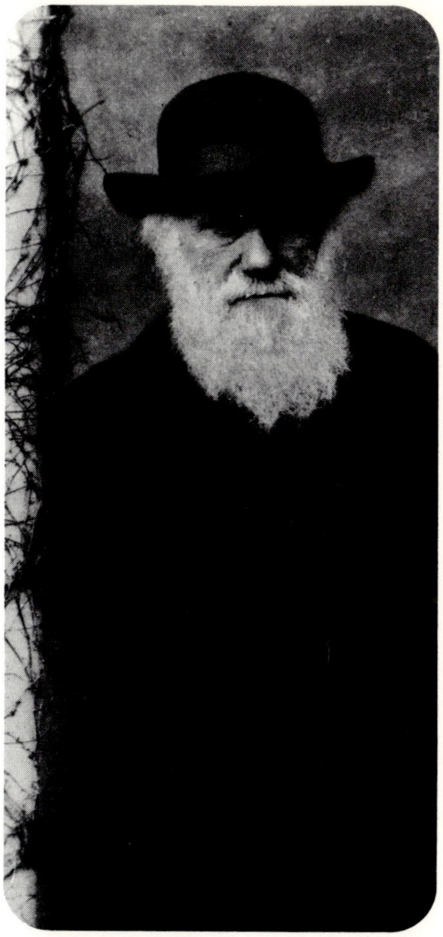

Hope, by George Frederic Watts, is a typical nineteenth-century painting, yet it was painted in 1886, sixteen years after Monet's *The Beach at Trouville* (both left). To the Victorian admirers of Watts the work of Monet must have seemed shockingly avant-garde

The nineteenth century seems to us now frightfully staid. In fact it was a century of revolutionary thought. Charles Darwin's book *The Origin of Species* upset traditions going back thousands of years (left). Van Gogh's pictures of peasants toiling for a bare existence (right) reflect the new social awareness of our great-grandfathers

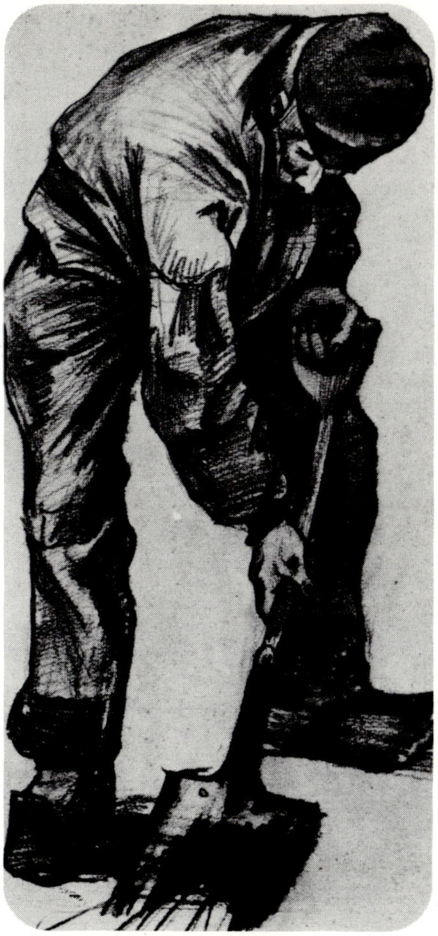

some of the workers which had been created by the industrial revolution. Van Gogh helped to portray some of the suffering of the agricultural and urban proletariate.

A vital link between the revolutionary theories of the Impressionists and the emerging revolutionaries of twentieth-century art was Paul Cézanne. He emphasised the simple fact that the history of art is really a history of the ways man has seen the world.

Herbert Read once wrote that a naïve person might object that there is only one way of seeing the world – the way it is presented to his own immediate vision. But in fact we learn to see, and vision becomes a habit and a convention. What we see is determined by our education and our environment and not the laws of optics.

Cézanne was a follower of the Impressionists for several years, but later reacted against their way of seeing the world. He wanted to impose an intellectual order on his painting, but allied with the Impressionist technique of painting directly from nature. And his achievement was instrumental in the direction modern art was to take during the first quarter of the twentieth century.

The scientific discoveries which were being made were reflected in the work of Pointillists like Seurat and Signac and their theory of 'optical mixture'. In 1890 the painter and theorist Maurice Denis said: 'It has to be remembered that a picture – before being a war-horse, a nude or some anecdote or other – is essentially a flat surface covered with colours put together in a certain order.'

Seurat's theory of an 'optical mixture', which involved breaking down the colours of nature into constituent hues and putting them in their primary state and in the form of dots on to the canvas, made specific demands of the spectator. Seurat was to have an enormous influence on the later trail-blazers of modern art: Picasso and Braque.

Clearly if we are to understand, not necessarily *commend,* modern art, we must examine it against the backcloth of the history of art and the specific movements and influences which formed it in the last century.

Modern art has widened the artist's subject matter and taken it into every corner of human experience. Because of the influence of Japanese prints which reached France in the 1850s, the discovery of African primitive sculpture and the art of the self-taught painter, artists have rejected the traditional ideas of beauty which were embodied in the art of classical Greece and the Renaissance. Rarely do artists consider whether an object, a scene or an emotion is ugly or beautiful, but simply whether it is interesting enough to paint.

Other influences which helped hurl twentieth-century art into new preoccupations and pursuits were the work of psychoanalysts like Freud, and the composers of avant-garde music. For the first time (perhaps with the single exception of Bosch) artists delved into dreams, repressions, hidden fears and desires as a valuable source of subject matter. Artists also wanted to make art like music, which could already convey emotions and feelings directly.

It was undoubtedly the camera which helped give the *coup de grâce* to many of art's traditional functions. Portrait painting is just one kind of painting unlikely to recover from the blow it suffered from the millions of people who suddenly discovered they could become photographers and produce their own pictures.

Between 1907 and 1913 Picasso and Braque evolved a new style known as Cubism. Carrying on the work of Cézanne they at last broke with the idea that a two-dimensional picture had to be a three-dimensional illusion. This painting (above), *Seated Nude,* by Picasso, now hangs in the Tate Gallery. Less and less people ask 'But what is it meant to be?'

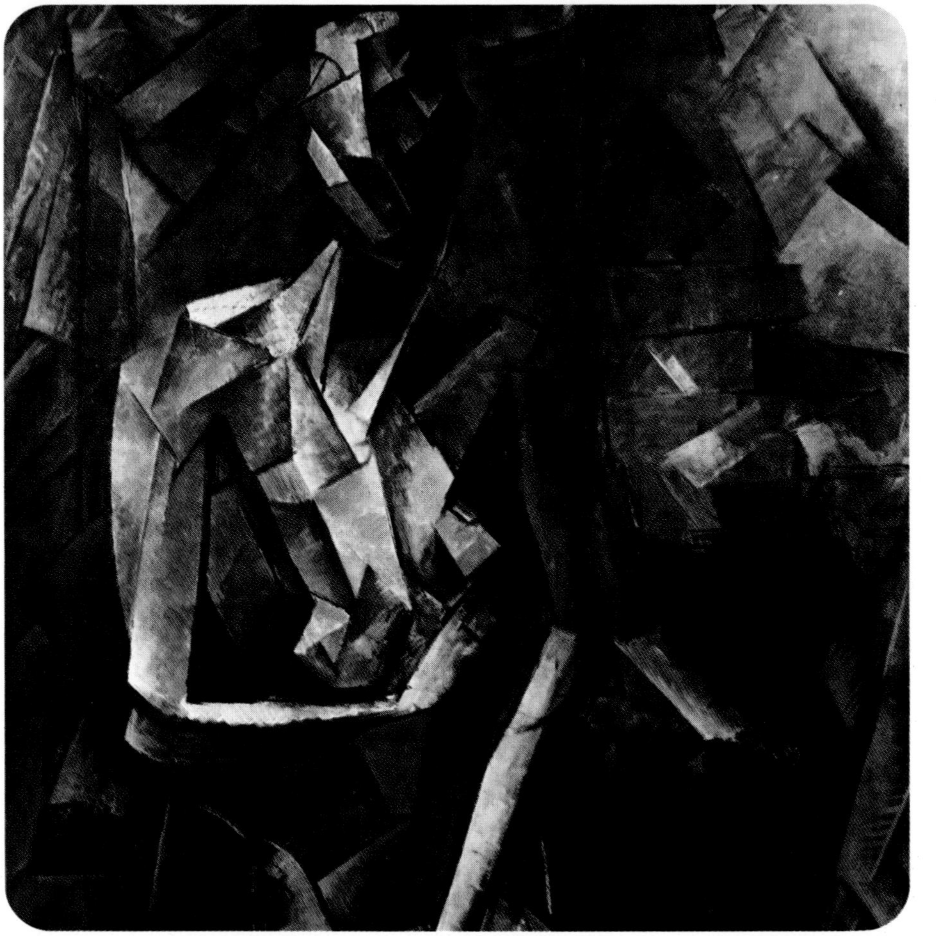

If the tradition that a picture must be three-dimensional dies hard, the idea that a picture has to depict a recognisable object still persists. Yet this abstract painting by Kandinsky, entitled *Première Aquarelle*, was painted nearly sixty years ago, before the First World War

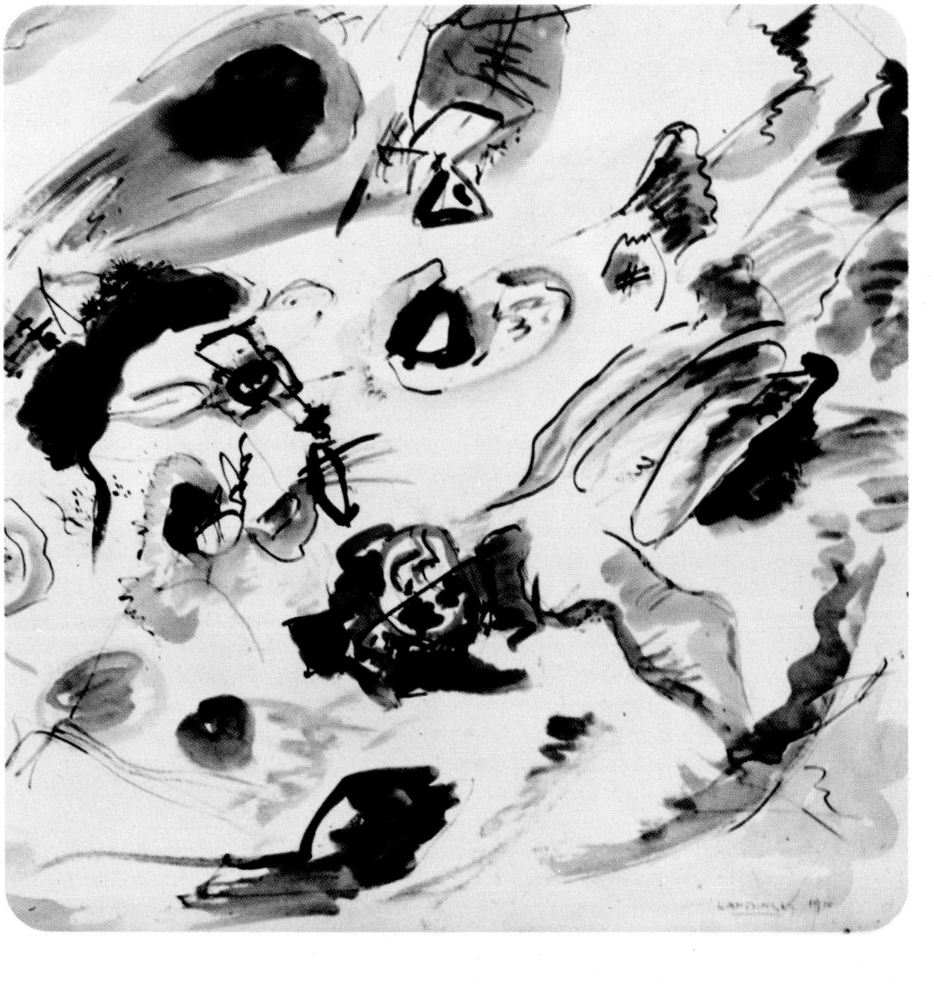

Since the Post-Impressionists, artists have had to find tasks which the camera cannot perform. This single fact helps explain their experiments with the texture of paintings and sculpture, the shape of a canvas, and their total rejection of imitating appearances. If there had to be a one-word explanation for the direction modern artists have taken in the twentieth century it might simply be, the camera.

Since 1913 artists have used an increasing range of new materials in their work: from the sand, wood and newspaper incorporated in pictures by Picasso and Braque to the different plastics, metals, woods and even industrial rolls of Kleenex which are being widely used today. What results is the sole criterion.

Paris and Munich were the first centres of modern art. Cubism—a style combining in one image several aspects of an object or a person—was evolved by Picasso and Braque between 1907 and 1913. Picasso's *Les Demoiselles d'Avignon* was the very first Cubist painting. And it was in Paris that Cubism rapidly became a major movement with adherents like Fernand Léger, Juan Gris, Jean Metzinger, and Albert Gleizes, among many others.

Munich attracted men like Wassily Kandinsky, Naum Gabo, Paul Klee and Alexei von Jawlensky, all of them major and influential figures. It was in Munich in 1911 that Kandinsky painted his first abstract picture, which launched another important movement.

Two other movements—Fauvism and Expressionism—arose shortly before the advent of Cubism and Abstraction. 'Les Fauves' (the wild beasts)—so-called because of the violent colours and shapes used in their pictures—was a self-conscious reaction against Pointillism, the style evolved by Seurat and Signac. Its leader Henri Matisse claimed that 'Fauvism shook off the tyranny of Pointillism'.

Whereas Fauvism appeared in Paris, Expressionism developed in Germany just before the First World War. Groups like Die Brücke in Dresden in 1905, and Der Blaue Reiter in Munich in 1911–12, continued a long North European tradition of expressing emotions and ideas through a vigorous and *expressive* style. Significantly, Expressionism in this century has reflected the unease and hostility which man may feel in his environment. Artists like Edvard Munch, Emil Nolde and Ernst Barlach were among the leaders of this movement, even though they often worked in isolation.

Art has rarely reflected the social and political undercurrents of its time as it did in Dadaism. Dada was really a protest movement which grew in Zürich, Cologne, Berlin, Hanover, New York and Paris during the First World War. Unlike Cubism, Dada artists adopted an attitude of mind rather than a distinct style.

Dada is one of the most misunderstood of all the modern movements. Preparing the way for Surrealism, Dadaists like Francis Picabia, Hans Arp, Kurt Schwitters, Marcel Duchamp, Max Ernst and Man Ray ridiculed traditional art and bourgeois conventions. Their basic contention, expressed in a number of bizarre ways, was that if European and American society could produce the senseless carnage of the 1914–1918 War, its art must be decadent and fit only for the rubbish heap. It was gestures like that of Marcel Duchamp giving a moustache to Leonardo da Vinci's *Mona Lisa*—perhaps the supreme symbol of traditional art—which characterised Dada.

Dada eventually gave way to Surrealism, which has taken many forms. André Breton—Dada's leading spokesman—claimed in the early 1920s that 'Dada was at the end of its evolution. It had foundered like a ship in distress. A reorientation was necessary.' Later Breton discovered his reorientation in psychoanalytical theories.

Surrealists have developed vastly differing styles to express themselves. Joan Miró, Marc Chagall, Max Ernst, Salvador Dali and Yves Tanguy are all leading Surrealists but with different aims and ideas. Nevertheless, such artists reflect the paradoxes and absurdities of men and societies in the twentieth century.

Mass-produced machines have been a powerful influence on the imagination of many modern painters. The Italian Futurists, a literary and artistic movement, were enthusiastic, for example, about such things as 'a motor racing car, its frame adorned with great pipes, like snakes with explosive breath . . . a roaring motor car, which looks as though running on shrapnel, is more beautiful than the *Winged Victory of Samothrace* . . . .' Since then other artists have made their own art machines, believing that oil painting will disappear in much the same way that wig-making did in the eighteenth century.

But it is Abstraction which may finally prove to be the art by which the first half of the present century will be remembered. Beginning with Kandinsky, abstract artists expressed their extreme discontent with the representational art of the official academies. It is worthwhile recording that the break-through to abstraction was something of an accident, a chance discovery. Wassily Kandinsky's description of his discovery is a key statement in the development of non-figurative painting:

> 'I was returning, immersed in thought, from my sketching, when on opening the studio door, I was suddenly confronted by a picture of indescribable and incandescent loveliness. Bewildered, I stopped, staring at it. The painting lacked all subject, depicted no identifiable object and was entirely composed of bright colour-patches. Finally I approached closer and only then recognised it for what it really was—my own painting, standing on its side on the easel. . . . One thing became clear to me—that objectiveness, the depiction of objects, needed no place in my paintings, and was indeed harmful to them.'

The artists who followed Kandinsky—pioneers like Kasimir Malevich, Piet Mondrian, Paul Klee and Naum Gabo—took different paths. Their influence spread almost everywhere—in England Ben Nicholson, Barbara Hepworth and Henry Moore were the leading representatives of the revolutionary techniques. In the United States it was men like Arshile Gorky and Mark Tobey who raised the flag of abstraction. But it was in Paris that most abstract artists worked, at least until the outbreak of war in 1939.

Because of developments in Central Europe in the nineteen-thirties many avant-garde painters and sculptors went to live in the relative security of the United States. Persecution by the Nazis in Germany, who considered *all* modern art to be decadent (ironically an opinion shared by Stalinists in the Soviet Union), encouraged the movement across the Atlantic.

The terrible carnage of the First World War (top) provoked violent reactions in thoughtful minds. One group of young rebels living in Switzerland started a movement known as Dada. They ridiculed not only contemporary bourgeois society, but also its art. One of them, a young man called Marcel Duchamp, claimed that some manufactured goods were more honestly artistic than much traditional painting and sculpture. His 'ready mades' included this *Bottlerack* (centre right)

The collapse of the German economy which led to the rise of National Socialism (bottom) was blamed on the greed of opportunist businessmen and financiers, who were brilliantly caricatured by George Grosz (centre left). As Europe moved closer to disaster, reactionary governments in Germany and the Soviet Union forbade avant-garde artists to express themselves freely. Many fled from Central Europe to America

The explosion of the atomic bomb at the end of the Second World War marks significantly a shift in the balance of power and influence to America. From 1945 several key figures—men like Jackson Pollock, Arshile Gorky, Willem de Kooning, David Smith, Barnett Newman and Mark Rothko—separately produced what is loosely called the New York 'school'.

All committed abstractionists, they emphasised the fact that New York was slowly replacing Paris as the important international centre for avant-garde ideas. Later Jasper Johns, Robert Rauschenberg and a few close followers—the post-war pioneers of assemblage (begun after the First World War by the Dadaist Marcel Duchamp)—helped consolidate the sudden importance and vitality of American art.

Beginning in the early nineteen-fifties, Pop art soon became the dominant artistic movement in the United States. Men like Roy Lichtenstein, Tom Wesselmann, James Rosenquist, Andy Warhol and Claes Oldenburg—all of them firmly committed to popular, representational images symbolic of our modern industrial society—have become internationally known.

Up to 1958 Oldenburg was painting conventional portraits and academic nudes when he fell in love, seemingly overnight, with the urban city. Today he says he is for the 'kool art'. . . 'I am for the red and white gasoline pumps and blinking biscuit signs . . . I am for Kool Art, 7-Up Art, Pepsi Art, Sunkist Art, Dro-Bomb Art, Pamryl Art, San-O-Med Art, 39 cents Art, and 9.99 Art.'

When you think of Oldenburg you automatically think of food—city food: hot dogs, chocolate éclairs, hamburgers and ice-cream sundaes. Oldenburg, Swedish-born and now 39, makes giant versions of them and exhibits them all over the world. 'If I didn't think what I was doing had something to do with enlarging the boundaries of art I wouldn't do it,' he says.

Pop art covers a whole multitude of different styles and attitudes. Assemblage—a technique where real objects, often junk, are used in a three-dimensional way—is widely considered as part of the Pop art world.

Many of the best-known assemblage artists are also known for their other contributions to modern art. Americans like Bruce Conner, George Cohen, Robert Moskowitz and Edward Kienholz; the Italians Baj and Rotella, the Englishman John Latham, and many others: Arman, de la Villegle, Spoerri, Niki de St Phalle, Christo, and Tinguely. Artists such as these group themselves under such names as: Commonism, Neo-Dada, OK art, Common Image, Pop Culture and, of course, Pop art.

Robert Indiana, now 39 years old, is a Pop artist with a difference. Whereas many of his contemporaries seem to be in love with the American Dream, the idea that Americans eat, sleep, fight and live better than anyone else, Indiana is sceptical. On several of his paintings he has stencilled: 'It is pretty hard to swallow the whole thing about the American Dream.' He said recently: 'The American Dream started from the day the Pilgrims landed, the dream, the idea that Americans have more to eat than anyone else. But I remember going to bed without enough to eat.'

Allen Jones, perhaps best known for his pictures of bright-red London buses and sexy girlies, is one of the few British painters to make a hit with his work in the United States. Mario Amaya made the point well when he wrote of Jones: 'Certain subjects continually reappear and there is a strong affection for what might be considered by some to be the cheap, meretricious, sleazy sexiness of the stripper or the pin-up. Yet, in his hands, such "forbidden" subjects "culled from magazines" suddenly seem pleasureful, sinless and full of wit and charm.'

Peter Blake is the demure king of British Pop, but his art owes as much to America as it does to solid British influences. He is one of the few modern artists who can show his work in the most zany avant-garde gallery in New York or Rome and still sell his work in that most traditional British institution, the Royal Academy.

Because Pop art takes its images, ideas and emotions from a particularly vocal and visual part of our culture, it is perhaps people living now who are best qualified to enjoy and judge its varied qualities. After all, a landscape is a landscape in any century. Pop art, by definition, is rooted in the present, *now*, in much the same way that a pop song is.

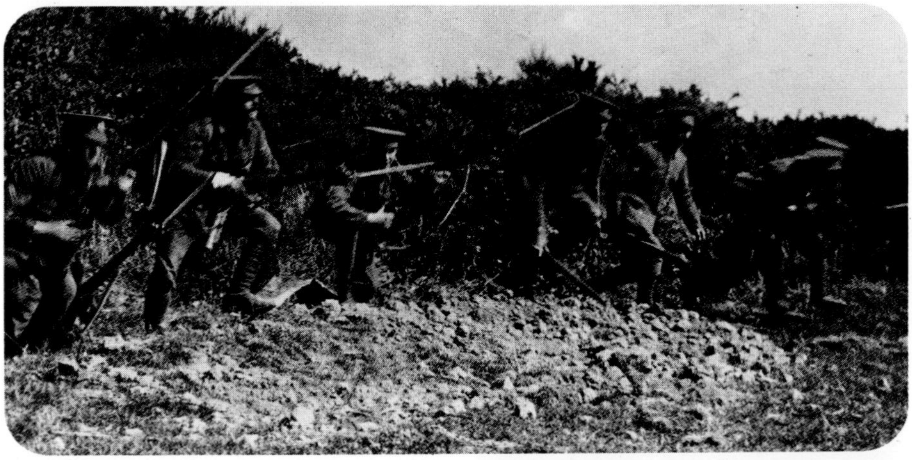

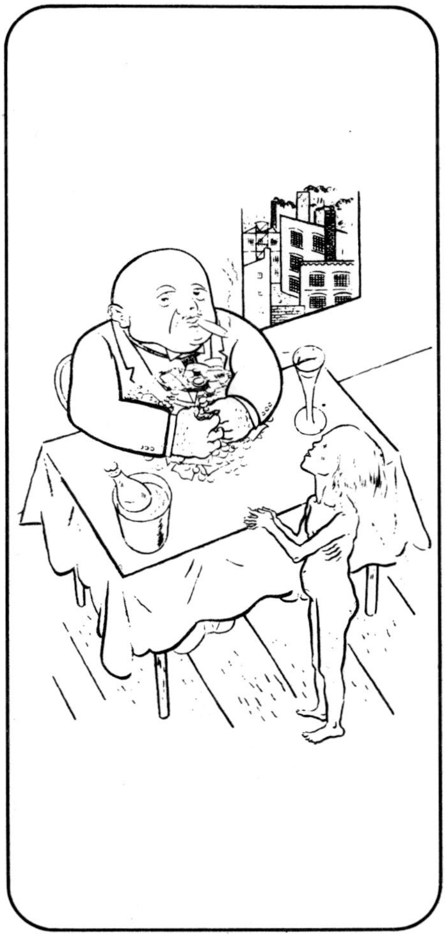

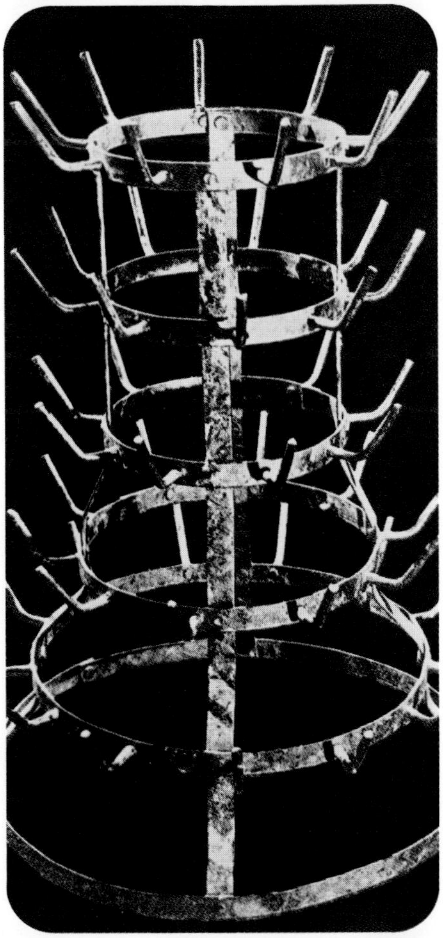

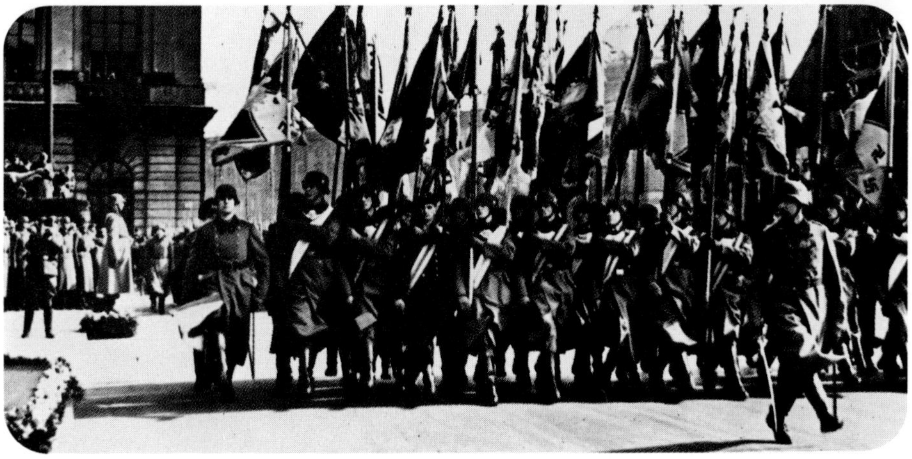

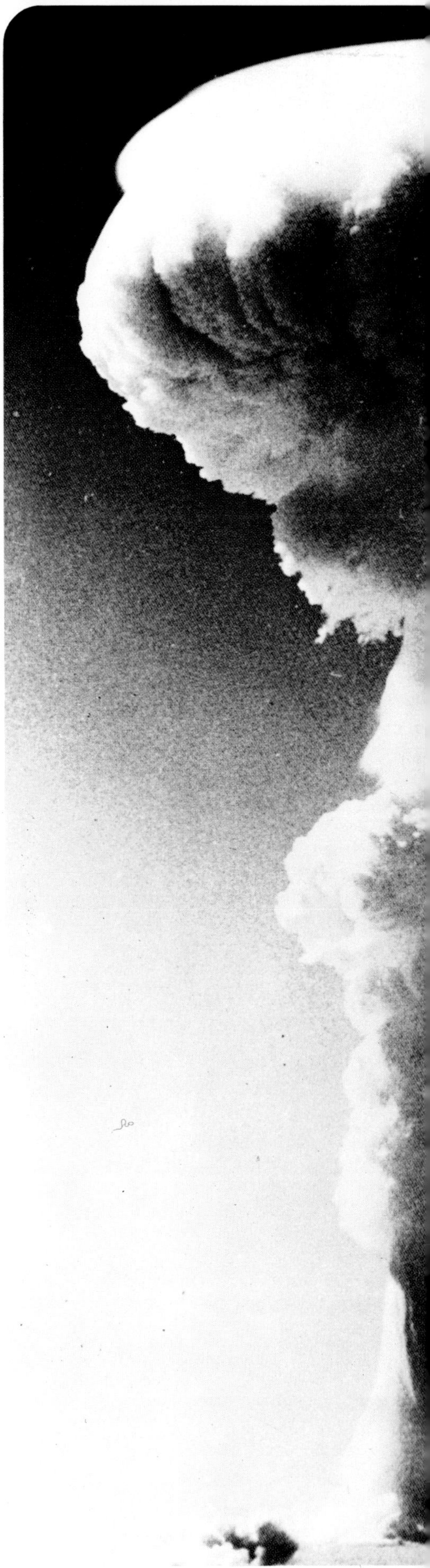

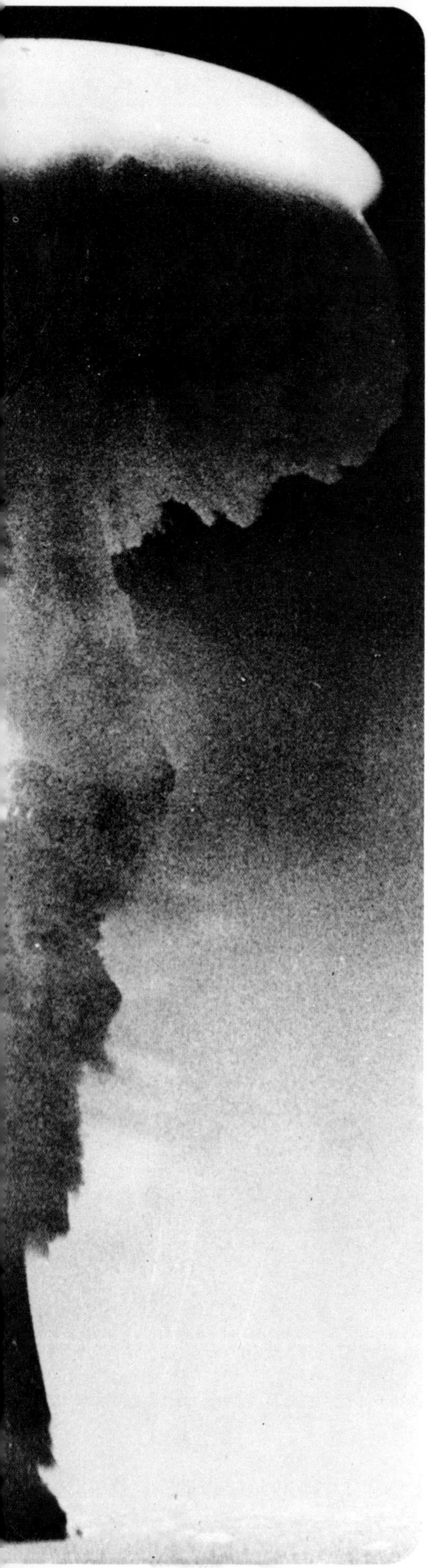

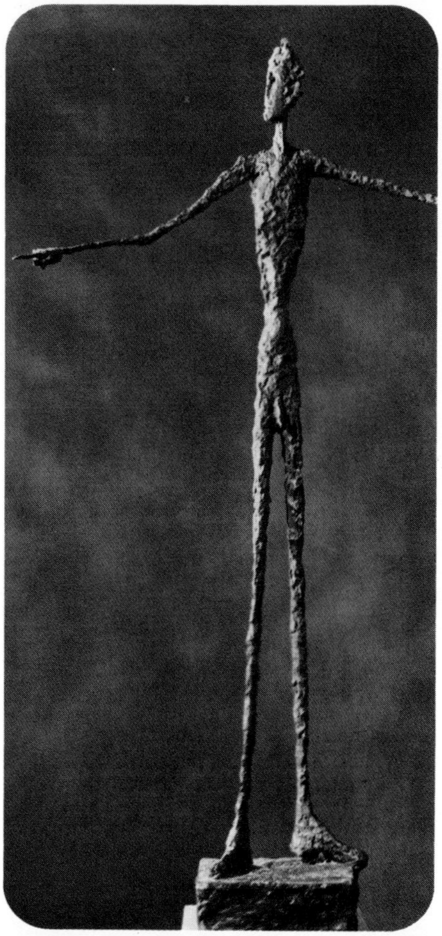

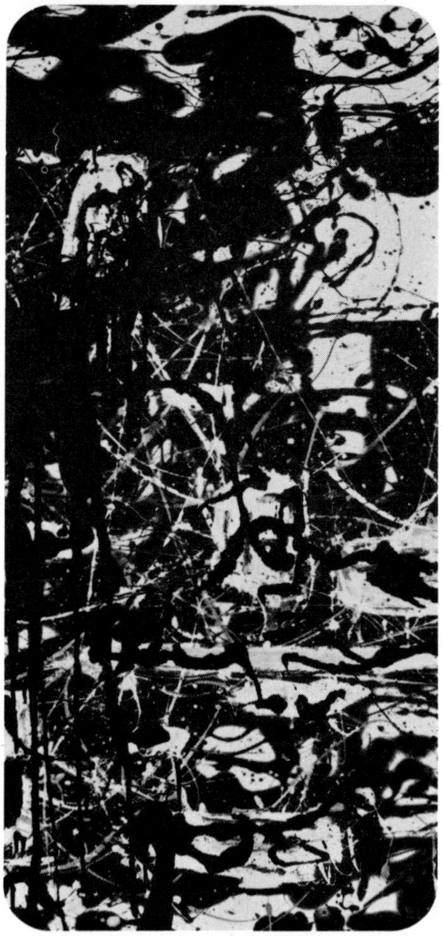

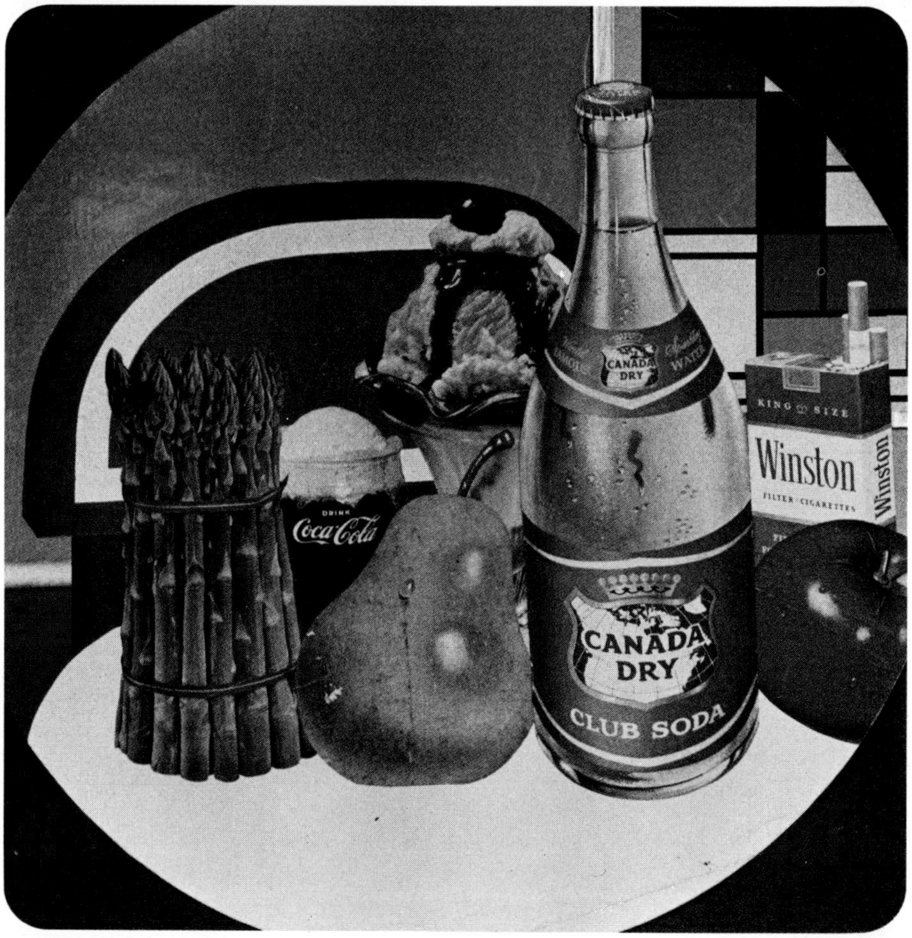
CANADA DRY
CLUB SODA
Coca-Cola
Winston
Winston
KING SIZE

Today there are more styles of art than ever before. Tachisme, Abstract Expressionism, New Realism, Neo-Dada, Kinetic and Optical art and Hard-Edge, to name but a few. More styles to cover those areas of life which art formerly had little to do with. Direct references, as in the pictures of Jim Dine, to sex and genitals is evidence of the often startling way modern art has increased its boundaries.

New Realists in Europe—artists like the late Yves Klein, Tinguely, Dufrene, Arman, Hains, Villegle, César, Mimmo Rotella, Deschamps and Christo—are interested in the *mythology* of a consumer-orientated, luxury-conscious industrial and urban society. Unlike many modern American painters, Europeans prefer to 'play' with mass-produced objects and symbols and give them an added dimension. An American Pop painter like Tom Wesselmann prefers to use direct references to international 'symbols' like Coca-Cola, Canada Dry and Winston cigarettes.

In Italy several avant-garde painters tackle the problem of depicting twentieth-century living and aspirations in an international style, which nevertheless does not forget their Italian heritage. Artists like Enrico Baj, Mimmo Rotella, Gianni Bertini, Giuseppe Romagnoni, Alberto Moretti, Mario Ceroli, Franco Angeli, Fabio Mauri and many others, are among the best known.

Lothar Quinte, Gerd Richter, Heinz Mack, Konrad Lueg, Siegmund Lympasik, Sigmar Polke, Herbert Kaufmann, Klaus Brehmer and Horst Hodicke are among the most prominent avant-garde artists in Germany now. Vitally and self-consciously concerned with the materialism of urban life, several German painters are also concerned with the social and political function of modern art.

In Belgium and Holland Hans van Eck, Paul von Hoeydonck, Woody van Amen and Pol Mara demonstrate their ability to reconcile their art with themes firmly rooted in contemporary city life. In Spain and Portugal a growing number of important figures like Rene Bertholo, Sansegundo, and Lourdes Castro are also interested in similar problems.

In Japan, Nobuaki Kojima, Ushio Shinohara and Keiichi Tanaami represent some of the best aspects of what is for Japan a new tradition in the visual arts. From South America kinetic artists like Jesus-Raphael Soto, Julio Le Parc and Sergio de Camargo, all of whom spend most of their time working in Europe, are involved with objects and machines which reflect the movement of our machine-conscious world.

Not surprisingly perhaps, many Canadian artists, especially those from English-speaking Canada, are heavily influenced by recent American trends in art. Armand Flint, Michael Snow, Sunao Urata and Dennis Burton are among the most prominent modern Canadian artists now working in their own country.

In Britain, internationally recognised painters such as Derek Boshier, Patrick Caulfield, Anthony Donaldson, Richard Hamilton, David Hockney, Patrick Proctor, Philip Sutton, Phillip King, Richard Smith, Eduardo Paolozzi, R. B. Kitaj, and Joe Tilson are influential in art schools all over the world. Reproductions and magazine articles bring their latest work to the notice of students and other artists, months, even weeks, after it is finished in their studios.

The artist in the 1960s undoubtedly feels less of an outsider. Few now feel they are fighting a hopeless battle against an indifferent public—as modern artists did in the past. Compared with the harsh experiences of the French Impressionists or the avant-garde at the turn of the century, they now live in a happier and more prosperous age.

People no longer expect an artist to live in dire poverty, like Van Gogh or Modigliani did. It's also unlikely that an artist will walk down the High Street with paint on his corduroys or with hair around his shoulders. He often leaves the business of looking like Toulouse-Lautrec to others. Most of them live with their wives and families in the suburbs of major cities and towns. The average artist looks much like the man next door. Art has moved into a boom period, but few can earn their living from painting pictures or making sculpture. Most get jobs in advertising, photography, fashion, stage or general design work. Others work in a factory or many teach art. Few either live in a garret or find a patron to keep them. Whatever our view of modern art, however, the influence of the artist on the way we feel about life and visual phenomena, has never been greater.

The explosion of the atomic bomb at the end of the Second World War marks significantly a shift in the balance of power from Europe to America. From 1945 such key figures as Arshile Gorky, Willem de Kooning and Jackson Pollock, whose abstract *Painting*, 1952 (top right) now hangs in the Tate Gallery, London, produced what is now called the New York 'school'

By the late nineteen-fifties Pop art had become the dominant artistic movement in the United States. A typical example is Tom Wesselmann's *Tondo*, painted in 1962

Meanwhile in Europe such famous sculptors as Barbara Hepworth, Henry Moore and Alberto Giacometti were examining the relation of man to space in sculpture. Giacometti's fragile figure *Man Pointing*, 1947 (top left), appears to take up more space than it really does

Some of the artists who have contrib

Larry Rivers, R. B. Kitaj
Kenneth Martin,
Martial Raysse

Heinz Mack, Patrick Proctor
Allen Jones, David Hockney

Fritz Hundertwasser
Anthony Caro, Bridget Riley,
Tinguely

Ser Hoogenboom, Kim Lim
P. J. Geissler, Barbara Hepworth

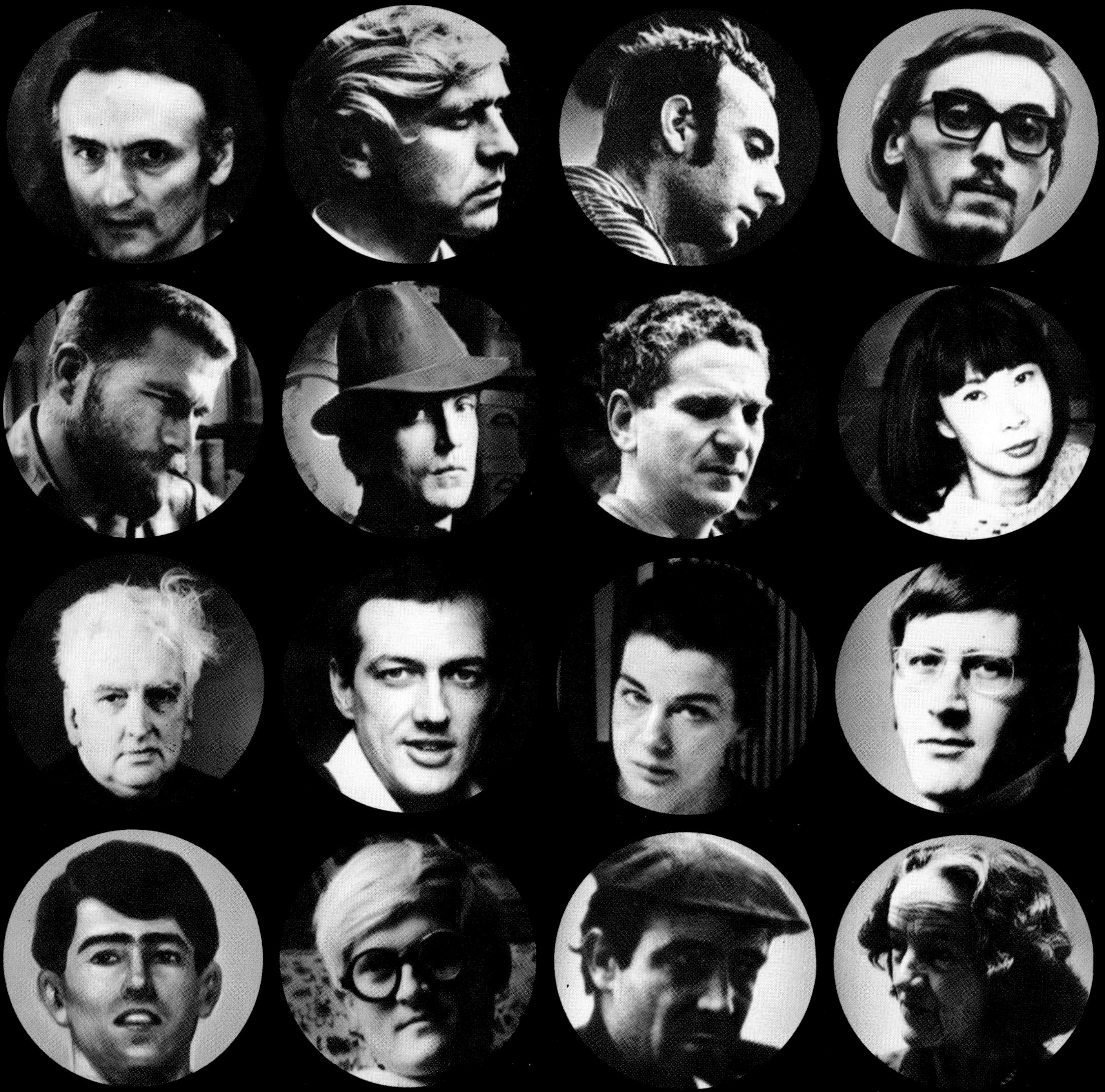

ed to the international art scene today

Russell Drysdale, Yvaral
(Jean-Pierre Vasarely)
Robert Rauschenberg
Frank Bowling

Louise Nevelson, Joe Tilson
Yaacov Agam, Richard Smith

Claes Oldenburg
Joseph Albers, Piero Gilardi
Michael Tyzack

Lydia Silvestri, Brett Whiteley
Cruz-Diez, Robert Indiana

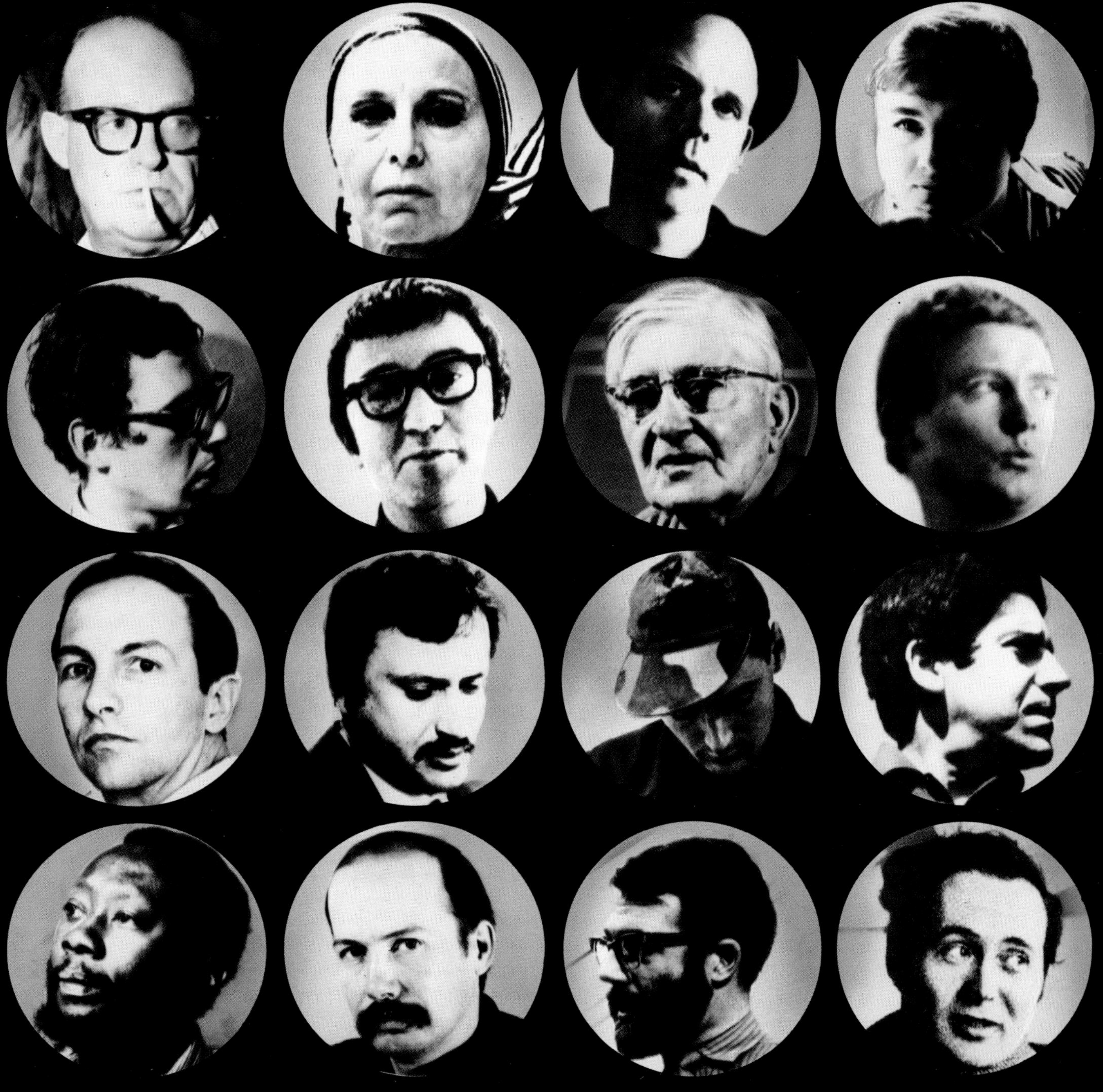

Pablo Picasso

Picasso's eyes are coal-black and fierce. They are the very first thing one notices about him: his black eyes. They dominate his whole body. Fixed and menacing, they appear to tear at one's face as though he wants to discover one's innermost thoughts. There is no escape from the eyes of Pablo Picasso.

To see him face to face is to understand something of the hypnotic effect he can have on others. Fernande Olivier's description of him is as true today as it must have been more than half a century ago. 'Socially it was difficult to place him, but this radiance, this internal fire that one felt in him, generated a kind of magnetism, which I could not resist. He was small, black, thick-set, restless, disquieting, with eyes dark, profound, piercing, strange, almost staring.'

Picasso was born in Malaga on October 25, 1881. He likes telling people that he was born at midnight; and on that day, so the tale runs, both the moon and the sun approached the nadir, and the light which shone on Malaga from the midnight sky came from a strange combination of planets and major stars, whose conjunctions and oppositions have provided astrologers with great room for speculation. Not surprisingly, Picasso has long believed that there is a direct relationship between these occult experiences and his own personality and life.

Picasso was, as one might expect, a child prodigy–and he has remained astonishingly prodigious ever since.

'My father was a painter but he gave it up because he said I outpainted him well before I was twenty years old. He just hung up his brushes and vowed he would never paint again. Because I went through all the academic tests there were at that time I just had to travel abroad.

'I first went to Paris in 1900, a few days before my nineteenth birthday. London was my eventual goal, Paris just a temporary stopping place. At the time I was fascinated with English furniture, clothes, the Pre-Raphaelites and English women.'

Picasso helped turn traditional art on its head. For centuries European art centred on religious themes until the Renaissance shattered its narrow orthodoxy. Secular art took various paths, leading eventually to movements like the Impressionists and the Post-Impressionists who painted landscapes and toiling peasants in an original way. Then Picasso came along at the turn of the century and began painting city life, mechanised society, city people, city poor and city tarts. His still-lifes of mass-produced cups, glasses, tables, chairs, newspapers were, after all, unmistakably twentieth-century objects.

Picasso also had to fight the photographer, who had become the artist's greatest rival. No longer did people want to have their portraits painted; the camera did it quicker and more cheaply. Picasso and his fellow professionals wanted to stay in business. They succeeded beyond their wildest dreams. Influenced by social and political movements, Freud and other modern signposts to the future, they yanked art into areas of life practically unknown to artists of the past. Their results are reflected in the way we look around us today, the way we feel about visual phenomena, and think about objects.

Picasso's own life has already supplied enough material and myth to fill a library and yet this has still not proved sufficient to feed his legend. Who were the ancestors of this modern god? Sabartes, Picasso's lifelong friend and biographer, has spent much time and research on this question. Not unexpectedly he discovered Picasso came from a noble lineage whose virtues included devotion, honesty, appreciation of the arts, religious beliefs and soldierly qualities. In a chronicle of King Pedro, son of King Alfonso of Castile, dating from 1591, there is an account of a battle fought in 1339 between Gonzalo Martinez de Oviedo, commander of the armies of the King of Andalusia, and the Prince Picaco, son of the Moorish King Albuhacen, who had arrived from Africa at the head of ten thousand knights. Picaco lost. Considering that Picasso is still alive the myths which already surround his life and work are really remarkable. Perhaps it will not be long before he joins Plato and Alexander the Great and is attributed with virgin birth and all the other trappings of legend.

Part of the Picasso mystery is to do with his extraordinary virility. Now eighty-five, he still seems to have a remarkable attraction for women. Throughout his life he has bowled over a steady succession of women:

Picasso has no real need of money. Whatever he wants he can draw. Twenty years ago he wanted a large house on the Côte d'Azur. He was able to pay for it with one still-life painting. He is seen here (above right) in his studio in the south of France

This drawing (below right), done in 1919 and inscribed 'A mon cher H. Pierre Roche', now belongs to a Mayfair art gallery

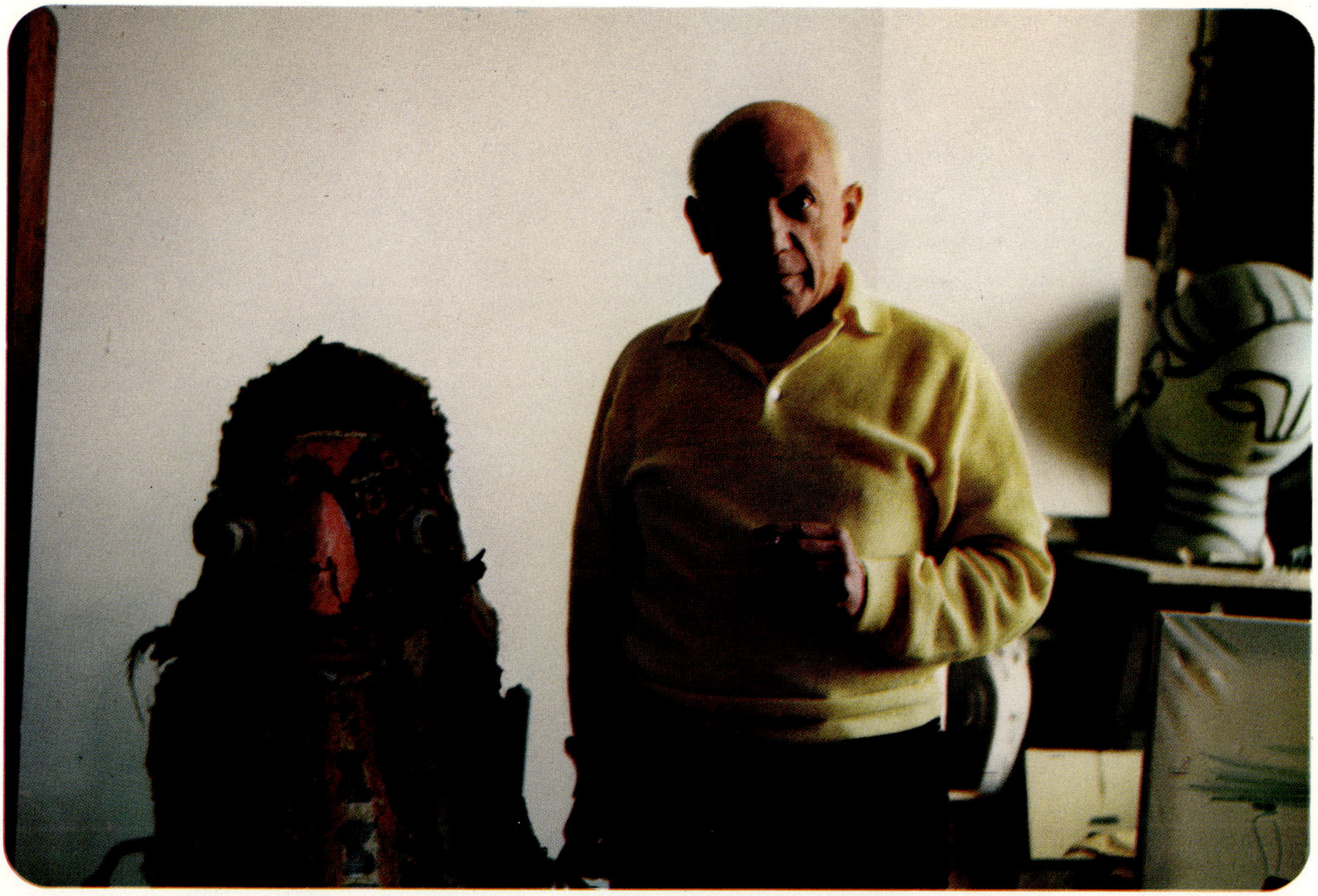

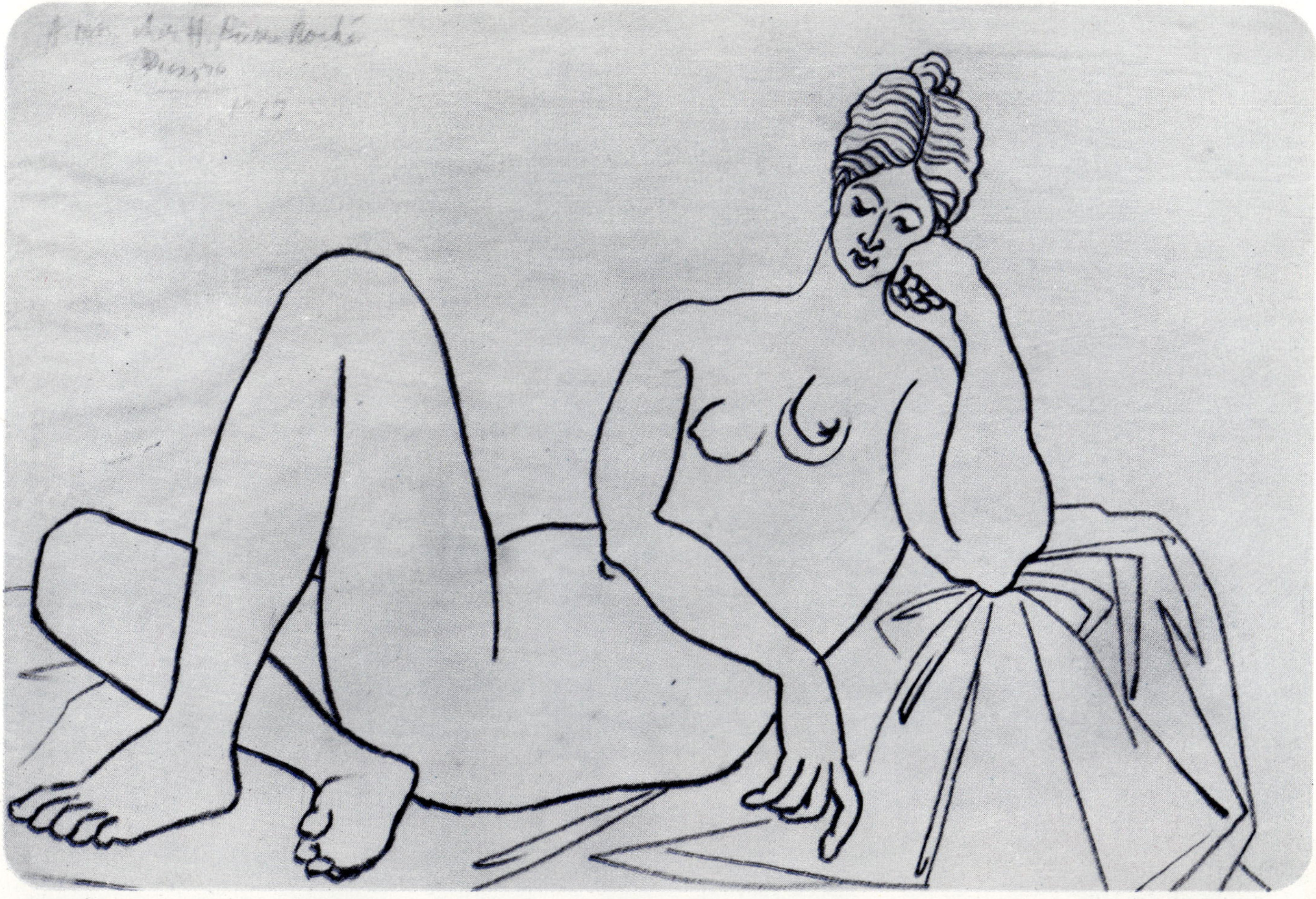

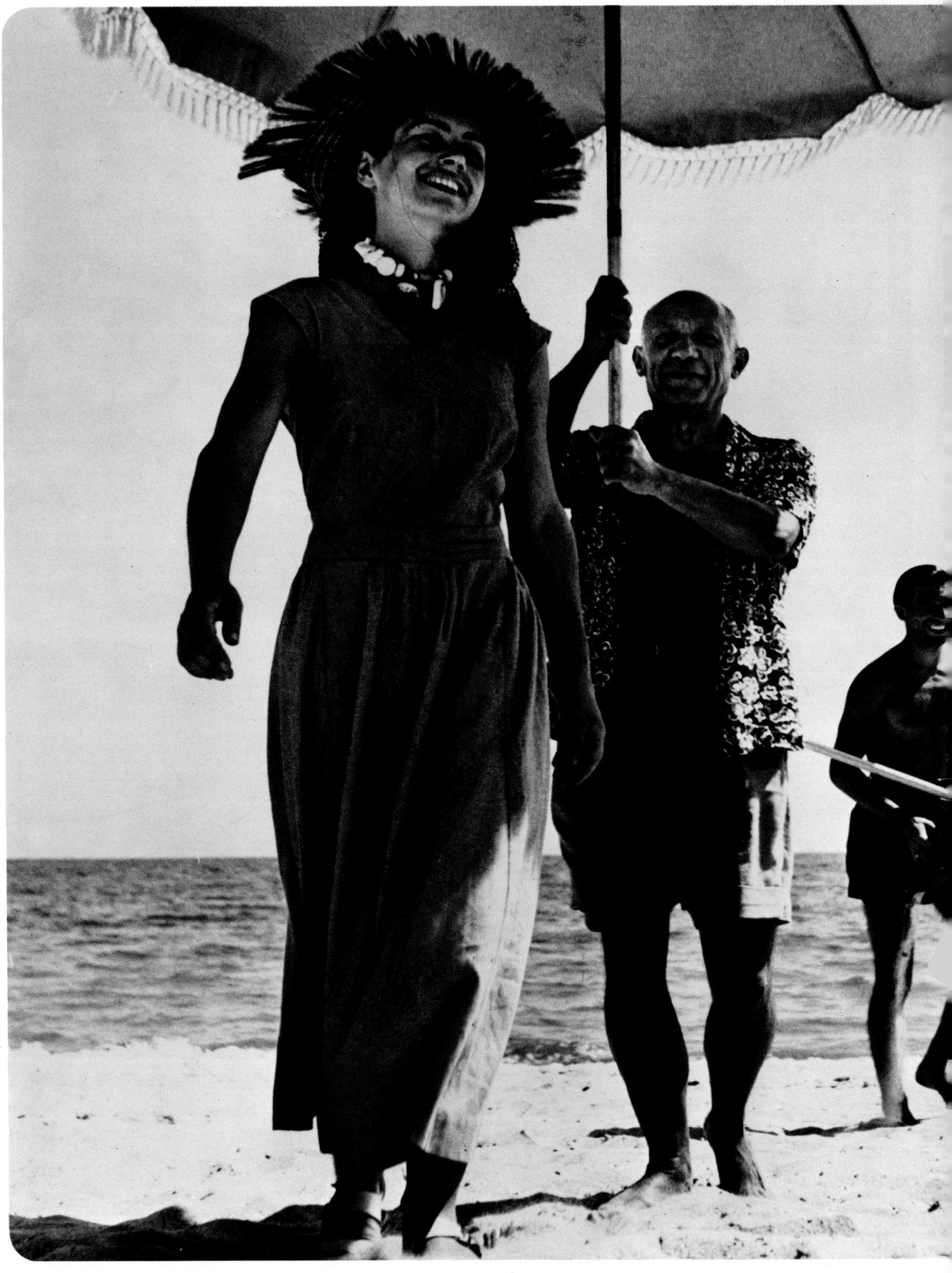

Fernande Olivier, Olga Kochlova, Dora Maar, Marie-Thérèse Walter, Françoise Gilot and Jacqueline Roque being perhaps the best known. Each of them has been immortalised in paint and sent round the world in millions of reproductions.

It is no accident that magazine editors like showing Picasso, even in his eighties, with a chestful of bushy hair. Picasso gives everyone hope: if he can keep impotence at bay in old age, perhaps we shall be able to, as well. If Picasso can attract young women, so can we when we reach his years. Women invariably think of Picasso as an attractive, powerful man, and never as a grandfather or an old age pensioner.

Picasso rarely meets any opposition to what he wants, what he does or what he says. People who know Picasso are terrified of losing his favour and his attention. When Françoise Gilot eventually left him for the painter Luc Simon, she was worried in case art dealers and collectors refused to have anything to do with her own paintings.

If Cesare Borgia had to kill the people who annoyed him, Picasso merely dismisses from his court those who tire him. He is more than a king or emperor because his domain stretches throughout the world. He can refuse to let one country, one city or a private person have one of his paintings–merely on a private whim. It was a private whim which allowed the Tate Gallery to buy its major Picasso, *The Three Dancers*: a matter of personalities.

Picasso is now beyond the reach of ordinary criticism. Countless books praise and worship the man, his work and his wisdom. Whatever he says is jotted down, then hallowed and published by his far-flung court of admirers. Paradoxically, although most people have heard of Picasso, few people could name or recognise his paintings.

Now at the centre of a world-wide cult, he has been mummified alive before he has had the chance of becoming a dead hero. Interest in Picasso has been steadily growing since the turn of the century and there is still no sign of it ending. But surrounded as he is by an inquisitive world, sycophants and a few remaining friends, he has become suspicious of and even indifferent to what is said and written about him.

'People are coming to see me all the time,' he says. 'They usually want something and so I don't want to see them. My friends are few now, many of them have died. Visitors are often like bullfighters, they prod the old bull and imagine he'll do something. I'm always being prodded to do something or say something. Nobody leaves me alone. It's been going on for years. That's why I left Paris years ago. Tourists were pestering me at my studio, my home, everywhere I went. I was one of the sights of Paris.'

Picasso has lived the life of the artist of popular legend–or so people like to believe. He has broken most of the Ten Commandments, both in his private life and in his art. He has coveted his neighbour's wife and mistress and he has pinched ideas from artists as far apart as Raphael and Van Gogh. He has been making graven images all his life, has bowed down to them and served them, and (through no great fault of his own) made himself into a modern god.

But Picasso is above such questions of conventional morality, just as he is above such worries as money. In fact, he has no real need of money. Whatever he wants, he can draw to obtain.

Twenty years ago Picasso wanted a large house in the south of France. He was able to pay for it with one still-life painting. Similarly, if he wanted a Rolls-Royce he could pay for it with a drawing only; a painting would be sufficient to pay for an aeroplane and he hates flying.

Picasso's 'Picassos' and his own collection of works by Van Gogh, Degas and Renoir–the list of modern works is endless–must be worth upwards of £30 million at current saleroom prices. Whatever he wants he can have. In his studio, specially built on to the house, paintings are piled on top of one another to form an ornamental pattern. To be there is one of the nearest experiences to being in Fort Knox. With paint he has become what Getty, Onassis and Gulbenkian became with oil and ships. But ordinary multi-millionaires are never held to be divine.

'I think I know what it is like to be God. I live at Notre Dame de Vie like a prisoner in my own home. Believe me, I wouldn't wish my fame on anybody, not even someone I loathe. I suffer from this imprisonment, both mentally and physically,' he declares.

L. S. Lowry. He is a recluse, brought up amid cotton mills, Lancashire grime and smoke, and back-to-back houses. For him loneliness is neither an attitude of mind nor something to be pitied; it is a condition

L. S. Lowry

L. S. Lowry is tall and haggard, with a merry knowing face and the deep-set eyes of a dreamer. He walks about awkwardly, covered from head to toe in a deflated grey trilby and an old crumpled overcoat which hangs untidily around his ankles and crinkled black leather boots. Standing against a background of crumbling Salford tenements to have his photograph taken, he is clearly wondering what all the damn fuss is about.

Lowry is a Royal Academician and a Mancunian Master of Arts. He is a recluse, brought up amid cotton mills, Lancashire grime and smoke, and back-to-back houses. He has been painting himself, his neighbours and the industrial North-West for more than half a century, and now lives alone in Longdendale: these are the barest details about one of Britain's best-loved painters.

In habits, in dress and in art, Lowry expresses well enough the baffling predicament in which many a modern artist has found himself. Unlike an elderly miner or a civil servant, Lowry cannot retire from his job even though he is fed-up with being an artist. He is perhaps the extreme example of a painter who finds himself famous but alone, honoured and yet at variance with the society and the people who have chosen to honour him.

The fact is that the British do not quite know what to do with an international figure like L. S. Lowry. He brings more prestige to this country than most of our politicians put together, and yet we are still not certain how to treat him. Our dithering and embarrassment are seen in the decision to show his work at the Tate Gallery twenty years after his major successes in the art world. In France or Brazil, someone as eminent as Lowry would have been asked to decorate the interior of a major building, or at least pay off his income tax in the form of paintings. He would not have been made to feel, and follow, the holy hermit life of a recluse.

At the turn of the century Lowry learnt the traditional secrets of antique drawing, the proportions of Apollo, and all the other High Renaissance hangovers which made up the curricula of Victorian-Edwardian art schools. He soon realised that it had little, if anything, to do with the art of the twentieth century. He was an-

noyed to discover he had to find his own way. Ignored for the greater part of his life Lowry suddenly found himself the central figure in a high-powered selling campaign. The goods were industrial landscapes, portraits and street scenes he had been painting between the two wars.

Lowry's art education was academic, but he ended up being able to draw. 'You've no idea how long I spent on freehand, antique anatomy and full-length studies,' he said. 'At art school, sir, they wanted accuracy more than anything else. They didn't start you doing a sketch out of your head, sort of slapdash, and then say, "Oh that's very good." If you were in the art school, you drew like you would in an art school. And we didn't all come out like Titian, sir!'

How does Lowry work when he begins a new painting? 'I've changed my methods of working through the years,' he explained. 'Up to 1919 I did a lot of painting outside, but I soon got fed-up with the whole paraphernalia. I said to myself: "Damn it, I'll drop out before I cart all that stuff about with me." And so when I started the industrial scenes I began taking a box of envelopes and things like that, doing a bit of sketching on the spot, and then going back home to paint. But now and then, if I'd seen a building that really interested me I'd do a careful, painstaking drawing out in the open.

'You know, my dear sir, I don't really know how I see my little people. I was asked once by a young lady in a school of art: "Why do you do your figures like you do, Mr. Lowry?" And I answered: "Well, because I can't do them in any other way." If I sit back and draw something they always seem to come out the same. It's really most odd. Do you like them? I'm never quite sure what people think.'

Lowry's studio is the back room of his house. It is small, dingy and chaotic. There is an old-fashioned easel, a paint-caked wooden table for his colours, and a single electric light bulb. 'Do you think my work is primitive? Some people do, I know. I really can't judge. There's no money in it anyway. The income tax people take it all. I won't have any more private exhibitions because of them. It's just not worth it. And the pounds you get aren't worth what they were in the old days. A pound is worth about four shillings now, I suppose. Terrible, isn't it, my dear sir!

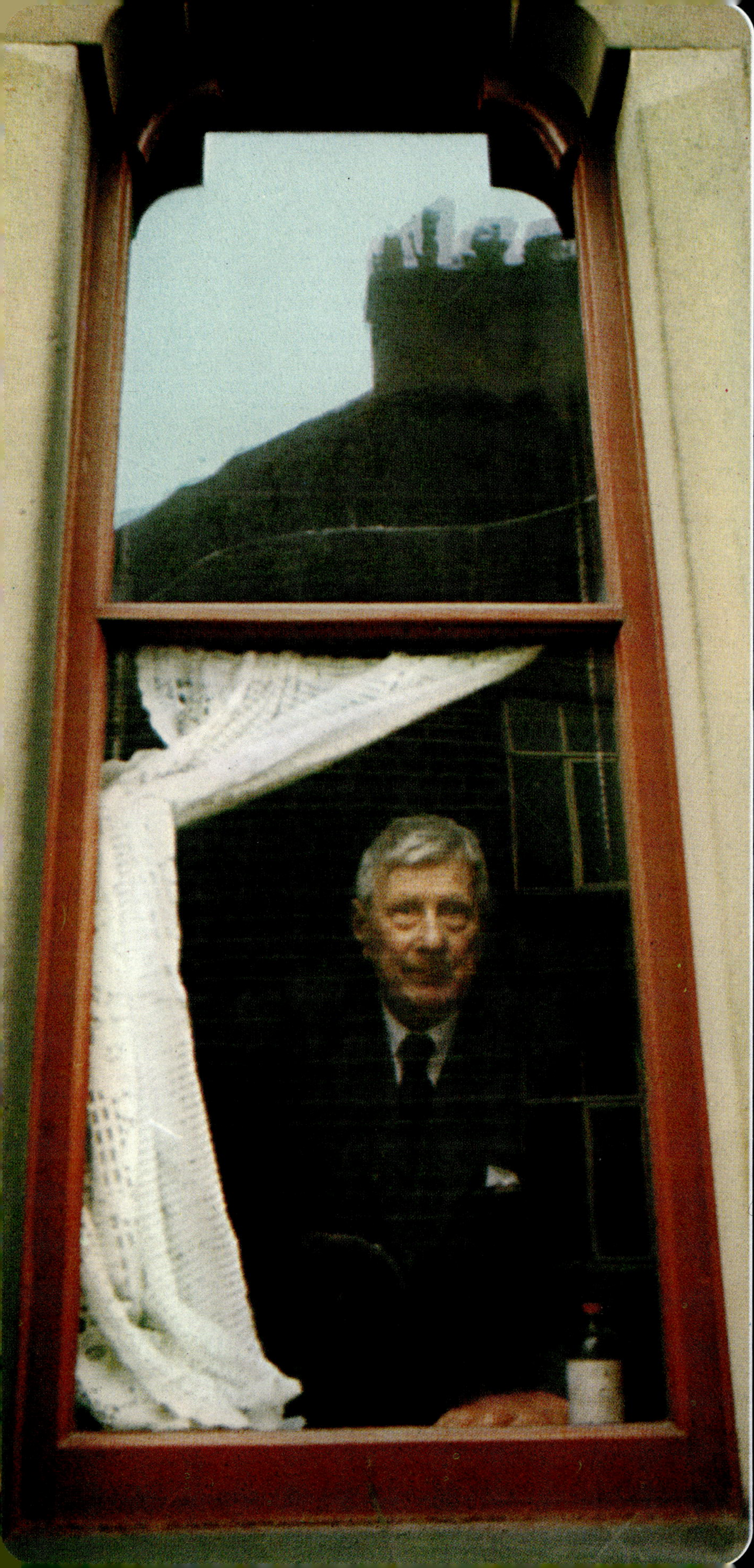
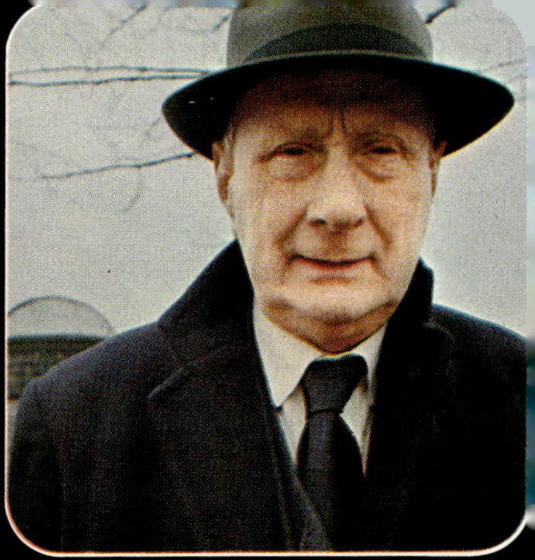
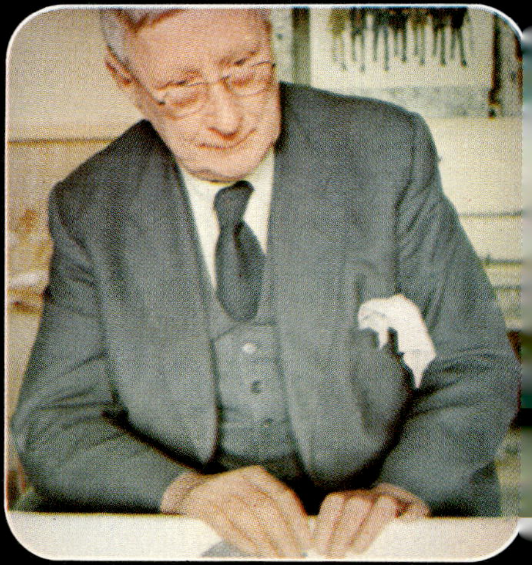
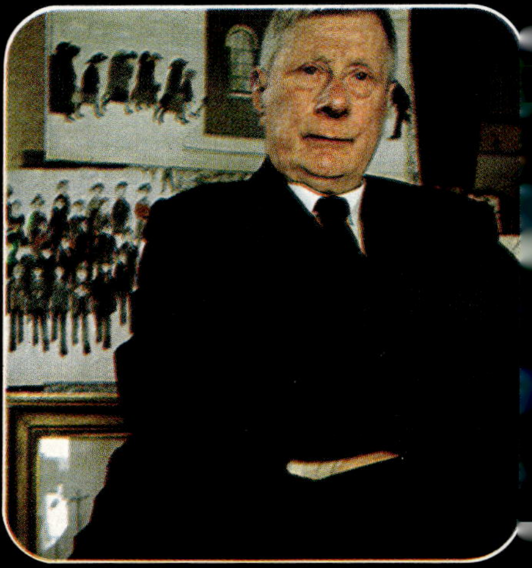
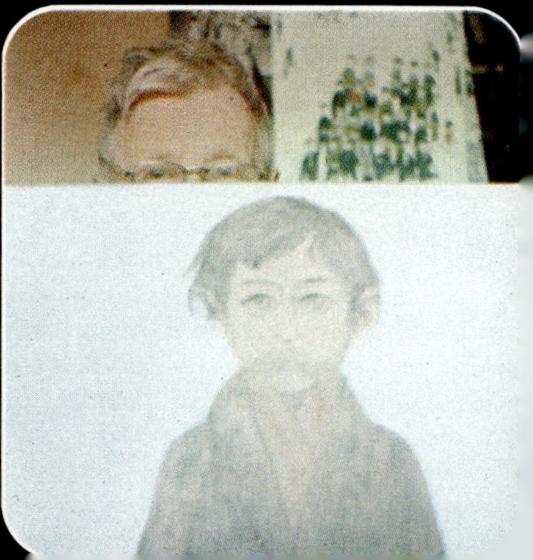

Roy Lichtenstein

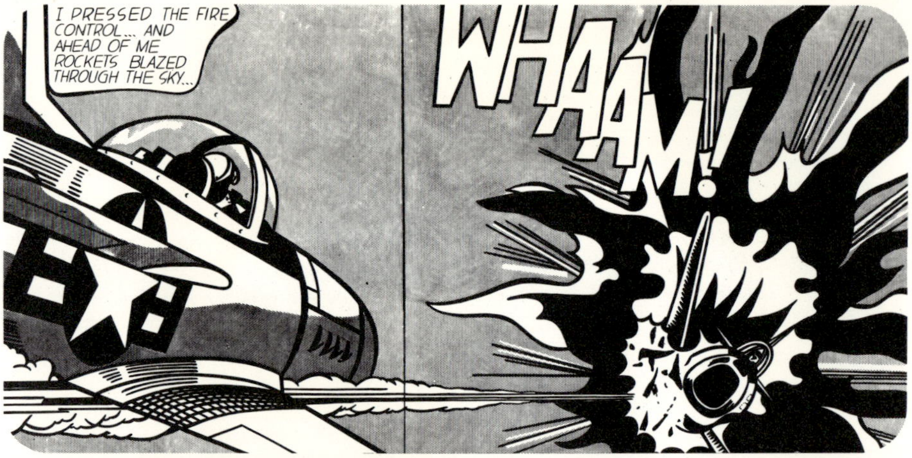

Roy Lichtenstein has rightly been called Mr Pop Art. He robs pop culture of many of its instantly-recognisable symbols: sleek ads, mass production and uniformity. By taking ready-made images from newspapers, public hoardings and fifty-cent comics, he produces pictures we wouldn't normally associate with the term fine art. 'I'm anti-contemplative, anti-nuance, anti-getting-away-from-the-tyranny-of-the-rectangle, anti-movement-and-light, anti-mystery, anti-paint-quality, anti-Zen, and anti all of those brilliant ideas of preceding movements which everyone understands so thoroughly.'

Now 44, Lichtenstein looks like a central European aristocrat, happier in tweed sports jackets and polo neck sweaters than blue jeans and all the other things many people associate with Pop painters, especially American Pop painters. He is slim, reserved and articulate.

'We like to think of industrialisation as being despicable. I don't really know what to make of it. There's something terribly brittle about it. I suppose I would still prefer to sit under a tree with a picnic basket rather than under a gas pump, but signs and comic strips are interesting as subject matter.

'The heroes depicted in comic books are fascist types, but I don't take them seriously in these paintings–maybe there is a point in not taking them seriously, a political point. I use them for purely formal reasons, and that's not what those heroes were invented for. . . . Pop art has very immediate and of-the-moment meanings which will vanish–that kind of thing is ephemeral–and Pop takes advantage of this "meaning", which is not supposed to last, to divert you from its formal content. I think the formal statement in my work will become clearer in time. Superficially, Pop seems to be all subject matter, whereas Abstract Expressionism, for example, seems to be all aesthetic.

'Everybody has called Pop art "American" painting, but it's actually industrial painting. America was hit by industrialism and capitalism harder and sooner and its values seem more askew. I think the meaning of my work is that it's industrial, it's what all the world will soon become. Europe will be the same way, soon. It will then be considered universal.'

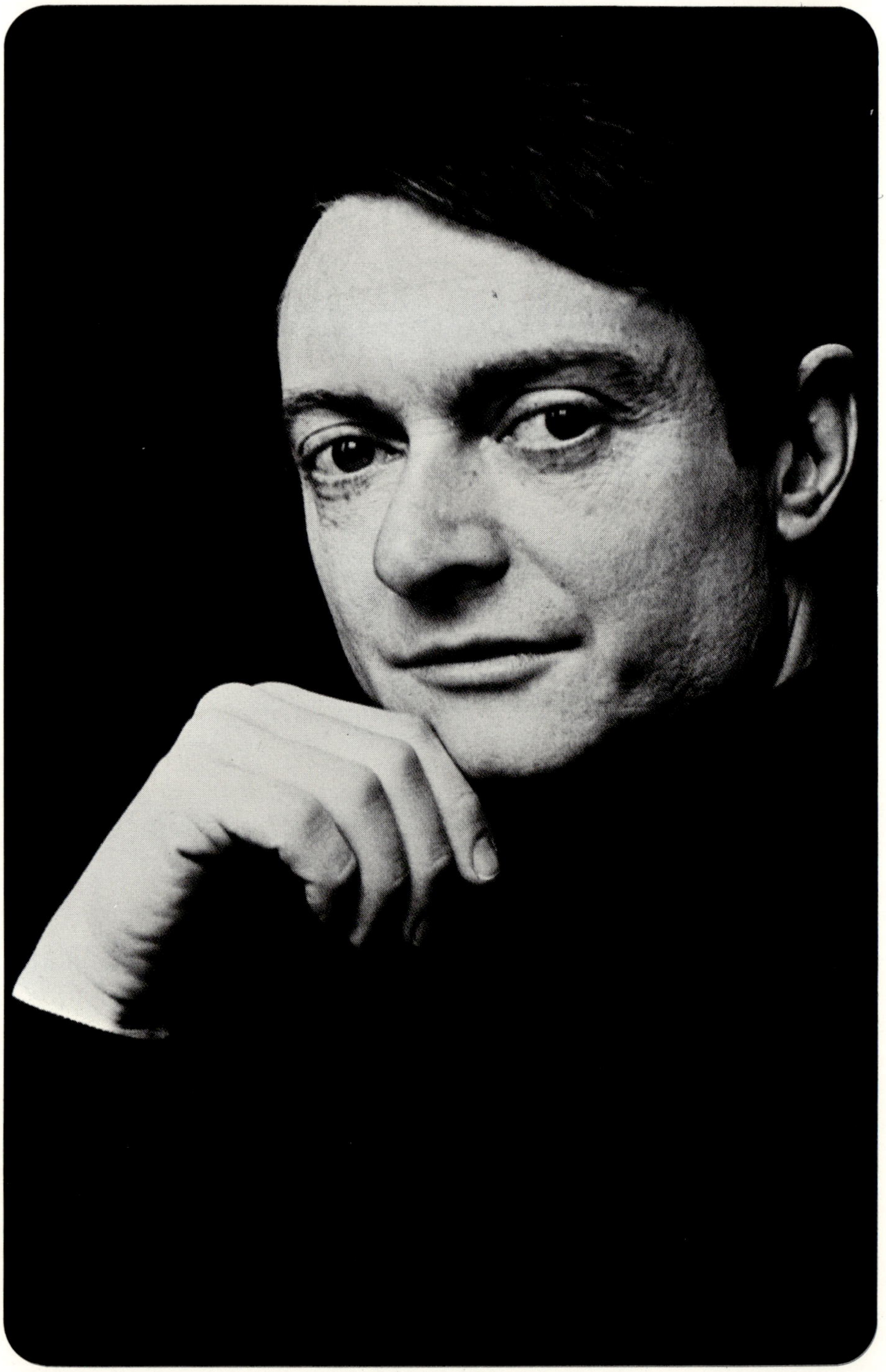

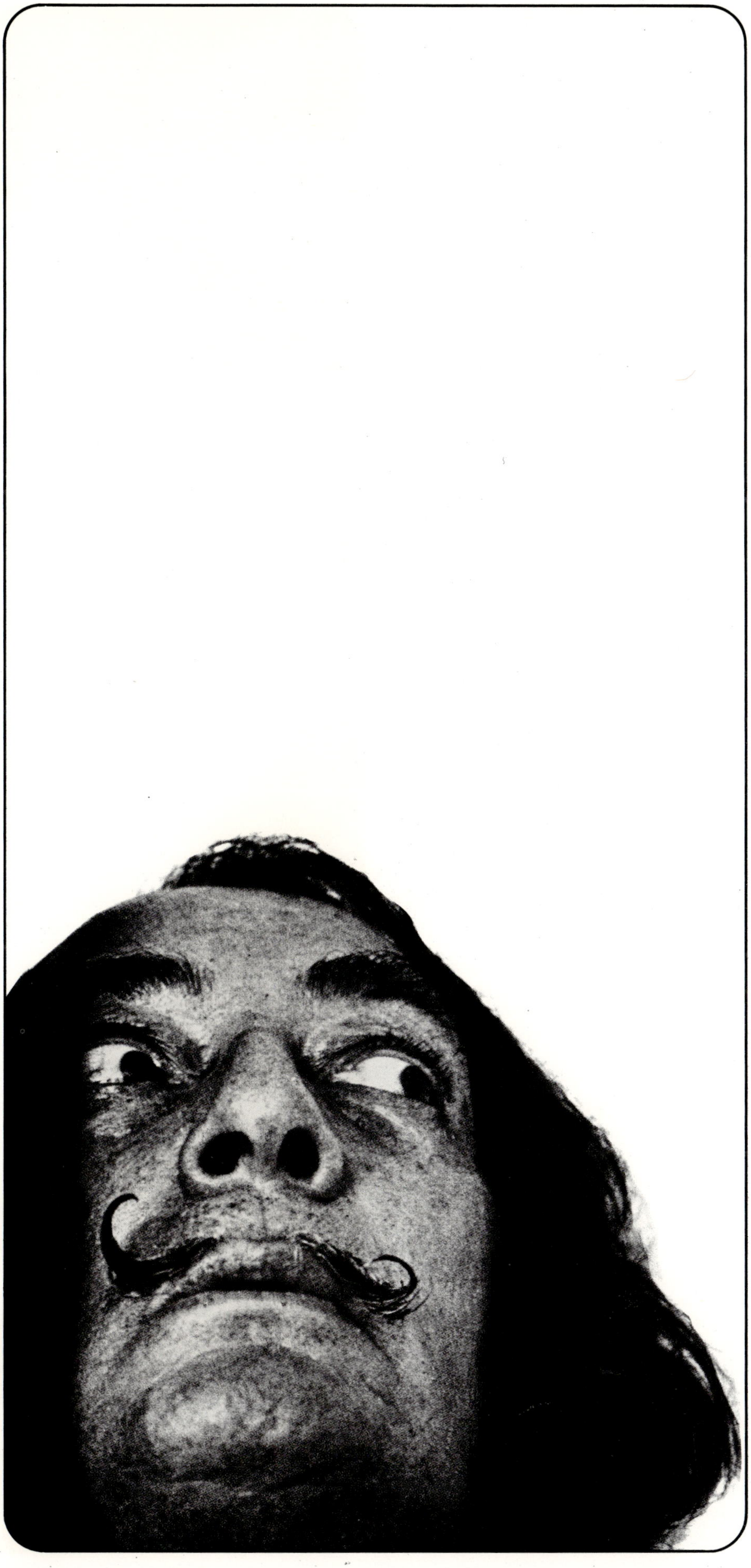

Salvador Dali

Salvador Dali, the Spanish Surrealist painter who has been likened to an excited prawn with his lengthy twitching moustache and black button eyes, is something of an enigma. Now in his sixties, Dali is widely regarded as a clown, a charlatan, mountebank, and a bit of a genius.

Dali's fooling in public and in private is, however, backed by many important paintings. Along with contemporaries like Man Ray and Magritte, he paints dreams, fantasies, and the jumbled disorder of the human unconscious.

Salvador Dali enjoys playing out some of the incongruities he discovers in the world, and in his own complicated personality, in public happenings. In fact, Dali was one of the earliest 'happening' artists.

Recently he gave a zany Press conference to announce his revolutionary ideas for opera and ballet décor. In a mixture of French, Spanish and English, he spoke of his new invention of using geometric forms created with liquid films of soap bubbles. 'As they dance,' he said, 'the dancers will dip big wire cubes into tanks of soap water. The membranes of water will form beautiful shapes.'

Dali began dipping one of his wire cubes into a plastic tank, but no beautiful shapes appeared. Just a pool of soapy water trickled on to the floor.

'That is American over-technicalisation for you. One of your major chemical companies made this solution for me,' said Dali in disgust.

Salvador Dali may play the fool, but he really is nobody's fool. He has many enemies, particularly among painters who dislike his publicity-seeking and commercial success. André Breton, the Surrealist leader, has been one of Dali's strongest critics. He condemned Dali and his work as worthless. 'Dali,' he said, 'is nothing more than an academic painter who has insinuated himself into the Surrealist milieu,'

His art–something he has himself described as 'paranoiac' inspiration–is now in demand all over the world. His prices and reputation, despite his detractors, are high. But whether Dali is a genius or a charlatan, inspired or just a clever technician with a brush, will be judged by time. In the meantime, Dali couldn't care less. Or so he says.

Henry Moore

Henry Moore is one of the giants of modern art. His name appears in newspapers and magazines with the regularity one normally expects of pop stars and international socialites. His art is now represented in private and public collections all over the world. Talk about modern sculpture and someone will almost certainly mention the name of Moore, however caustically or eulogistically. People are quick to say what they feel about his sculpture: they either love or hate it. For others, Henry Moore is just a damn good form of investment. Buying his sculptures is as good, they believe, as putting money in the bank–probably better if his post-war record is any guide.

Money apart, which is difficult enough in the art scene, many critics believe that Moore is probably the most important artist Britain has produced since Constable and Turner. His achievements are all the more remarkable when it is remembered that Britain, unlike France and Italy, has no great sculptural background.

Moore was born at Castleford in the West Riding of Yorkshire in 1898. His father was a coal miner and his mother worked as a domestic servant. At the age of eleven he won a scholarship to the local secondary school, now the Castleford Grammar School, where he remained until he was eighteen. Moore became interested in drawing and sculpture when he was at school. And through early impressions of his Yorkshire birthplace, Moore's sculptures were to become deeply imbued with reminiscences. A feeling for the solid, the rugged and weathered landscape of the nearby dales and moors has appeared at different periods of his development.

Conscripted into the army in 1916, he served in France until the end of the First World War. Moore then went to the Leeds College of Art, intent on becoming a professional artist. In 1921 he was awarded a 'Royal exhibition scholarship' with which he could study at the Royal College of Art in London.

During his early years as a sculptor he was influenced by medieval carvings, negro and Mexican sculpture, and the work of Michelangelo and Rodin. He also came into contact with the work of Epstein, Picasso, Gaudier-Brzeska and Modigliani and their art was a revelation.

Although Moore is rightly considered a modern artist, tradition has played a significant part in his development over the years. Most of his sculpture follows in the mainstream of the European tradition. For example, he has always been primarily interested in the human figure and its condition. His Mother and Child series, to give only one example, can be compared with the work of some Renaissance masters. Thus his art is much less abstract than is perhaps widely believed.

Moore's early years as a sculptor weren't as difficult as some writers have since suggested. 'My first one-man exhibition came in 1928 when I was thirty; the next one came in 1931, and then I had one-man exhibitions of sculpture every two years up till the war. Then, in some way, the war made the difference. It may have been that the shelter drawings that I did at that time which, to me, were a great excitement, or at least that period was, brought my name into general knowledge, and since those days it wasn't necessary for me to teach. I could earn my living out of sculpture alone.

'Nowadays, there's a tremendous change in art. Before the war one could have counted British sculptors on one hand, and now there are at least a hundred or more young sculptors having exhibitions every year in London.

'I now believe that it doesn't matter how you produce your sculpture, whether it's carving, modelling, welding, construction or in wax or in plasticine. What matters really is what it is, what kind of form, how good it is a sculpture, not the way it's done or the material. At one time I thought that carving was the best method of producing good sculpture. I no longer think that carving is superior as a method to everything else.

'As a sculptor, I want to produce good sculpture. The really great sculpture of the past has in it, for me, some sort of reflection of belief in life and in the worthwhileness of life. Artists like Michelangelo and Rembrandt; these people are great humanists because they have a tremendous understanding and expression of human problems, of the human happiness and tragedy of our lives.'

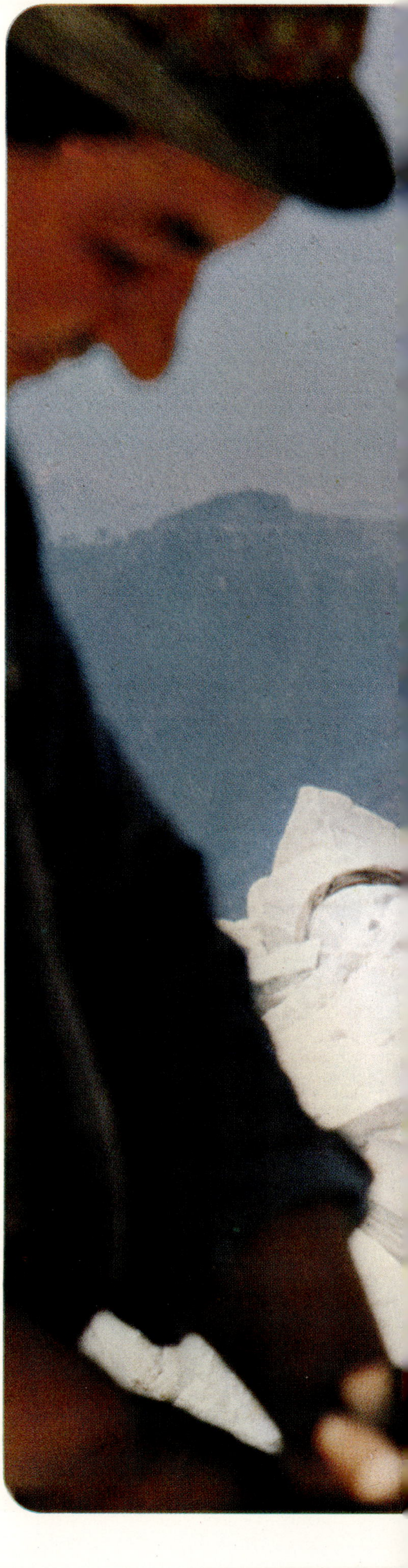

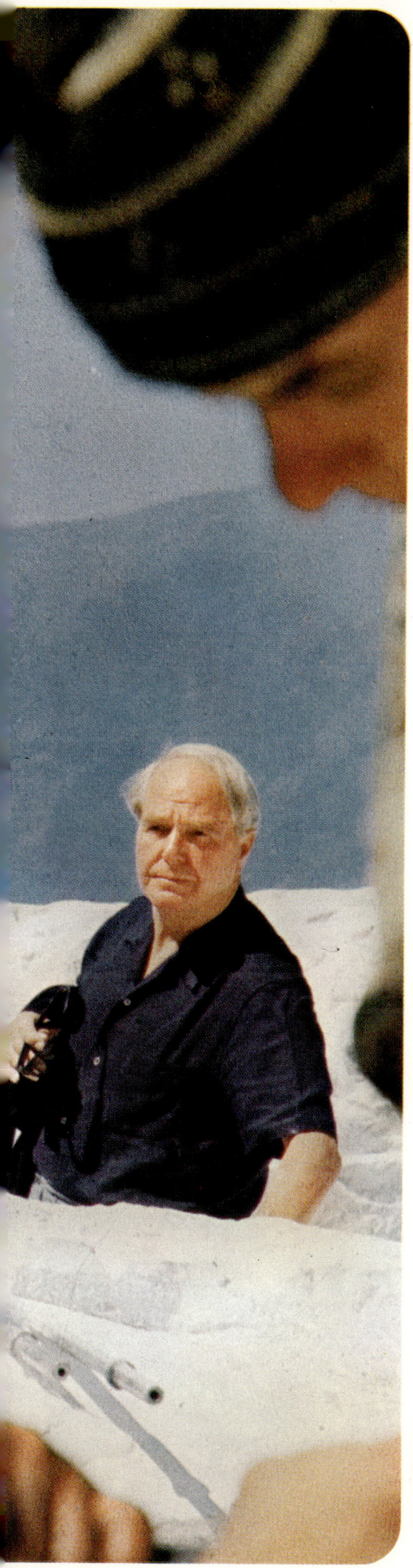
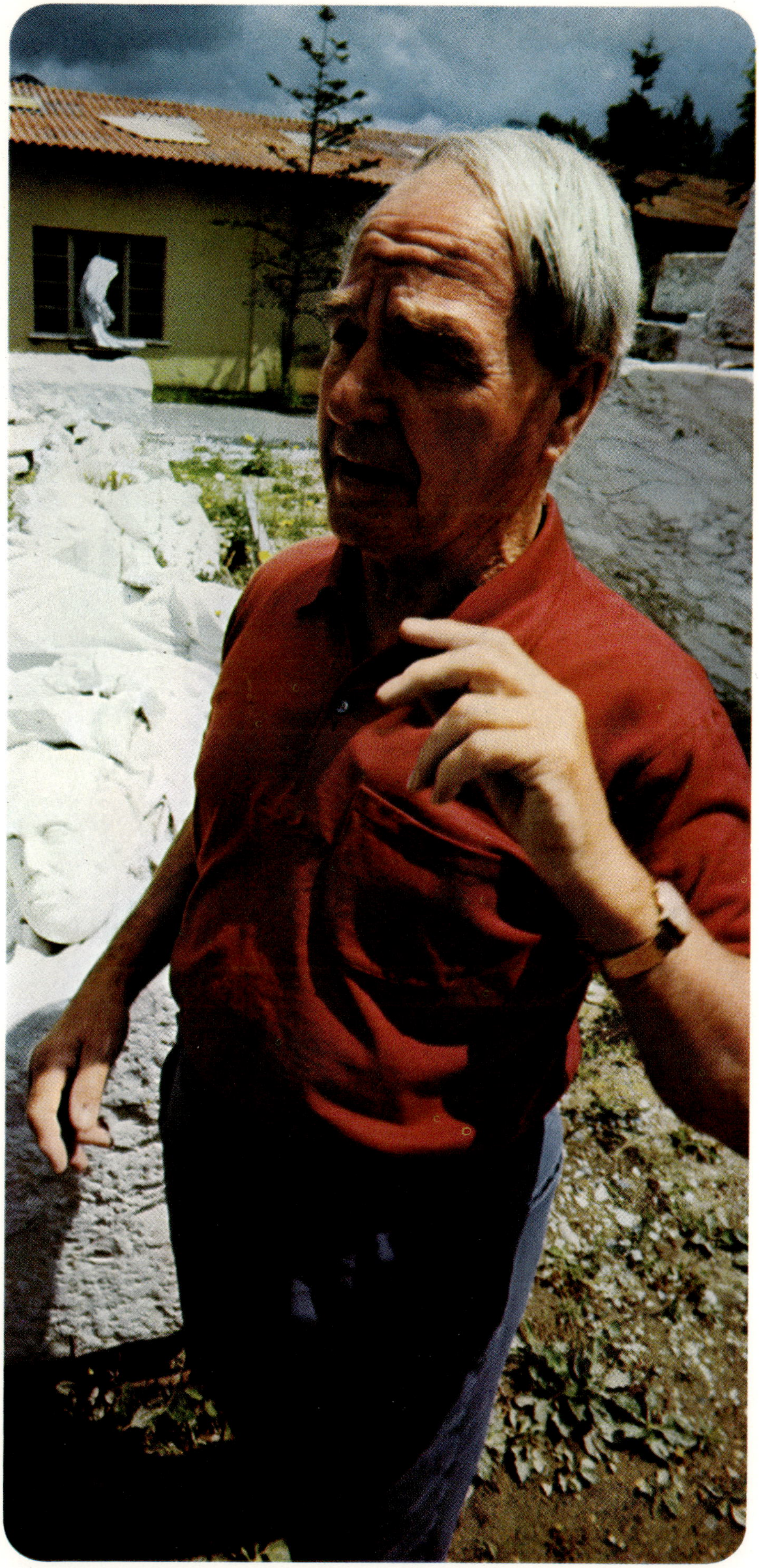

Ralph Ortiz

Ralph Ortiz, acknowledged spokesman for the Destruction in Art Movement, claims that destruction is essential to the nature of things. 'We destroy in order to create. Destruction is built into our species,' he says. 'If we could not destroy we would not survive for one moment. Our species destroys in the most fundamental sense to live. We destroy in order to realise ourselves.

'It is within this framework that I perceive a value for destructivist art. I believe destructivist art gives our destructive instinct its essential expression while coming to terms with destruction's most primitive maladaptive aspects, aspects that ordinarily would prove to work for the destruction of the species rather than for its survival.'

At a series of 'Destruction Events' Ortiz deliberately broke up a chair. About this event he wrote: 'Each axe swing unmakes this thing called an upholstered chair; each destruction unmakes my relationship to it. It is no longer for sitting; it is no longer hard or soft, beautifully designed or ugly, mid-Victorian or French Provincial. Each axe swing takes me away from the chairness of the chair to the transcending complexity internal in all things.'

Ortiz believes that the fine arts today play a passive if not irresponsible role in contemporary civilisation. They succeed only in insulating us from the reality of life and its horror. Ortiz's 'Henny Penny Piano Destruction Concert' brings us face to face with this horror. For him the chicken symbolises everyone caught up in the vast machine of modern life; the piano is that vast complex of history and tradition that dominates us.

The chicken 'attacks' the piano, but is ultimately sacrificed to it. Finally Ortiz becomes the avenger, shattering the piano with an axe, the violence filling his studio with the sound of splintering wood and the vibrating strings. 'Now,' says Ortiz, 'the concert is over: all that is left is sculpture.'

Whatever the sociological significance of these ultra-avant-garde 'artists', they are something of a nightmare to the vast majority of commercial art dealers. 'If you can't sell it, it must be rubbish,' one well-known international art dealer was heard to declare.

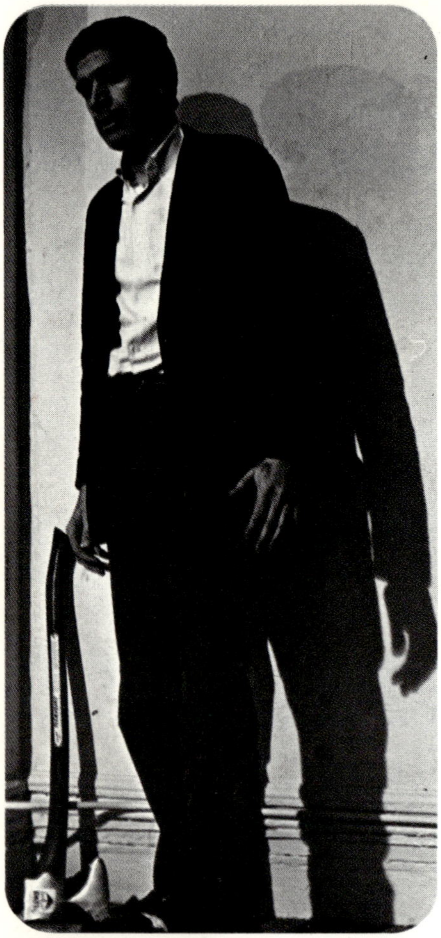

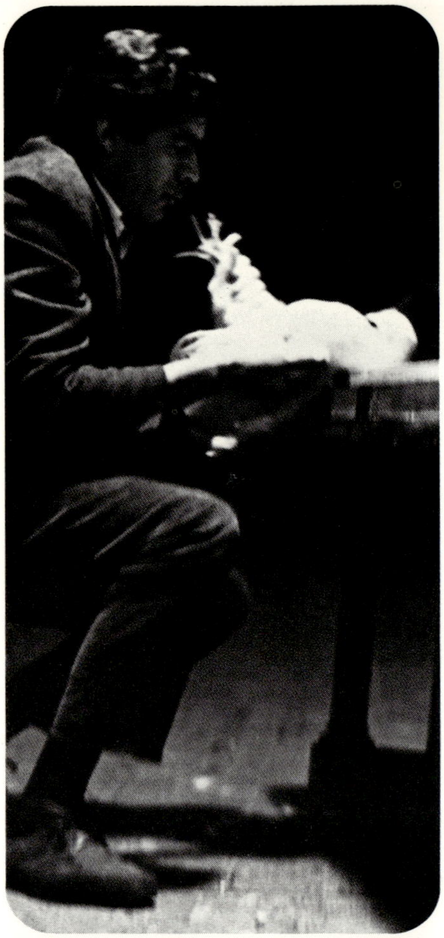

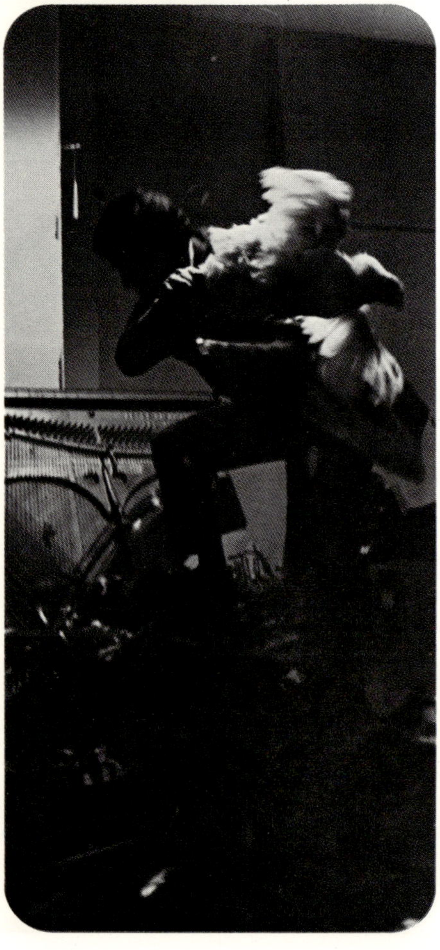

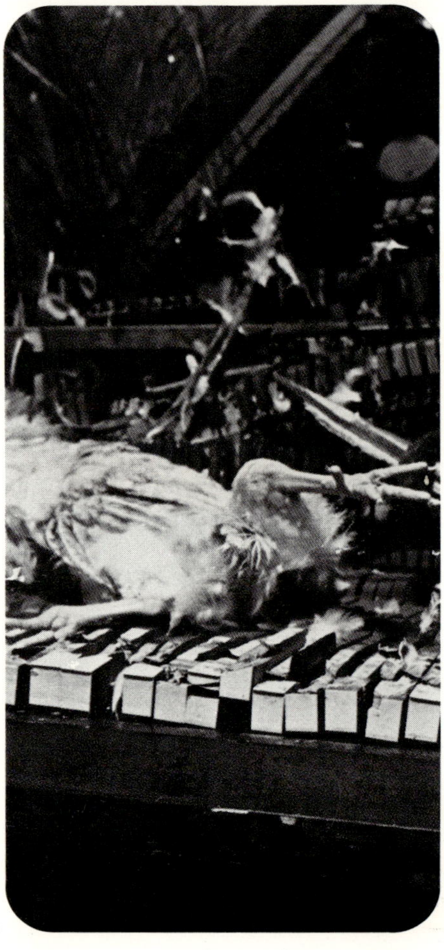

Julio Le Parc

Julio Le Parc, who has won the Venice Biennale's Grand Prix for painting, is an Argentinian artist who now lives in Paris. He is the unofficial spokesman for the 'Groupe Recherche d'Art Visuel', which in the last two years has become increasingly prominent.

The group was founded as a spearhead for Kinetic art in 1960. Basically, it is interested in the logical developments of Op art with mechanically aided visual effects. It is in keeping with the group's activities and beliefs that although Le Parc won the Venice prize for painting, he does not use paint, brushes or canvas.

Le Parc wants to withdraw the word 'art', with its present-day meaning, from our vocabulary. 'We wish to interest the spectator, to help him overcome his inhibitions and develop beyond. We wish to make him participate. We wish him to join in with other spectators. When entering an exhibition of our work he will put into practice these instructions. It is forbidden not to participate. It is forbidden not to touch.' To 'participate' you have to press buttons, roll balls, or switch on the electrically motivated exhibits. It is rather like being in the Science Museum at Kensington where all the models work at the turn of a handle. It is a 'happening' that goes on happening.

Ensemble-cinq mouvements-surprises, one of Le Parc's art objects, consists of five buttons and five sections, which in turn or together produce a variety of optical illusions. It is a kind of futuristic puppet show. Press one button and a sheet of polished aluminium begins to shimmer furiously. Press another button and white hoops start to rattle along a metal rod –'rather like commuters on the train every morning,' says Le Parc.

Another exhibit is a box in which ping-pong balls shoot about from corner to corner. A large red ball bounces yoyo-like on a piece of elastic. Mirrors hang in one corner and the effect on the spectator is rather like the curved mirrors at a fair.

Le Parc has made pairs of spectacles which create colourful optical illusions for the wearer. As the spectator enters the gallery he can step on to uneven black blocks of wood which shake and move and give 'a feeling of unreality'.

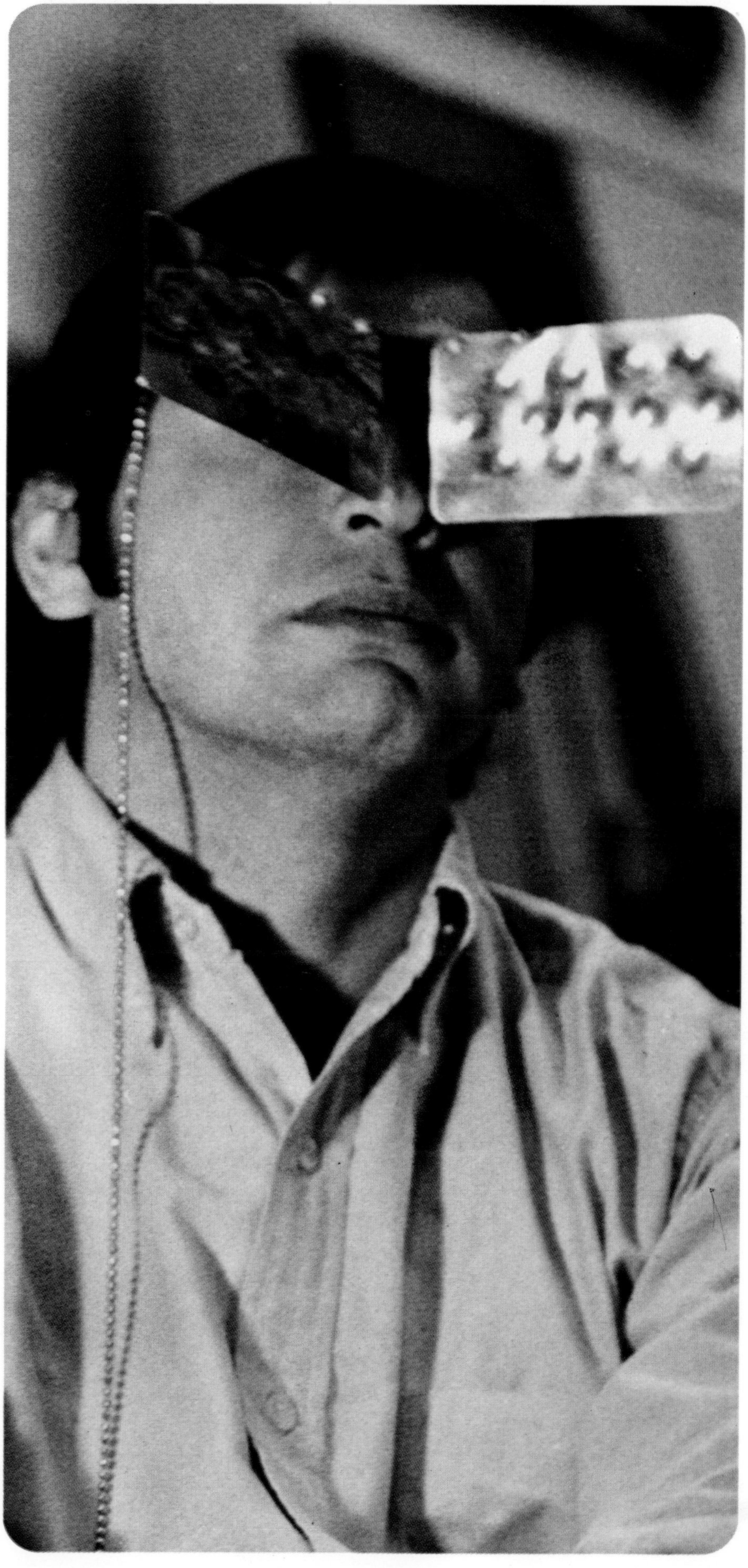

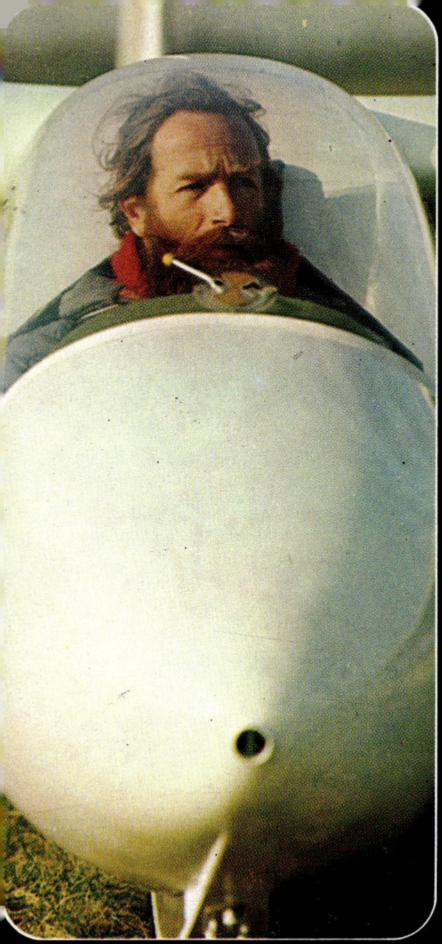

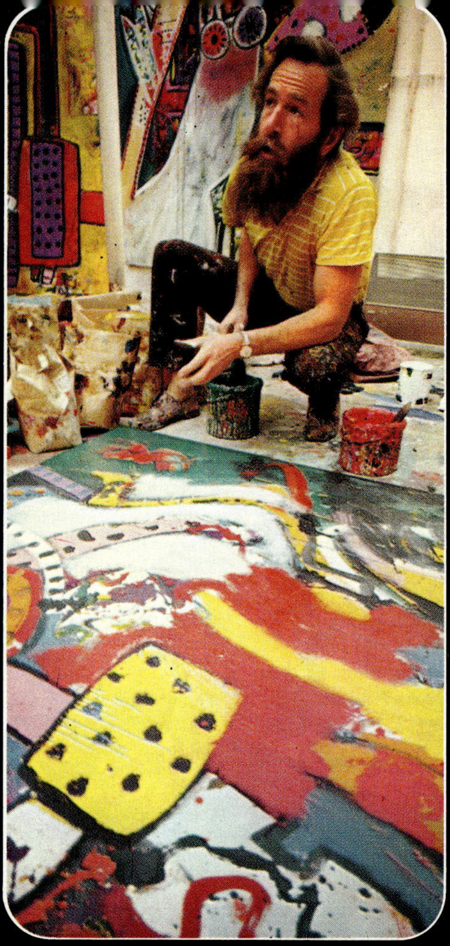

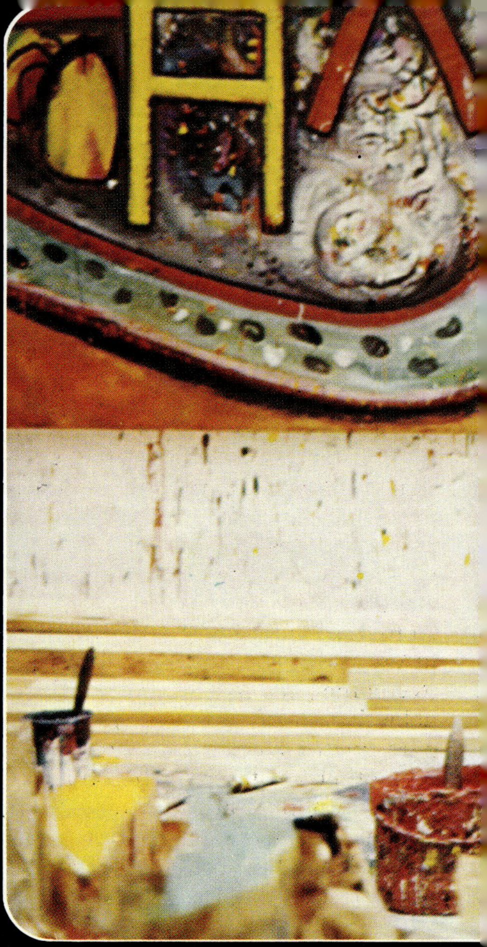

Alan Davie, pictured here in his glider (above), is seldom seen at art functions. Most of his spare time is spent gliding, driving his E-type Jaguar, and studying Zen Buddhism. Six feet tall, with piercing blue eyes, Davie spreads his paintings all over his large studios (centre and right). 'The act of painting is for me a religious expression of life itself,' he claims.

Alan Davie

Alan Davie, the Scottish-born painter, was considered in the early 1950s, by the few critics and collectors who knew his work, to be the *enfant terrible* of British art. In retrospect, this hardly seems surprising when one remembers the storm which Abstract Expressionism started. Many Abstract Expressionists followed the example of Jackson Pollock in America and threw paint at the canvas instead of using the conventional brush. At that time, there were many more people than there are today who considered such actions sacrilegious to art.

Alan Davie was one of the few Abstract Expressionists in England to ride the storm successfully, and go on painting (with a brush) in more or less the same inimitable style.

Married with two children, Davie lives in comfortable domesticity just outside Ware, in Hertfordshire. He is seldom seen at art functions; most of his spare time is spent gliding, driving his E-type Jaguar, and studying Zen Buddhism. Now at 48, he finds himself securely placed above the middle rung of the art ladder. His paintings are to be found in many of the world's major modern art museums.

Six feet tall, with piercing blue eyes and balding slightly amid an otherwise luxuriant head of hair, Davie inadvertently spreads his paintings all over his large studios. After working on small sketches he begins on three or four canvases rolled out on the floor. Inevitably paint is dripped over the floor, on his clothes and even on the walls.

'Being an artist is a kind of hell,' he says. 'One's always on the verge of producing something marvellous and yet it doesn't quite come off. One's destroying beautiful things all the time. The mental anxiety is considerable.

'The act of painting is for me a symbolic, religious expression of life itself. I have no religion in any formal sense, but I consider the act of painting to be religious. It is not a matter of expressing something that is known but reaching out into the unknown. People today look at paintings with their brain. I believe this to be wrong. In my work as an artist I strive to lose myself, not find myself. I am painting for myself, not for others, and it is

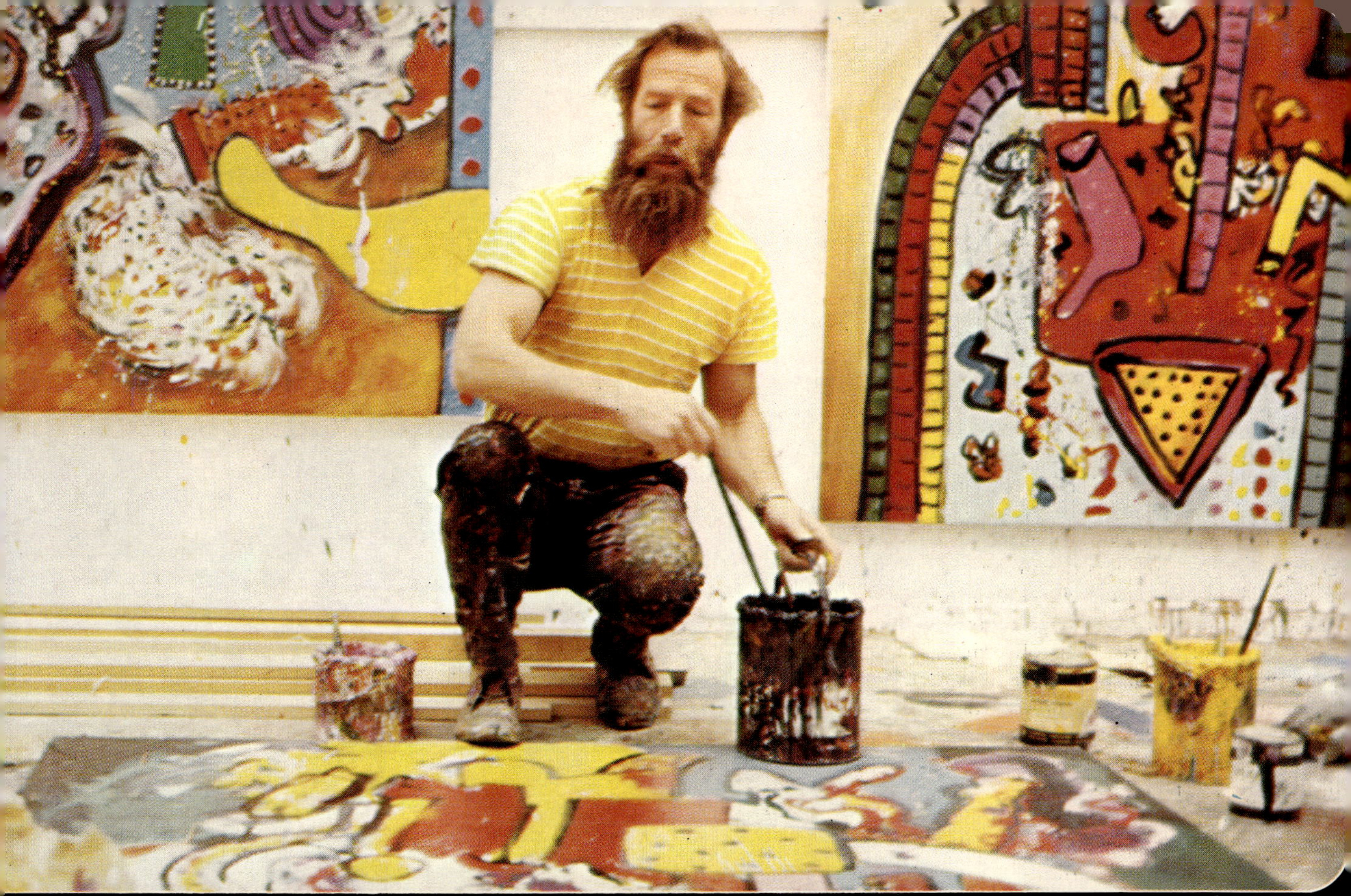

only incidentally that I strike a wider note that others understand.

'The problems of the artist today are the outcome of his possessing too much knowledge. Knowing as we do that creation is basically intuitive and that intuition is not born of knowing (there is no "know how"), we have come to certain conclusions as to the kind of mental attitude to adopt whilst actually painting. It has been clear to us that one must concern oneself with the activity of painting, be it a physical one, like a dance, or an improvisation with ideas or concepts, and we must continue to pay as little attention as possible to the end towards which we are moving, allowing the end to come when it comes, that is, at the end, when the right moment arrives. And at that moment I must say one has no aim, striving, or expectation. A painting–a work of art–should never to my mind be finished. I think it was Bonnard who once said that a finished work of art is usually *dead*. Painting for me is a continuum. I am continually trying to lose myself in my work, looking always for perfection.'

Asked his opinion about the main the need to paint, Davie answered: 'In what way can I describe what I feel art to be? Perhaps I could say: art is the evocation of the inexpressible. But no definition can in itself be entirely satisfactory. Actually, what I am trying to get at is best expressed by the idea of pure intuition. We could define the function of art as being: to arouse the faculty of direct knowledge by intuition, and what we feel by intuition requires pointers or symbols more than concrete ideas for its proper expression; and these pointers have to be enigmatic and non-rational. They are shy of intellectual interpretation and come to us, as one Japanese writer has put it, like "flashes of lightning". Sometimes I think I paint simply to find enlightenment and revelation. I do not practise painting as an art; and the Zen Buddhist likewise does not practise archery as an exercise of skill but as a means of enlightenment. The right art is purposeless, aimless. The more obstinately one tries to learn how to paint for the sake of producing a work of art, the less one will succeed.'

Davie has been variously described chiste, and even an Abstract painter. As an artist these labels mean very little to him. 'Labels, particularly in the art world, are usually meaningless, and misleading. For example, to my mind there's really no such thing as abstract act. I find Rembrandt can be as "abstract" as Mondrian is so generally thought to be. The popular term Action Painting is generally tagged on to my work and the writers imply in the term the outward show and expression of the artist's physical activity and emotion. Nothing could be farther from the truth as far as I am concerned. Activity and emotion have always inevitably played a part in the creative process. But they in themselves are only part of the mechanism of creativity and the processes involved. The struggle, the joy and the despair that went into the work are seldom apparent in the completed image and there is no question of the picture expressing the activity of its production or even the emotions of the artist at the time. Can you imagine a piece of music expressing the pianist's activity of manipulating the keys of his instrument? Self-expression is something contrary to

Paul Wunderlich

Paul Wunderlich was born in Berlin in 1927. He was, therefore, twelve years old at the outbreak of the Second World War and seventeen when the attempt was made on Hitler's life in 1944. This event seems to have left a permanent mark on his work and he once did a series of lithographs entitled *20 July, 1944*, full of dismembered and tortured bodies—the generals who were hung on meat-hooks and, for the Führer's pleasure, photographed while they choked to death. It is as though Wunderlich wants to turn sadistic into aesthetic satisfaction, just as he attempts in his more recent work to use bodily functions or sexual obscenities in socially acceptable works of art. For Wunderlich, terrible, unacceptable things must become something else; no less horrible perhaps, but palatable. Maybe a clue to his art lies in his statement that he never dreams, but were he unable to work he would be plagued by nightmares. It seems, then, that Wunderlich is a master of sublimation. If his pictures resemble the works of Surrealist painters this is purely accidental. He claims to follow no school, nor to know why he paints. Like many artists he prefers not to talk about his work, but this is not because he cannot express himself in words, but because to do so might place it in jeopardy. He sees a strange beauty where others see only horror, and manages to let us share his vision. It is the vision of Dürer and Grünewald. The figures in Wunderlich's work are contorted and twisted like the central figures in the *Isenheim Altar* crucifixion, or in the South German engravings of the Dance of Death. There is horror indeed, but so much beauty, delicate colour and careful technique. The German critic Max Bense wrote: 'The dialectical relationship between beauty and deformity belongs to the essential characteristics of Wunderlich's style.' Frank Whitford, writing in the catalogue for a recent Wunderlich exhibition, has commented: 'The dialectic removes the subject one stage further from the spectator. It prevents daydreams from becoming nightmares.' Just as he protects himself by painting, his paintings shield and protect us in a world that has become so threatening that we are afraid to contemplate it any more.

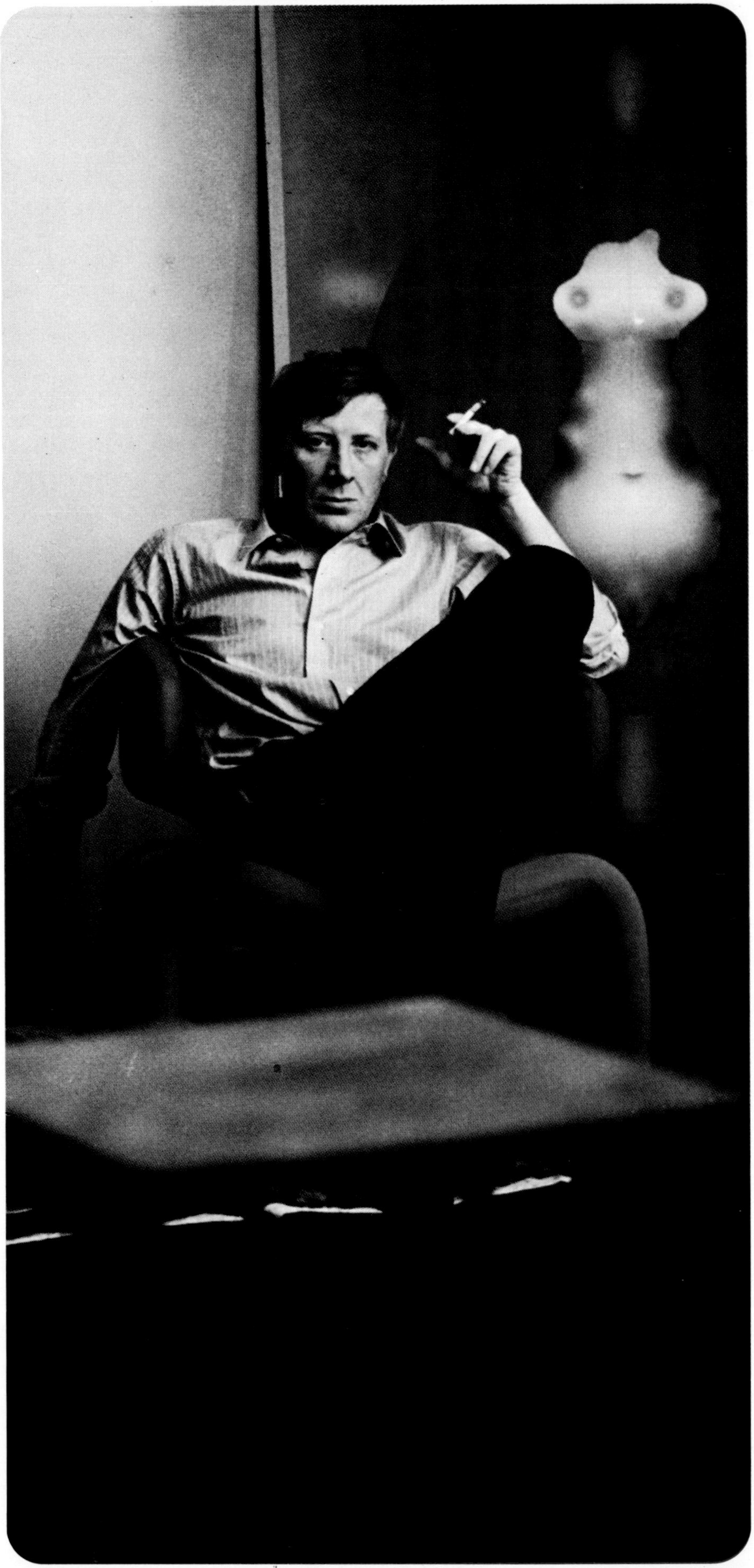

THE ART SCHOOLS

46,000 art students. In the USA there are more than 200,000; in Germany 62,000; even Japan has several thousand art students. More people than ever want to be professional artists.
Few ever realise what is little more than a dream. The vast majority will get jobs in industry, photography, advertising, general design and teaching in art schools. Not more than a minority will paint a professional picture when they complete their studies and an even smaller minority will be able to write 'professional painter' on their National Insurance card or passport. Many art students never really leave school. They remain, usually on a part-time basis, to teach other students to become painters, who in turn teach other students to become painters . . . and so it goes on. Some, especially in Britain, even look forward to this. Artists still feel they ought to earn their living in a more recognisably productive way in a country where puritanism still runs deep. In the United States, for example, professional painters and sculptors are noticeably more reticent about their 'responsibilities' to younger artists.
The Hornsey College of Art is typical of the new wave of British art schools. Little-known before the war, it has come up fast recently to rank with the other famous London schools, the Central, the Slade, St Martin's, Chelsea and, most sought-after, the Royal College of Art. Today it gets 2,500 applications for 250 first-year places. Hornsey is closely in touch with the professional art world. Several successful painters teach there, part-time – it has Bridget Riley, Philip Sutton, Bryan Kneale, Tess Jaray, Alan Reynolds. Unlike the Royal College of Art or Chelsea, both of which are housed in new concrete and glass palaces, Hornsey is billeted in Victorian-Edwardian buildings scattered around the district. One of the college annexes is in the old Badminton Hall at Alexandra Palace. Twice the size of a municipal swimming pool, its floor space is divided into painting compartments and gives the appearance of an African shanty town. Students tend to barricade themselves behind makeshift wooden boards tied up with string and covering an area about eight feet by ten feet. The vast network of 'studios' are loud with the squeal of spray guns, and littered with strange, man-made materials. Occasionally the already shrill atmosphere is punctuated by booms from the sculpture section, isolated at one end of the hall.
Proof of the dissatisfaction which some art students feel about art education was seen in the Hornsey College rebellion of May 1968. Students demanded the elimination of compulsory examinations, and the removal of the distinction between vocational and diploma courses. Not only were they supported by many members of the staff, but even the local town council gave them a sympathetic hearing.
On November 2, 1967 the Royal College of Art, Britain's most prestigious art school, celebrated its royal charter and newly-acquired university status by installing its first Provost, Sir Colin Anderson, and its first Visitor, the Duke of Edinburgh. *The Times* published an eight page survey on the College.
Sir Paul Reilly, Director of the Council of Industrial Design, underlined the RCA's position as a national asset: '. . . The college now serves very widely the demands and needs of industry, and, though the reputation of its fine art schools has seldom been

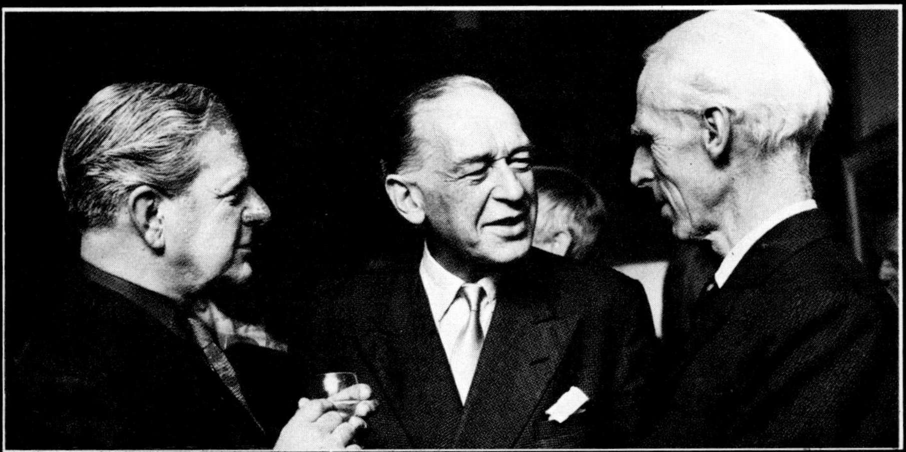

Tuition in art schools is becoming more and more professional. Here Edward Morss, Principal of the St Martin's School of Art, talks with Robert Medley and John Piper, both artists of note

Today few art students spend time learning the traditional secrets of the old masters; instead they are being trained for work in industrial design, advertising or television

Although the Bohemian image of art is nearly as dead as Toulouse-Lautrec, some of the traditional features remain. Here students draw from the model, as they have done since the days of Raphael and Michelangelo, while others work in the sculpture workshop of a modern art school

Peter Blake (top right), well-known British Pop artist, teaches at the Royal College of Art, London. He is seen here talking to brilliant young gallery owner Robert Fraser (seated). An open-air exhibition in the King's Road, Chelsea (bottom right)

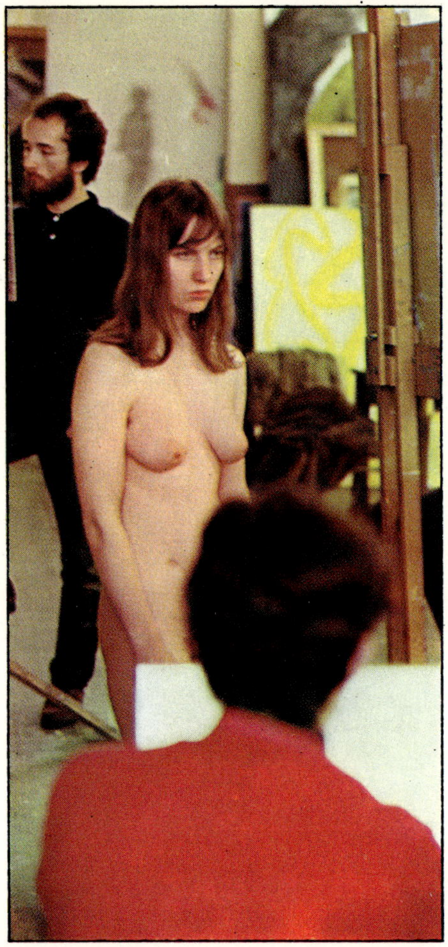

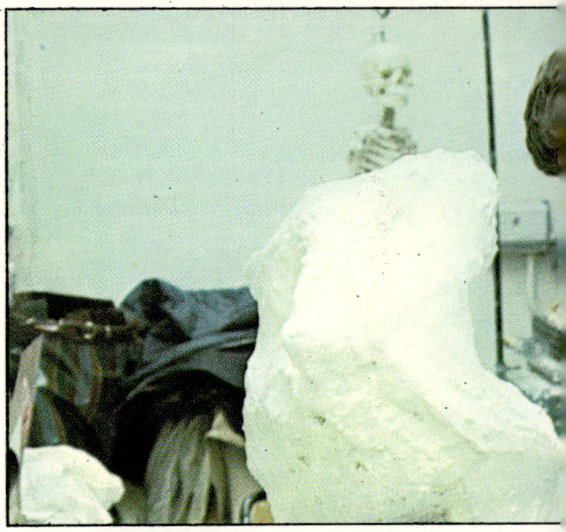

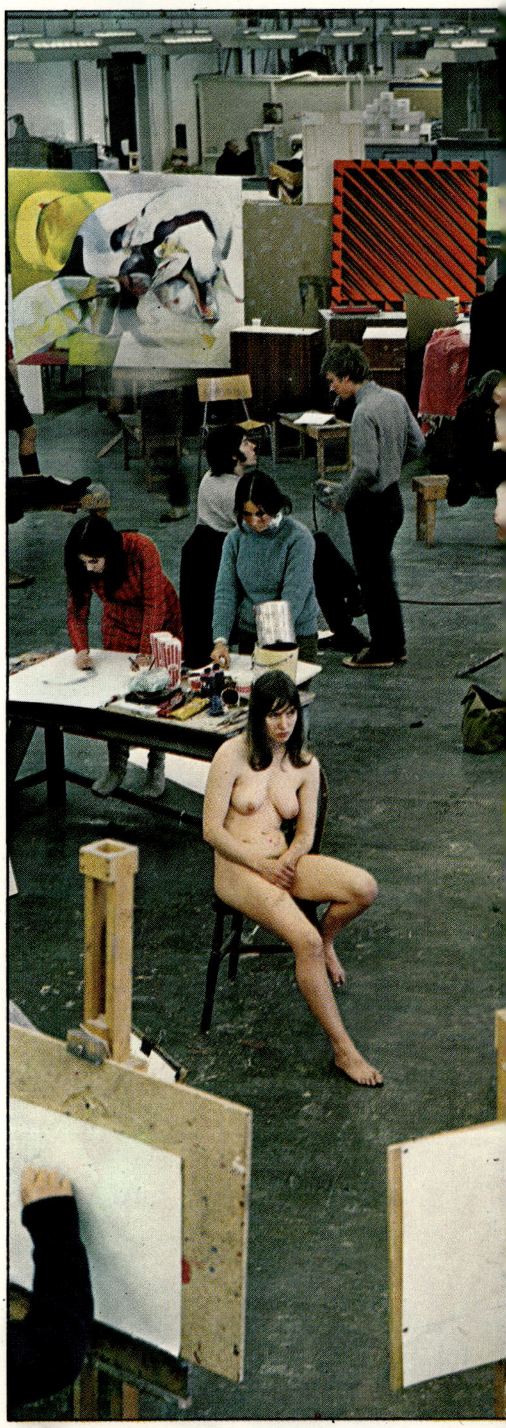

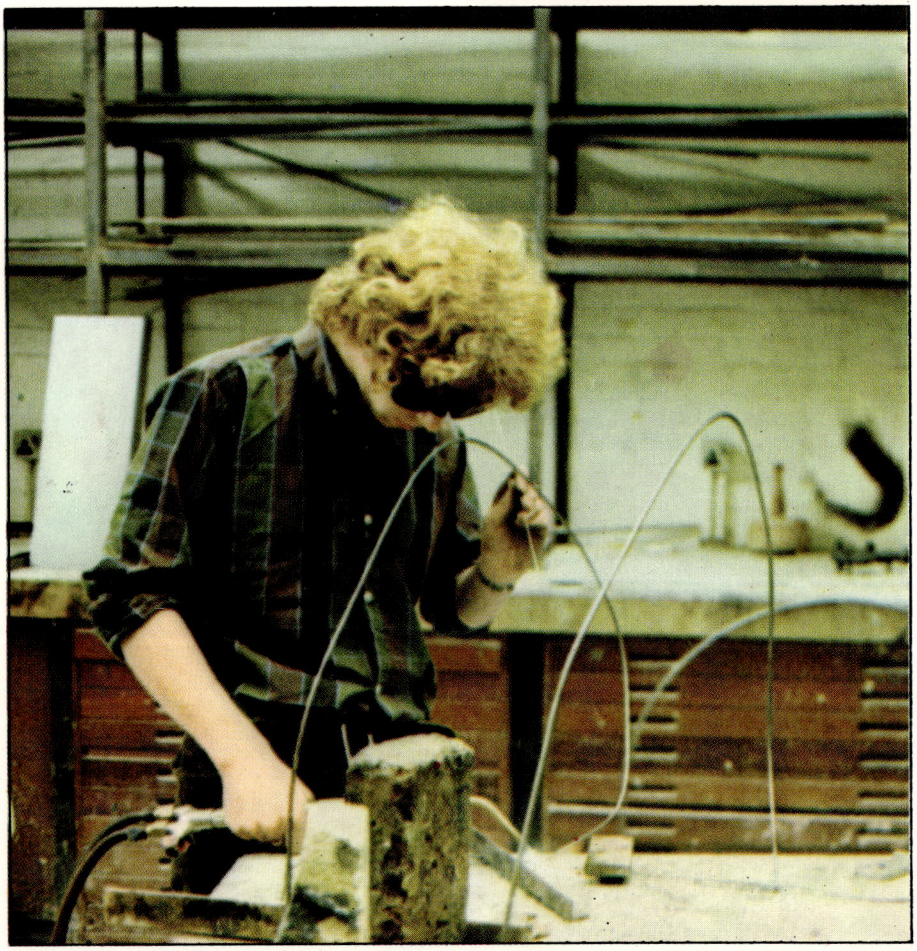

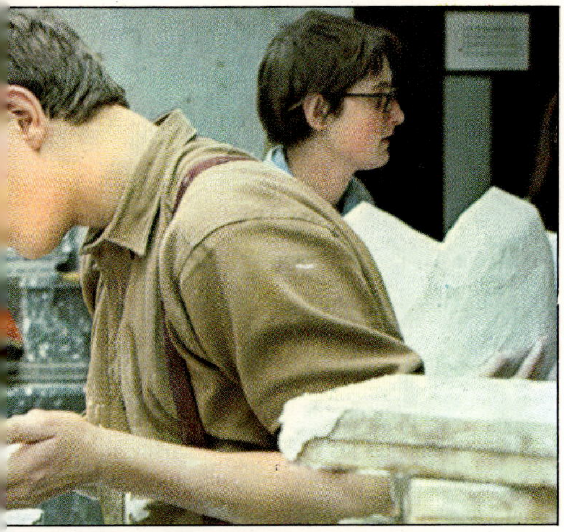

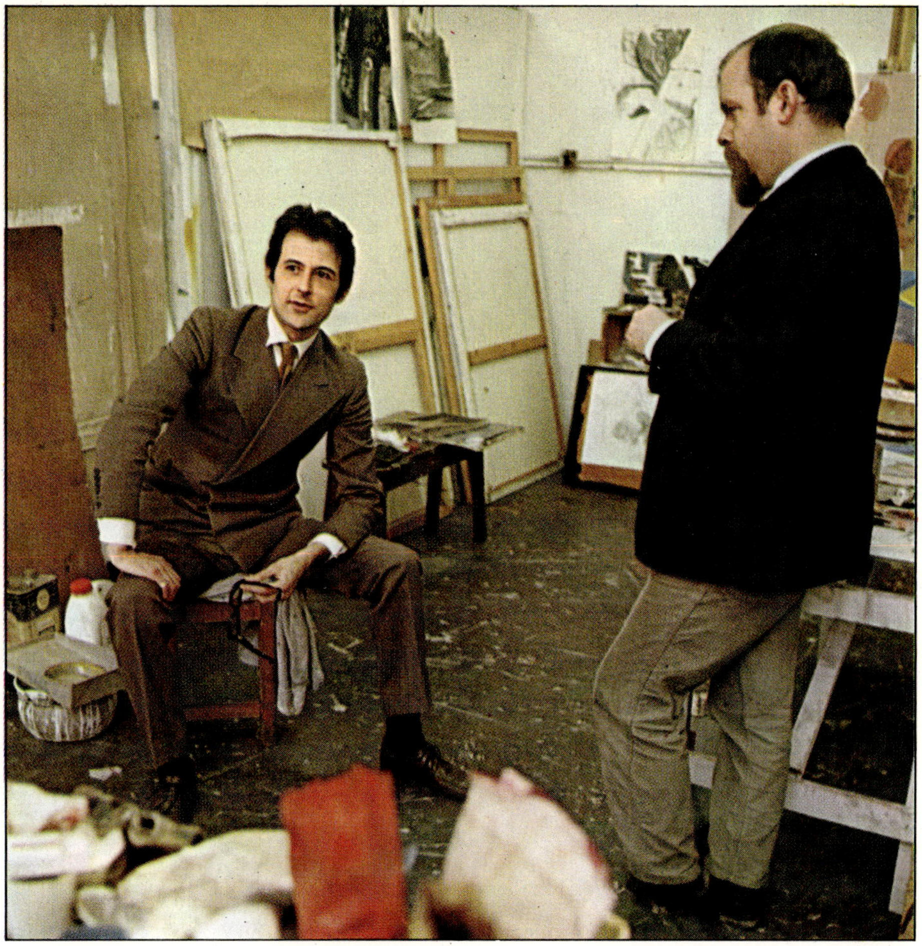

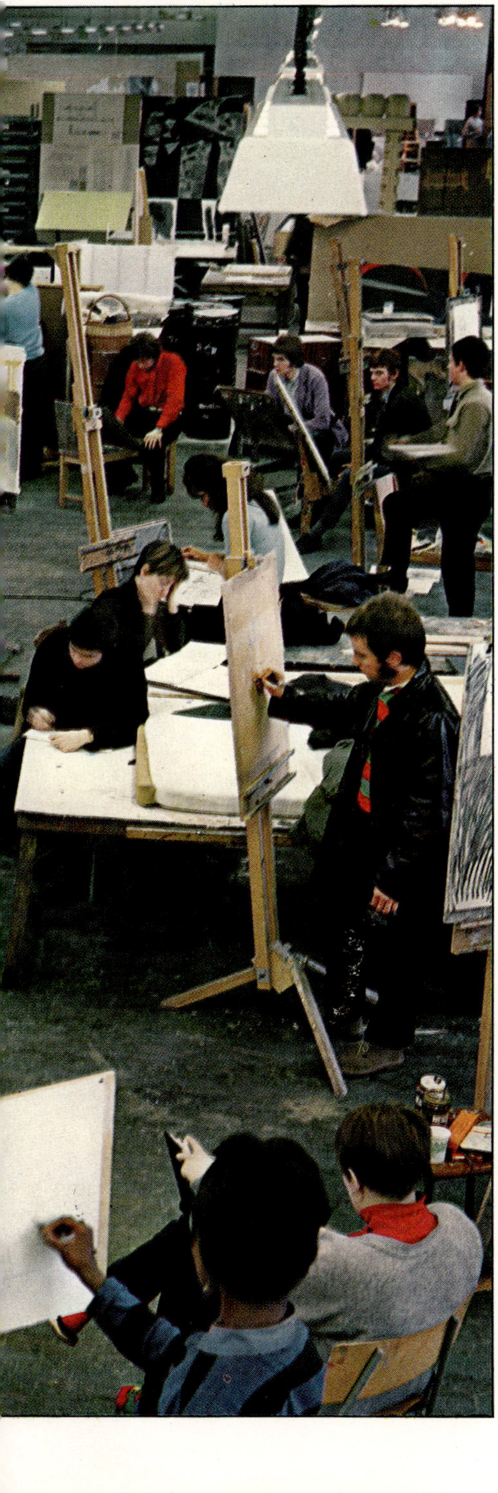

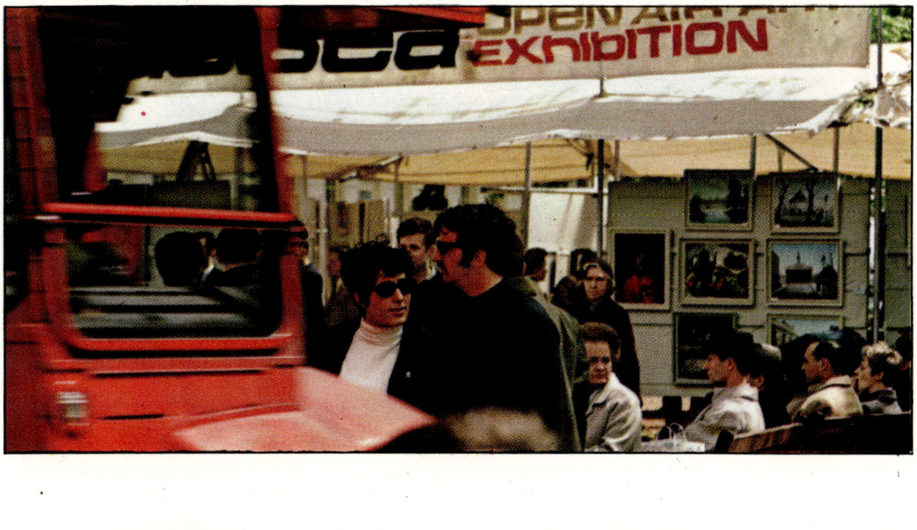
EXHIBITION

livelier or more influential than in the past decade, it is in the industrial, commercial world that the college is making its most direct contribution to the national economy.'

Several satisfied ex-students of the RCA, including Henry Moore, sung its praises. David Hockney, a popular avant-garde painter on both sides of the Atlantic, said: 'I liked the casualness of the school. The fact that only three or four paintings from life (the traditional art school subject) were demanded a year was a great help to students finding a new attitude to subject matter.

'I enjoyed working there. And I'm sure that if I had not been a student there during those three years, it would have taken me a little longer to discover some small knowledge of painting.'

Joe Tilson, a prominent British artist, is more critical of the present state of the RCA and other London art schools. Naturally perhaps, his criticisms are aimed at the fine art departments. When I spoke to him he said: 'The Painting School of the Royal College of Art has changed from the easy-going 1950s under Professor Rodrigo Moynihan to a rigid dull regime and a list of the most nowhere artists to be found at the Royal Academy.

'Around 1954 Riley, Blake, Denny, Smith and myself were there. There was no teaching but great freedom to do what you wanted to and much interchange of ideas amongst the students. Jones and Hockney were at College around 1960-61. Jones left after his first year and Hockney was failed in his Final written exams but the Principal, Sir Robin Darwin, gave in and passed him.

'The Slade teaching has a much more positive effect, though not necessarily a good one. The Sculpture Department is appallingly bad. The Slade has been more lively lately due mainly to Harold Cohen teaching there plus other Visiting Teachers such as Kitaj, Hodgkin, Auerbach and myself.

'St Martin's Painting School is zero on anyone's list. St Martin's Sculpture School is the best I have seen and so are the results, both in work and the interchange of ideas between teacher and students, and teachers and teachers, because it is this second thing that has helped most in London to develop people's attitudes and ideas. In London, as opposed to New York, everybody teaches. There are obvious disadvantages to this, but one advantage is that you are forced to meet other painters and sculptors every week in a situation where serious discussion can take place.'

The Bohemian image of art is as dead as Toulouse-Lautrec. Art is now playing a greater part in teacher-training colleges and in schools all over the world. Mental hospitals and rehabilitation centres encourage their patients to paint, sculpt and make things. More and more people believe that art has magical properties: solace for the insane, comfort for the rich who can graciously blood-let their bank accounts by buying works of art, and satisfaction for the producer—the artist. Art is the cure-all for many of society's ills.

Following behind the professional art schools who try and process students—the raw material—into artists are the private schools and art masters who offer to do the same job on a different level. Postal courses, residential courses and evening institute classes eager to make men and women into artists. The art magazines and some of the more serious newspapers carry such attractive and rosy advertisements as:

Lessons given in drawing, painting and sculpture. Individual tuition given in extensive studios by a staff of distinguished artists. Prospectus on application.

The present situation is a curious one. Thousands of men and women want to create works of art and yet proportionately we have seen much less original talent in the last decade than at any time in the twentieth century. We know that only one student a year leaving a *prominent* art school makes a professional reputation, however modest. Part of the answer lies in the simple fact that the art market is already saturated with modern works of art. If all the paintings produced in five art schools in one year were heaped together we would have enough material to fill every private and public gallery in the world.

Times are getting harder for the artist leaving art school. Small wonder that many of them disappear into the financially rich worlds of advertising, television and design. But what will be the ultimate effects on art in the second half of the twentieth century?

Looking, teaching, working, or just relaxing are all part of art school life. More people than ever before want to be professional artists. Art students have to find their own way and create work for themselves. Many never really leave school. They remain, to teach other students to become painters. Teachers shown here include Sir Hugh Casson, David Pye, Keith Lucas, Carel Weight, Misha Black, Richard Guyatt (back row), Roger Nicholson, Robert Goodden, Bernard Meadows and Christopher Cornford (middle row), with Professor Lord Queensberry

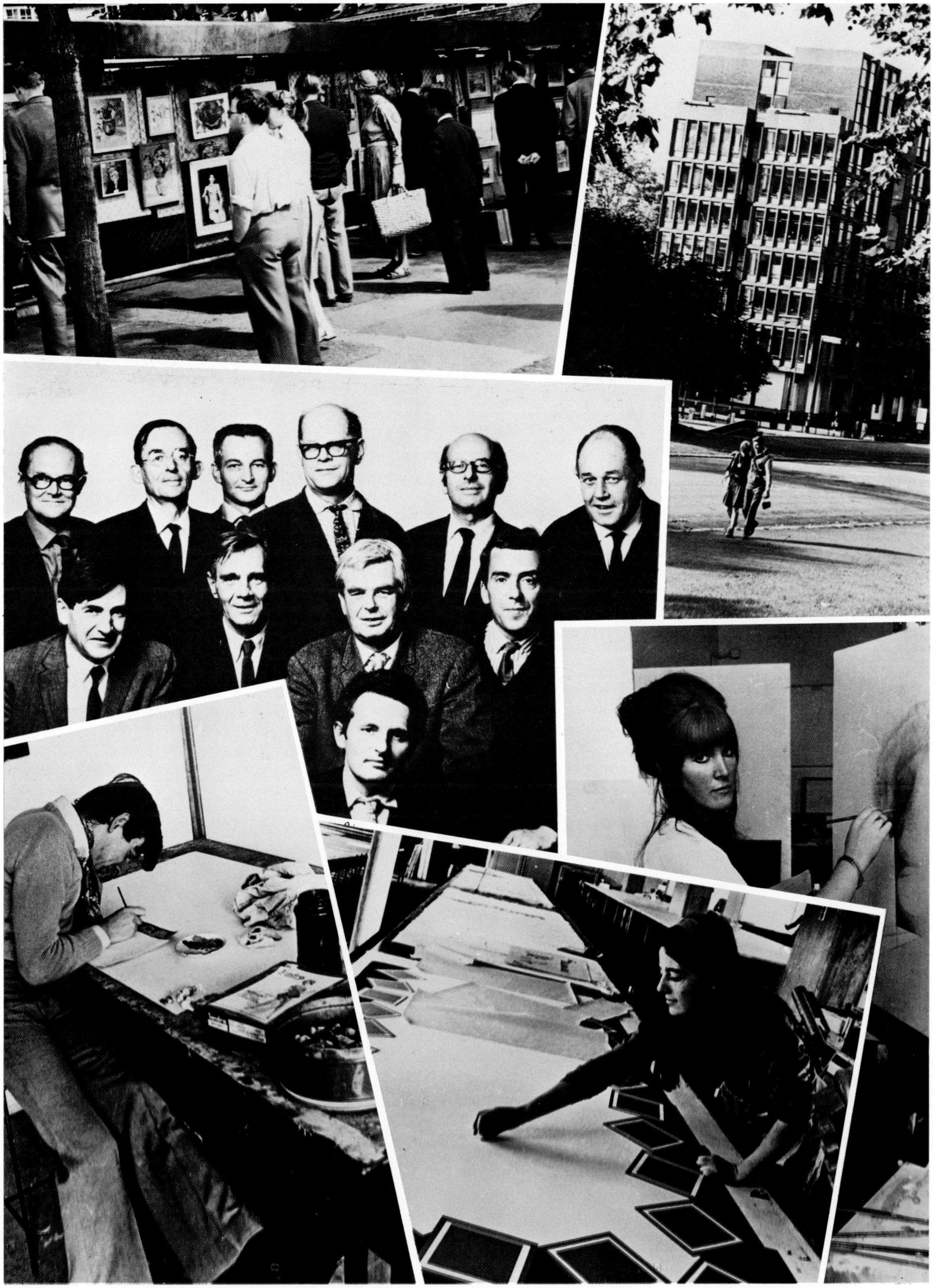

AUCTIONEERS & SALEROOMS

Fine art salerooms are now at the bustling centre of the art market. Dealers, collectors, speculators and sellers visit them assiduously. And the record prices in London, New York or Paris regularly make headlines. Rembrandt's *Aristotle Contemplating the Bust of Homer* fetched £821,400 ($2,300,000) at the Parke-Bernet Galleries in New York; Van Gogh's *Portrait of Mademoiselle Ravoux* 150,000 guineas ($441,000) at Christie's; Rembrandt's *Portrait of the Artist's Son, Titus* 760,000 guineas ($2,234,400); Picasso's *Mère et Enfant de Profil* £190,000; Léger's *L'Escalier* $100,000; Miró's *Autoportrait No. 2* $85,000; Pollock's *Composition No. 16* $32,000 . . . the list is almost endless. Auctioneers are in business to discover the price of every work of art.

If you have an old master or even a comparatively scarce modern picture to sell, the chances are that you will take it to an auctioneer rather than a private gallery. In fact, since 1945 firms like Christie's, Sotheby's and Parke-Bernet have profitably trespassed on traditional gallery territory. Items knocked down for between £15 and £20 constitute the bulk of the leading salerooms' turnover. It is now as easy to take a modern picture in demand to Christie's or Sotheby's as it is to enter a Rubens or a Canaletto, with the one proviso that it is relatively scarce and likely to fetch more than £15.

An examination of the world's leading auction houses leads to one firm conclusion. At the moment London is the richest and most important centre of the international art trade and has regained the important position in the art market she enjoyed at the end of the eighteenth century. Before jet travel, London was not a convenient stopping place on the route between Paris and New York. But London Airport has helped make British art a vital centre of the international art world; air transport is efficient and easy and London is geographically well situated. Moreover, sellers and buyers have a powerful tax incentive to do business in England. There is no import or export tax on works of art and no export licence is needed unless something is valued at more than £2,000 and rates of commission are very low.

London now has an annual turnover of more than £100 million in pictures, silver, jewellery, furniture, porcelain and other works of art, and the salerooms take a large slice of that. In fact, the combined turnover of the New York and Paris auction houses is less than the annual turnover of London.

The principal auction rooms of the world are: W. & F. C. Bonham & Sons Ltd, of Knightsbridge, London; Christie, Manson & Woods Ltd, of St James's, London; Dorotheum Kunstabteilung, of Vienna; Galerie Charpentier, of Paris; Hôtel Drouot, of Paris; Dr Ernst Hauswedell, of Hamburg; Knight, Frank & Rutley, of Mayfair, London; Kunsthaus Lempertz, of Cologne; Palais Galliéra, of Paris; Parke-Bernet Galleries, Inc., of New York; Phillips, Son & Neale Ltd, of London; Sotheby & Co., of London; K. G. Venator, of Cologne.

In the last few years competition from Continental dealers and collectors has notably increased in London and New York auction houses. France, West Germany, Holland and Italy were particularly well represented and there is little doubt that buyers from these countries will eventually become formidable competitors to British and American ones.

Auction sales in West Germany, France, Austria and Italy are becoming more important, and there is a steady supply of objects at prices which would be considered low in American and British salerooms. Should Britain enter the Common Market it will no doubt encourage a freer art trade between the countries of Western Europe, and also widen the boundaries of taste in European art and culture.

Although prices realised in the top foreign salerooms are overall much lower than in Britain and America, *individual* items occasionally do extremely well. For example, £122,000 was paid for Monet's *Le Pont d'Argenteuil* at a sale held by Maître Ader at the Palais Galliéra in Paris. The same picture was sold for £860 in 1897. In a sale held by Finarte in Milan, organised by the Finanziario per l'Arte, £12,000 (21m. lire) was paid for a Modigliani nude. Chagall's *Jeunes filles aux fleurs* fetched £10,178 at the Galerie Charpentier in Paris, rather a high price for that artist.

For the most part auction rooms like the Dorotheum Kunstabteilung of

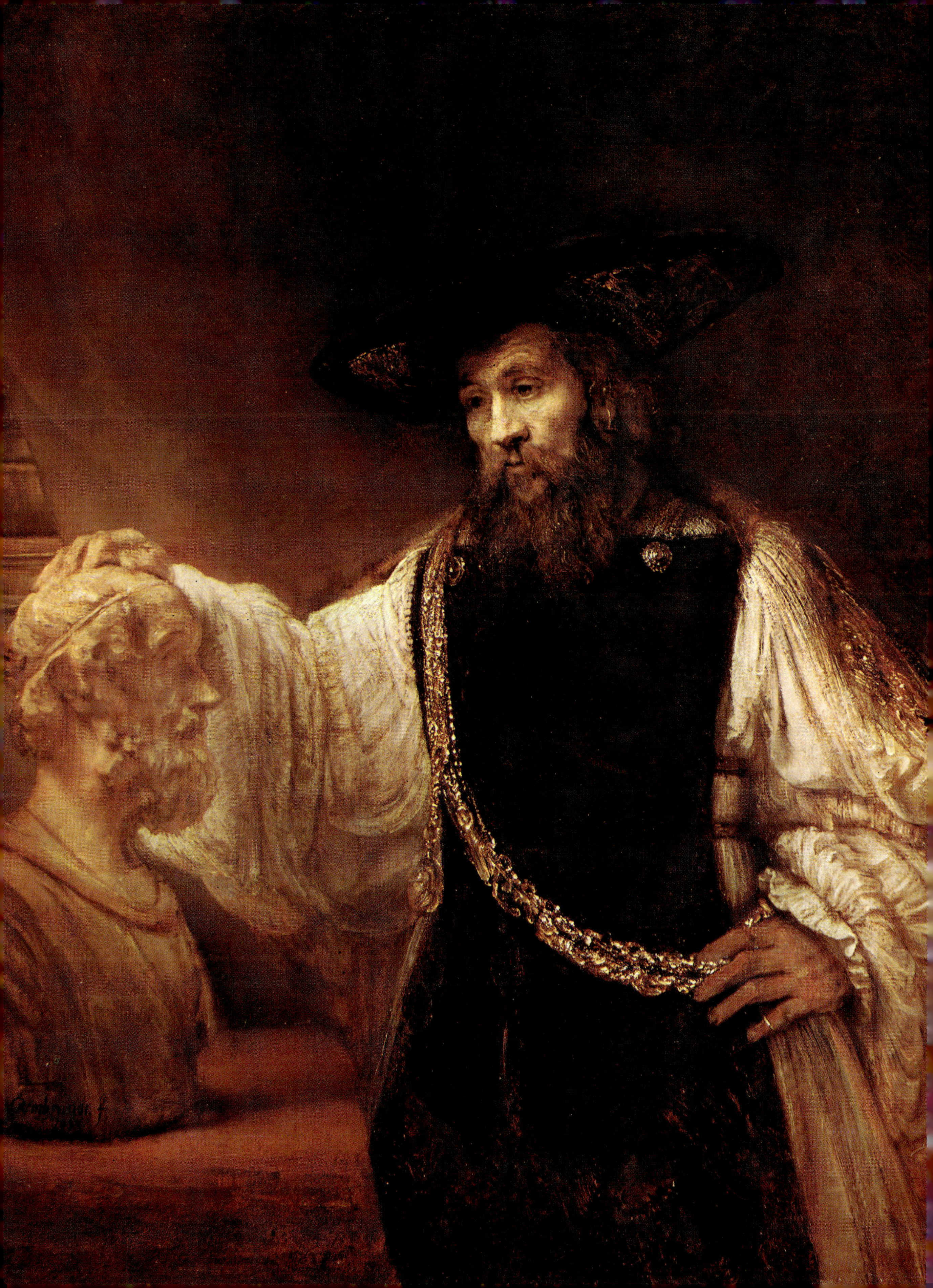

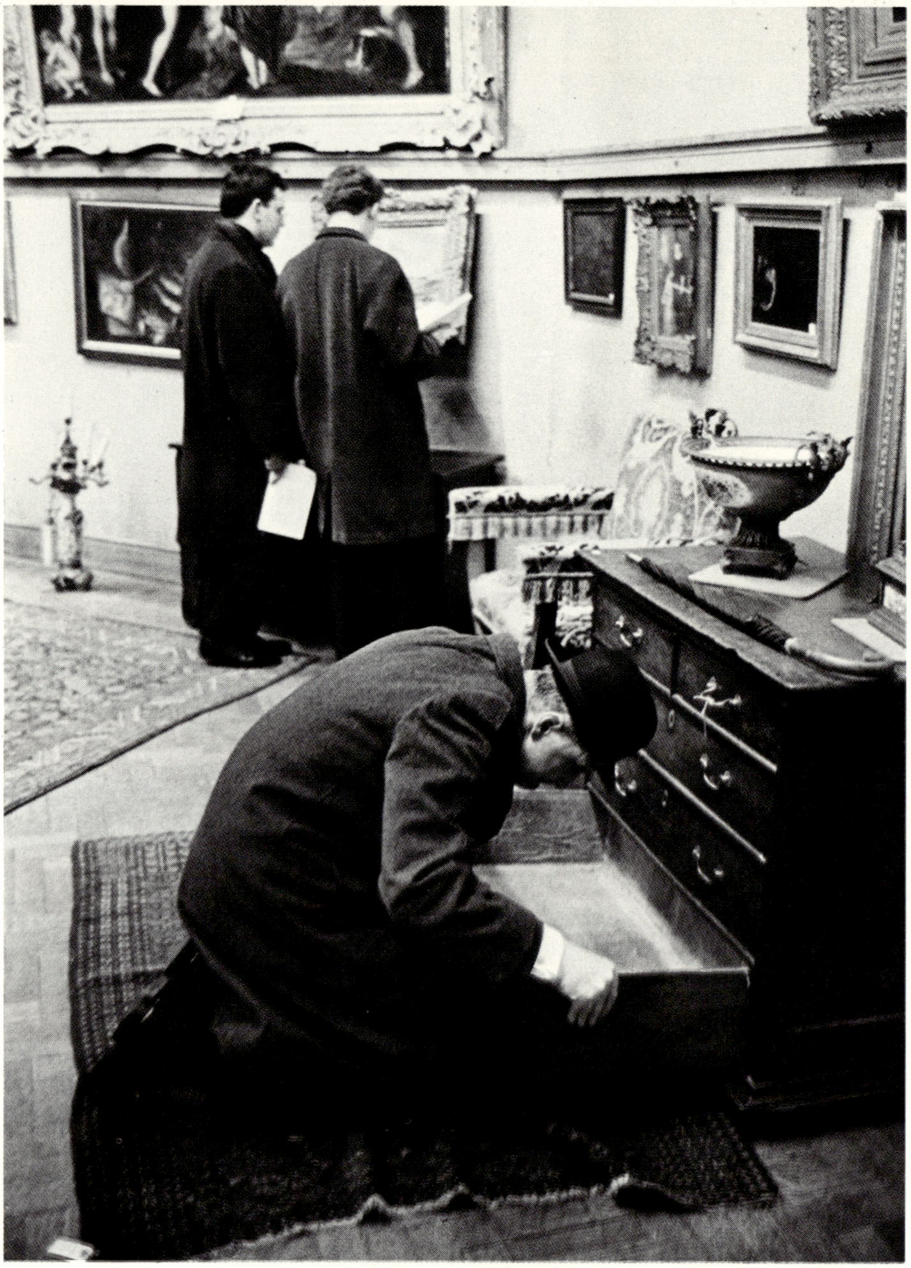

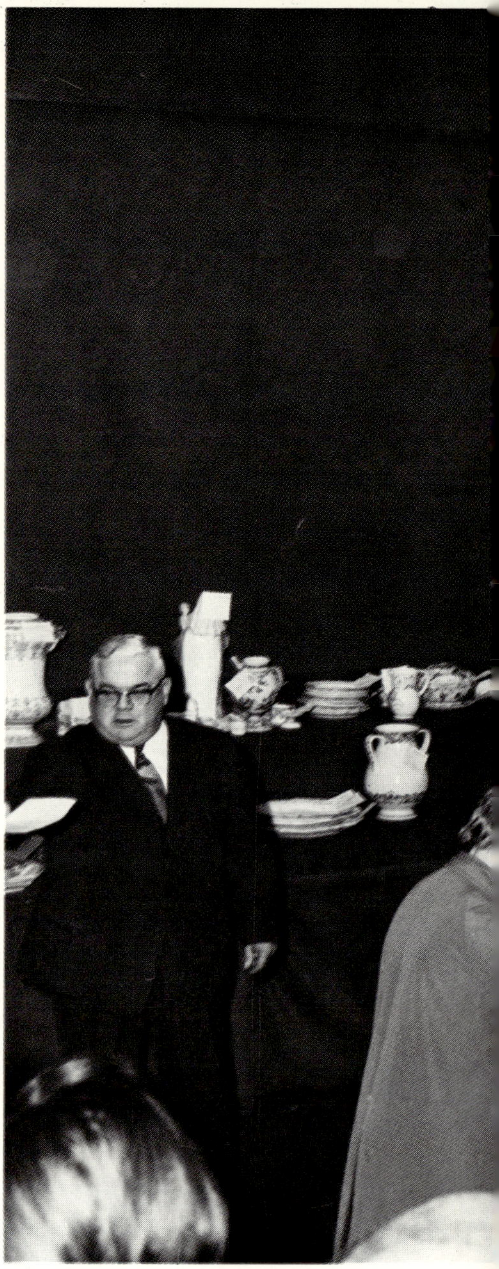

Vienna, and Hauswedell of Hamburg, concentrate on, what to British and American eyes, seem to be specialised old masters.

Recent sales have included Gothic reliefs in limewood, life-size heads of Buddha and stone figures of Vishnu, areas of taste which are still not widely popular outside central Europe.

Despite these somewhat restricted areas of taste, the international art market is becoming increasingly *international*. A Degas, a Henry Moore, a Rothko, or a Rembrandt will almost certainly fetch much the same price in any one of the world's major auction rooms. Buyers come from all over the world–Sotheby's claim they have buyers from more than 70 countries–and this has made works of art an international currency to be exchanged almost anywhere.

In England auction houses have become the bustling centres of the art trade. But in South America and countries like Spain and Portugal, dealers do not have the direct competition of public salerooms. If people do not buy or sell to home dealers, they often send works of art to the London, Paris, or New York salerooms.

Sometimes, an individual dealer in a country without an auction house will organise his own public sale of art works. For example sales are organised by the Finanziario per l'Arte in Milan, which exists for the express purpose of financing transactions in art and antiques. But there is much more to an auction house than the mere buying or selling of art.

In the world's major auction houses, art scholars and historians are on the staff to help buyers and sellers alike. Identifying works of art accurately is any auctioneer's constant problem. Experts are also available for valuations for insurance, probate or family division. A definite identification of a work of art by one of the leading auction houses is usually worth its weight in gold. Positive identification and proof of a picture's origin–usually called its provenance–is usually a collector's safeguard when he buys.

'The auction houses have encouraged people to come from all parts of the world to bring their fine art, and

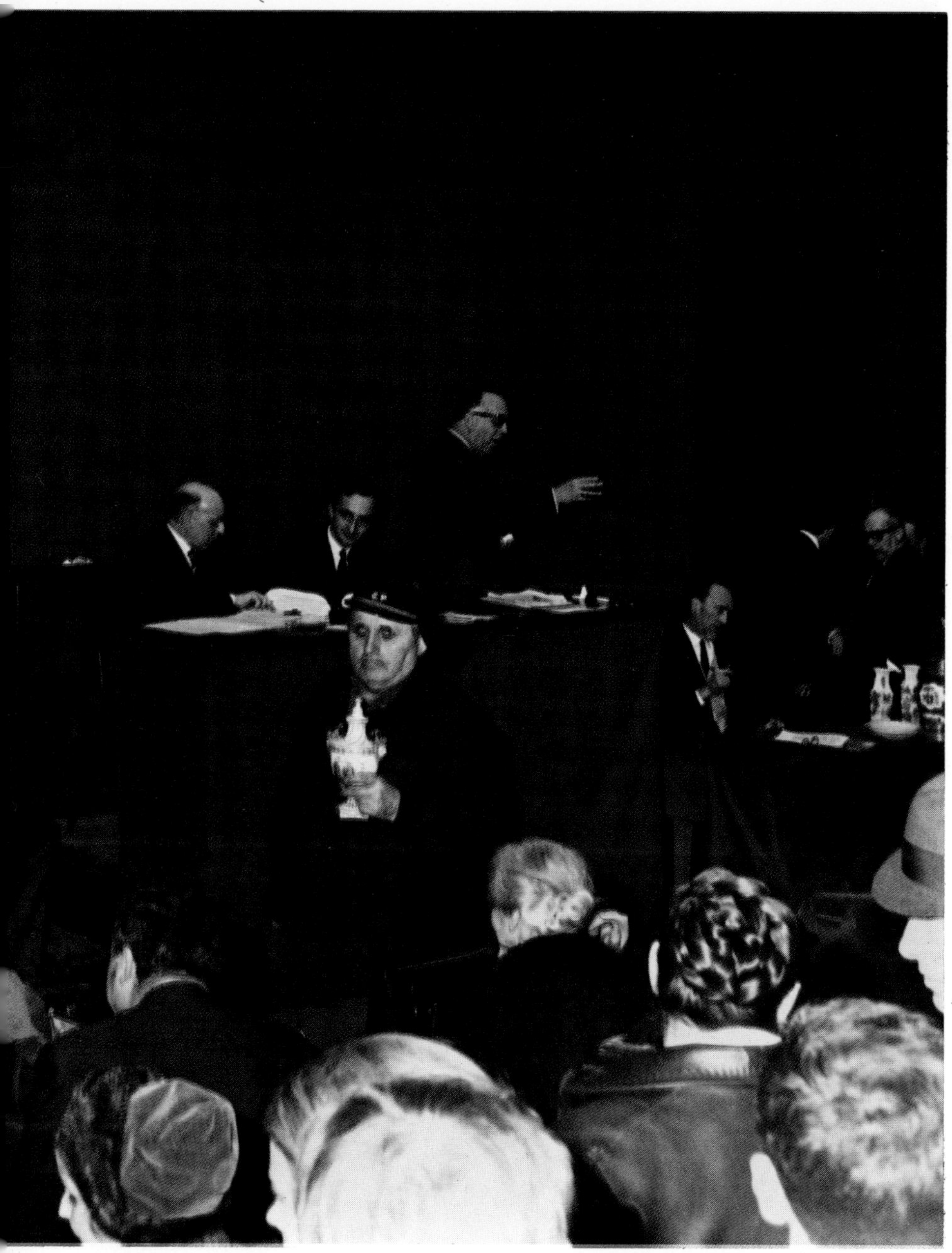

also to buy it,' says Stanley Clark of Sotheby's. 'After all, Britain also has the greatest reservoir of fine art of any country in the world. We've also a pretty good reputation abroad for fair and honest business.

'Selling modern art in the saleroom has been very successful. The first sale of British pictures fetched £19,000 for about 130 pictures. There has been a sale every year since then and every total has gone up year by year. In 1965, 130 pictures realised £84,000.

'Sotheby's turnover for the 1965-66 season ended by reaching a record of £21,426,720 of which the London total was £13,026,720 and Sotheby's Parke-Bernet Galleries in New York £8,400,000. The London turnover was £914,555 more than the year before, and that in New York, a record for North America, showed an increase of £3,500,000 on the previous season. Apart from Sotheby's, the Parke-Bernet turnover is higher than that of any other auction house in the world.

'Sotheby's went out to make a house to which anyone who was interested in fine art could come to buy and sell. Therefore in 1966, out of a turnover of £21½ million, 75 per cent of the lots were sold for less than £100. In fact, 28 per cent were for £20 or less. More than 70 countries send sellers to Sotheby's and almost as many send buyers. Even the Soviet Union, Hungary and Czechoslovakia send fine art to London.'

'The basic function of an auctioneer

Fine art salerooms are now at the bustling centre of the art market, and the record prices in London, New York or Paris regularly make headlines. Rembrandt's *Aristotle Contemplating the Bust of Homer* shown on page 111 fetched more than two million dollars at the Parke-Bernet Galleries, New York (now in the Metropolitan Museum of Art, purchased with special funds and gifts of friends of the Museum, 1961)

Before an auction astute bidders carefully sift through the lots which are soon to come under the hammer (left)

The uninitiated must tread carefully in the salerooms. Traps and tribulations await anyone who does not know the basic rules. Here (right), in a French auction room, valuable porcelain is up for sale is to sell works of art, on behalf of owners, for the highest possible price,' says Bruce Chatwin, until recently a director of Sotheby's. 'That is to say, it is different from a dealer who wants to buy a work of art as cheaply as possible.

'Sometimes we track collections down to the ends of the earth; we're always on the look-out for new collections to sell.'

Suppose somebody buys a picture which he believes to be by Goya, and which is attributed to Goya in the saleroom catalogue, and later finds out as near as can be judged possible that it is not by Goya. Has he any grounds for bringing the painting back? Fortunately, with the Misrepresentation Act in Britain the buyer now has the right to send back an item if it were proved that it wasn't by the artist named in the catalogue.

Art dealers use the salerooms as a grand clearing for works they cannot or choose not to sell in their own private galleries. They also use the auction house to do a bit of price-fixing.

A dealer may have three watercolours by a minor old master, which would probably make £80 at auction. He puts one in a sale and with an accomplice bids himself until the price has reached, say, double what the trade would expect. The dealer has bought his own picture back (and paid commission), but he has also succeeded in raising, for however short a period, the market value of his two other watercolours.

The prices of pictures sold at Sotheby's, Parke-Bernet, Christie's or at any of the minor auction houses provide a rough guide to what we might expect to pay in a private gallery. For example, if a dealer is selling a Graham Sutherland gouache for £250 and an almost identical picture sells at Christie's for £320 he will almost certainly raise his price to bring it in line with the saleroom.

If you are selling a picture remember that the auctioneer charges a commission, normally 12 per cent for lots under £100, 10 per cent for items over £100, and 8 per cent for the trade, on the prices realised. Above all, remember to place a reserve price. Otherwise, the picture which you believe has a market value anywhere between £100 and £150 may be knocked down for as little as £10.

The commission rates charged by auction houses vary considerably from country to country. On the opposite page are the charges of auction houses in nine countries.

International demand for works of art and antiques has risen at the same time as, and in some cases as a direct consequence of, the huge demand for gold all over the world. One New York dealer told me that inflation was a dealer's best friend. 'If you don't believe me, ask any American auctioneer,' he added.

Mr Eric Shrubsole, of the New York branch of S. J. Shrubsole, has just repurchased a George II coffee pot which he sold to an American collector in 1956 for $275. Recently he paid $3,600 for it and expects to sell it again at a fair profit.

In 1957 he sold a silver cup and cover for £1,750 and recently repurchased the same piece for $3,750. 'Twenty years ago antique silver was the cheapest item of all the arts,' he says. 'Today it is a fantastic money investment, partly because of its disappearance from the international market.'

A spokesman for Parke-Bernet, the New York auctioneers, said: 'Many items which come up for sale, particularly pictures, are baffling many of our clients because they don't know the names of old masters who painted them. In other words little or unknown artists' work is fetching some astonishing prices. This is in keeping with an overall rise in prices: economic uncertainty on the stock exchange and elsewhere is a major cause of the recent and growing scramble for art works.'

But as art writer Gerald Reitlinger wrote recently: 'Those who gasp in wonder at the latest auction prices, seldom reflect that their green crisp pound notes mean little more than the half crowns of the days of the sovereign-purse. The figures have a mystique and a poetry of their own simply as figures.'

Mr Stanley Clark, of Sotheby's, says prices and activity have increased since devaluation of the British pound. 'More people have been coming to the sales, and more people are buying than ever before,' he says.

'Since devaluation we've had more than 1,000 new clients every month. Less wealthy people are buying. In fact, 70 per cent of the things sold at auction by us go for less than £100. We expect more sales and a lower average price.

'Recently we've seen an enormous increase in the prices of relatively and hitherto unknown works of art. For example, a year ago we couldn't sell the work of William Huggins, the Victorian animal painter.

'Today his paintings are fetching at least £800 or £900. Provincial schools like the Norwich school or the Smyth brothers, of Ipswich, are rising in price phenomenally. I paid £5 10s. for a picture by one of the Smyth brothers two years ago, now it would fetch more than £1,000. Modern English drawings are going up all the time.

'Two magnificent L. S. Lowry paintings fetched £260 and £250 respectively in 1960. Now, they just couldn't go for less than £6,000. With inflationary fears they could go for as much as £7,000.'

Before the appearance of British artists like Henry Moore, Ben Nicholson, Barbara Hepworth, Francis Bacon and even Sir Winston Churchill, the top saleroom performers were always French, Russian or Spanish.

Despite an overall price rise in the world's auction houses, certain areas of taste have taken a tumble. A change in the taste of influential collectors invariably has an immediate effect on prices. For example, the majority of 18th century British portraits which art dealers like Duveen and others sold to American multi-millionaires in the first quarter of this century have *fallen* in value since the war. But they had a long way to fall because they had been sold at prices—especially artificial prices—which still surprise saleroom observers who are practically immune from the shock of 'millionaire' art prices.

When the Stotesbury Collection was sold in New York in the 1940s the result was a chilly warning to art speculators who have come to think of salerooms as Aladdins' caves. Following his initial investment of many millions of dollars Stotesbury lost no less than several million dollars. The moral is clear: buy what you like, but buy it cheaply.

But the uninitiated must tread softly in the salerooms. Traps and tribulations await anyone who does not know the basic rules.

Even men familiar with saleroom techniques and bidding habits occasionally trip up. When the collector

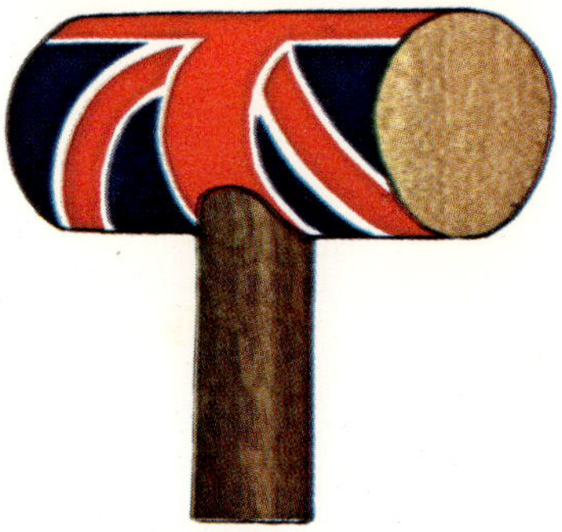

GREAT BRITAIN
12 per cent commission up to £100
10 per cent commission over £100
8 per cent commission to the trade
No taxes for foreign sellers
No taxes for domestic buyers
No Customs duties

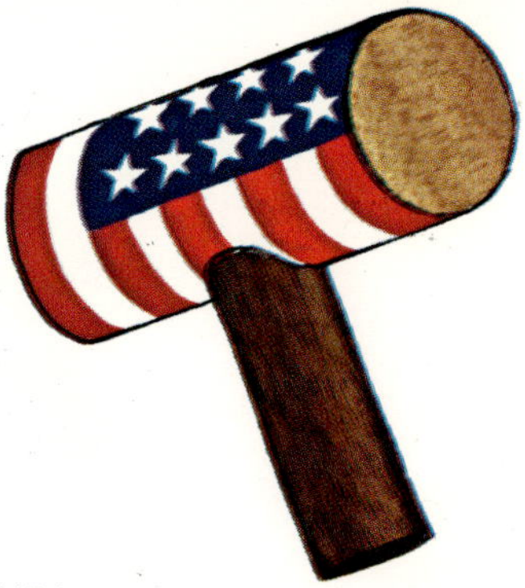

USA
$12\frac{1}{2}$-15 per cent commission rate
+10 per cent Federal sales tax (silver and jewellery)
+ 4 per cent New York City sales tax (on all works of art)

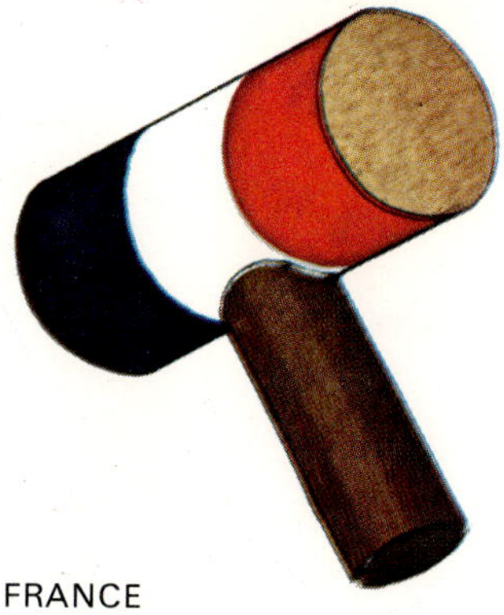

FRANCE
Average of 11 per cent commission rate
Buyer's tax:
16 per cent up to 6,000 francs
$11\frac{1}{2}$ per cent from 6,000–20,000 francs
10 per cent above 20,000 francs

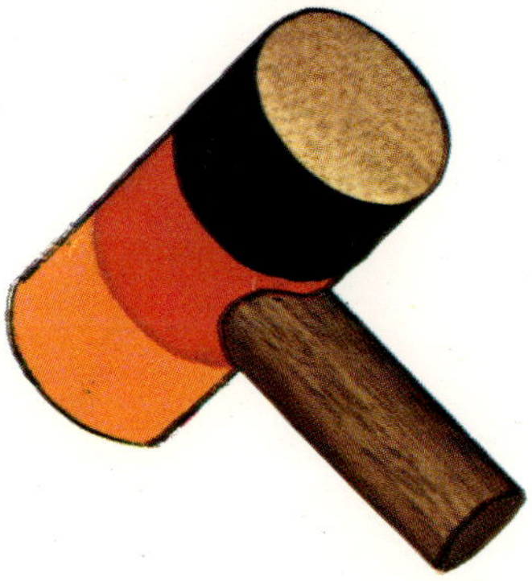

GERMANY
15 per cent commission rate
+ 10 per cent Federal tax

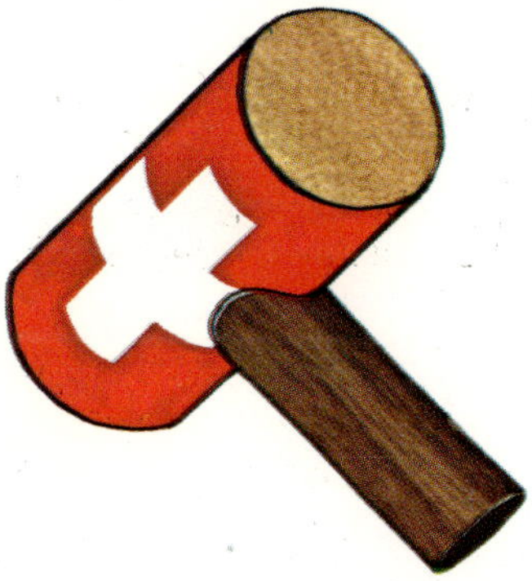

SWITZERLAND
15 per cent commission rate (Prints, drawings and illustrated books)
20 per cent commission rate (Collections of items fetching less than £40)
10 per cent commission rate (Items fetching more than £2,500)
+ 10 per cent Federal tax

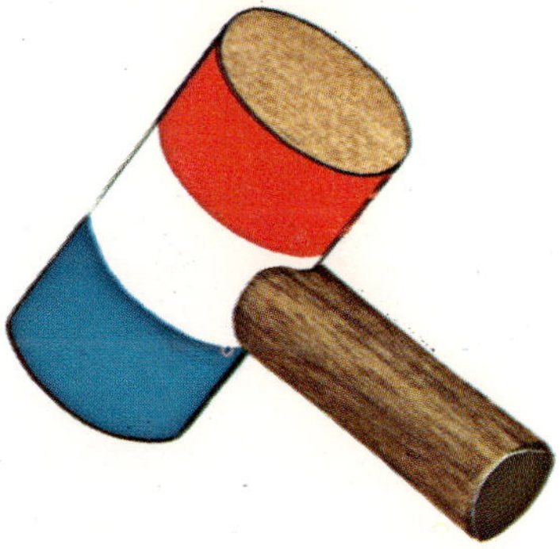

HOLLAND
16 per cent commission rate (private persons)
11 per cent commission rate (dealers)

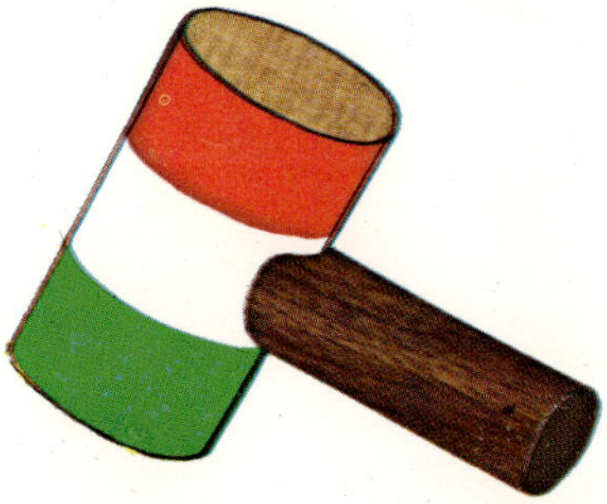

ITALY
15 per cent commission rate
+ 10 per cent buyers' and vendors' taxes
Also up to 30 per cent Excise tax on works of art

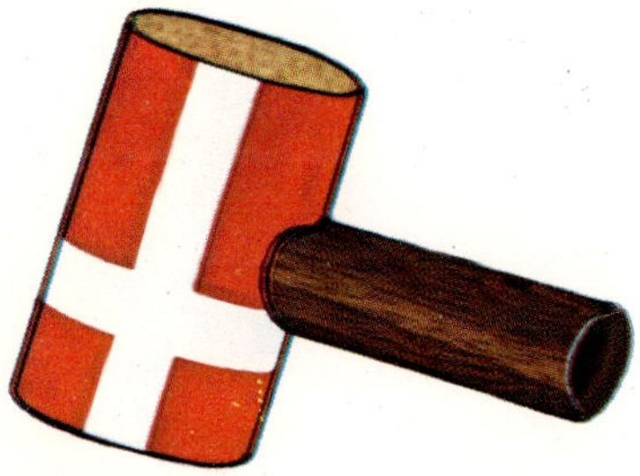

DENMARK
Commission rate + taxes 20 per cent

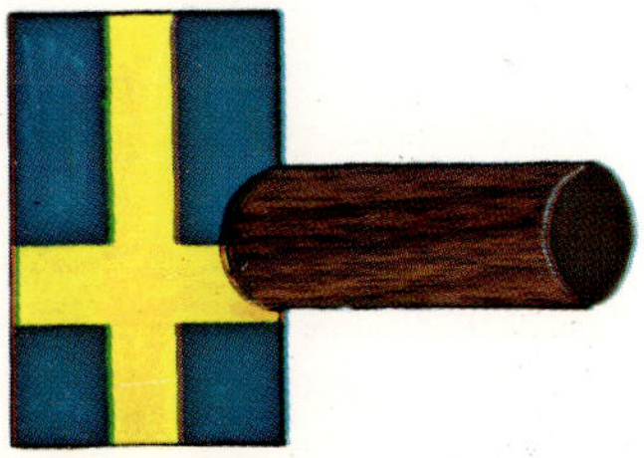

SWEDEN
Commission rate + taxes 20 per cent

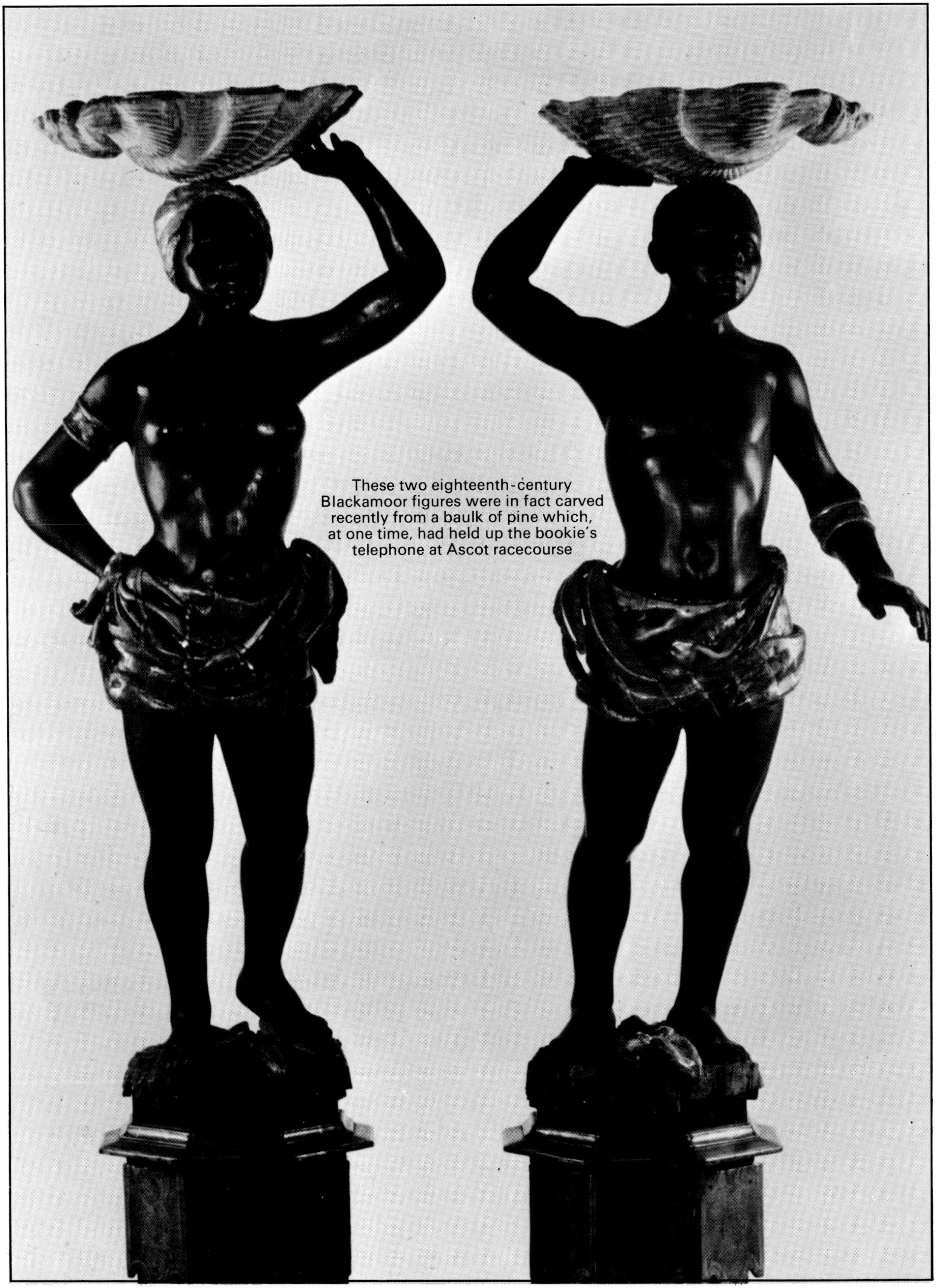

These two eighteenth-century Blackamoor figures were in fact carved recently from a baulk of pine which, at one time, had held up the bookie's telephone at Ascot racecourse

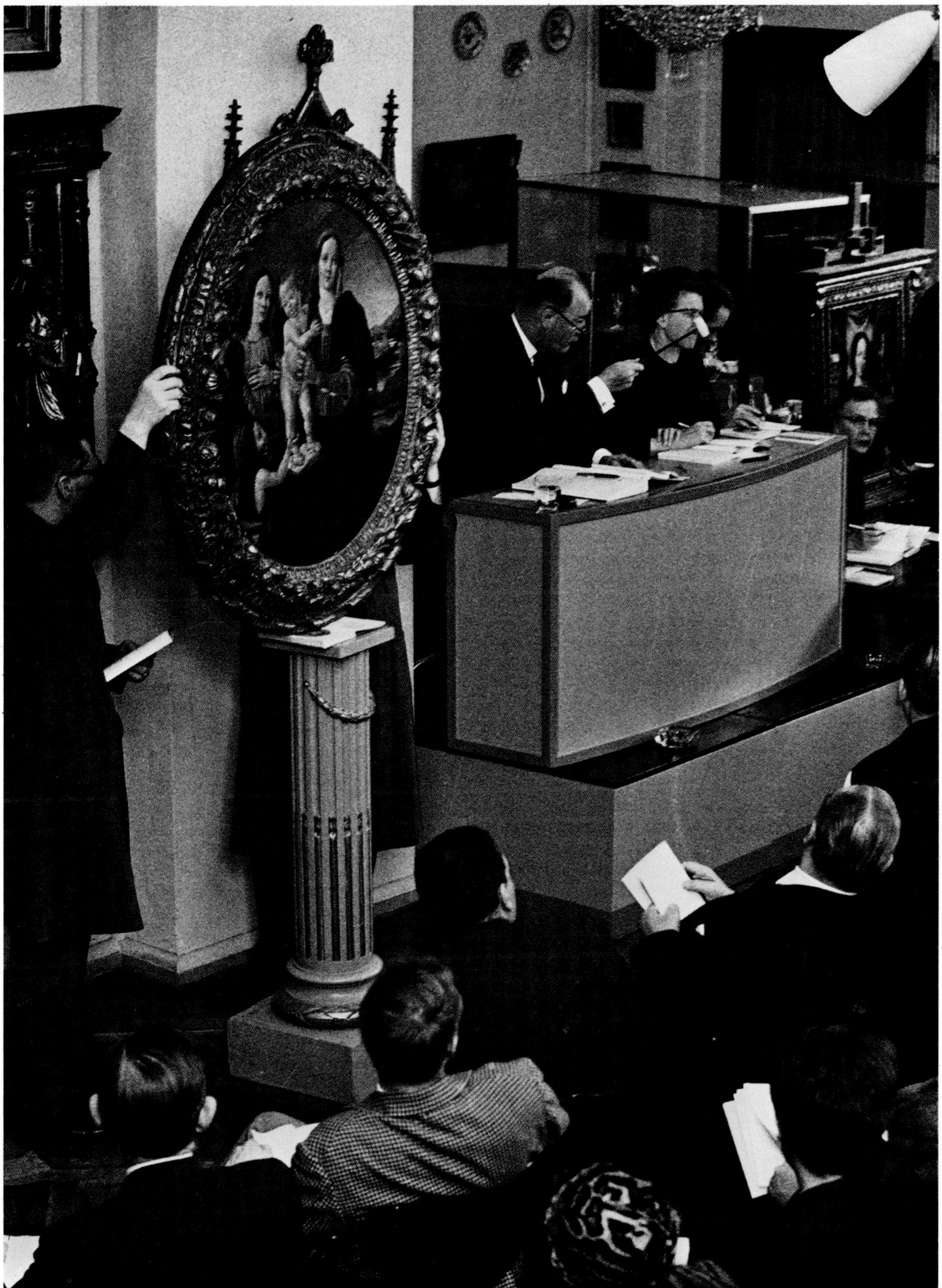

There's not much redundancy among the ranks of the art forgers these days. There is plenty of work for the man who can restore a drawing into a watercolour, add an impressive signature to an unsigned painting, or, better still, produce an 'original' forgery.

Of course, forgers like the Dutchman Han van Meegeren, who successfully fooled several experts with his 'Vermeers', or the Frenchman Jean-Pierre Schecroun, who swindled many art collectors with his Picasso, Braque and Miró forgeries, are few and far between. Most forgers today find it difficult enough to change a cheap print into an expensive lithograph. (Done by removing the printer's mark with a strip of scotch tape run neatly along the bottom edge of the print.)

There's no shortage of artists who are technically capable of painting in the style of anyone you care to name, but the fact is that few are tempted to fake pictures. The art trade also has its own resistance towards fakes, partly because they can glut the market and lessen the scarcity value. Not surprisingly, art forgers are always more active during an art boom. Reports of international art forgers, dishonest dealers and saleroom swindles regularly make the headlines in newspapers and magazines. Recent examples have included 'The great art-fake game' in the *Sunday Times*; 'Not very bright art gang–woman expert sums up' in *The Times*; and in the London *Evening Standard*: 'The Texan, the playboy, the $1m. collection–I unravel the art story of the century' by Lord Kilbracken.

Before discussing the modern epidemic of fakes it is worth looking at a few cases in the past. Someone said recently: 'Faking, of course, is as old as art: it is perhaps the second oldest profession. And, like the oldest, it has its boom periods.'

When Michelangelo was 20 he carved a cupid in marble. The cupid, which was a copy of an ancient sculpture, was buried for a short time to make it look old. Michelangelo was then paid 30 ducats by a dealer who, in turn, sold the cupid to Cardinal Riario for 200 ducats. Riario, a noted collector of ancient sculpture, imagined he had acquired an important addition to his collection.

The lion's share of the profits from forgery rarely go to the artist. In fact, few forgers even meet or come into contact with collectors. It is the dealer or his agent who carries off most of the proceeds from forgeries. Their function has been likened to a 'fence' in the criminal world; they are the 'respectable' link between the forger and the client.

During an art boom prices are determined by supply and demand and popular trends. Michelangelo 'faked' an ancient sculpture because this happened to be in great demand. More recently, the forgery of more modern works of art has followed the tremendous demand for them. Forgers concentrate on artists whose work now fetches high prices.

The ease with which today's forgers sometimes swindle art collectors and dealers can be judged from several recent exposures in the press and in the courts. Today's art world is wide open to the unscrupulous. This was proved by an experiment with a fake picture. Robert Dumont-Smith, professional painter and a regular contributor to the Royal Academy's summer exhibition, was commissioned to paint a picture in the style of Christopher Wood.

Wood was only 29 years old when he died in 1930 and his pictures now fetch anything up to £5,000 in the salerooms. He is a difficult artist to fake because a largely complete record of his work exists and the chances of an unknown oil painting suddenly turning up are remote.

Dumont-Smith painted a 24 × 36-inch picture in the style of Wood in under two hours. The picture was painted over a Victorian portrait, the brittle-hard paint of which was allowed to show through the Wood to give a feeling of age. The back was then covered with brown paper, a few rusty nails and some dust and then put into a period wooden frame. It was ready for its début.

The Redfern Gallery, who had handled Wood's pictures both before and after the war, and Terence Mullaly, the art critic of the *Daily Telegraph*, were both sent a large photograph of the work. An accompanying letter asked that the picture be identified. The Redfern Gallery thought it might be an unknown painting by Christopher Wood and invited the owner to bring the picture into the gallery for closer examination. Mullaly thought that the painting was by Wood, but it must be emphasised that both were judging from a photograph.

Later the Redfern saw the picture and were suspicious about its origins. (In fact they have a complete record of all Christopher Wood's paintings.) The research girl who took the picture to the Redfern told them that it had been given to her by her boy friend but she didn't have his name or address. Two days after this meeting the Redfern Gallery, to their credit, asked for the picture to be taken away from their premises.

It was then entered at Sotheby's for

The fake Christopher Wood painting that had experts guessing was produced in less than two hours. The various stages from drawing to finished work are shown here

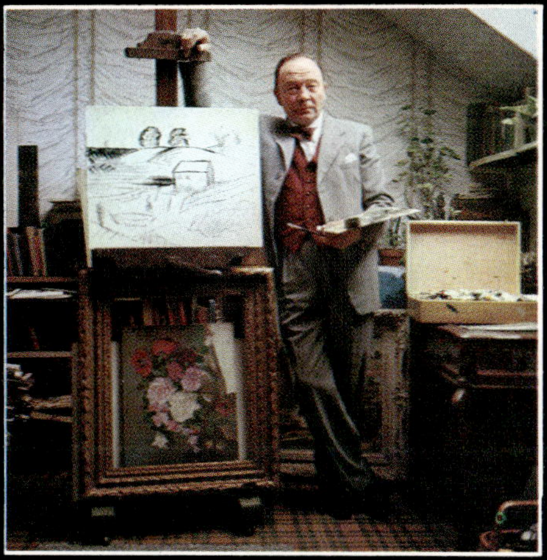

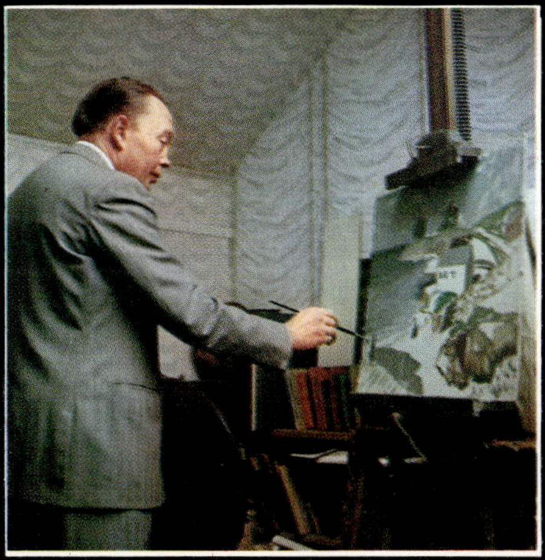

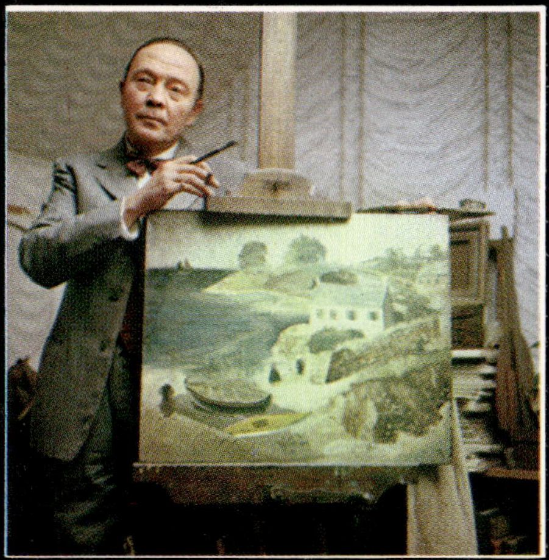

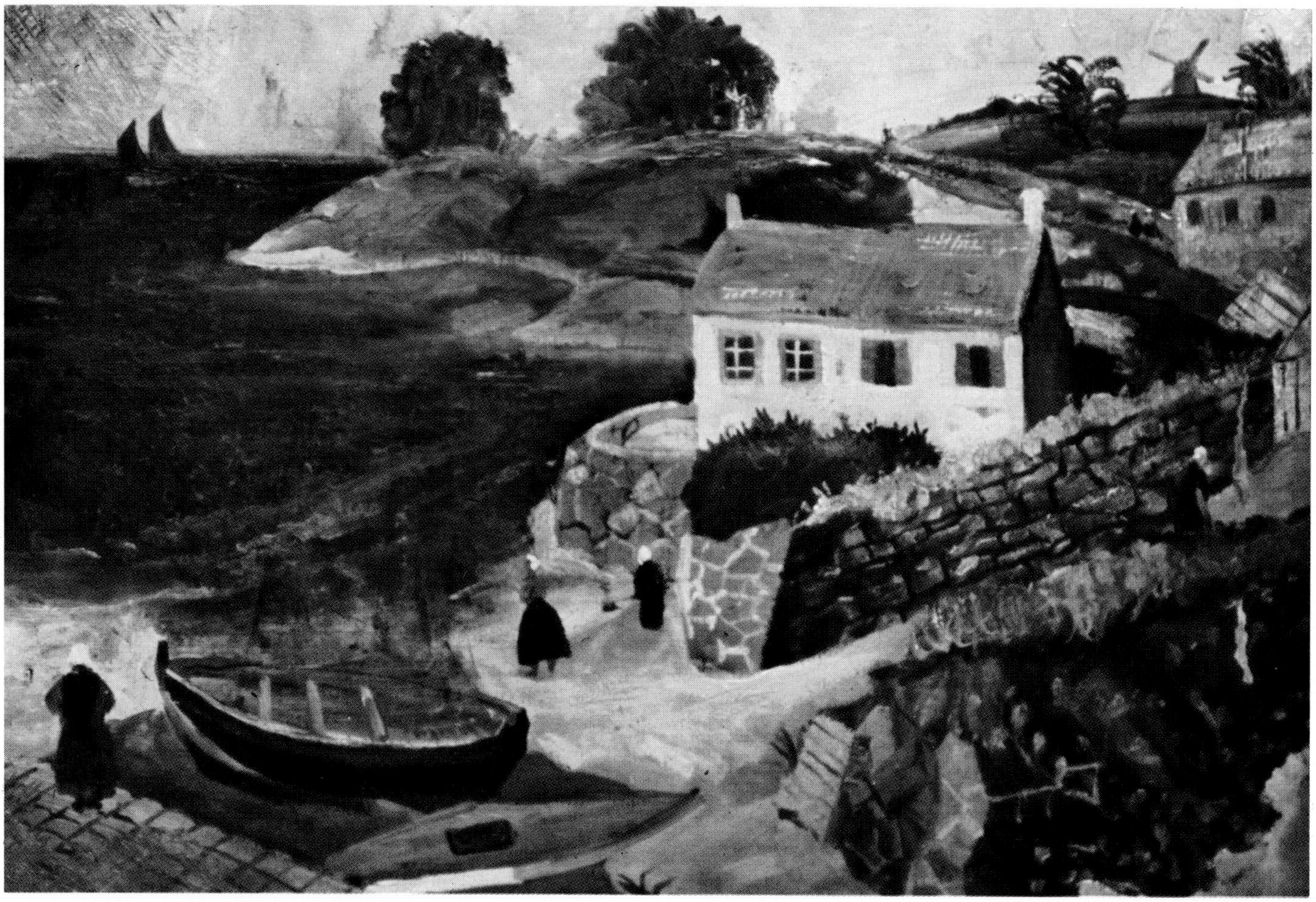

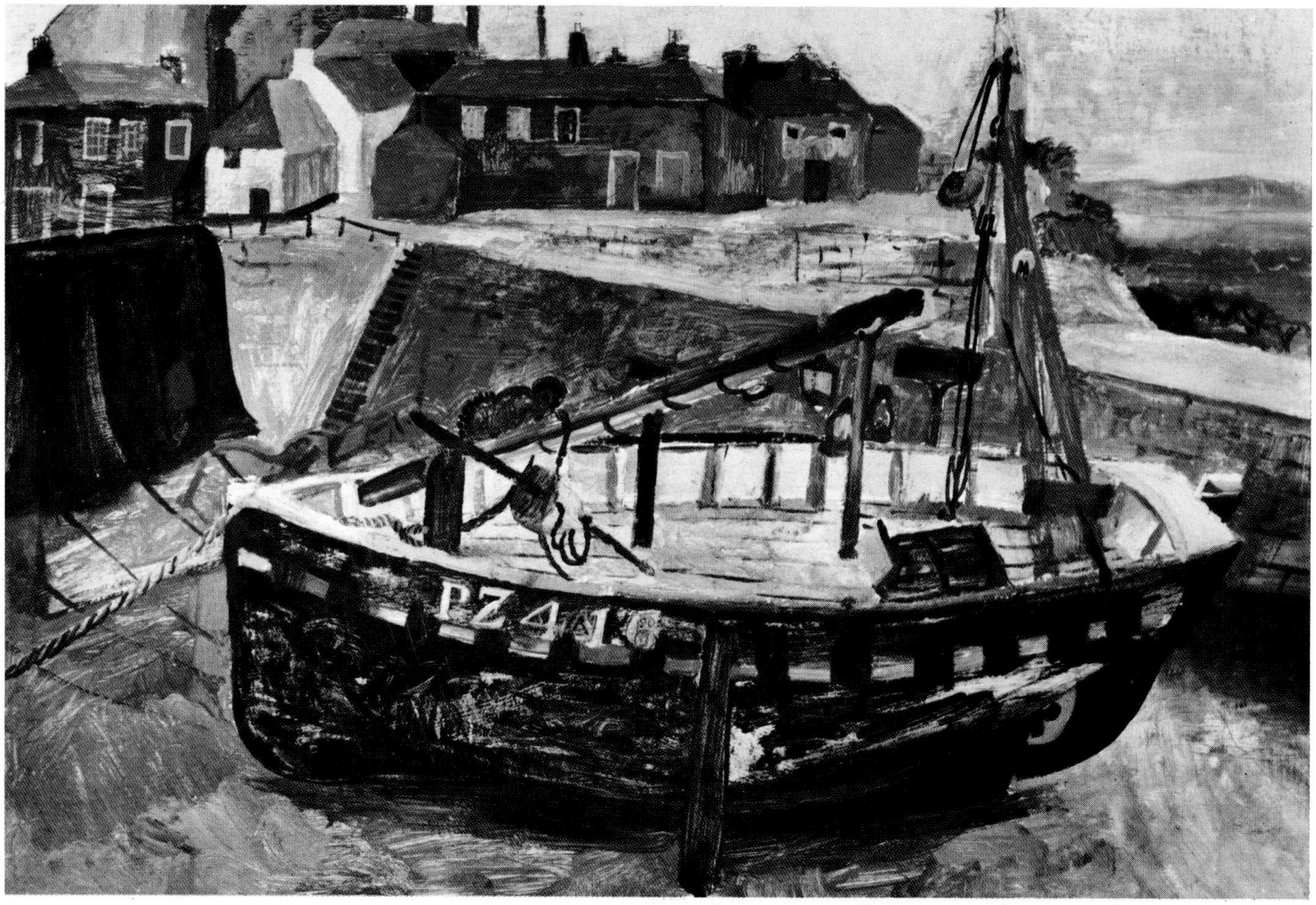
PZ41

The fake Christopher Wood painting (above) incorporates several well-known characteristics such as black-shawled fisherwomen, a canoe, a fishing boat and a typical view of Treboul in Brittany, a favourite spot of the artist. For comparison, a genuine painting by Wood entitled *PZ416 Cornwall*. It was painted in 1930

a forthcoming sale of modern pictures. After keeping the picture for several weeks, a normal procedure, Sotheby's fixed a note to the picture saying 'check this with the Redfern Gallery', but not before one of Sotheby's assistants thought that it was 'definitely a Christopher Wood and should fetch about £500 in the Salerooms'. If it had been by Wood it would fetch at least £2,500. Presumably the picture was checked with the Redfern because the picture was finally refused entry into the sale.

Another research assistant then approached six well-known London art galleries. Four of them believed that the picture was probably by Christopher Wood, although the researcher made no mention of his name. Only the Crane Kalman Gallery suggested that it was a fake.

The Grosvenor Gallery suggested that the Treboul scene could have been by Christopher Wood but was probably by a contemporary. The Alwin Gallery made no comment and added that they charged a fee for identifying pictures.

A girl at the Piccadilly Gallery thought that the painting looked like a Christopher Wood and would be worth between £400 and £500. The Lefevre Gallery thought that at first glance it looked like a Christopher Wood, but it could be by someone else but they didn't know who. Gimpel Fils assumed that it was by Christopher Wood.

The experiment with the Christopher Wood goes some way to support what many people already believe: that comparatively few dealers are scholars and anyway it is difficult to distinguish between the genuine and the fake. If the Christopher Wood had been produced for fraud and not as an experiment, in a year rather than in two hours, had been chemically treated, baked in an oven, given a provenance and likely story, it could be in a public collection today.

Buyers of art-works must remember the old Latin tag *caveat emptor* (let the buyer beware). However, with the new Misrepresentation Act which came into force in Britain in April 1967 the buyer can now revoke a contract within a reasonable time irrespective of whether the mistaken attribution was made fraudulently or in good faith. But if you're buying a picture by a well-known artist *insist* that the receipt includes a provenance, its history from the time it left the artist's studio and a list of the experts who have pronounced it genuine. Of course, if the provenance has been forged, which is not unknown, you have problems.

The major salerooms *reject* on average about a fake a day. The problem is not really the fake itself, but its provenance. 'Making a mongrel into a poodle is one thing,' said one well-known American dealer, 'but acquiring a respectable pedigree makes an operation tricky for the forgers.'

Nowhere was this more obvious than in the case of Jean-Pierre Schecroun, one of the big names in the history of international forgery. Schecroun was sentenced in 1962 to a two-year jail sentence and a fine of £4,000 for a number of astonishing exploits in the fakes market. He was alleged to be able to paint a picture in the style of Picasso, Braque, Léger, Miró, Picabia and Soulages, not bothering with cheap copies or the alteration of well-known paintings. Presumably many of his pictures are still circulating in the art world.

One visit Schecroun made to London in 1961 had both interesting and profitable results. Setting up in a well-known London hotel, Schecroun sent his assistants around the West-End art galleries to find out their particular interests and the level of their stocks. Were they short of Picasso watercolours, Braque gouaches, Léger paintings or Miró watercolours? Armed with this information Schecroun apparently began producing his work for the London dealers and drying it on the hotel radiators. Later, his assistants, elegantly dressed and breathing French respectability, delivered the watercolours and gouaches to the dealers for inspection.

In some cases the assistants also included impressive provenances with their wares. The gang stole rubber stamps and official headed writing paper from the Galerie Maeght in Paris, then Braque's agents. The whole operation was efficient, swift and professional. Altogether Schecroun and his assistants made £20,000 during their ten-day visit.

Two dealers in London who bought work from Schecroun's assistants were Jacques O'Hana of the O'Hana Gallery and Robert Estorick of the Grosvenor Gallery. O'Hana was especially pleased with a Braque he'd bought and showed it to Estorick. Suddenly one of them noticed that

Making copies of Greek sculpture played an important part in the art of Imperial Rome. This Roman head of Dionysus (below) was made in a style fashionable in Athens five or six centuries before. Jean-Pierre Schecroun (right), who was alleged to have swindled many art collectors with his Picasso, Braque and Miró forgeries, is seen here looking at their signatures which he has painted on the wall of his Paris studio

Not all fakers create new pictures, many merely make copies of pictures by well-known artists. Here (below), an Otto Wacker copy of a painting by Van Gogh is almost exactly the same as the genuine thing (above)

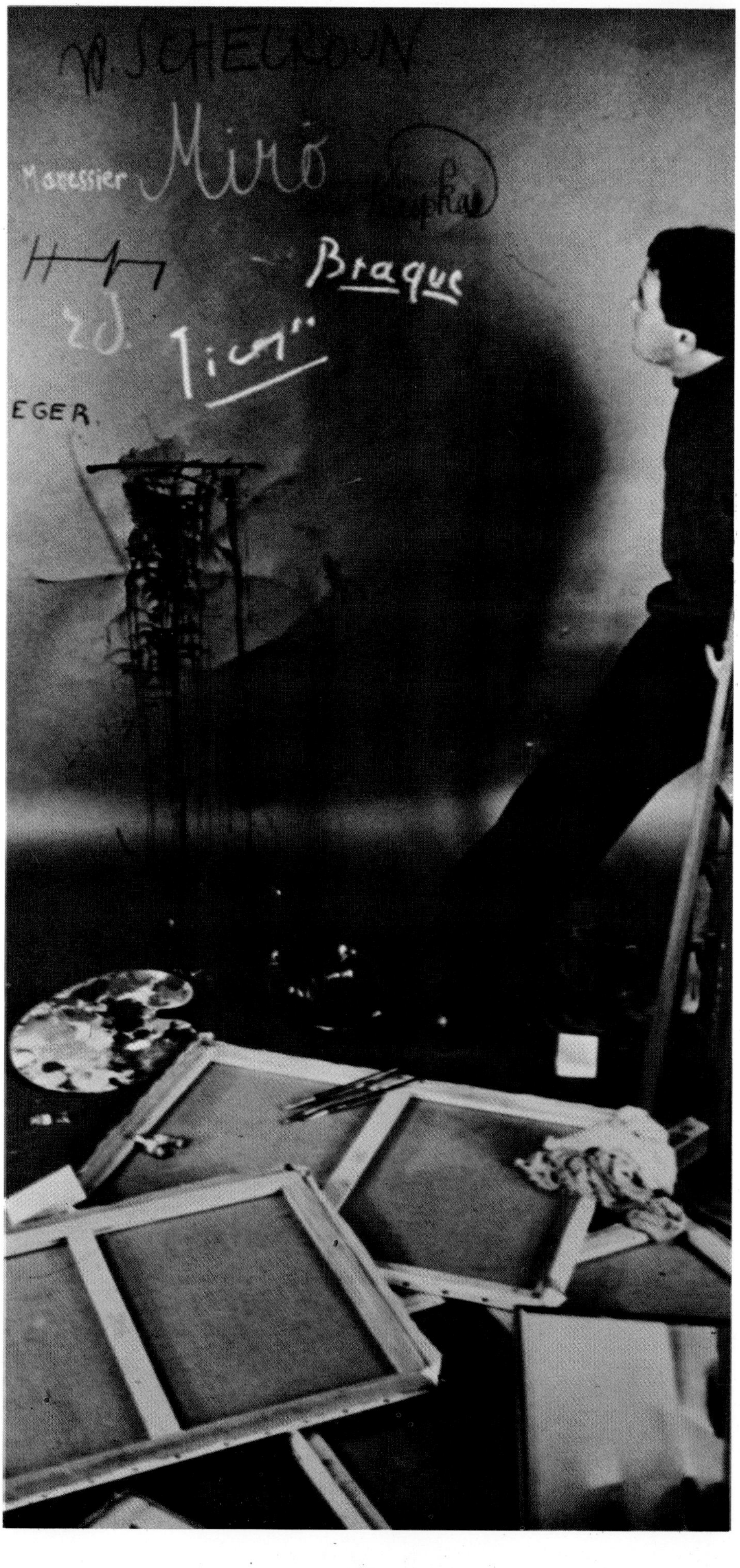

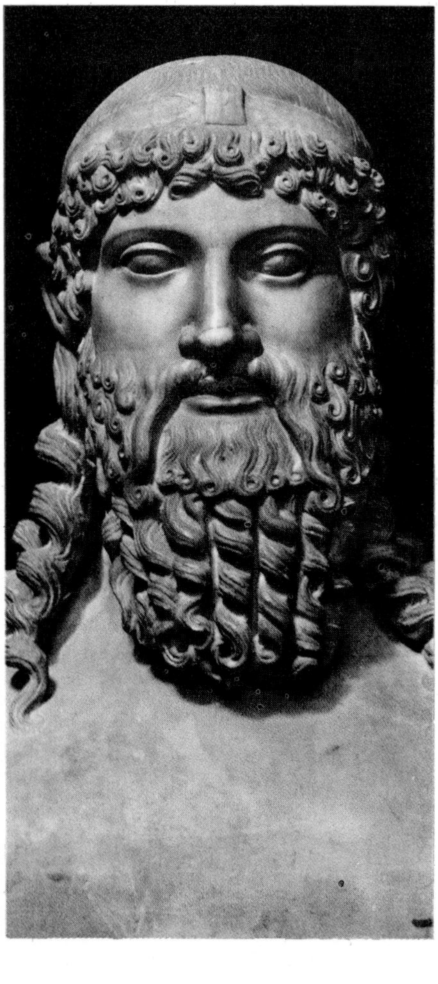

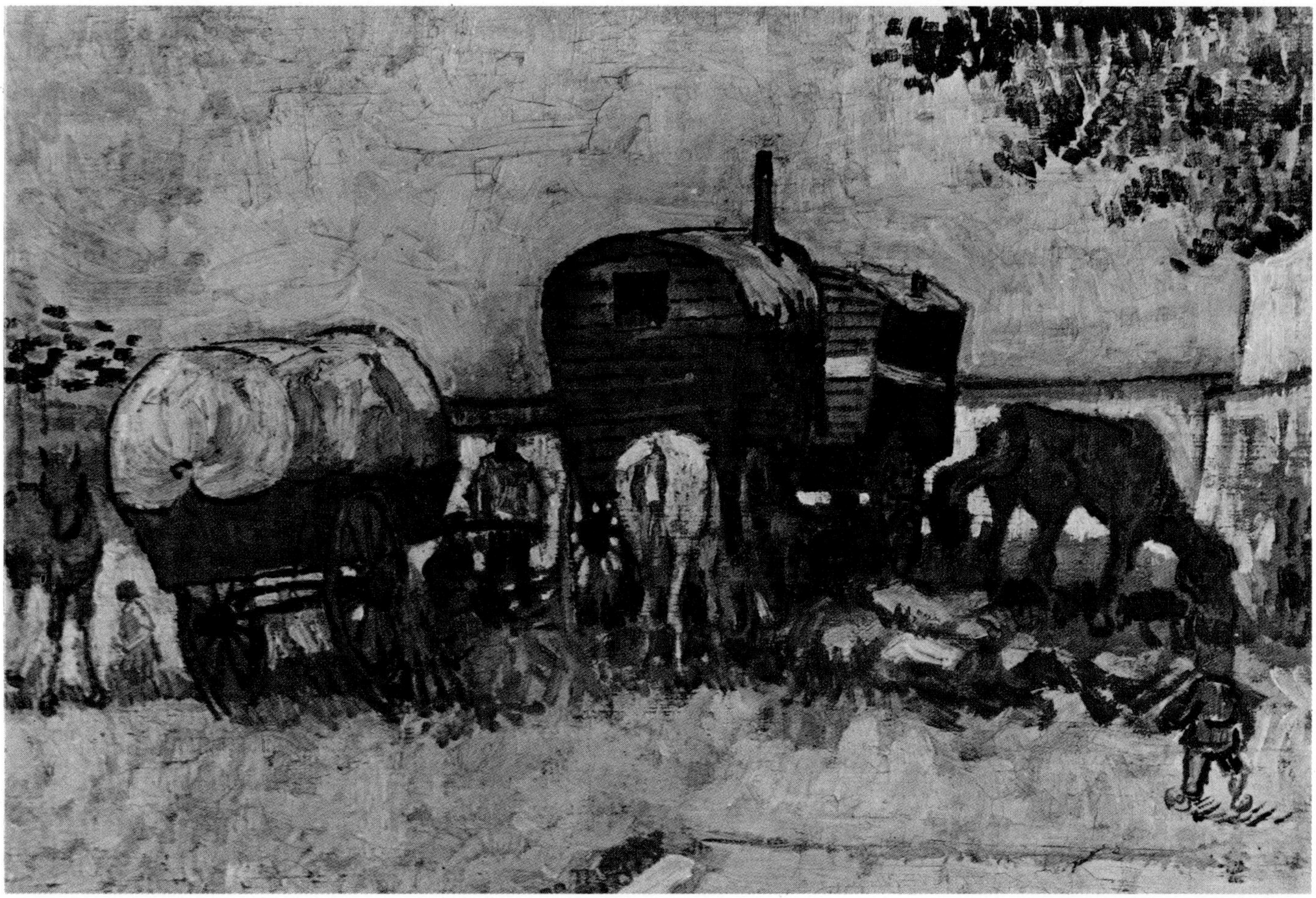

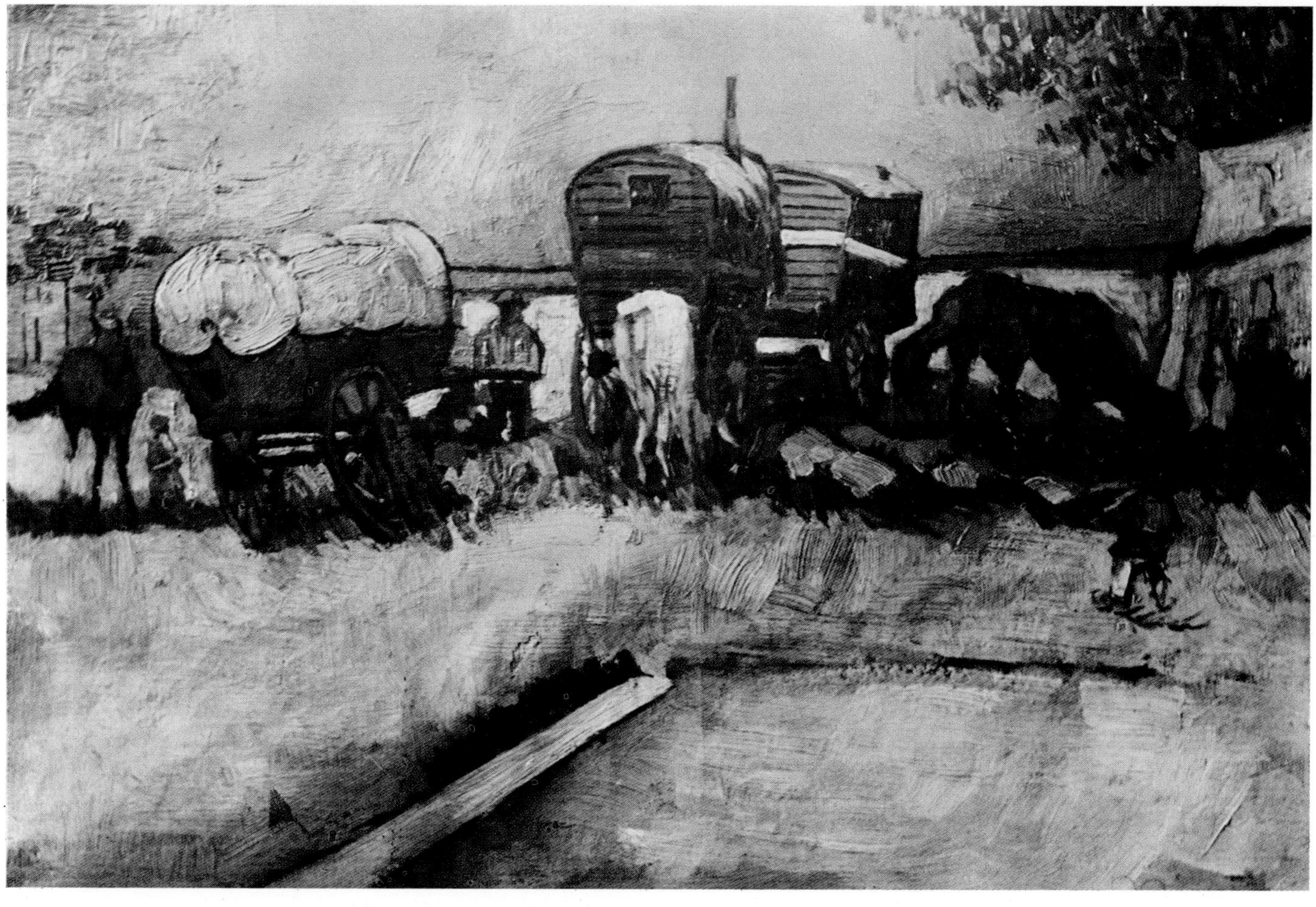

their latest purchases were all on the same kind of paper. Immediately they called in the police who started investigations.

Schecroun himself was eventually caught in his Paris apartment.

Van Gogh has certainly not escaped the attention of forgers. Unknown and despised during his lifetime, some of Van Gogh's work was destroyed when he died. Fortunately for the forgers, no record of his paintings was kept.

Furthermore, Van Gogh often painted the same subject many times over and this made the forger's task even simpler. Versions of well-known paintings by Van Gogh still turn up in junk shops, 'flea' markets and even minor salerooms. Several variations of his famous self-portraits, painted at different times during his life, have appeared since his death. Dealers often claim that a hitherto unknown 'Van Gogh' has been discovered in one of the regions in France, Belgium or Holland where he was known to have lived.

One of the biggest scandals in the history of art forgery was centred around fake Van Goghs. During an exhibition of paintings by Van Gogh at the Paul Cassirer Gallery in Berlin in 1927 some of the exhibits were considered to be forgeries. Experts who had doubted the authenticity of thirty-three of the one hundred Van Goghs discovered that all the questionable Van Goghs were from the collection of Otto Wacker, a part-time dealer, which was said to have come from a Russian living in Switzerland. If his name was divulged he and his family (who still lived in the Soviet Union apparently) would suffer the most serious consequences for exporting works of art without an official permit. Wacker also claimed that the pictures did not have a provenance because, for the sake of the pictures' safety in Russia, it had been destroyed, Police investigations followed and Wacker was eventually sentenced to a term of one year's imprisonment.

The case of Otto Wacker's Van Goghs did not end with his imprisonment. Seven years afterwards the dispute flared up again and whereas most German experts considered the Van Goghs to be fakes, other experts, notably Dutch, considered they were genuine. Nationalism seemed to take the place of scholarship.

Van Gogh's nephew has been exposing every instance of forgery of his uncle's work he has been able to uncover. Some years ago he said: 'I had indisputable proofs of their activities in my hands. But I found myself faced with impregnable defences erected by rich and powerful persons, in whose interest it was that certain secrets should not be revealed.'

Rich and powerful persons were involved in the case of Han van Meegeren and it was this fact alone which led to his arrest and eventual imprisonment. Van Meegeren's downfall came in 1945 when two Dutch police officers called upon him at his Amsterdam studio, 321 Keizersgracht. He was charged with collaboration with the German Occupation forces by selling a picture by Johannes Vermeer of Delft (1632–75) representing *Christ and the Adulteress* to Alois Miedl who was well known as a buyer for the German Nazi Hermann Goering. The price was $495,000.

Rather than face a charge of high treason Van Meegeren 'confessed' that he had painted the Vermeer. 'The painting discovered among Goering's possessions in Germany,' he said, 'representing *Christ and the Adulteress* is not a Vermeer, as you assume, but a Han van Meegeren. I myself executed it.' Not surprisingly, he was laughed out of court. 'You must and shall believe what I say! I defrauded the German Marshal Goering but not the Dutch Government,' he claimed.

In the early 1930s Van Meegeren was an unsuccessful painter who found life difficult, largely because he felt his work had been ignored by collectors and critics alike. He decided to paint pictures in the style of Vermeer and hoped to fool the so-called art experts.

Van Meegeren's first Vermeer *Christ at Emmaus* was sold to a leading Amsterdam art dealer in Paris and then to the Boymans Foundation for 550,000 guilders. Abraham Bredius, a leading specialist of 17th-century Dutch painting, said the picture was a masterpiece.

Forgers of the quality of Van Meegeren are few and far between. Psychological motives behind his Vermeers were almost as important as the financial rewards. Although Van Meegeren produced another one of his Vermeers–this time it was called *The Young Christ Teaching in the Temple*–he did not convince everyone that all the Vermeers he confessed to painting were *really* by him.

Van Meegeren was meticulous about the smallest details in his Vermeer pictures. The pigment he used was exactly that used by 17th-century Dutch masters, so was the canvas, and even the brushes he used were made of badger hair, which Vermeer used. Van Meegeren baked his finished pictures in an oven so that ordinary solvents, including alcohol, would not remove them. He discovered that if he dipped his brush into a mixture of phenol and formaldehyde he could pass his paint off as seventeenth century. He also invented a middle period of Vermeer's development: this was probably his final masterstroke and the one which convinced many experts that the so-called Vermeers were genuine. Ironically, one of Van Meegeren's forgeries was sold in 1950 at an Amsterdam auction house for only £5. The art world soon washes its hands of frauds which have been uncovered. In the case of Han van Meegeren an unknown painter had, for a short time, been cast into the role of genius.

Controversy about whether a picture is spurious or genuine does not always end in a case of fraud. When the American multi-millionaire and art collector H. E. Huntington bought a picture of two ladies by Romney for $100,000 he didn't doubt the work's authenticity. The art dealer Lord Duveen did. The painting, said to be of the actress Mrs Siddons and her sister Miss Kemble, might be Romneyesque, but Duveen remarked, it was *not* by Romney.

The matter eventually reached the court. By this time, Huntington was convinced that his picture was not a Romney even though some experts claimed it was. Everyone agreed it was a fine picture, but Huntington wanted a Romney and not just a fine picture.

Huntington discovered that on the day Romney was supposed to have painted Miss Kemble and Mrs Siddons, both ladies were out of town. Mrs Siddons was acting in a play in Birmingham and Miss Kemble was on holiday in France. The dealers admitted defeat immediately.

They offered Huntington his $100,000, plus £10,000 costs and

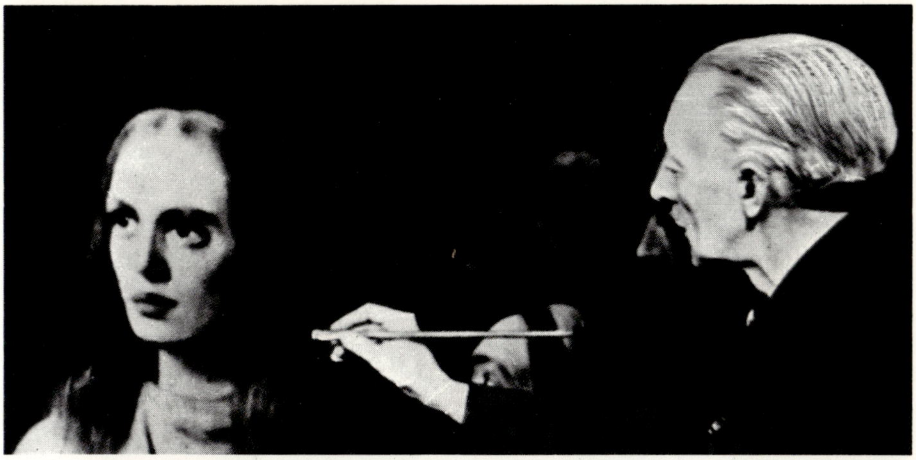

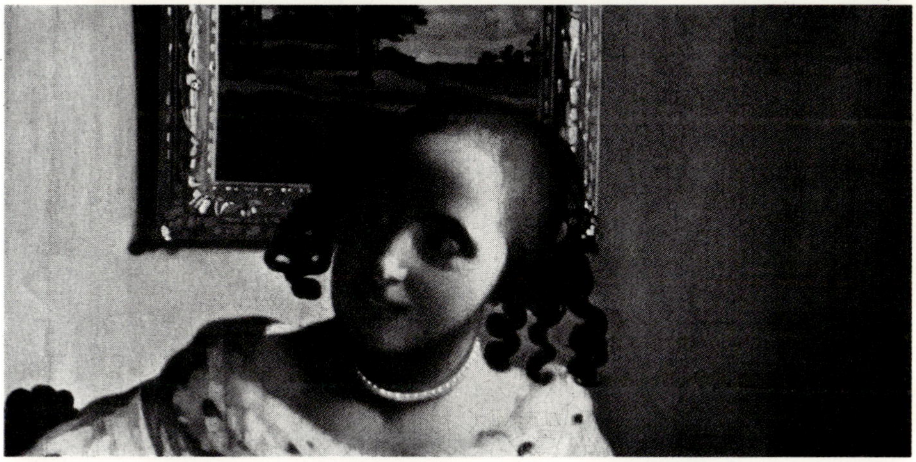

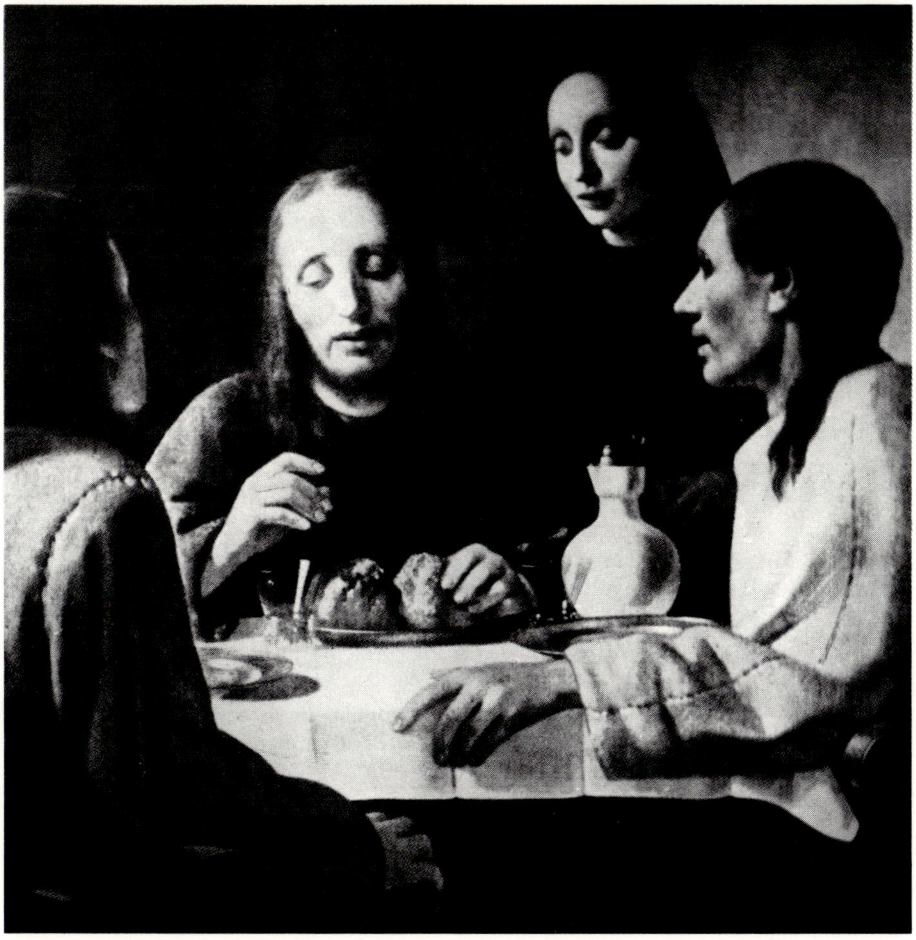

A faker paints away his freedom. Here Van Meegeren fakes a Vermeer in order to make sceptical experts accept his claim. Later he was convicted. He died in prison. This head of a girl (centre) is from a genuine Vermeer, *The Guitar Player*, belonging to the Iveagh Bequest, Kenwood, London.
Christ and his disciples at Emmaus was sold to the Boymans-van Beuningen Museum, Rotterdam, in 1938. After the war van Meegeren confessed that the painting was by him

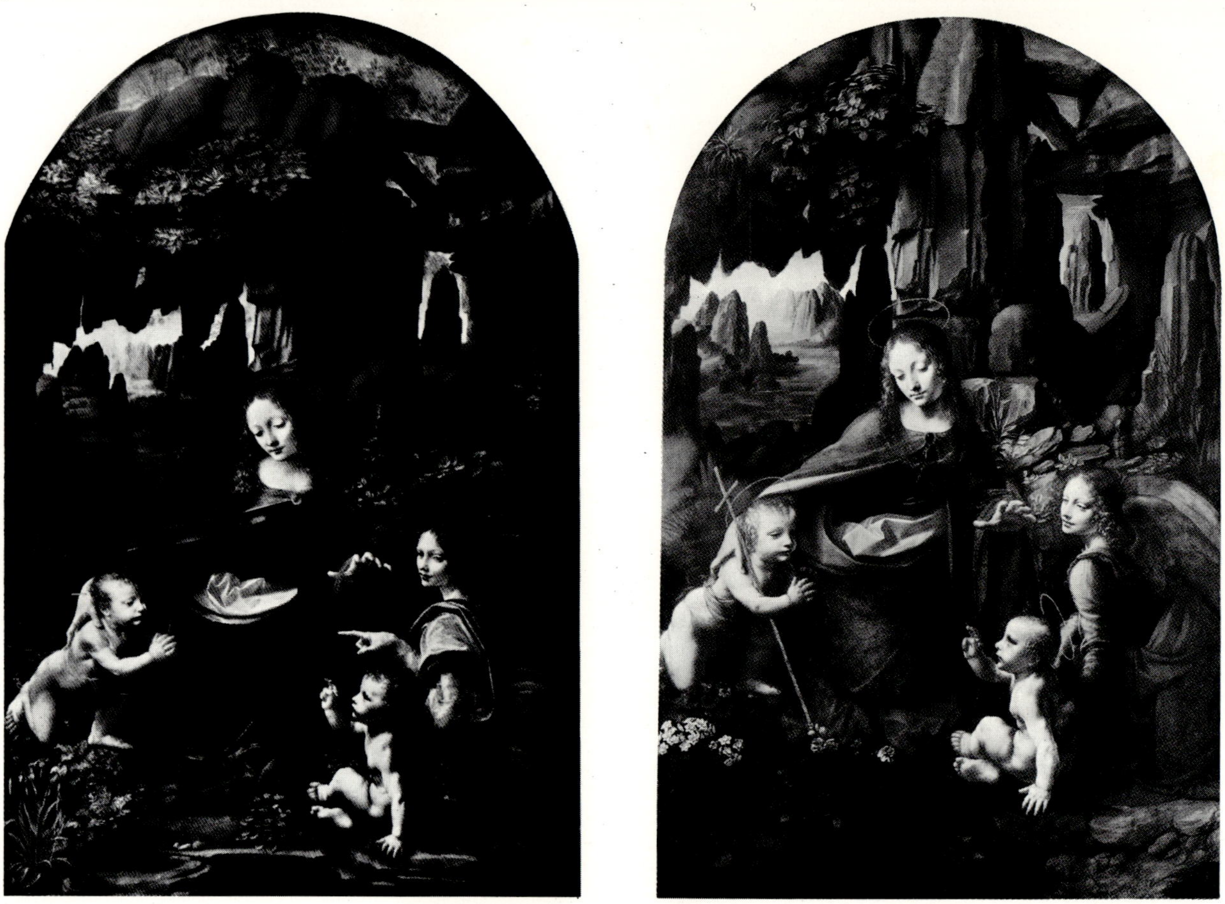

interest. The art dealers who sold Huntington the picture by Romney, which turned out to be by a friend of Romney's, Ozias Humphry, went out of business. Nevertheless Dr George C. Williamson, scholar and art adviser, claimed both during and after the trial that parts of the portrait could be by Romney.

Whether the picture is by Humphry or Romney, or by the united efforts of Romney and Humphry, it is clear that no fraud was intended. Similarly, the twin versions of Leonardo's masterpiece *The Virgin of the Rocks,* in the Louvre and the National Gallery, London, fall outside the realm of fraud. After all, both pictures are said to be by the world's most expensive painter, Leonardo da Vinci. They are an important and valuable part of the two collections and tremendous crowd-pullers.

Few people would deny that museums and their great pictures have a lot to do with a country's prestige, tourism and economy. In fact, never before have the international public given so much time to looking at history's more valuable litter. And never before have the public been so ready to believe what they're told by museum-men and art experts. Most of them are highly qualified and experienced but unfortunately they are not infallible.

Can we be sure that the National Gallery's only painting by Leonardo is *really* by Leonardo? And what about the same picture in the Louvre in Paris: Is that *really* by Leonardo too?

Several British experts believe that the Louvre Leonardo is either spurious or a copy of the London Leonardo. While many European experts think that the London Leonardo is a copy of the Louvre Leonardo. Then again, other people are certain that both paintings are out-and-out fakes. It is unlikely if the truth will ever be known.

It wouldn't be the first time the Louvre has shown a dud. Their experts, to give just one example, bought the Tiara of Saitaphernes, imagining it was a genuine Greek crown of about 200 B.C. In fact, it was made in 1896 by Israel Ruchomovsky at his home in Ouspenskaia Street in Odessa. Eventually the French admitted they'd boobed. But not before the tiara was placed in a prominent position at the Louvre and visited specially by 30,000 people a day.

Of course, the French might well reply: 'What about your Francesco Francia in the National Gallery?' In May 1955 *The Times* published a reproduction of the National Gallery's *Virgin with Child and Angels* by Francesco Francia (1453–1518), a pupil of Leonardo, and a reproduction of another *Virgin with Child and Angels* which was sold at Christie's the previous year. Tests showed that the National's twin didn't have the genuine touch. It was taken off the walls.

Similarly, the National Gallery's *Portrait of Cornelius Van der Geest* by Van Dyck once had a body to it. No longer. The Gallery had to cut it off because they discovered that only the head was painted by Van Dyck. Cornelius Van der Geest's body had been added, as X-ray photographs showed, 200 years ago by skilfully joining two wooden panels together.

Boob for boob the National Gallery and the Louvre probably come out even. But there's still the thorny question of the two Leonardos. Both great museums would have us

These two pictures, both entitled *The Virgin of the Rocks,* are in the Louvre, Paris (left) and the National Gallery, London (right). Can we be absolutely sure, however, that both paintings are by Leonardo da Vinci?

This drawing *Head of a Girl* by Emil Nolde (left) was used by Jupp Jenniches for his forgery (right)

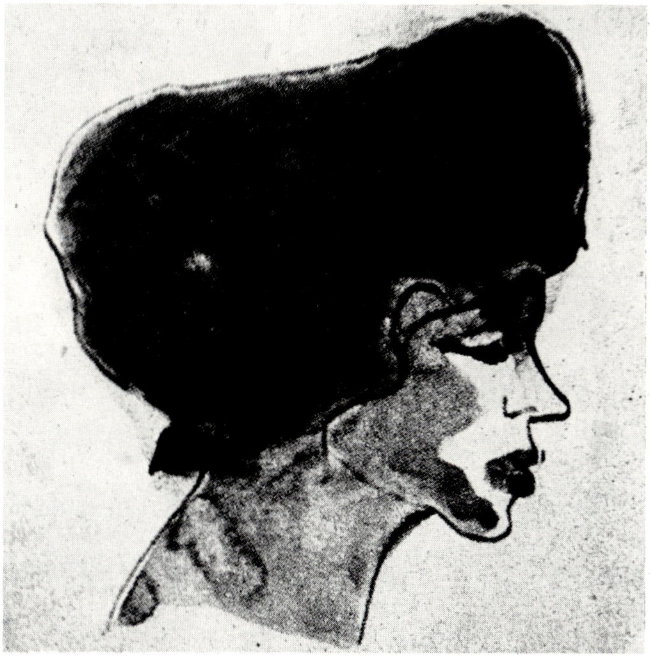

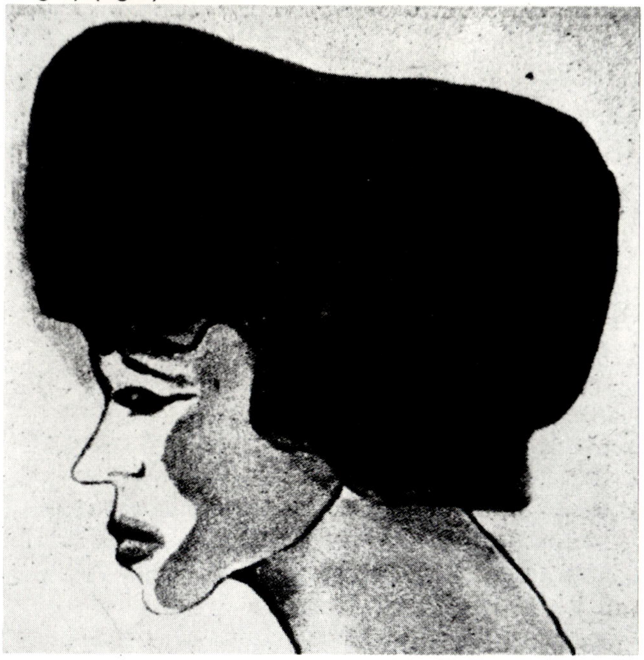

believe that they've got the original and their rival across the English Channel an inferior copy, possibly a fake. Lined up behind them are small armies of specialists reverentially rooting for their favourite twin. For the sake of us outsiders perhaps they could let us in on their scholarly controversy and label each painting: 'This may or may not be by Leonardo da Vinci (1452–1519)'.

The modern art world has lent itself to forgery, copyright and dishonesty more than any period in the past. This is largely because art is now so organised and works of art have an immediate and international value. The most powerful sections of the art scene know the price of practically anything on canvas. Small wonder that the art scene is wide open to the unscrupulous. Juliette Claude Latour, a woman who produced modern art fakes in France after the war, claimed that it was one of the easiest jobs in the world to do.

A German museum attendant also found it easy to copy modern works of art. Jupp Jenniches worked for the Cologne Art Club for more than twenty-five years. His main job was to pack paintings, frame them and sometimes to restore them. Shortly after his release from an Allied prisoner-of-war camp he began 're-storing' pictures which had been damaged in the cellars.

Jenniches was so successful at restoring pictures that he began working for a dealer and collector called Robert Schuppner. Schuppner had already served a sentence of three years in 1942 for dealing in forged works of art. He is alleged to have commissioned Jenniches to produce paintings by Nolde and Klee and several other highly-priced European artists.

Fraud was first suspected by Professor Leopold Reidemeister, Director of the Cologne Museum, but not before several of Jenniches's paintings had entered notable collections. Reidemeister thought a watercolour said to be by Nolde was a fake. He sent it to Nolde who replied that he did not paint it. Other works owned by Schuppner were examined and found to be forgeries.

Many of Jenniches's pictures were just copies. On one occasion he simply traced a female head by Nolde and then reversed it. He could not invent new Noldes or Klees, only copy an original and then alter it to fool the dealers and collectors. His court sentence was light because the judge held that post-war conditions were so severe in Germany that they encouraged swindles of this kind. Schuppner was said to have swopped a Max Ernst for a sack of runner beans, half-a-pound of butter for a George Grosz and a Nolde for some fruit.

The scandal of the museum attendant who could produce modern works of art only increased public suspicion of modern art and the experts who could not distinguish the genuine from the spurious. Matters were made even worse, especially in Germany, by statements made by an unknown artist-restorer called Lothar Malskat. In May 1952 he claimed that the medieval frescoes in the church of St Mary at Lübeck were nothing but forgeries by Dietrich Fey and himself. Few took any notice of his allegations because it was widely known that Lothar Malskat had had violent arguments and disagreements with Dietrich Fey.

Because he was ignored, Malskat confessed to forging medieval paintings while restoring works in Ratzeburg

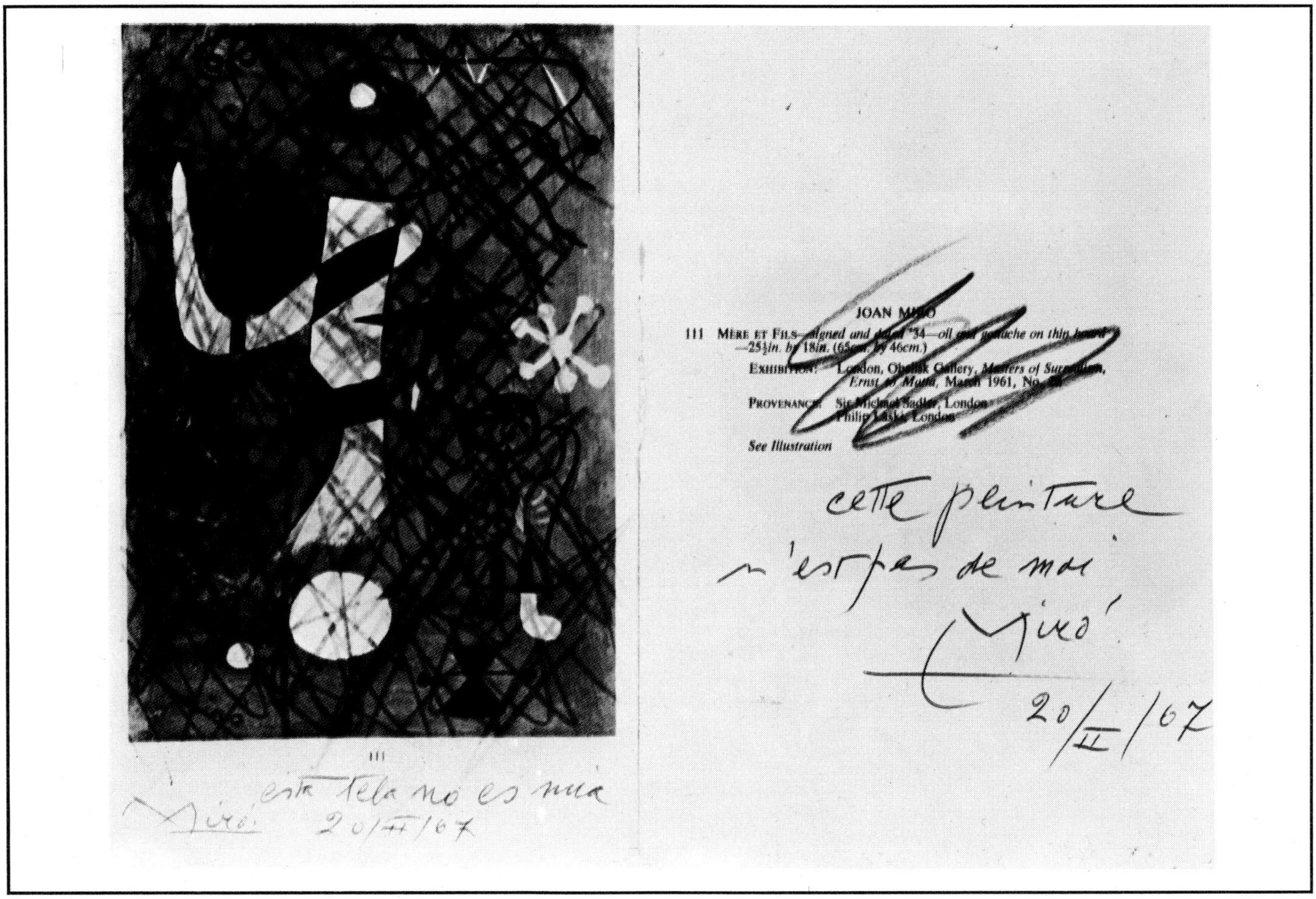

The 'Miró' disowned by Miró. When this painting appeared in a New York gallery the artist Joan Miró was so annoyed that he wrote 'This painting is not by me', all over the page in the catalogue

A bronze horse which scholars considered to be 2,400 years old has been declared a fake by Mr Joseph V. Noble of the Metropolitan Museum of Art, New York. He believes the horse was made shortly before the museum acquired it in 1923. Marks on the bronze show that it had been manufactured by the sand-mould process, which was not invented until the 14th century.

and Schleswig cathedrals. Not only had he forged paintings there, he added, but also in the cathedral and the hospital of the Holy Spirit in Lübeck. Other churches in Lübeck were also mentioned. Although *Die Welt* published reports of his allegations and reproduced photographs of the so-called forgeries alongside reproductions of the ninth-century portrait of a Coptic saint which Malskat claimed he used, few experts were at that time convinced or even suspicious. Malskat confessed to yet more forgeries, this time of more modern painters he had imitated. Finally, Fey and Malskat were sentenced to short terms of imprisonment in 1955.

Meanwhile, Chancellor Adenauer had attended the rededication of the restored medieval murals in Lübeck's St Mary's church. Two million anniversary stamps were issued for the occasion and the event was seen as of special religious and political significance. Then the truth came out: the murals in St Mary's church were forgeries. The Establishment had been taken for a ride–Germany was stunned by the news.

The case of the fake Miró was featured by the *Sunday Times* Insight team in April 1967. The painting first appeared at a London auction on December 19, 1960. It was catalogued as French School; abstract subject–*Woman and Child*, and was sold for £375. A few months later, it turned up at an exhibition called Masters of Surrealism held at a London gallery. In the catalogue it was said to be *Mother and Child* by Joan Miró the Spanish Surrealist. It was sold for £1,500. Six years later, the painting was sold at a Christie's auction of Important Impressionist and Modern Works to the Findlay Gallery of New York for £4,725. Delighted with their purchase, the gallery sent a photograph of the work to Miró himself. Miró immediately disowned the painting and scrawled 'this painting is not by me', all over the photograph in French and Spanish. Thus the affair ended. This is one painting that the highly reputable Findlay Gallery will never sell.

The international scope and far-reaching power of dishonest members of the art scene may be revealed by the Meadows Case–which may yet

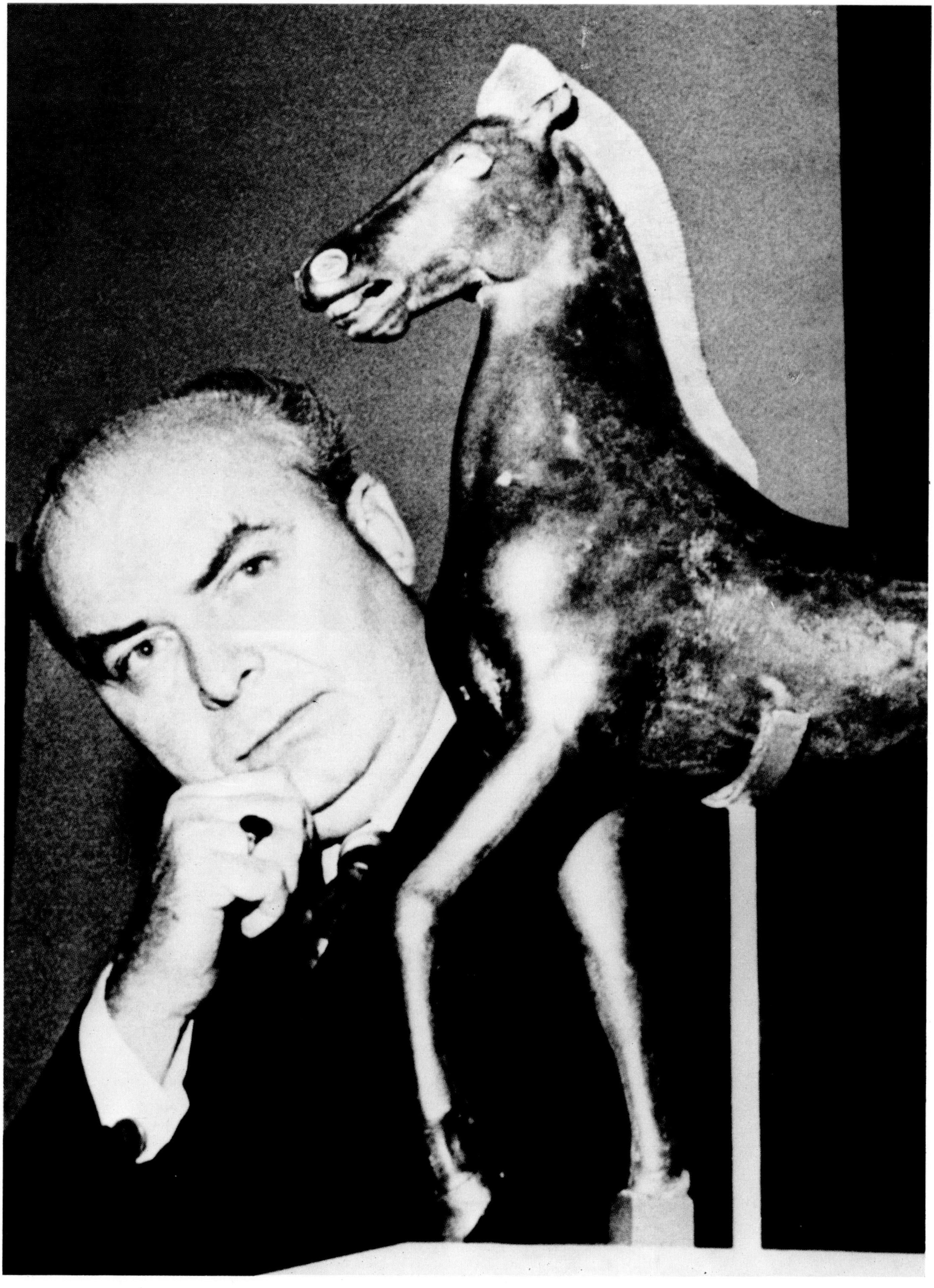

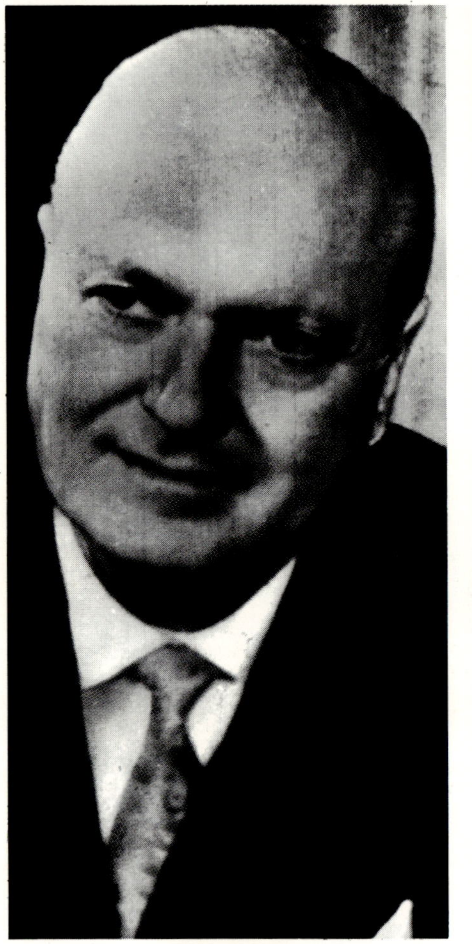

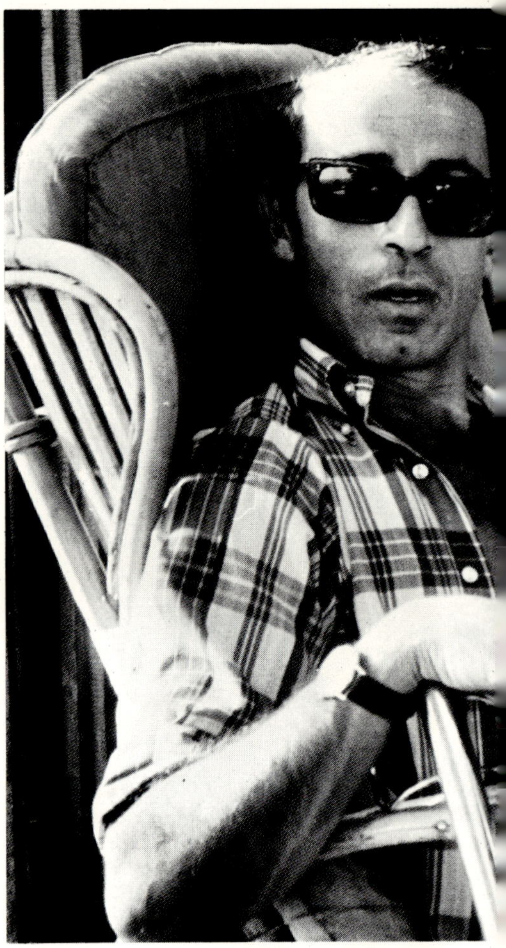

Algur Hurtle Meadows, the multi-millionaire Texas oilman (left) who paid one million dollars for his art collection. More than forty paintings were suspected to be fakes. Was it merely a coincidence that many of them had been obtained from the same dealer—international playboy Fernand Legros (centre)

Meditation (right), once believed to be by Corot, is now admitted by the Cleveland Museum of Art to be a fake. This museum also owns another Corot, *A View of the Roman Countryside*. Obviously there are murmurs

emerge as one of the art scandals of the century. Algur Hurtle Meadows, a multi-millionaire Texan oilman, built up a collection of Impressionist, Post Impressionist and Modern pictures in a relatively short time. But in January 1967 it was stated in several newspaper reports that his collection included more than 40 fakes for which he had paid $1,000,000 (£357,000). Meadows was alleged to have bought them from the same dealer, Fernand Legros.

Legros says that the pictures he sold Meadows are not fakes. Nonetheless, the Art Dealers Association of America (ADAA) have denounced the majority of pictures bought from Legros by Meadows, although they agree that a few of the pictures are 'original' although incorrectly attributed. Legros sells works of art on a very large scale all over the world, yet it is only the Meadows pictures which have been declared fakes by the ADAA he says.

In his mid-thirties, balding and a chain-smoker, Legros has been an American citizen for 15 years, having been born in Egypt of a French father and a Greek mother. He lives the life of an international playboy and has homes in the Bahamas, Austria, New York, Paris and Ibiza.

In September 1963, an associate of Legros bought a portrait by Delaunay for $3,900. Legros entered the picture in a sale of modern pictures. It was bid up to about $20,000, a very high price for such a picture. Legros declined to sell, but later he let Meadows have the portrait for about $30,000.

Legros points out that most of the paintings he sold to Meadows had sound provenances with them. He has even mentioned three of the experts who have given provenances. These are Andre Pacitti, Paul Ebstein and Maurice Malingue. In a report in the *Evening Standard*, Lord Kilbracken states, 'Pacitti and Ebstein did not know that paintings with certificates said to be theirs were among those sold to Meadows.'

Meanwhile, Legros's associate, Lessard, had been arrested and imprisoned. The French police claim that they found in Lessard's Paris apartment four forgeries, forged provenances and customs papers inside a packing case addressed to Dallas, Texas. Later Lessard was released pending his forthcoming trial in

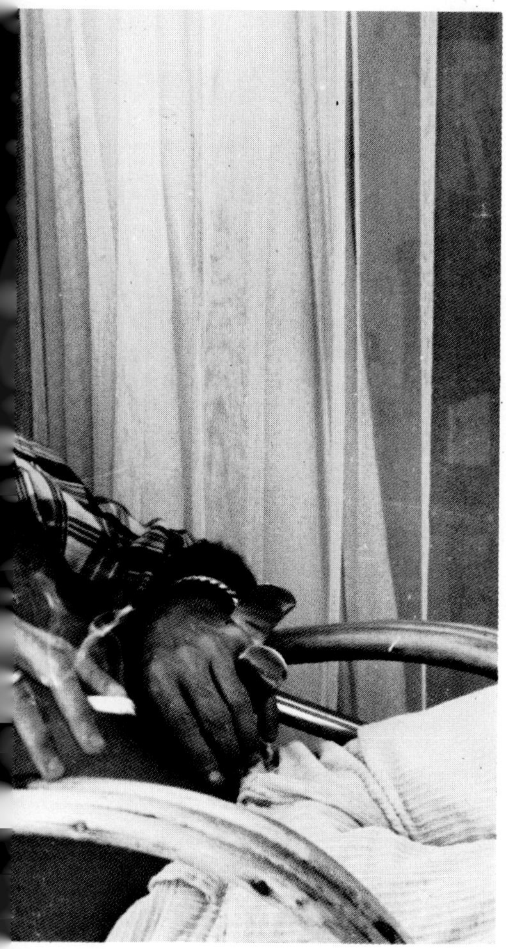

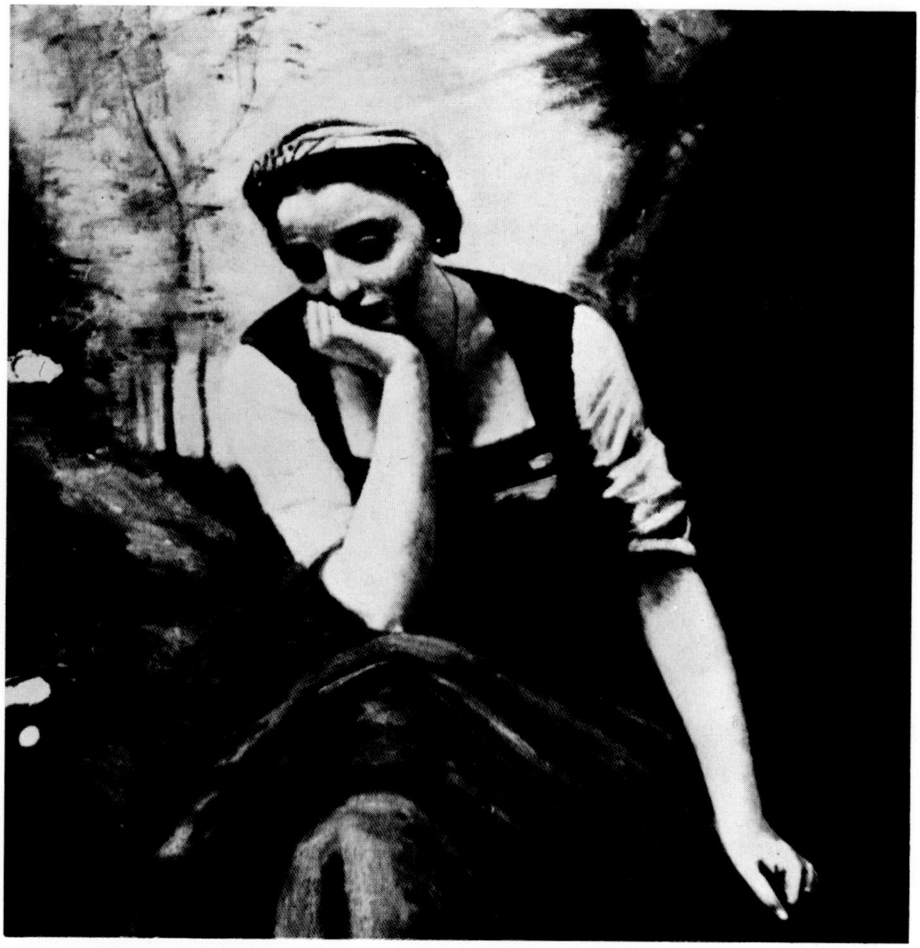

Paris. Meanwhile, French authorities made further investigations and eventually issued a warrant for Legros' arrest.

Earlier Legros had even offered to buy back the supposed fake pictures from Meadows. The price mentioned was in the region of $300,000, approximately one third of the price Meadows originally paid.

Meadows, however, is now buying some more paintings from the well-known firm of Wildenstein's, and has already spent another $1,000,000 according to newspaper reports. Wildenstein's are also examining the paintings sold to Meadows by Legros. According to M. Philippe Huissman, director of Wildenstein's in Paris, two paintings, Dufy's portrait of *J. S. Bach* and *Paysage* by Vlaminck (both of them described as forgeries by the ADAA), are believed to be genuine.

Lord Kilbracken's report in the *Evening Standard* quotes Meadows as saying, 'Of course, I'm not an expert. I know nothing about art but I do know what I like. I do not insist upon him (Legros) returning all I paid. If Legros could substitute just a few authentic paintings, I guess that would be a start. I made the proposal to him in Paris last June (1966) and he offered six paintings of which he produced photographs and certificates. But four of them turned out to be probable fakes, in the opinion of the expert I consulted. The two others were genuine Bonnards. But since then we've heard nothing from Legros and we haven't even been shown the paintings themselves. If Legros would make any reasonable offer, we would feel inclined to accept it. And then all the known fakes could be publicly destroyed—yes, we'd burn them. And that's what I'd really like.'

In March 1968, Legros was arrested in Geneva, allegedly wearing a wig and carrying a British passport. He has since been found in his cell suffering from an overdose of drugs. Meanwhile the controversy continues.

Famous museums are also not beyond the reach of clever fakers and their organisations. The Cleveland Museum in the United States have now admitted that a Corot in their collection is nothing but a fake. Corot has suffered terribly from the activities of the forgers and the remark: 'Corot painted 2,000 pictures during his life, of which 5,000 are in America', is probably an underestimation.

The Cleveland Museum's Corot—titled *Meditation*—has an interesting history. Corot's agents sold a picture called *Meditation* to H. S. Henry, an art collector and Philadelphia railway owner. In 1907 it was apparently sold to another industrialist, Matthew C. Borden, for nearly $16,000. Later the picture entered the collection of Jacob Goldschmidt in New York. In 1948 it was sold to the Cleveland Museum of Ohio by an art dealer acting on behalf of Goldschmidt.

The Cleveland people now know the real history and background to their picture. H. S. Henry did own a genuine Corot which he'd bought from Corot's agents but later a fake picture in the style of Corot was substituted. It is not known who was responsible for the substitution.

Jean Dieterle, one of several Corot authorities, still has a photograph of the painting that Henry bought in France. Now in his eighties, Dieterle saw the Corot fake when it was borrowed by the British Arts Council for a Corot exhibition which was seen in Edinburgh and at the National

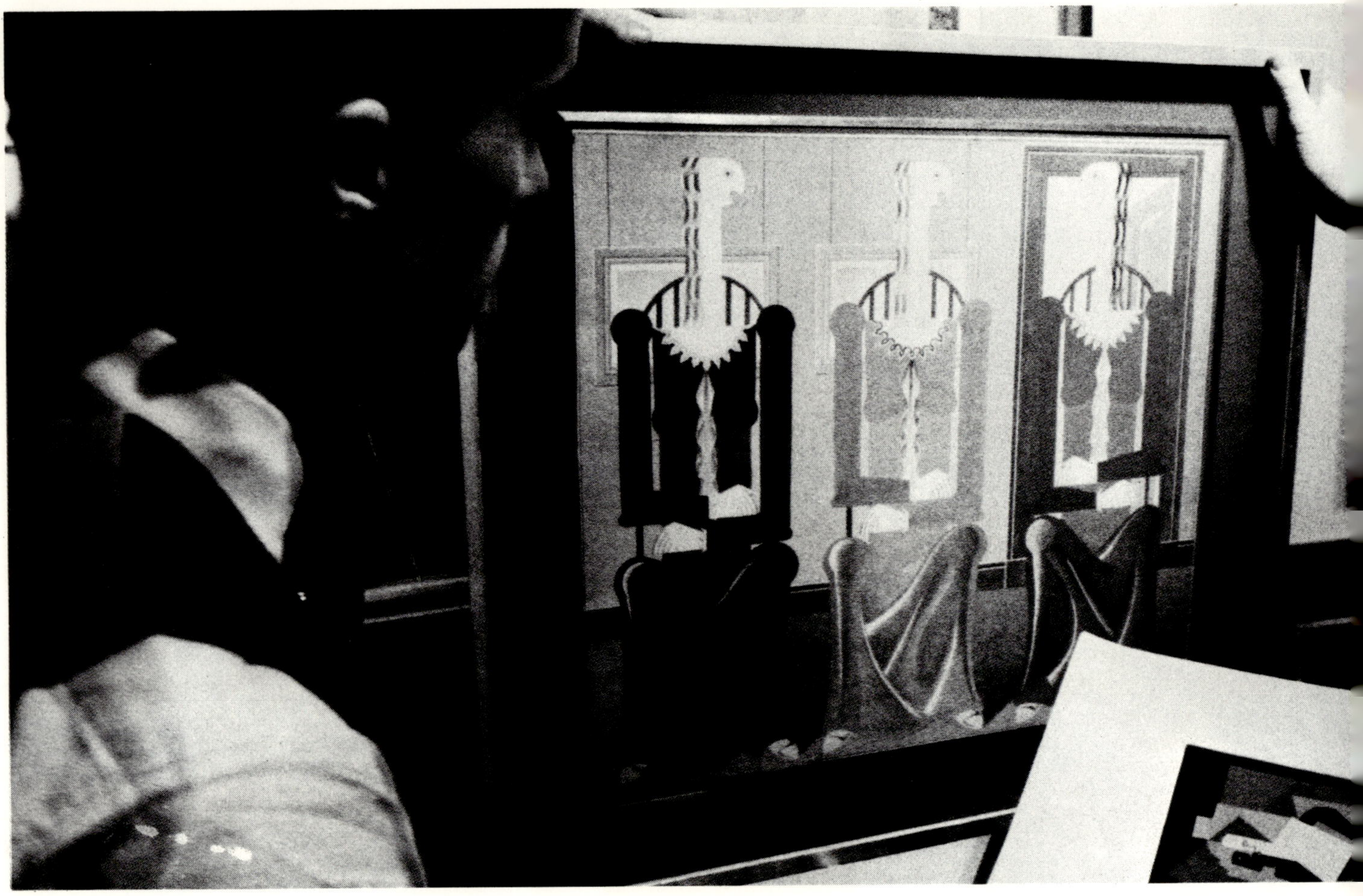

Gallery in London. Dieterle said that the Arts Council exhibition included several fake Corots. 'I think that at least six pictures in that exhibition were not by Corot,' he was reported as saying. He was especially adamant about a Corot pen and wash study in the exhibition. 'Corot never did a pen and wash study in his whole career,' he declared.

The Cleveland Museum are also 'troubled' by another picture which is attributed to Corot. The *Sunday Times* published the following account beneath a photograph of the Corot: '*A View of the Roman Countryside*, valued at £50,000 and attributed to Corot by the museum and the American dealers Rosenburg, who bought it from London dealer Marshall Spink. Cleveland's claim is that it belonged to collector Clément Jourdan, who showed it at the Paris Fair in 1889. But some scholars say the real picture was destroyed by fire before the Fair, and that in fact the Fair committee rejected the Jourdan picture as it does not appear in the catalogue. Examined by five Corot experts between 1951 and 1956, including world authority Jean Dieterle, Knoedlers and the Marlborough Gallery, all thought it a 19th-century fake though at that time it was signed Corot – a feature which has vanished.'

Paintings can be declared fakes and therefore comparatively worthless or genuine and therefore valuable on the opinion of experts. But whether something is genuine or spurious is often controversial and never finally settled or even likely to be settled.

Recently, disagreement, admittedly lop-sided, broke out in Paris over a number of paintings said by some to be by Manet. One of them, a study of a dog with a red collar, was sold in 1965 at a London gallery for a price reported to be more than £30,000. Jacques Mathey, a well-known French expert, considers that the painting of a dog is by Manet and not by a follower of Manet's style or a forgery. On the other hand, Manet specialists like Durand-Ruel, Dennis Rouart and Daniel Wildenstein believe that the picture is *not* by Manet. If they are right, the picture is worth, at very most, about £500.

The picture of a dog appeared in a sale at the Hôtel Drouot, a well-known Paris saleroom, in June, 1964. It had, however, been seen in a Paris gallery exhibition before that sale. There were several Manets in the same sale and the auctioneers called in several specialists to examine them. The little dog in a red collar was eventually entered in the catalogue as: 'French School, showing signs of restoration and traces of a signature'. It was sold to a wealthy lady named Mme Dagieu Sully for £185 – who soon sold it to the Manet specialist Jacques Mathey through a Paris dealer.

Dudley Tooth, of the Arthur Tooth Gallery in London, bought the picture from Mathey for the sum of £7,000. They entered the painting in their spring catalogue as being painted by Manet in 1876. Named *Fofolle* it was bought by a client for £30,000, which was a reasonable price *if* the work really is by Manet and not someone else. Naturally, Arthur W. Tooth & Sons have been perfectly correct in their dealings with the Manet picture and enjoy a high reputation in the art world. Nevertheless this case demonstrates that even the most expert and knowledgeable opinion is not beyond challenge.

Another example of doubtful identifi-

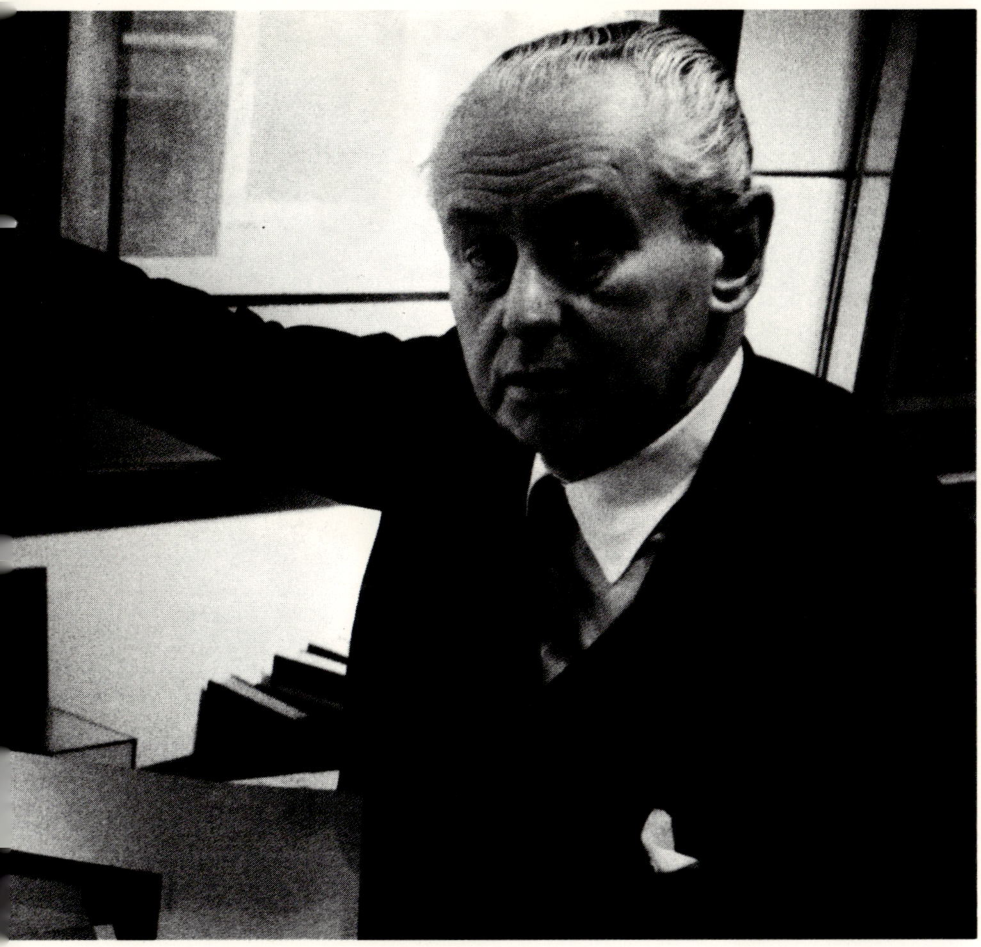

cation is the Gleizes or Bisson affair. Roderick Bisson, a man of about 60 who works for a Liverpool departmental store and writes regularly about art for the *Liverpool Daily Post* under the nom-de-plume 'Z', was on a visit to London in 1963. Visiting the Redfern Gallery he noticed a watercolour of three seated figures entitled *Babillage* and attributed to the French Cubist Albert Gleizes, who died in 1953. 'I was told that it cost 600 guineas,' says Bisson. When he hinted that its value was rather less because he had painted it in Liverpool in 1925, he was asked by an incredulous assistant to leave.
When the picture, now priced at 750 guineas, appeared in another exhibition in 1967 he wrote to Rex Nan Kivell, who is recognised in the London art trade as a modern art expert. Nan Kivell immediately withdrew the picture from sale. 'I looked the picture up in our records and found that we bought it from a Paris gallery. They had obtained it from the estate of a well-known collector.'
By this time Nan Kivell was getting excited. If Roderick Bisson had painted this picture, he might have more work of a similar style and date. He wrote to Bisson: 'I am most interested that you should have created an idiom like this as early as 1925. Were you consciously influenced by Gleizes at that time? Better still, have you portfolios of your work done at that time put away? That would be a find . . . Do let me know if you have any early work you are willing to show.'
Bisson has never replied. Yet if he has portfolios of similar work he would almost certainly become an art world personality overnight. Bisson merely confirms that he still has such things in his possession, but refuses to show them to outsiders. 'I don't want to get involved,' he says. 'I'm sorry, I just don't want to get involved.'
It is worth pointing out that no chicanery was involved and both parties acted with scrupulous correctness. Nevertheless this story does demonstrate the fact that nobody is ever certain that a work of art he has bought is *really*, in the final analysis, by the artist he is told painted it. Nobody, that is to say, unless a collector watches an artist paint a picture from start to finish—a highly unlikely possibility.

Rex Nan Kivell displays a picture, attributed to the French Cubist painter Albert Gleizes, which a Liverpool art critic claims that he painted in 1925

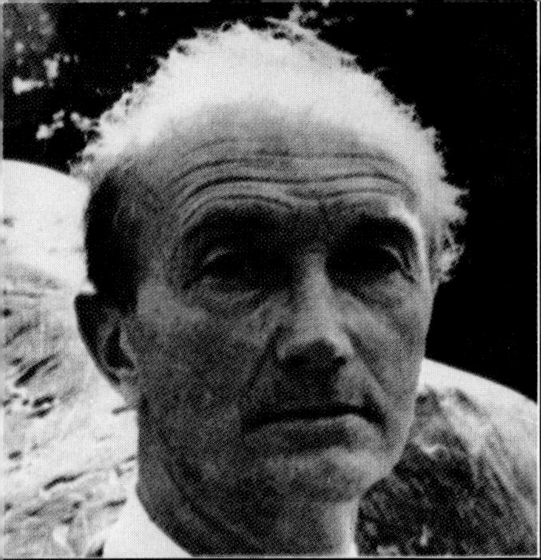

THE ART CRITICS

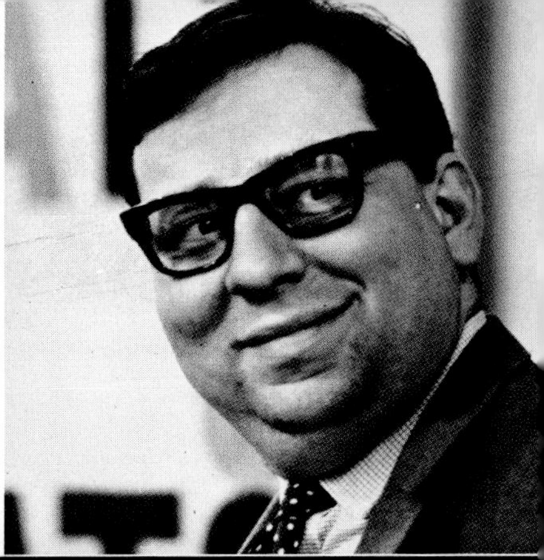

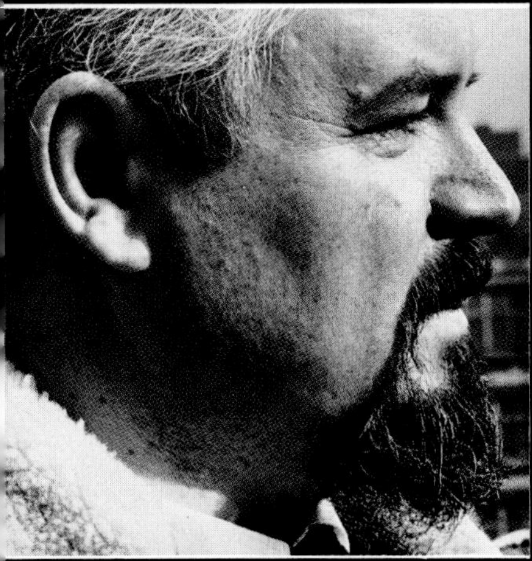

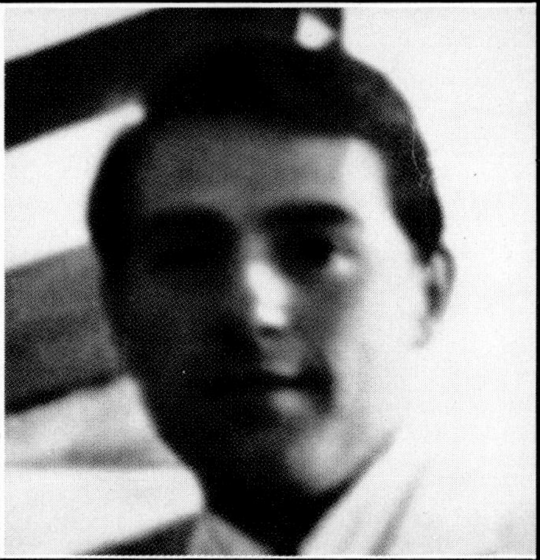

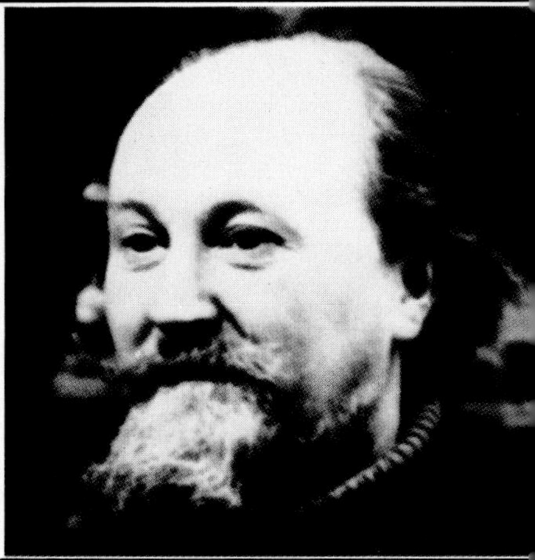

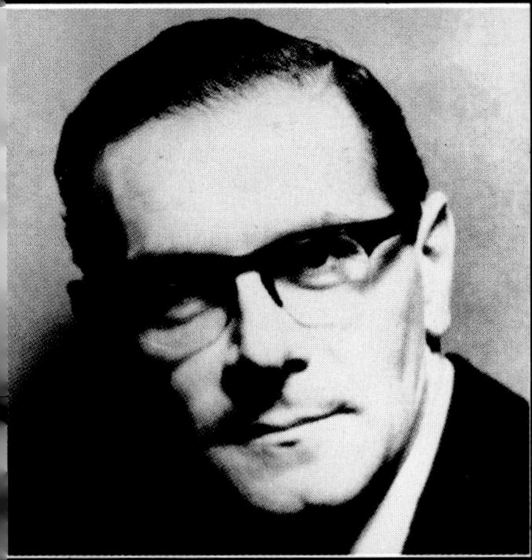

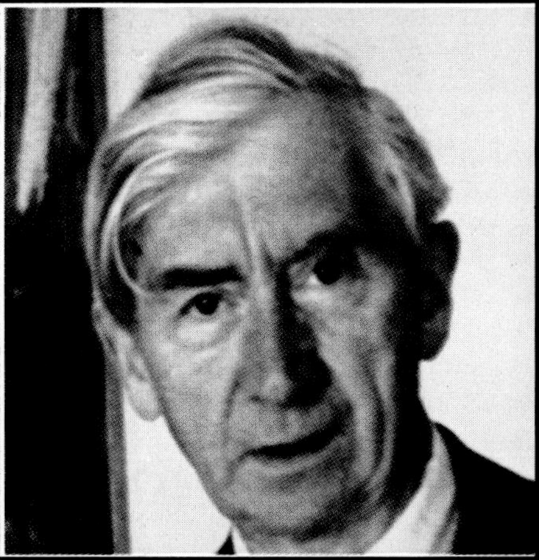

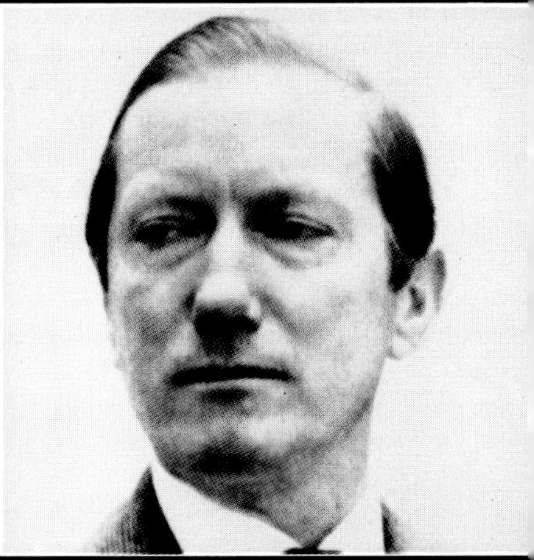

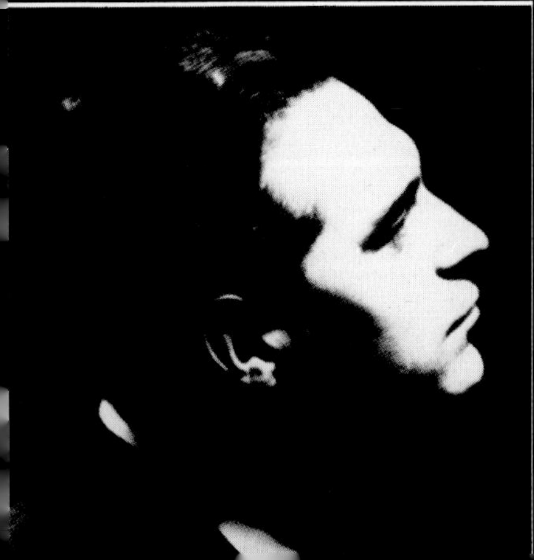

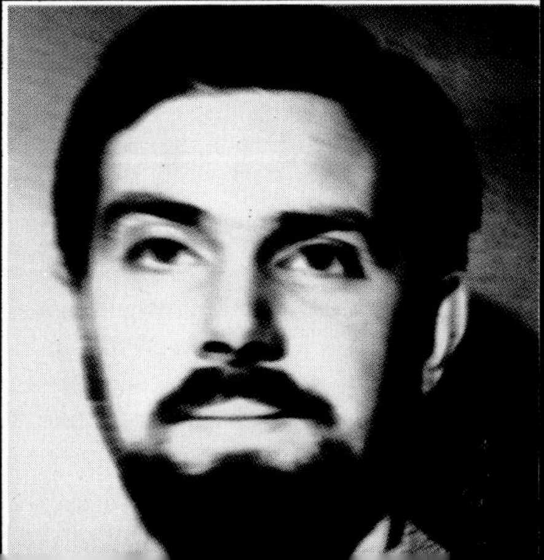

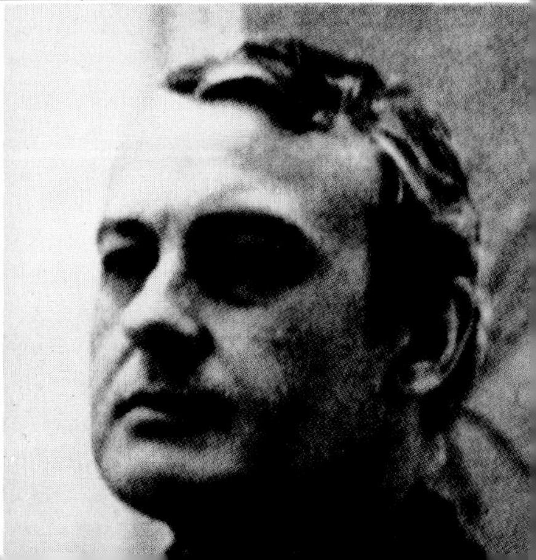

Whatever their faults art critics have helped take the gospel of modern art all over the world. Whether or not they regard themselves as missionaries, the eleven critics shown here (left) certainly influence the taste of millions of readers

Left-hand column: Nigel Gosling, *The Observer;* Denys Sutton, *Financial Times* and editor of *Apollo;* Charles Spencer, *New York Times*; Terence Mullaly, *The Daily Telegraph. Centre column:* Mario Amaya, former editor of *Art and Artists;* Sir Herbert Read, art historian, critic and writer; Stig Barfoed, *Aalborg Stifstidende. Right-hand column:* Edward Lucie-Smith, *The Times;* Max Wykes-Joyce, *New York Herald Tribune;* John Russell, *Sunday Times;* Bryan Robertson, *The Spectator*

Art critics do a very different job from racing correspondents, who are paid to tell their newspaper readers which horse might win the three-thirty race. Rarely will a critic tip an artist for posterity, a short-term investment or a prize at a top art competition like the Venice Biennale.

D. H. Lawrence once wrote that a 'man has to have a gizzard like an ostrich to digest all the brass tacks and wire nails of modern art theories.' Many painters and sculptors are hostile towards critics. So are many art dealers.

But whatever their faults art critics have helped take the gospel of modern art all over the world. Articulate and intelligent writers like Harold Rosenberg and Clement Greenberg in America, and Hans Richter in Europe, have made art more intelligible.

Sir Herbert Read, who died recently, was an outstanding example of a critic who early in his career pinned his faith on several artists he felt were important. In countless magazine and newspaper articles and in a series of books and lectures he helped explain what the avant-garde were doing in art.

Read lived among artists like Henry Moore, Ben Nicholson, Barbara Hepworth, Piet Mondrian and Naum Gabo. Critics rarely have the good fortune to watch the creative process in such an intimate and involved way. By definition, critics tend to be detached observers.

In the United States and Britain many prominent newspapers and magazines employ an art critic on a salary or contract basis. Their job is to report and comment upon current exhibitions in museums or private galleries and to generally bring art and artists to the attention of their readers. On the continent of Europe, however, many publications prefer to commission distinguished art historians to write art criticism for them. This means that a newspaper like the *Frankfurter Allgemeine Zeitung* will have several critics writing for it. This does not mean that all English art critics are merely journalists with a good knowledge of art. For example, Denys Sutton, the distinguished editor of *Apollo*, is also art critic for the *Financial Times*.

John Russell is in many ways typical of the American and British critic. His regular column in the *Sunday Times* gives his readers a continuity of ideas and opinions, whatever their own conclusions may be.

'Most things about the art world have changed for the better since the war,' says Russell. 'The condition of the newspaper critic has unfortunately changed for the worse. Sixty years ago the coverage given to art in serious newspapers was up to ten and twenty times what it is now.

'My task as I see it is to get people to visit exhibitions which I personally like and recommend. I loathe about ninety per cent of the shows which I see, but it is the ones I write about every week that I would usually recommend to my readers.'

Although critics like Russell believe that the position of the newspaper critic has changed for the worse since the war it is nevertheless true that most newspapers and magazines devote some space nowadays to art, however sensationally. Art is often big news.

Nigel Gosling, art critic of *The Observer,* believes that the task of a critic must change because of the rapidly changing art world. 'With more than 150 galleries in London, 200 in Paris and more than 400 in New York, the art critic can no longer cover the old ground as before,' he says.

Max Wykes-Joyce is a freelance art critic who writes regularly for several specialist art magazines and is now the London art critic of the International Edition of the *New York Herald Tribune*. Now 54, he is a well-known and popular figure in and around London art galleries.

'I've been a member of the Birmingham Repertory Company, a student at London and Cambridge Universities, and in the early 1960s I had a part-time job in an art gallery,' he says. 'I did train for a year as a painter and sculptor, but whereas it troubles me if I'm not able to write a few sentences a day, it doesn't worry me if I don't put brush to canvas or chisel to stone.'

Terence Mullaly, the art critic of the *Daily Telegraph*, has been a controversial art critic for some years. More conservative in his outlook than many of his colleagues, Mullaly has ridden against the tide of art criticism of the 1960s and survived. Influential and respected, sometimes through pursed lips and gnashing teeth, a kind review from him can make an exhibition successful. For many of the avant-garde, however, Mullaly epitomises the supposed respectability and ultra-conservatism of many art critics. The reason for this is obvious: many of them have felt the lash of his tongue.

Writing about the Young Contemporaries show, held annually in London, he said that as far as he was concerned a large amount of money had been entirely wasted on the students exhibiting. Similarly, when reviewing the work of Francis Souza on exhibition at the Grosvenor Gallery he said that Souza's best paintings were the black ones. You can't see them, he added.

'I think the occasional touch of humour never did an art column any harm,' says Mullaly. 'A point has to be made forcefully sometimes, you know. Most art criticism to my mind is too dull for words nowadays.'

Bryan Robertson, energetic director of the Whitechapel Gallery, art critic of *The Spectator* and for several years a pioneer in bringing the main aspects of British and American avant-garde painting to a wider audience, is unhappy about the art critic's diminishing role in the Press.

He put the point plainly in the book *Private View*. 'Newspaper critics have a tough time: insufficient space, and sometimes inadequate backing or half-baked interference from ignorant literary editors under whose wing they have to function. Even a serious television programme like *Monitor* rarely had the courage to tackle art as *art*, rather than in terms of personality, notoriety or some equally irrelevant handle.'

Critics are constantly under attack from painters and sculptors. Many artists feel that if their exhibitions are ignored by critics it is part of a plot organised by rival artists and dealers. Often it is simply the fact that a critic's space is limited and that there are so many private exhibitions opening every week.

Francis Souza, the Goan-born painter who now lives in New York, has been fighting a running battle with art critics for many years. 'Critics are an extraordinary crowd,' says Souza. 'Some of them are more guilty of distortion and inaccuracy than others. One English critic reviewing the Tate Gallery's exhibition of American painting wrote in 1956 that Jackson Pollock, America's most famous postwar painter, should be slapped.

'Five years later the same critic wrote an article under the banner headline: "The Agony of Jackson Pollock". A paean of praise, it failed to mention his earlier insulting remarks about this artist. Critics are just like harlots: not much responsibility.'

One problem which faces the art critic is his relationship with the private art dealer. Many critics depend on their writing for a living and few of them have the courage to speak against dealers when the situation deserves it.

Proof of the pressure which dealers can exercise is not difficult to find. Allegations that several London art dealers threatened to vilify a leading art critic if he did not write favourably about their exhibitions were made in February 1968 by Sheldon Williams, former Liberal candidate for Richmond and former London art critic of the International Edition of the *New York Herald Tribune*. Twenty prominent art dealers, including Mr Harry Fischer, of Marlborough Fine Art, Mr Leonard Foster, of Wildenstein, and Mr Patrick Phillips, of the Leicester Galleries, signed a petition to defend Williams' reputation. It was circulated by the Crane Kalman Gallery, Knightsbridge, London.

Sir Roland Penrose, the collector and former director of the Institute of Contemporary Arts, wrote to the editor of the *New York Herald Tribune* in support of Williams, whom he described as 'a critic well-known for his integrity'.

Williams said: 'Early last year an influential dealer asked me why I didn't write more about his shows and more favourably. He also asked me to retract some of the criticisms I'd made in the past. I declined politely, but he telephoned me several times until I finally told him what I thought of him. He then told me that he would see to it that I was hounded out of the art world. Several dealers then began a campaign against me. A few people kept their word and tried to unpick me bone from flesh.'

The art critic of a leading daily paper told me of the pressure to which art critics can be subjected from dealers. 'Bribery and threats are very unusual, but not unknown,' he said. 'I was once sent a cheque for £500 by a Mayfair dealer with a note saying: "I think we understand each other now". I banked it and sent another cheque back for £500 and 6d. and a note saying: "I think we understand each other perfectly".'

Jasia Reichardt (left), Polish-born art critic and the assistant director of the Institute of Contemporary Arts in London, is considered to be one of the most avant-garde writers on art today. A regular contributor to magazines like *Architectural Design* and *Studio International*, she has also edited several monographs on living artists for a well-known publisher

Doing his best to liven up the art scene is Anthony Fawcett (right). Barely in his twenties, he is possibly the youngest of Britain's art critics. Formerly critic and art editor of *Isis*, Oxford University's famous magazine, he also worked for a short spell as public relations officer for the newly-opened Museum of Modern Art in Oxford. As an art critic his field is mainly contemporary painting, sculpture, and especially Kinetic or experimental movements. He has recently been working with Beatle John Lennon and Yoko Ono at the headquarters of their organisation, Apple

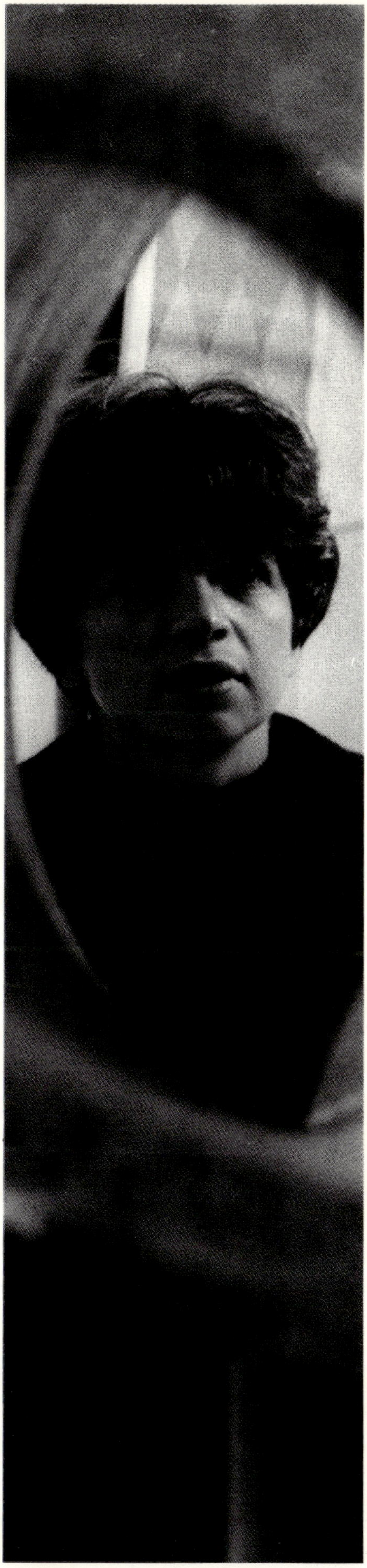

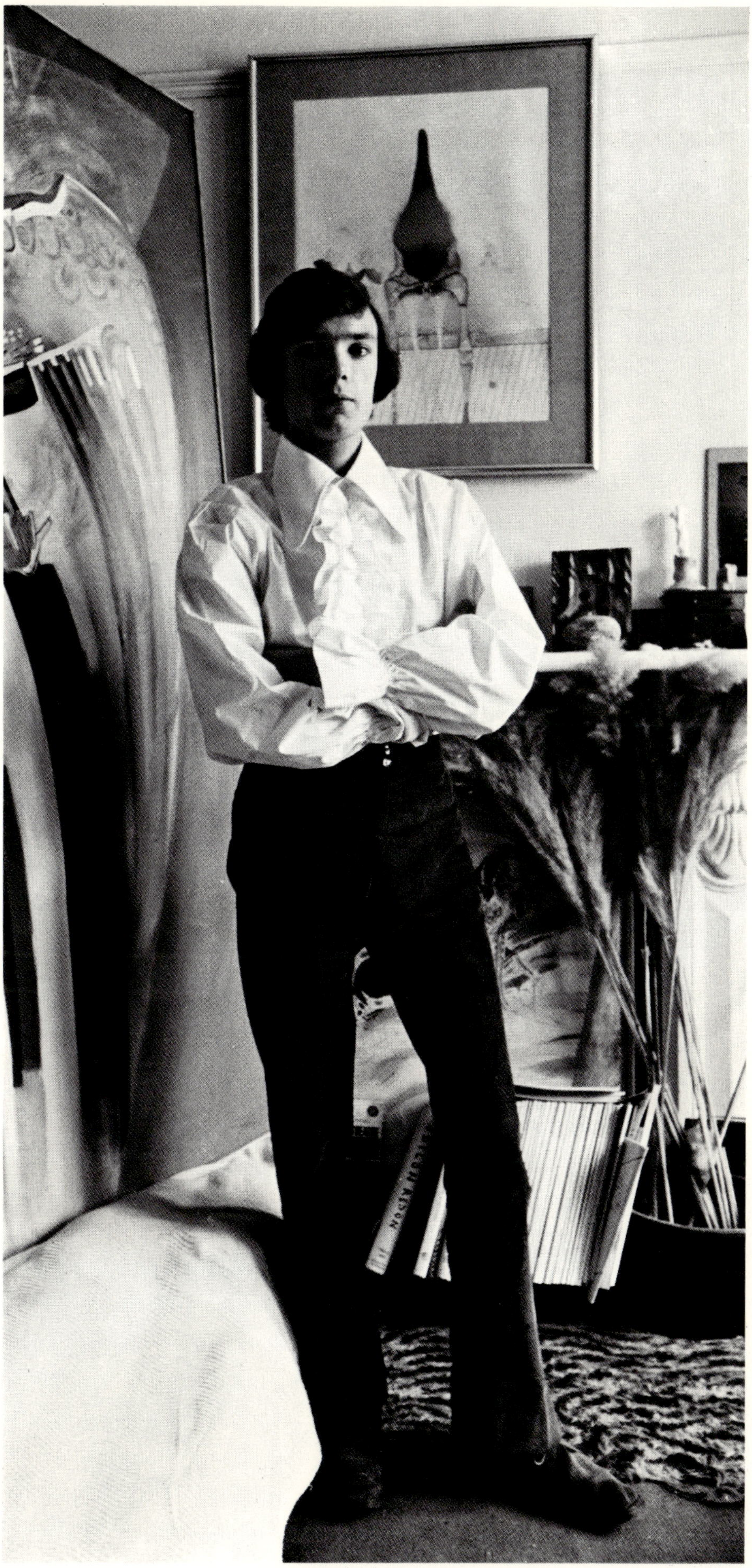

BOOKS PRINTS & POSTERS

Never before has so much art been produced and never before has so much been written about it. By selling millions of art books, prints and posters, publishing companies have helped stimulate further the enormous interest in the plastic arts. Giorgio Vasari, the painter and writer, who wrote the first important art book in 1550, appealed only to a privileged minority. Even as late as the nineteenth century, art writers aimed at a small, specialised and academic market. Rarely did the art criticism of Jacob Burckhardt, Charles Baudelaire, Heinrich Wöfflin and John Ruskin reach the layman. Although scholars continue to produce books today which are of academic interest to a comparative few, they are nevertheless fully aware of their responsibilities outside their own narrow circles. Writers like Bernard Berenson, Germain Bazin, Antonio Morassi, Herman Voss, Hofstede de Groot, E. H. Gombrich and John Pope-Hennessy—to name only a few well-known scholars—have all made their knowledge available to the ordinary reader.

The popular design and outlook of many art books and magazines, and

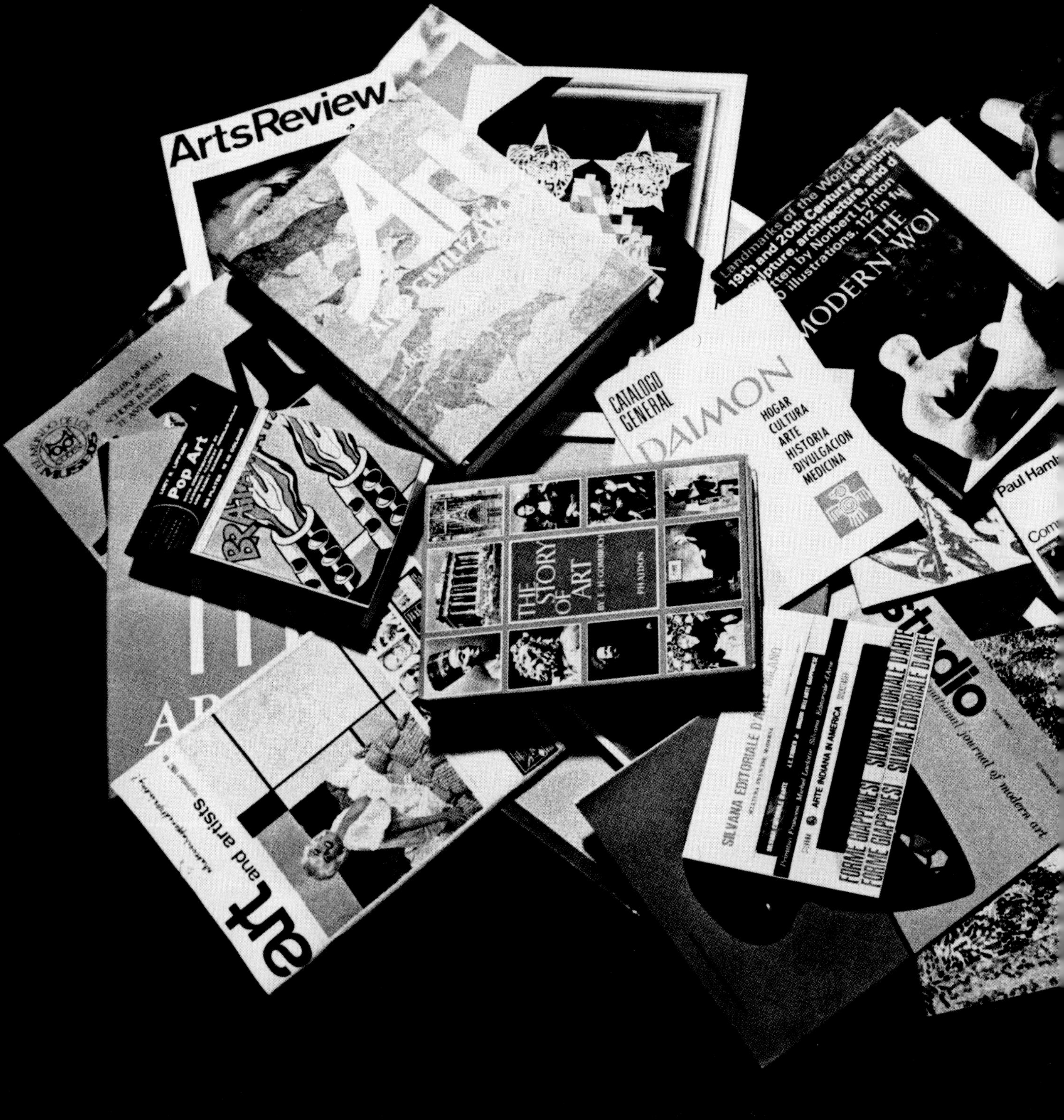

their increasing number and variety, reflect their appeal to a wider audience than ever before. Simultaneous publication of the same book in several language helps lower the retail price of art books.

Publishers like the Phaidon Press, Thames and Hudson, and Paul Hamlyn in England, Fabbri, Sansoni and Mondadori in Italy, Bertelsmann and Dumont Schauberg in Germany, Schroll and Verlag Zsolnay in Austria, Skira in Switzerland, Artia in Czechoslovakia, and McGraw-Hill and Harry Abrams in the United States have been responsible for the revolution which has taken place in international publishing. For the price of a theatre ticket people can now buy lavishly illustrated books on a variety of subjects from Icon painters or Cimabue and Donatello to Salvador Dali and Pop art.

The extraordinary appeal of art today has created a complex and seemingly insatiable demand for art objects. Multiple editions of graphics, many of them signed by the artist, are helping to both satisfy and stimulate this demand. Most modern artists have produced limited editions of lithographs and etchings.

Graphics have become an important sideshow in the modern art trade. Because they are multiple, more people are able to afford them. Signed lithographs in editions of less than seventy-five can often be bought in leading galleries for less than ten pounds each. Unsigned lithographs by the giants of modern art, including Picasso, Braque, Miró, Chagall and Henry Moore, can now be bought for less than fifty pounds each.

Publishing companies, many of them small, now publish large amounts of graphic work. Leading companies

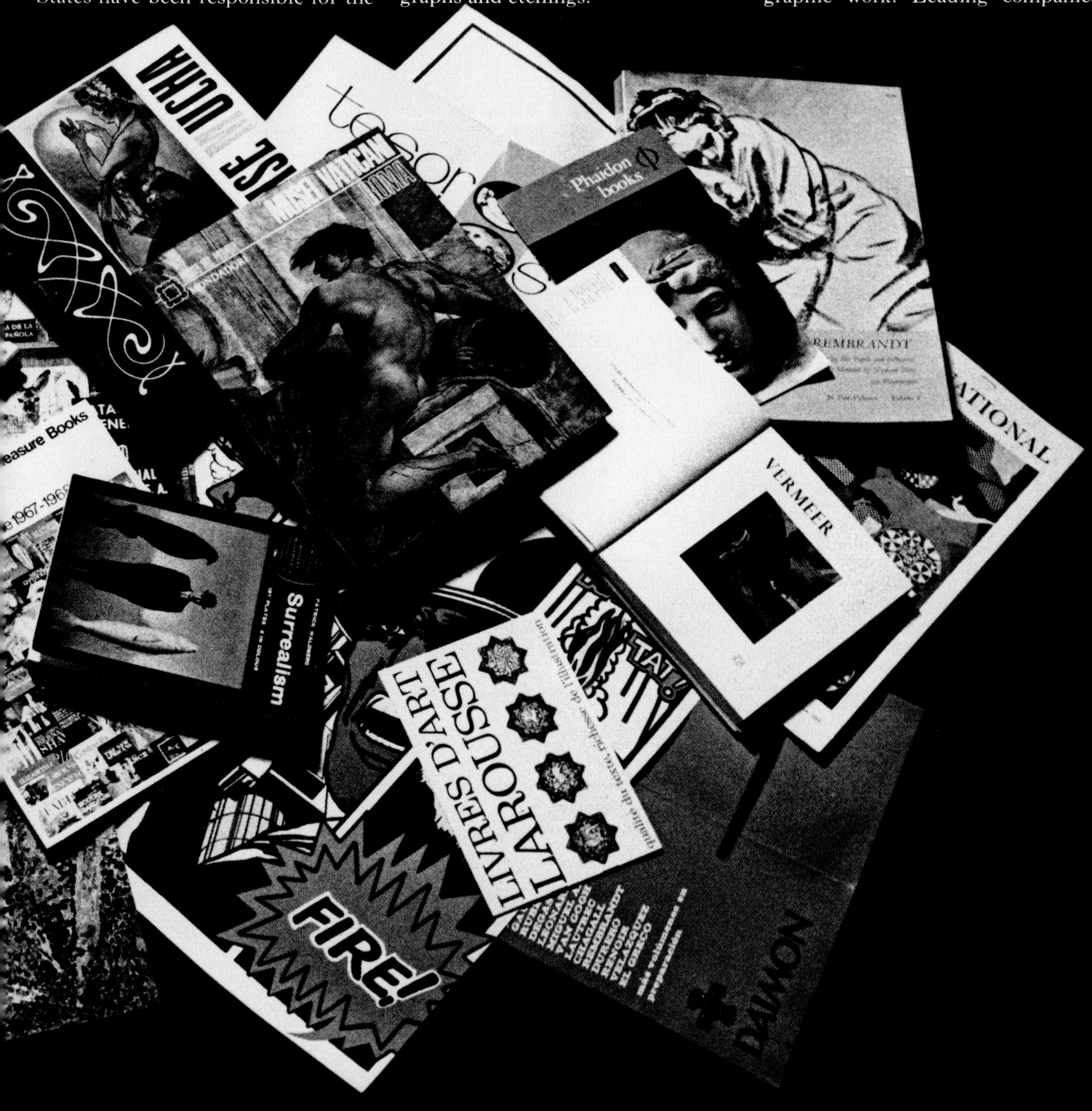

like Editions Alecto, Marlborough Fine Art, the Curwen Press and London Graphic Art, have encouraged the widening interest in 'original' prints.

Proof of the investment value of some modern prints can be judged from a curious phenomenon in many auction houses. Reproductions of work by Picasso, Braque and other well-known names are being bought for a few shillings in bookshops and then entered as original lithographs in the salerooms. But when they come up for auction they have 'acquired' an impressive 'Braque' or 'Picasso' signature and figures in one corner of the print to suggest that it is part of a limited edition. It is the rising value of genuine original prints which stimulates this kind of activity.

Not all the reproductions now available are by instantly recognisable names. Athena Reproductions, for example, aim to publish reproductions at the lowest possible prices by printing thousands of prints. Although work by Picasso, Van Gogh, Klee, Modigliani and Bernard Buffet is included in their modern art series, they also publish prints by less well-known artists such as Vasarely, Diaz, Marini and Mondrian. Athena eventually hope to commission the most avant-garde artists of today.

The recent appearance of original posters, many of them worthy enough to be called works of art in the way that Toulouse-Lautrec posters are works of art, is especially important. It suggests that large numbers of people feel the need for lively pictures to put around them.

These new posters of the 1960s were originally intended for publicity –for dances, 'happenings' and the theatre. Often they are not signed and their style is a harmonious mixture of Pop, Op, and Camp. One writer has described the style of the modern poster as neo-Art Nouveau. And there is little doubt that the most obvious influence is Aubrey Beardsley, who died in 1898. Poster artists would probably prefer to describe their art as psychedelic.

San Francisco has become the cult centre of posters, although posters are to be found in most major cities in America and Europe. One of the best and most prolific artists involved with posters is Wes Wilson who works for the Fillmore Auditorium in San Francisco. Steve Renick and Ned Lamont are also outstanding.

The common impact of a modern poster is the way that the 'message' of the poster is implied visually. One *senses* what the artist is communicating–whether it is a dance, a happening or a show–and despite the fact that most posters have lettering. In fact, figures and lettering in a poster often merge together–or appear to–rhythmically.

Propaganda through the medium of specialised art magazines has also played a role in spreading the gospel of the plastic arts. Some of these magazines and journals are very distinguished indeed, and receive contributions from scholars all over the world. *The Burlington Magazine* is one of the most famous. Edited by Benedict Nicolson, an article in its pages is the ambition of many young art historians. Both *Apollo*, edited by Denys Sutton, and *The Connoisseur*, edited by L. G. G. Ramsey, have large international circulations and are read by scholars, museum men, and dealers. In fact, all these journals receive considerable revenue from the advertisements placed in them by leading dealers and auction houses on both sides of the Atlantic.

James Fitzgibbons' *Art International*, with editorial offices in Lugano, is devoted to contemporary art. It has a team of correspondents in Rome, New York, Paris, London and Zürich. Norbert Lynton, their London correspondent, is also art critic of *The Guardian*. Similar in scope, but with a slightly different approach, is *Art Forum*. It is published in New York and edited by Philip Leider.

Mario Amaya, author of a successful book on Pop art, has edited *Art and Artists*. This journal, aimed as a much wider market than others mentioned so far, has done a lot to make contemporary art acceptable to the general public. Its closest rival is probably *Studio International*, edited by Peter Townsend. Founded in 1893, *Studio International* has changed its format, price, editorial policy and even its name over the years–and survived. It now finds itself in a world in which there is a greatly increased interest in the arts but many more art journals to cater for it. Competition for advertising revenue is fierce, and there will probably be some casualties. Nevertheless, new and better journals will always be necessary to keep pace with the flood of new developments on the international art scene.

The poster craze sweeps across Europe and America leaving a trail of exuberant psychedelia in its wake

God Is Love. A design for a love poster by Keith Davis (top left): Californian hippy-type poster by Wes Wilson published by Mouse Productions (top right); Underground art movement poster by Jon Goodchild published by Splash Posters (below left); Poetry poster by Tom Adams with poem by Edward Lucie-Smith (below right)

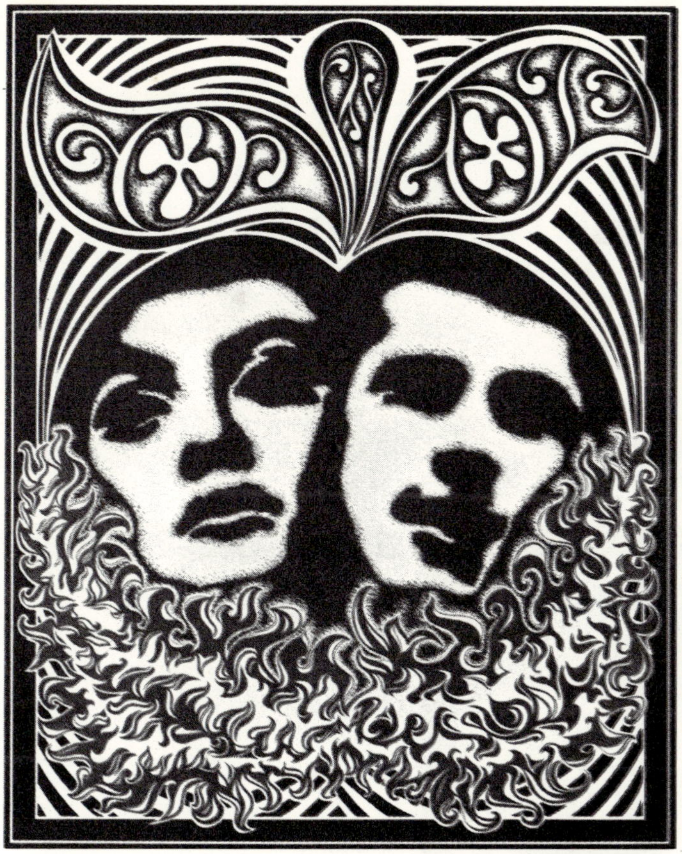

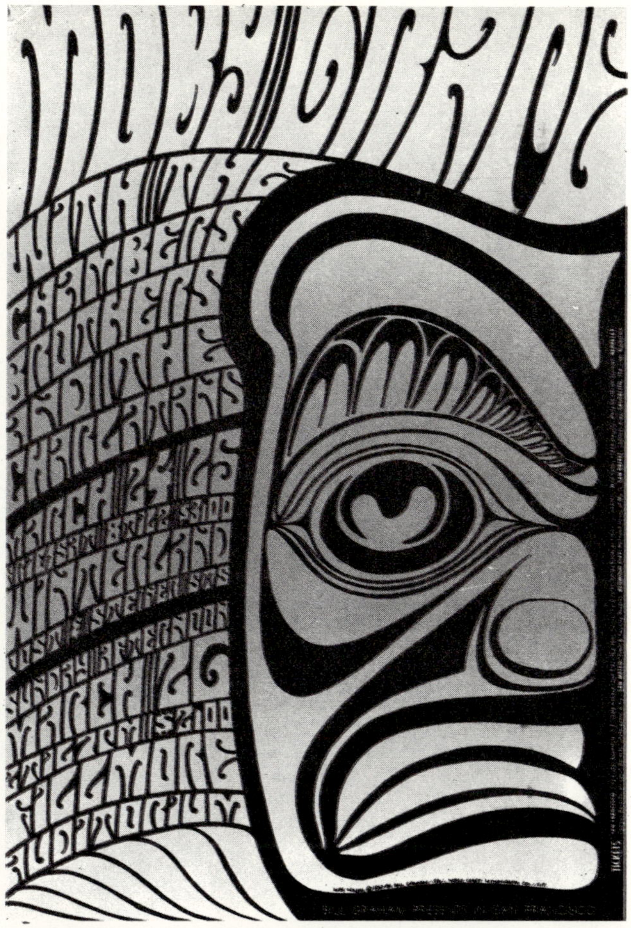

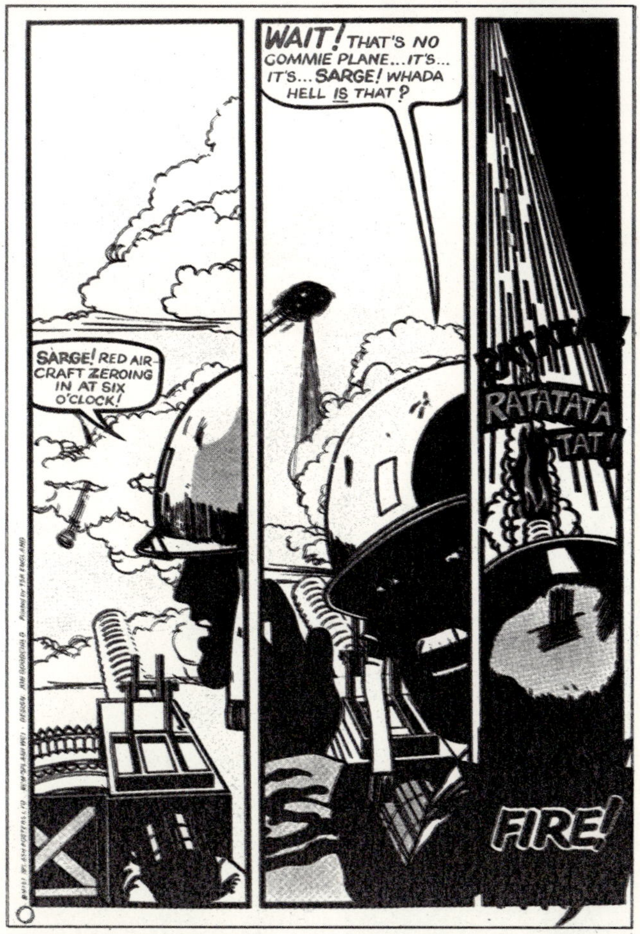
SARGE! RED AIRCRAFT ZEROING IN AT SIX O'CLOCK!
WAIT! THAT'S NO COMMIE PLANE...IT'S... IT'S...SARGE! WHADA HELL IS THAT?
RATATATA TAT!
FIRE!

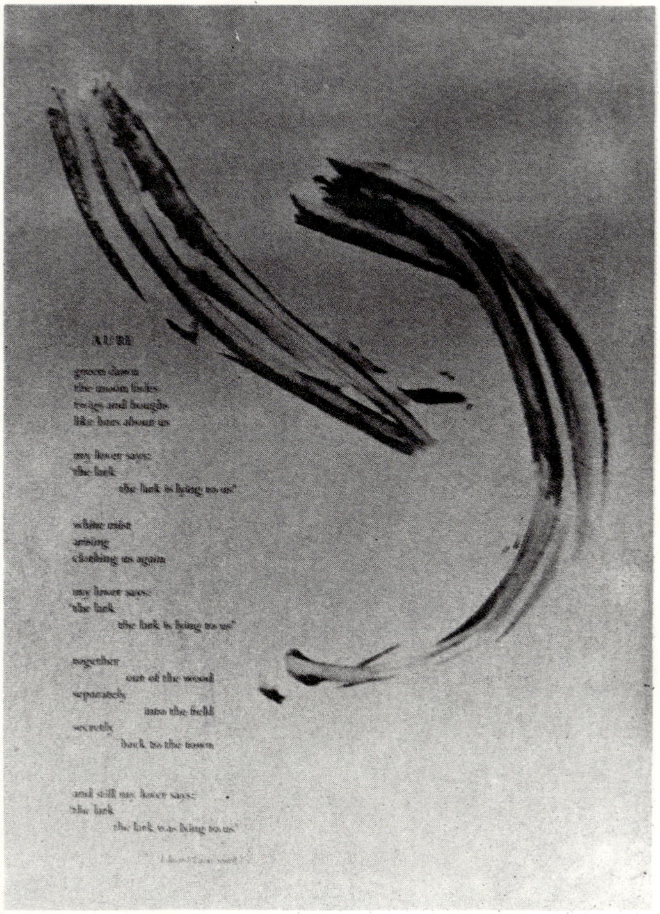
AUBE
green dawn
the moon hides
twigs and boughs
like bars about us
my lover says:
'the lark
the lark is lying to us'
white mist
arising
clothing us again
my lover says:
'the lark
the lark is lying to us'
together
out of the wood
separately
into the field
secretly
back to the town
and still my lover says:
'the lark
the lark was lying to us'

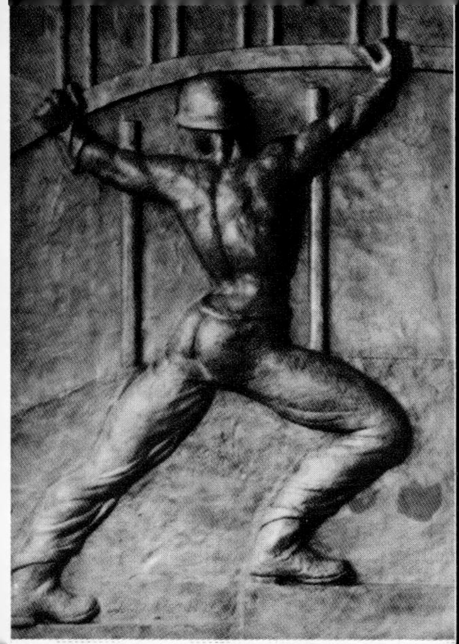

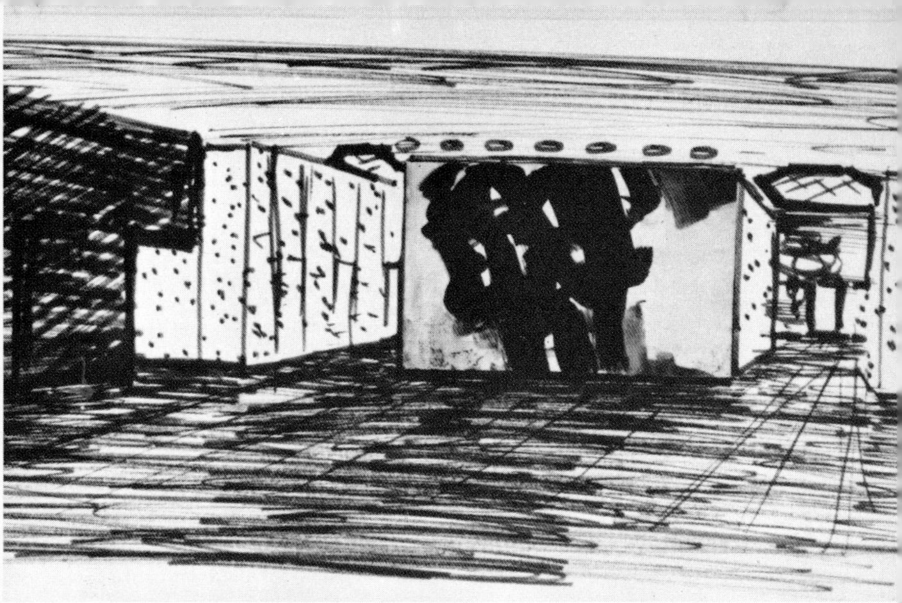

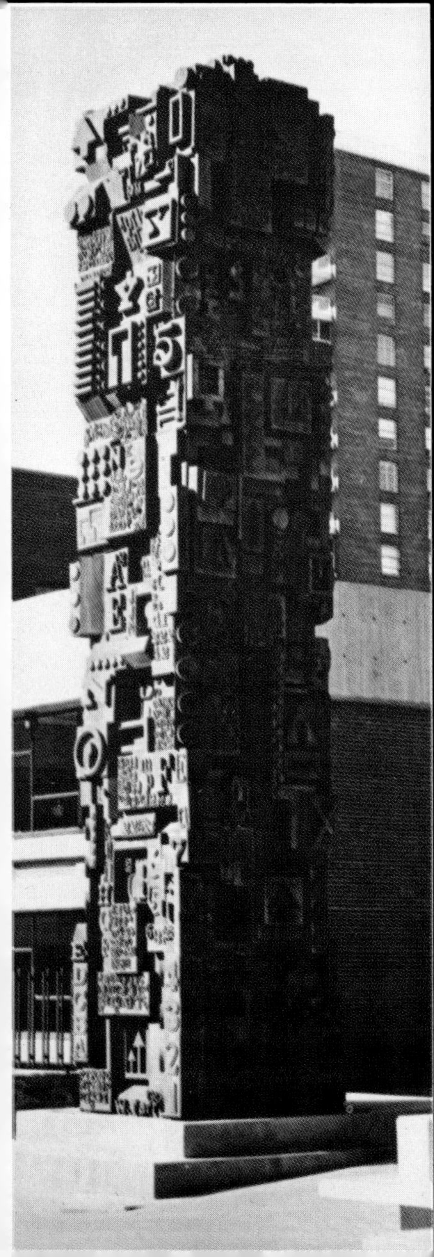

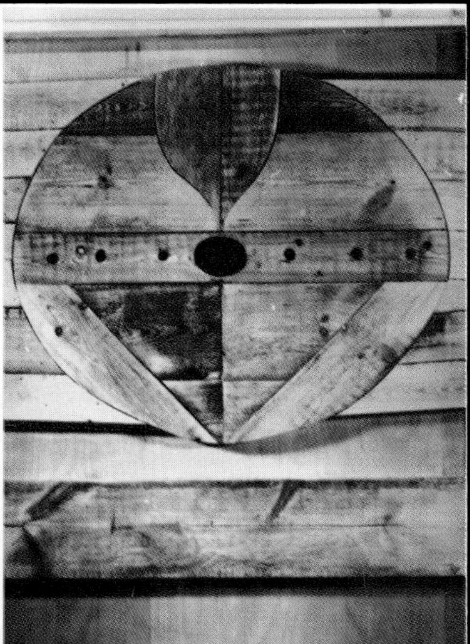

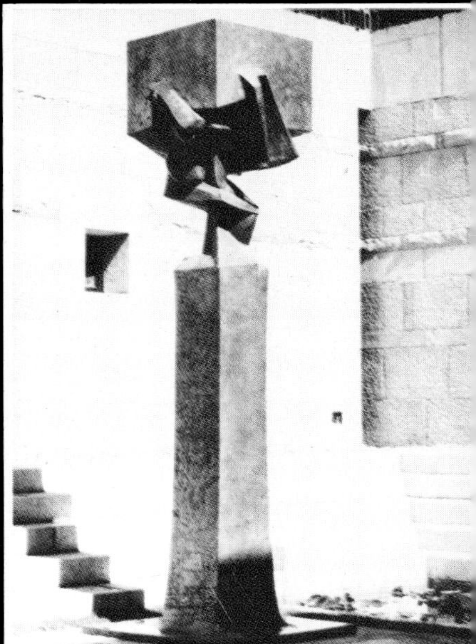

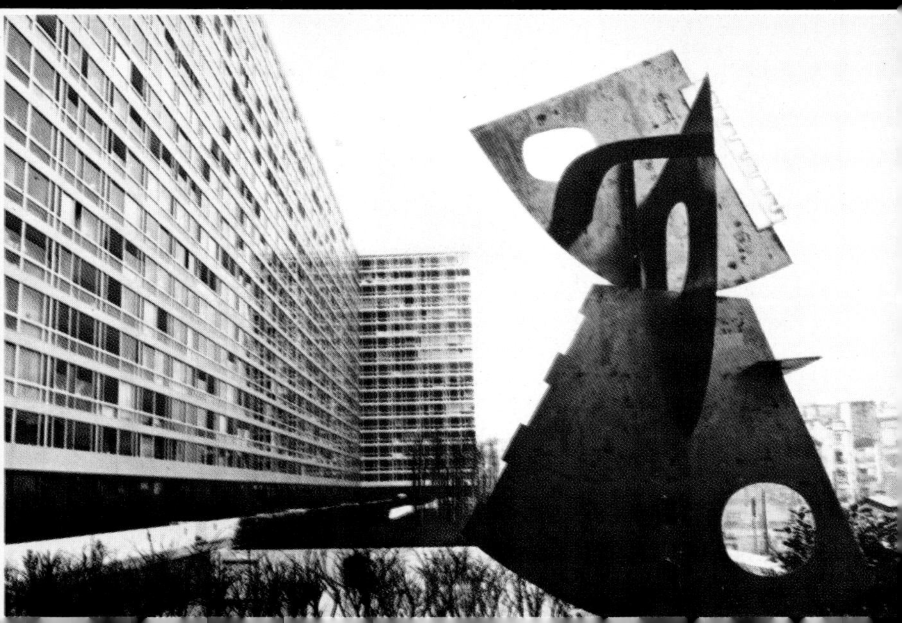

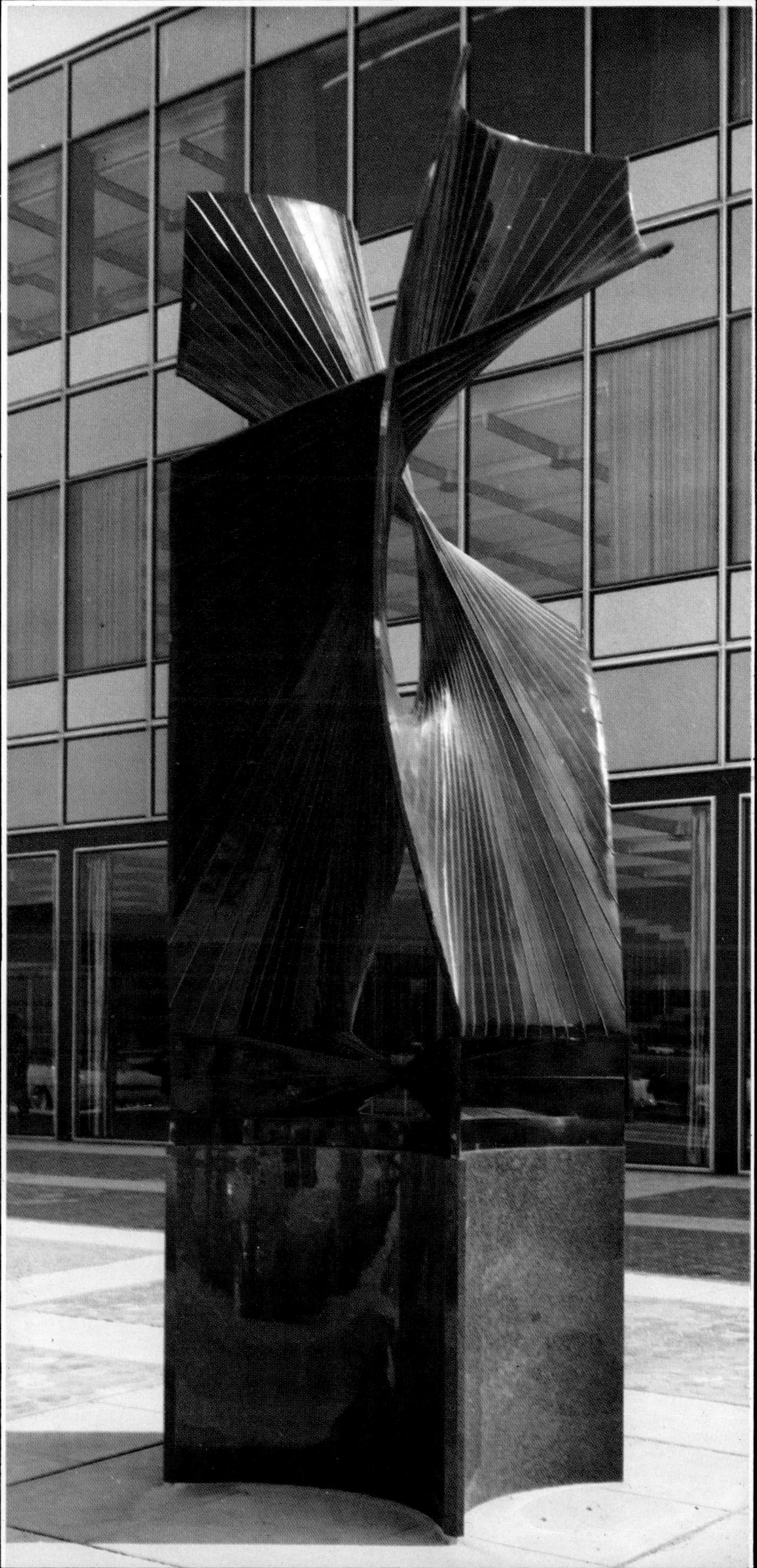

PATRONS AND PUBLIC

The new art patrons are governments and business corporations rather than private individuals. This fine example of modern sculpture by Antoine Pevsner stands before the General Motors Technical Centre in Detroit. Other works of art commissioned or bought by organisations appear on the opposite page

Top row. Bas relief by Dora Gordine at the Esso Refinery, Milford Haven, Wales. Commissioned by Esso as a tribute to the men who built the refinery and those who operate it. Sketch for a ceramic tile mural by Pierre Soulages for the main entrance hall of the Oliver Tyrone Corporation Building, Pittsburgh

Second row. Sculptured steel column by William Tarr, commissioned by the New York City Board of Education. Weighing more than ten tons, it was built entirely by Tarr over a period of eighteen months.
A wood relief by Joe Tilson, bought by the Peter Stuyvesant Foundation. Fritz Koenig, *Large Column Caryatid,* 1965–66. This bronze sculpture was commissioned for the West German Embassy in Madrid

Bottom, right. Sculpture by Berto Lardera in the grounds of a multi-unit housing project at Maine-Montparnasse, Paris

The new-style art patrons are governments and business corporations rather than private individuals. Unlike the ordinary collector, the patron is prepared to help artists by offering them money, awards, competitions, promotion and official acquisitions.

The Ford Motor Company is a keen supporter of American art and regularly gives grants to students and artists. Ford's now have a gigantic collection of more than 8,000 items which they have collected in the past twenty years. Even ultra-modern artists like Bruce Conner have been given $10,000 awards to support them in their experiments in the arts.

Hallmark Cards Incorporated, which manufactures greetings cards, has been organising art competitions for more than twenty years. In 1949, the year of the first competition administered by Wildenstein's, the well-known art dealers, it attracted more than 10,000 entries.

Since Hallmark began its competitions it has spent between a quarter and half a million dollars in commissions, prizes and promotions. The firm also awards three art scholarships every year to art students and it also buys student works for exhibiting in museums, schools and institutions up and down the country.

International Business Machines Corporation of America (IBM) has been patronising the fine arts since before the war. Its major function is to buy works of art from countries where it operates. The IBM travelling exhibitions have been seen all over the United States and more than three million Americans are known to have visited them.

The H. J. Heinz Company of Pittsburgh began buying works of art in the late 1950s. Through the enthusiasm of Mr and Mrs Heinz the firm's collection has grown quickly. Not surprisingly perhaps, the company has been buying well-known modern artists like Boudin, Rouault, Braque, Stuart Davis, Soulages and John Kane to form a solid basis for later purchases.

It is business corporations like the Standard Oil Company of New Jersey, the Manufacturers Trust Company in New York, the John Hancock Mutual Life Insurance Company and the General Electric Company, which have helped stimulate interest in modern art in the United States. The

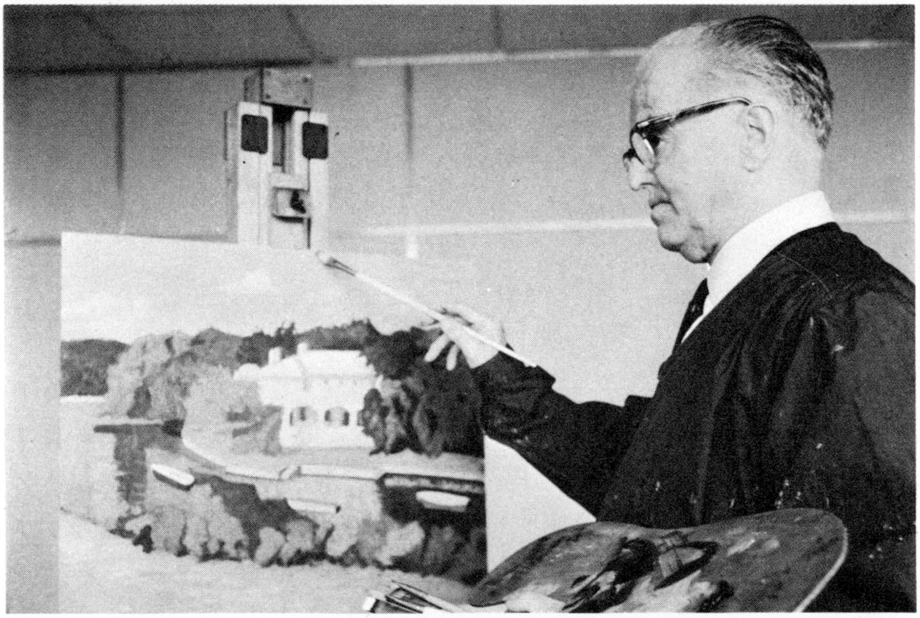

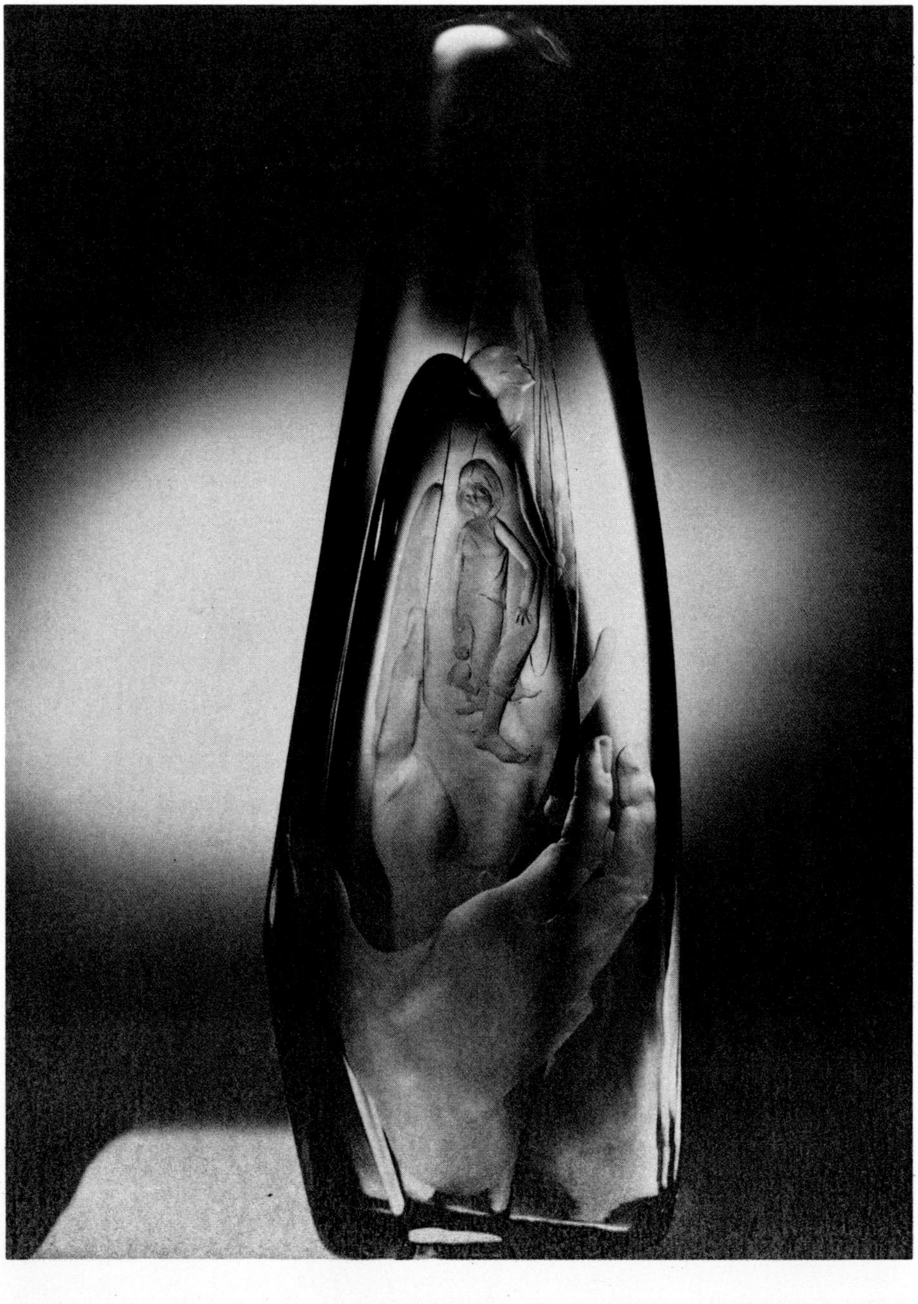

General Electric Company, for example, commissions twelve paintings each year for its calendar and now has a collection of some five hundred works which regularly tour the United States and Canada.

John Moores, a Liverpool businessman, is the only British art patron to finance and organise a national competition for contemporary paintings and sculpture. Energetic supporters of the avant-garde, such as Edinburgh's Richard Demarco of the Richard Demarco Gallery, have organised competitions, but they have been with collective rather than individual support from one patron.

The John Moores Liverpool exhibitions have been running since 1957 with a good deal of publicity and optimism and are now a firm biennial date in the art scene calendar in Britain. The aim has always been: 'To attract the best artists to show their work in Liverpool, and to support and encourage living artists, particularly the young and progressive.'

'I was fed-up with people saying that little happens in art in the North of England,' says John Moores. 'The best exhibitions all seemed to be in London and I decided to start a Liverpool show. Now the best British artists send their work here and if people want to see a representative selection of British painting they have to come to Liverpool. The show doesn't go to the capital.'

Although the John Moores Liverpool shows do not necessarily give a good or representative view of British art, they have brought the gospel of modern art to a city and a region where it was rarely seen or heard before. But few would call Liverpool anything but a backwater of the British art scene.

Attendances at the John Moores Biennale have risen steeply since 1957, but they seem unlikely to compete with football crowds or even darts players in Liverpool.

Since 1957 the prizes for winners in the different sections of the John Moores competitions have varied slightly. In 1967 the Pop artist David Hockney won the first prize of £1,500 followed by Malcolm Hughes (£750) and Joe Tilson (£500).

Paul Mellon is a multi-millionaire and the owner of the world's richest privately-owned collection of English old master paintings. The bulk of his collection centres around eighteenth- and nineteenth-century pictures, which caught his attention when a student at Clare College, Cambridge.

'I'm a passionate Anglophile,' says Mellon. 'I've got strong childhood memories of travelling in England with my mother and father. My mother was English. The contrast between the green English landscape and the smoky atmosphere of my native Pittsburgh will always stay in my mind. English painting of the past seemed to emphasise the special qualities of the English countryside.

'When I got married my father gave me several pictures by Marshall. They were hunting and horse racing scenes, and I remember my father saying how dangerous riding was. "Every damn fool knows some horses run faster than others." But it helped stimulate my growing interest in English art.'

Paul Mellon was encouraged in forming a collection by Basil Taylor, the English critic and art historian. And just how rich and varied is the collection he has brought together can be judged by a comment in *The Times* recently. 'The Mellon Collection does with splendid profusion what the Tate Gallery can as yet hardly claim to do.'

Every major British painter from 1700–1900 is represented, sometimes magnificently, in the collection, but Mellon has also collected innumerable examples of less-known artists. Names like Samuel Collings, George Haugh and Joseph Nickolls. Then there are paintings by the so-called conversation painters including Wheatley, Zoffany, Devis, Mortimer, Phillips and Wright of Derby.

The Mellon Collection is one of the world's finest private collections. Its magnificence has a warning for governments, museums and committees responsible for buying works of art, whether they are old masters or modern works. Paul Mellon was able to buy many of the pictures in his collection without noticeable opposition or competition from institutions who should have been in the market for such major acquisitions. Of course, when it comes to buying the problem is invariably, though not entirely, a matter of money. It is high time that governments gave the same attention and resources to art that they seem so willing to do towards the less ethereal and more mundane aspects of our lives.

John Moores (top left), a businessman with a great love of the arts, started a Liverpool art show which has now become a firm date in the British art scene calendar

The National Trophy for Road Safety for Children (bottom left) is presented each year by Shell-Mex and British Petroleum Limited to encourage and acknowledge outstanding work performed in the cause of the safety of children on the roads

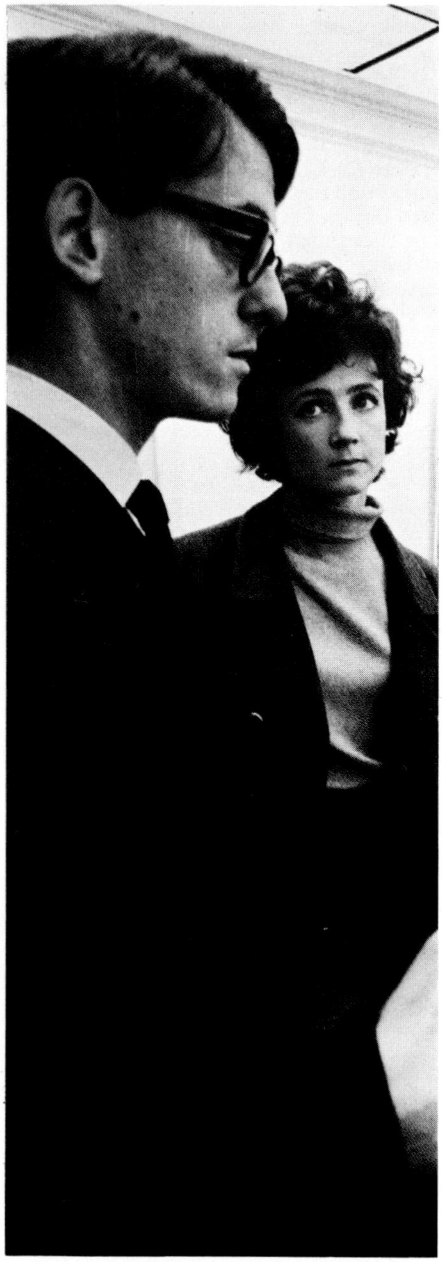

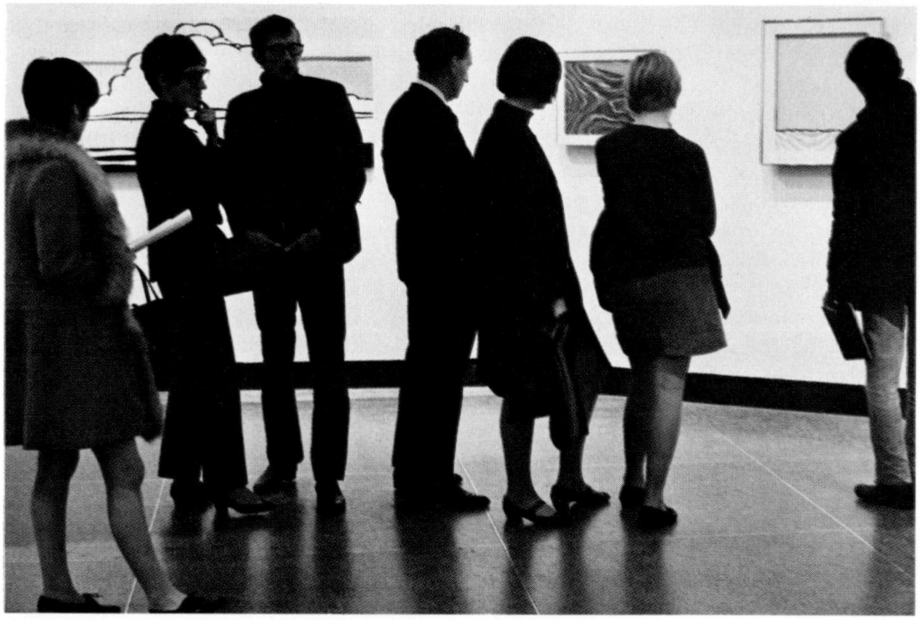

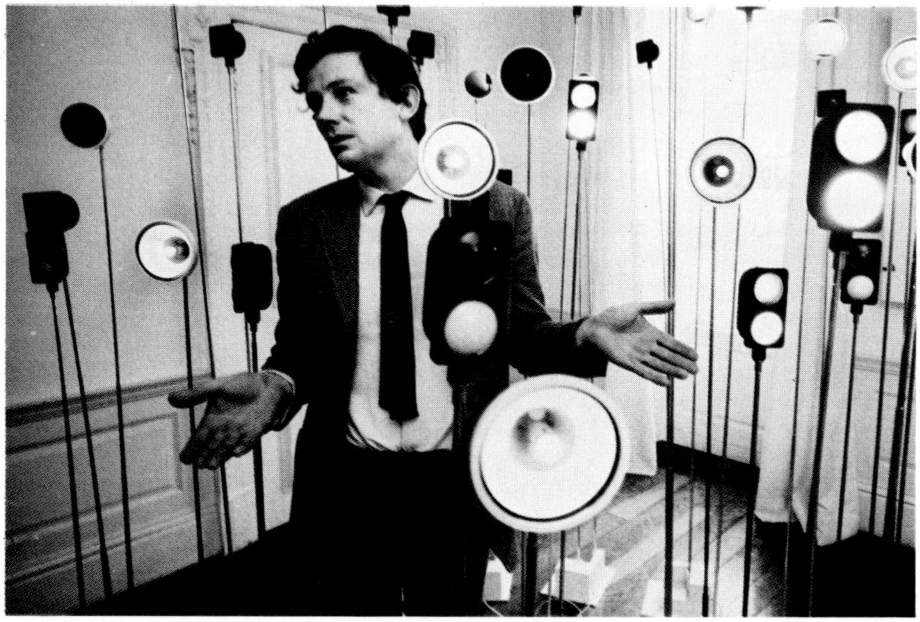

Lord Dufferin, young patron of the avant-garde and a partner in the Kasmin Gallery, Bond Street. A group of students (above right) at the recent, outstandingly successful Lichtenstein exhibition held at the Tate Gallery, London. Jeremy Fry (below right) surrounded by a group of Kinetic sculptures by Takis

Opposite page. Pauline Vogelpoel, organising secretary of the Contemporary Art Society. Guests attending a Friends of the Tate soirée in London

Jeremy Fry, who is both engineer and modern art patron, is behind the Kinetic sculptures now being made at his Bath home, Widcombe Manor, and a nearby factory. A year ago the work he is selling cost £800 in a West-End gallery, but today he is selling it at prices between £12 and £19. The pencil-thin, electrically operated sculptures resemble futuristic and flashing lights, and their effect is close to twinkling coloured lights on a Christmas tree.

Fry explained his reasons for trying to take art from its hand-built Rolls-Royce phase to a level he feels more in keeping with a mass-production conscious society. 'Making unlimited editions as cheaply as possible is the beginning of a new breakthrough in selling works of art,' he says. 'Only the present economic set-up in the art world prevents artists producing their work cheaply and in multiple editions. At the moment some galleries sell small limited editions of sculpture with a hand-written signature in order to maintain its price within the context of the exclusive art-gallery market.'

Leslie Waddington does not feel that Fry's scheme is a threat to modern dealers. 'Not more than fifty people buy avant-garde sculpture in Britain, so I can't see this as a viable economic proposition or as dangerous competition. I wonder if these new-style art merchants will support and finance their artists as we are doing, even when their work doesn't sell well.'

Art tastes are gradually becoming uniform, with touring exhibitions of

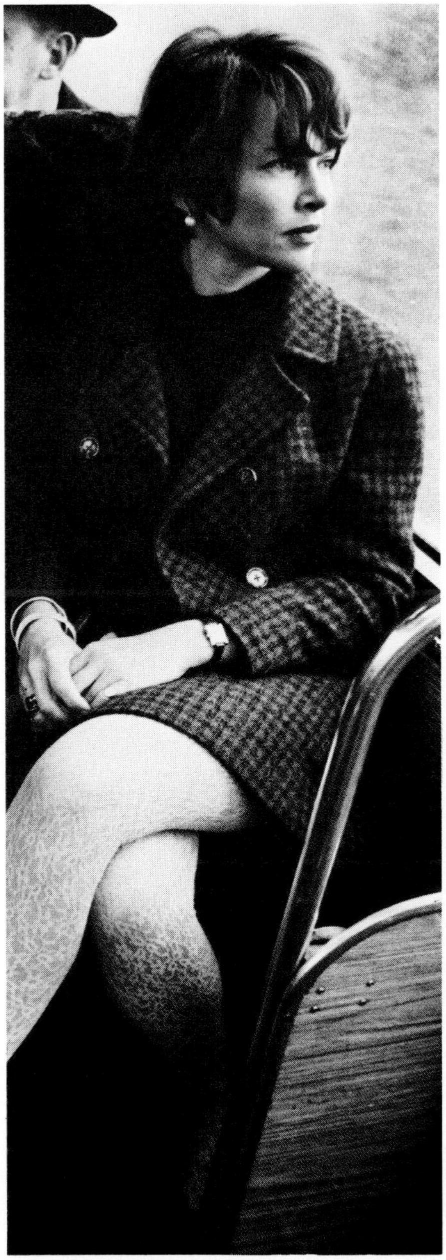

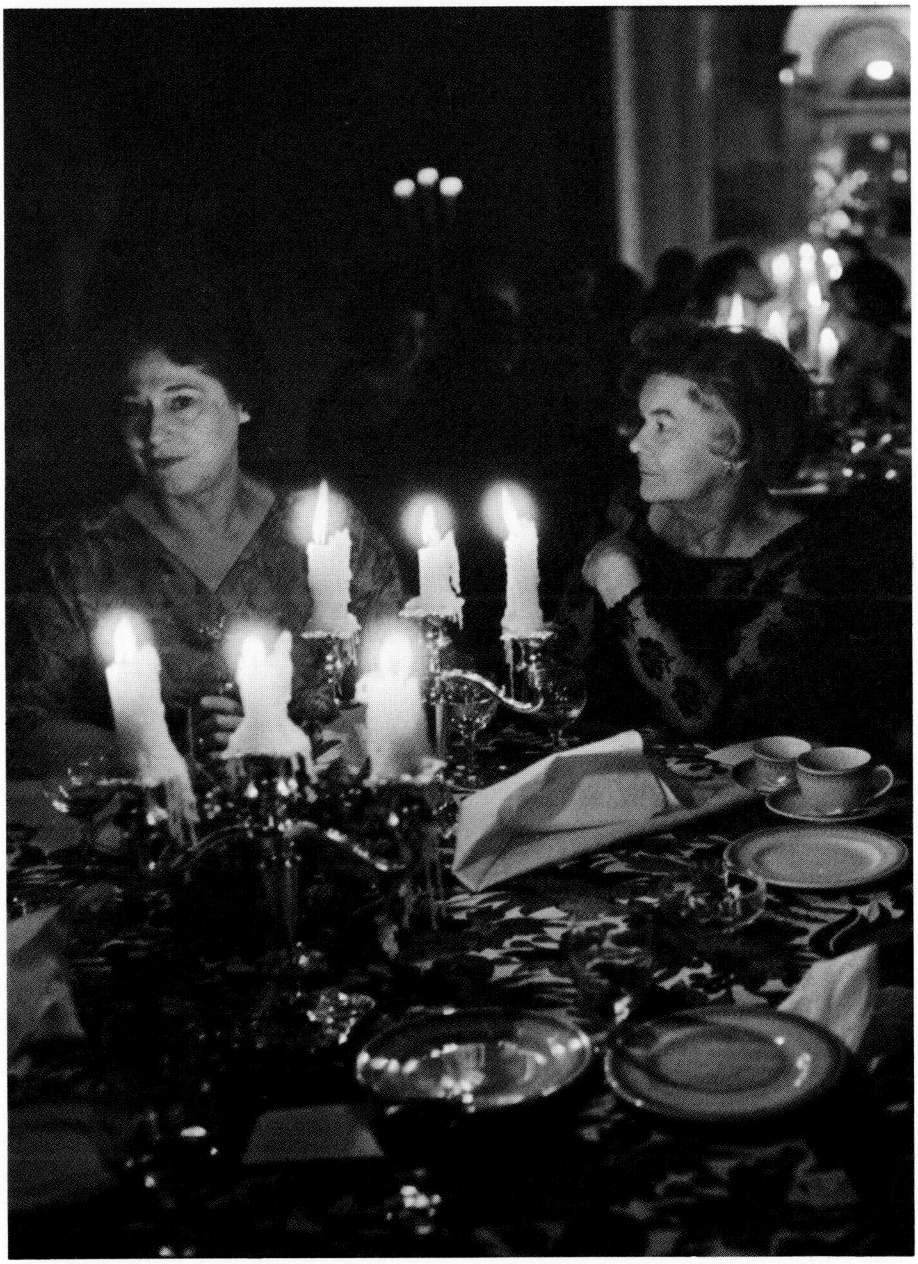

paintings and sculpture visiting countries like so many old-fashioned music hall companies. Recently the Roy Lichtenstein show was seen in America, then at the Stedelijk Museum, Amsterdam, the Tate Gallery, London, the Kunsthalle, Berne, and the Kestner Gesellschaft, Hanover.

No longer must people travel to London, Paris, New York or Boston to see all the best shows, because art is now being taken to many small towns. In Britain the government-financed Arts Council makes awards to artists and public galleries, and also buys paintings and sculpture for its own collection. Its touring shows are an important part of the art calendar in Britain.

The British Council is in the export field for cultural prestige although it does not earn foreign currency, at least not directly. But it has helped establish British artists abroad with extraordinary success. Since 1945 the Council has done valuable missionary work for artists who were little-known or forgotten.

The Contemporary Art Society, with its headquarters at the Tate Gallery, has been attracting modern art fans since 1910. As well as encouraging members to show interest in art it also buys contemporary works of art and presents them to galleries all over Britain and the Commonwealth. It also organises exhibitions like the British Sculpture in the Sixties exhibition at the Tate Gallery.

The CAS's organising secretary is Pauline Vogelpoel, who arranges visits to art galleries and private collections all over the world. 'The Society's main job is to buy and distribute modern works of art; we also make special grants towards the acquisition of rather special pictures – like Picasso's *The Three Dancers*, which is now in the Tate Gallery,' she says.

The Friends of the Tate Gallery is an increasingly important patron in Britain. With a membership of more than 1,000, it has an ordinary membership, Corporate Members, Associates, Patrons and Benefactors. Privileges, in proportion to their contributions (according to their official report), are given to the different levels of membership of the Friends of the Tate Gallery. The Friends buy works of art and present them to the Tate.

The world's museums are now in the leading ranks of art patrons. Twentieth-century bricks have largely replaced the flesh-and-bones of great patrons of the past. There are now fewer than one hundred individuals who are in the market for highly priced works of art, but even they find it difficult to compete with the top museums.

When the Museum of Fine Arts in Boston, the Art Institute, Chicago, the Metropolitan or the Museum of Modern Art, New York, the National Gallery, Washington, the Rijksmuseum, Amsterdam, the National Gallery, London, or the Louvre in Paris, decide to bid for a work of art on the market, there are probably less than ten private individuals who can compete. Through death duties, gifts and private bequests, the museums are rarely out-manoeuvred by private patrons.

The world's major museums are to be found in Europe and the United States. Institutions like the Boston Museum of Fine Arts, for example, possess not only an outstanding collection of European and American paintings, but also a collection devoted to the arts of the ancient Near East, Egypt, Asia and the Far East. Apart from the magnificent collection owned by the National Museum in Tokyo, the Boston Museum has brought together the richest collection of Chinese and Japanese sculpture and painting that is to be found anywhere in the world.

The Boston Museum is perhaps best known, however, for its collection of Impressionist and Post-Impressionist paintings. Famous pictures like Renoir's *Le Bal à Bougival*, Gauguin's *Where do we come from? What are we? Where are we going?* and Vincent Van Gogh's *The Postman Roulin* are among the Museum's masterpieces. The Boston Museum also owns an important fine art reference library and photographic collection, and regularly issues art publications of interest to both scholar and layman.

The Art Institute of Chicago has become one of America's best-known museums through the patronage of local businessmen. Established in 1879 as an art school, the Art Institute began its own collection through bequests, purchases and gifts made by many local citizens. Today, this comprehensive collection bought from all over the world, is perhaps best known for its remarkable examples of French art.

New York has several museums of importance. The Frick Collection, a small gallery on East 70th Street; the Metropolitan Museum of Art, on Fifth Avenue at 82nd Street; and the Museum of Modern Art are among the more notable collections.

The Museum of Modern Art on West 53rd Street was founded in 1929 and has one of the most controversial collections of works of art in the world. Its policy is to buy work by outstanding contemporary artists, many of them comparatively young.

Two other important American collections are the Philadelphia Museum of Art, which is on Parkway and Fairmont Avenue, and the National Gallery of Art, on Constitution Avenue, between Fourth and Seventy Streets, in Washington D.C.

In Europe the outstanding museums to be seen include the Rijksmuseum in Amsterdam; the Museum of Fine Arts in Antwerp, the Museum of Fine Arts in Brussels; the Uffizi Gallery in Florence; the Prado Museum in Madrid; the Art History Museum in Vienna; the Vatican Museums in Rome; and the Bavarian State Art Gallery in Munich, commonly known as the Alte Pinakothek.

In Paris the most important museum is, of course, the Louvre. Many of the world's best-known works of art, including the *Venus de Milo* and the *Mona Lisa*, are to be seen there. In London, the National Gallery in Trafalgar Square contains one of the world's major collections of European art. The Gallery is also well known for its daily lectures, free and open to the general public, on different art subjects. Other museums in London include the British Museum, the Victoria and Albert Museum, the Tate Gallery, the Wallace Collection, and the Courtauld Institute Gallery. It is major museums like these which have helped stimulate the growing interest in art throughout the world. Although many museums and galleries are now under criticism for the traditional way they show their treasures, changes in exhibiting techniques are gradually taking place. Already some institutions provide tape-recorded audio aids for the use of visitors. Well-organised information services, such as the one at the Metropolitan Museum of Art in New York, are also being introduced in more galleries.

Major museums like these have helped stimulate the growing interest in art throughout the world.
Top row. National Gallery, London; the Prado, Madrid; the Pitti Palace Florence.
Second row. Victoria and Albert Museum, London; the Guggenheim Museum, New York; the Louvre, Paris.
Bottom row. National Gallery of Art, Washington; the Uffizi, Florence; the Tate Gallery, London

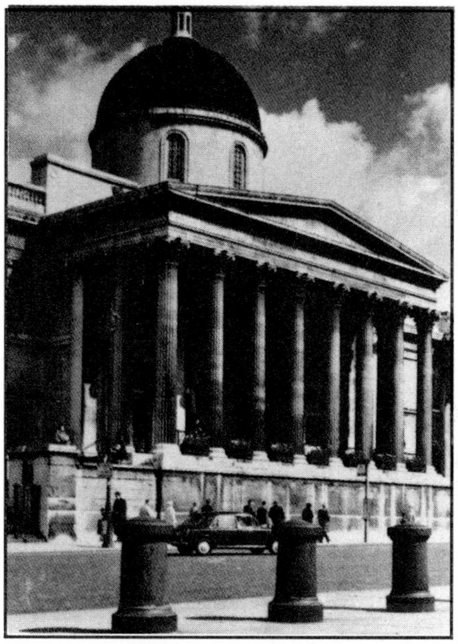
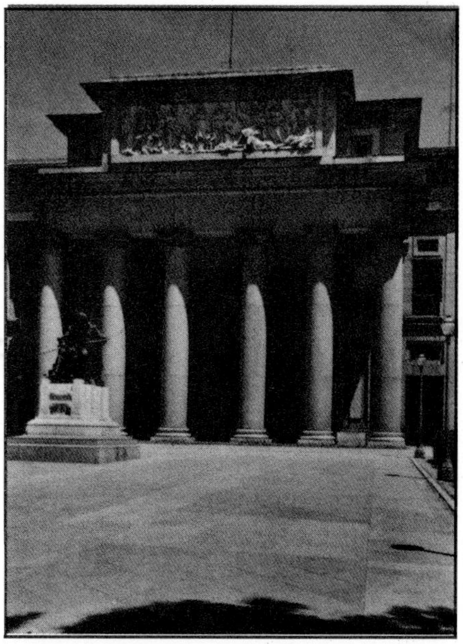
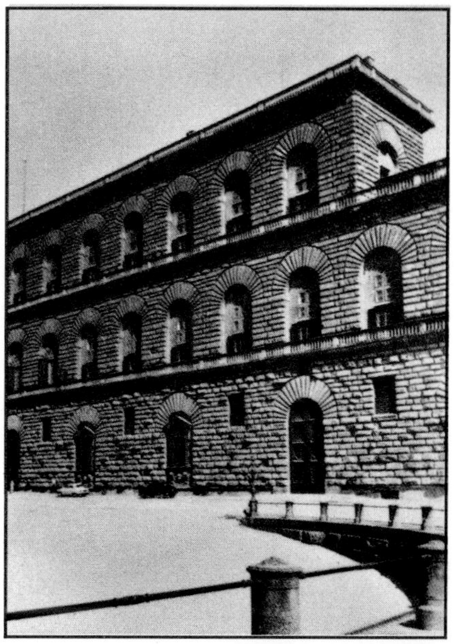
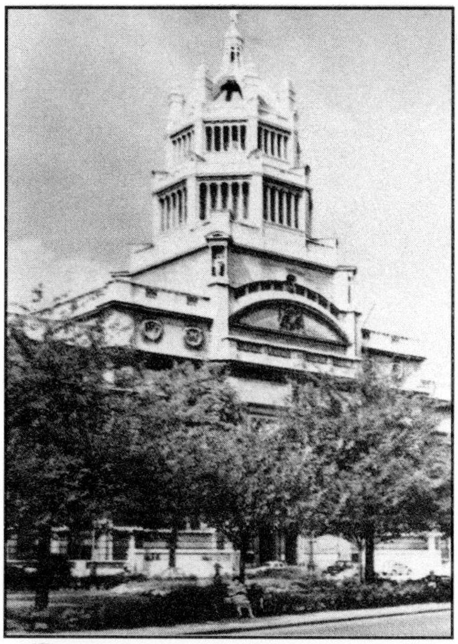
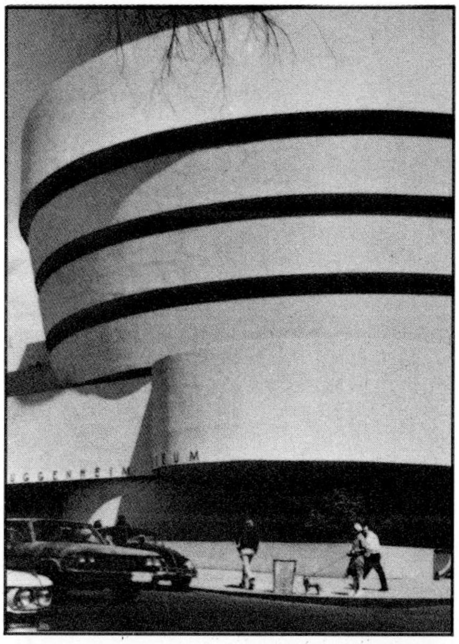
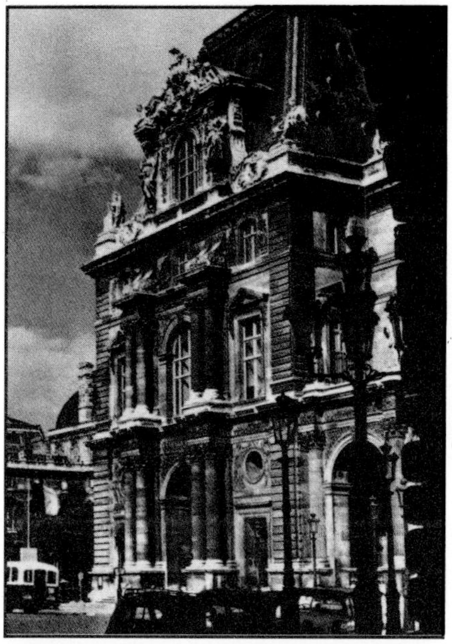
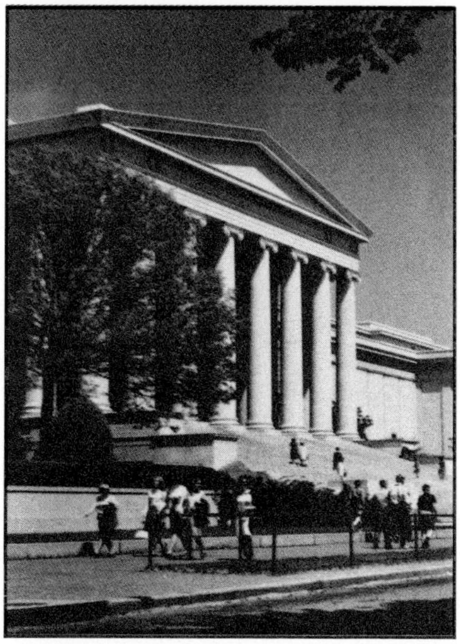
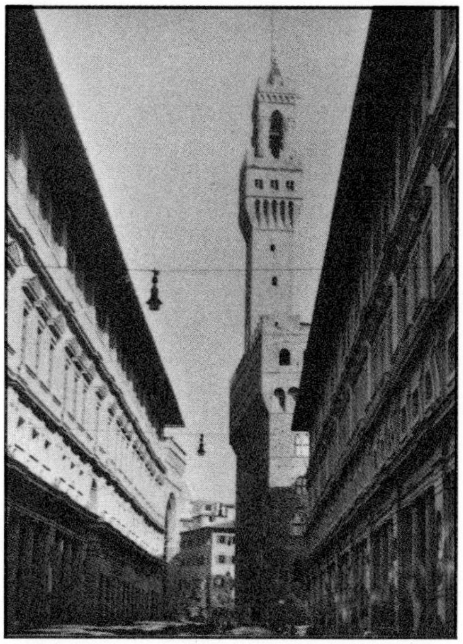
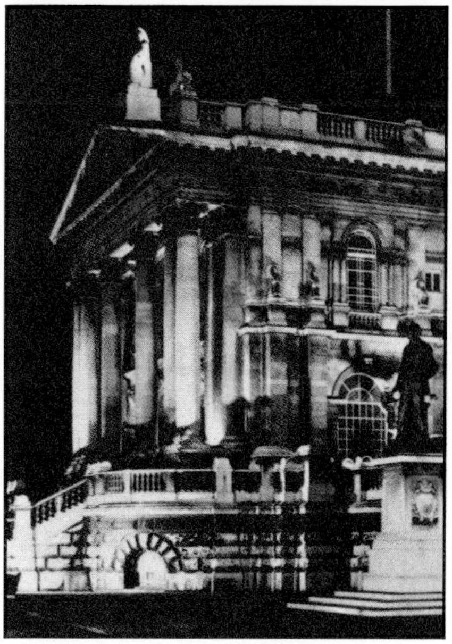

Acknowledgements

The author and publishers wish to express their appreciation of the courtesy of the following in supplying photographs and granting permission for their publication in this book.

Front jacket
Top row (left to right): Detail from *Aristotle Contemplating the Bust of Homer* (see caption: p.113), Life Class (see caption p.106)
Middle row (left to right)
Gold Box by Clive Barker
Picasso in his studio
Bottom (left to right)
Geoffrey Agnew (see caption p.41), Andy Warhol (see caption p.11)

Back Jacket
Pop culture posters in London

Aalborg Stiftstidende
Galerie Aenne Abels, Cologne
Albany Studio
Alinari-Giraudon
Arne Bruun Rasmussen, Copenhagen
Art International
Art Voices
Associated Newspapers
Associated Press
Australian News & Information Bureau
Axiom Gallery, London

Ian Berry—Magnum
John Bignell
Blackstone-Shelburne, New York
Jane Bown

Camera Press
Bryn Campbell
J. Allan Cash
Roberto E. Castro, Paris
Jean-Marie Chourgnoz, Paris
Christie Manson & Woods Ltd., London
Carlo Cisventi
Adolf Clemens
Geoffrey Clements
Cleveland Museum of Art, Gift of Hanna Fund
Compagnie des Commissaires Priseurs au Départment de la Seine, Paris
A. C. Cooper Ltd.
Patrick Coyle

Keith Davis
Daily Telegraph
Dresden Pinacoteca

Esso Petroleum Co. Ltd.
Crispin Eurich

Richard Feigen Gallery, Chicago
Hans Feurer
Robert Fraser Gallery, London
John R. Freeman

Mr and Mrs Victor Ganz
General Motors Ltd.
John van Gerallen
Photographie Giraudon
Burt Glinn—Magnum
Jon Goodchild
Greater London Council and Trustees of the Iveagh Bequest, Kenwood
Grosvenor Gallery, London
Guildhall Art Gallery, Corporation of London

Karen Hagon
Studio Hamlet
Hanover Gallery, London
André Held—Ziolo
Christian Herdeg
David Hockney
Michael Holford

Galerie Iolas, Paris

Martha Jackson Gallery, New York
Sidney Janis Gallery, New York
Colin Jones

Kasmin Gallery, London
Martin Kay
Graham Keen
A. F. Kersting
Keystone Press Agency
Lord Kilbracken
Malcolm Kirk
J. A. Kirkegaard
Martin Koretz

Alfred Lammer
Leicester Galleries
J. S. Lewinski
Rudolf Lichtsteiner
London Express & News Feature Service
The Louvre, Paris

Magnum
Sameer Makarius
Man Ray
Erling Mandelmann
Mansell-Alinari
The Mansell Collection
Marlborough Fine Art Ltd., London
Keith McMillan
Lotte Meitner-Graf
Metropolitan Museum of Art, New York
Ronald Miglionico
Djordje Milićerić
David Mist
Jack Mitchell
Peter Moore, New York
Keith Morris
Mouse Productions
Antonia Mulas,
Ugo Mulas
Musée d'Impressionisme, Paris
Museo Nazionale, Naples
Museum of Modern Art, New York

John Naar
Hans Namuth
The Trustees of The National Gallery, London
National Gallery of Art, Washington D.C., Andrew Mellon Collection
Hugh Newberry
Nova

Observer
Odeon, Prague
Desmond O'Neill

Pace Gallery, New York
Parke Bernet Galleries, New York
Pitti Palace, Florence
Popperfotos
Roger Pring
Proscenium Galleries, London

Edward Quinn

Radio Times Hulton Picture Library
Redfern Gallery, London
Galerie Denise René, Paris
Bridget Riley
James Robinson
Roy Round
Royal Academy of Arts
Royal Holloway College

Scala
John D. Schiff, New York
Sepp Schuller and Ehrenwirth Verlag
Shell International Petroleum Company Ltd.
Shunk-Kender
David Newell Smith
Galerie Ileana Sonnabend, Paris
Sotheby & Co.
Splash Posters
Staempli Gallery, New York
Mark Strizik
Studio International
Peter Stuyvesant Foundation
Sunday Times
Swaebe
Syndication International
Karin Szekessy

The Trustees of The Tate Gallery
The Times
Galerie Alexandre Tolas, Paris
Arthur Tooth and Sons Ltd., London
Topix

United Press International (U.K.) Ltd.
United States Information Service

Vincent Van Gogh Foundation, Amsterdam
Jeff Vickers Photography

Robert Walker
The Trustees of The Wallace Collection
Andy Warhol
Watson Bros.,
Wes Wilson

Special thanks are due to Keith Morris for his photographic work on the opening spreads and throughout the book.

Index

Not in the Australian edition*
Only in the Australian edition†